Agricultural Buildings and Structures

Agricultural Buildings and Structures

James H. Whitaker

Emeritus Professor of Agricultural Engineering
University of Connecticut
Storrs, Connecticut

Reston Publishing Company

A Prentice-Hall Company
Reston, Virginia

Library of Congress Cataloging in Publication Data

Whitaker, James H
  Agricultural buildings and structures.

  Includes bibliographies and index.
  1. Farm buildings—Design and construction. 2. Farm
layout. I. Title.
TH4911.W46   690′.8′9   78–27301
ISBN 0–8359–0176–9

© 1979 by
Reston Publishing Company
A Prentice-Hall Company
Reston, Virginia

10 9 8 7 6 5 4 3 2 1

Printed in the United States of America

Contents

LIST OF TABLES

Preface

This text is designed to furnish the fundamental subject matter for a general course in farm structures for junior and senior students in agricultural mechanization or related agricultural curriculums.

It is intended to give a logical approach to the planning and design of structures in keeping with modern agriculture. While many design procedures are examined and illustrated, it is recognized that in some courses *method* rather than *theory* may be emphasized. For this reason, table material and standard practice designs are included in many cases. Although not intended as a handbook, a considerable amount of data required for design parameters are included. The book should be of value as a reference to vocational agriculture teachers, extension workers, and others interested in agricultural building design.

In recognition of the use of the SI metric system in Canada and in anticipation of conversion to this system in the United States, customary and SI Units are presented side by side throughout the book.

The book is organized in two parts. The first part begins with a brief review of the development of farm buildings in North America. After chapters devoted to the economic feasibility of buildings and farmstead planning, much of the balance of Part I deals wtih materials of construction and basic structural design. In addition, chapters covering heat transfer and solar energy, air-moisture relationships, and ventilation are included. And finally the subject of construction cost estimating is examined.

Part II is introduced with a discussion of a "systems approach" to planning and its importance in selecting, laying out, and designing buildings for specific farm enterprises. Housing requirements for dairy, poultry, and general livestock are included along with those for the storage of crops, and finally, greenhouses and several miscellaneous buildings are dealt with.

I am indebted to many people who have aided the progress of this book in its various stages. Appreciation and a sense of deep obligation are expressed to the authors of the numerous and varied resources used in the preparation of this volume. I extend my sincerest thanks to my colleagues at the University of Connecticut who have read parts of the manuscript and offered helpful suggestions and encouragement. I wish in particular to acknowledge the help of John W. Bartok, Jr., George A. Ecker, James A. Lindley, Ralph P. Prince, and William C. Wheeler as well as Robert G. Light of the University of Massachusetts.

My appreciation is also extended to the following persons from across the United States and Canada who supplied regional information: Gerald R. Bodman, University of Nebraska; Kenneth G. Boyd, Lambton County, Ontario; Theodore J. Brevik, University of Wisconsin; Frank D. Ciambriello, Orange, Connecticut; Keith A. Clark, Vineland Station, Ontario; George A. Duncan, University of Kentucky; W.C. Fairbank, University of California; George F. Grandle, University of Tennessee; Marvin E. Heft, Allegan County, Michigan Extension Service; Dexter W. Johnson, North Dakota State University; Franklin Kains, Regional Municipality of Waterloo, Ontario; Michael A. McNamee, University of Wyoming; Richard Phillips, University of Missouri; John Ed Ryan, National Forest Products Association; Frank H. Theakston, University of Guelph; and James F. Thompson, University of California.

And finally, I am deeply grateful to my daughter, Carol, for the illustrations in the first chapter and to my wife, Alice, for her loyal assistance and encouragement during this endeavor.

James H. Whitaker
University of Connecticut

Part One

Planning, Materials, and Basic Design

Part I presents basic principles relating to economic feasibility, farmstead planning and construction cost estimating. The characteristics and applications of building materials commonly used in agricultural construction are examined. Heat transfer and the control of building environment through ventilation are discussed. Inevitably, new building materials with superior characteristics will be introduced and continued research will develop refinements in the methods used to control environment. Nevertheless, the fundamental principles discussed will remain useful in developing plans, selecting materials, and designing safe, efficient, and effective buildings for modern agricultural needs.

Chapter One

Introduction

Buildings are an integral part of modern agriculture and contribute greatly to the efficiency of operation, the quality of the products produced, and the health and comfort of the workers and livestock. While the buildings of today are no more functional than the barns of past generations, they tend to be much more specialized. Often a *system* is chosen for an agricultural enterprise and then a building is selected or designed to provide the necessary conditions for the system. These conditions may range from little more than protection from wind and rain to sophisticated control of the building's total environment.

Eric Sloane (1966) accurately states, "The successful farmer has been transformed into a businessman and the barn has become a factory." Agricultural buildings have changed over the years as differing requirements have been imposed and new methods and materials have been developed. However, a close look at how the needs for crop and animal shelter were met by early farmers reveals a surprising number of ideas that are still valid today. A brief study of early barns should be interesting and worthwhile.

EARLY BARNS

The design of the earliest barns was largely influenced by the labor and materials at hand. At first, only the very minimal requirements were met. The first settlers probably provided only shelter for themselves and their families, waiting until the first crops were harvested to construct the necessary storage. As a quick and easy way of getting that first storage, wattle and daub were sometimes used. (Wattle refers to small branches woven together to form a wall, and daub is the mud or plaster used to seal the surface.)

However, in the forested areas of the East, barns were usually constructed of logs supported on low stone piers. As farmers prospered, more stone was used for the walls of the first floor. Eventually the ends, and finally the entire barn, was constructed of stone. Stone barns were popular in the Pennsylvania area in the late 18th and 19th centuries.

Figure 1-1.   An early log barn.

The first roofs were usually covered with slabs of bark, although thatching was also employed to a limited extent, particularly in Canada. Some roofs were constructed with warped or scooped-out wooden slabs laid with the hollow sides alternately up and down and overlapped, much as tile is used today. This carried the rain water off with little leakage. However, shakes, which were thin slabs split from logs 3 feet or less in length, soon became the most common roofing material.

In the middle west and south-eastern areas of the country corn was the predominant crop and the earliest buildings were log corn cribs. As hay became more important, a mow was constructed over two or more cribs. Frequently the mows were cantilevered well beyond the crib walls.

In the middle of the 19th century, as the pioneers pushed west, sod

Figure 1-2.   Log corn cribs and catilevered hay mow of Appalachia.

houses and barns became common on the treeless prairies. With characteristic ingenuity, the pioneer used wide strips of sod laid one upon another to build up a thick wall. Sod was also used in various ways to cover the roof. The "soddies," as they were called, were common until the early 20th century. As the soddies were gradually replaced, it was common to see wood frame construction used first for the barn and later for the house. This sequence of change probably occurred because the sod houses were considerably warmer and required less heat during the bitter winters. But while the sod made an excellent wall for house and barn, leaky roofs were almost inevitable, and dust and debris from the roof filtered down into the rooms.

During the 18th and early 19th centuries, little or no winter production was expected from livestock. Buildings were therefore constructed only for the protection of grain and equipment, while the forage was stacked in the yard and the stock was given minimal shelter. As the agriculture of the country developed, larger barns were constructed with hay storage and threshing floors. Horses were the first to be given protection, while cows were provided only an open shed. Later, as barn design evolved, stables for cows were added as lean-tos, and these gradually became an integral part of the barn.

Although local materials were used, a distinct European influence reflecting the settler's origins began to appear at an early date. One of the earliest examples was the Dutch influence evidenced by low side walls and a steep-pitched roof. These barns were common in eastern New York. The hewn timber frame provided a floor plan reminiscent of

European basilicas with a center nave and narrower side aisles. Fitting with this was a single door in one end of the barn. The steep pitch helped prevent damage from heavy snow and leaks from imperfect roof covering.

The English influence appeared in the form of both wooden and stone barns designed with higher walls and lower pitched roofs. These barns had doors near the middle of each side for drive-through access to the threshing floor. Bays on either side of the threshing floor were used to store unthreshed grain or hay. Mow storage for hay may also have been provided above the grainery or cow stable at one end of the barn. Frequently barns and sheds of this period were built to form an "L" or "U" shape, giving more protection from the weather.

Figure 1-3.   Dutch barn of eastern New York State.

Figure 1-4.   English type barn with its drive-through threshing floor.

The Victorian influence appeared in the form of steep-pitched roofs, many gables and dormers, a cupola, and perhaps sash windows. There appears to have been a considerable prestige factor involved in owning one of these charming buildings.

Figure 1-5. Victorian influence on the English type barn.

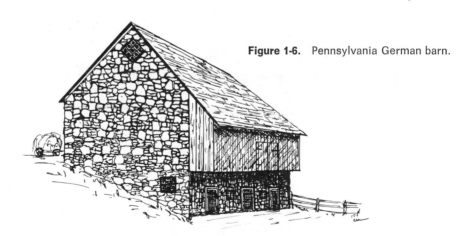

Figure 1-6. Pennsylvania German barn.

The Pennsylvania barn was influenced by the heritage of settlers arriving from numerous European countries. However, it is generally conceded that the South German and North Swiss influence was predominant. Today this influence is popularly known as Pennsylvania Dutch, a corrupted form of Pennsylvania Deutsch (German).

The characteristic most often associated with the Pennsylvania barn is the cantilevered overhang that provided shelter for the stock. However, probably just as typical is the use of stone for much or all of the walls. Usually there is also a drive floor entrance above the stable reached from a bank or hill on one side. In many cases intricate ventilation openings were built into the stone end walls. The hex signs, appearing in the mid-19th century, were for decorative effect only.

Gambrel roof barns appeared late in the 19th century as farms increased in size and greater storage space was needed. With the increased use of balers and combines in the mid-20th century, many of these barns, still standing and in good condition, seem unnecessarily large and high.

Examples of the connected barn are still to be seen in Quebec and northern New England although they have a somewhat different origin in each area. Those found in Quebec probably relate to a European heritage where the living quarters are found in one end of a single, large building. In contrast, the New England connected barn seems to have been born from the rugged winters and consists of a string of several small buildings connecting the house to the main barn. With this design one can walk from house to barn without trudging through the deep snow.

Figure 1-7.   New England connected barn.

Prairie barns seem to rest near the earth, probably because stones for a foundation were scarce, and the low profile reduced the effect of strong winds. Typically they had doors at the ends to allow wagons to be driven through and a hay door in the gable end through which the hay mow could be loaded from outside the barn. They often had a lean-to on one or both sides for sheltering the stock.

It would be negligent to overlook the round barns that were found in many areas of eastern Canada and the northeastern United States. Probably the earliest of these was built of stone in 1825 in Hancock,

Figure 1-8. Prairie barn.

Figure 1-9. Round barn with a central silo.

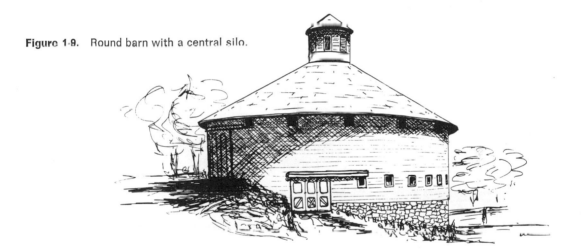

Massachusetts, by the Shakers, a religious community with an industrious and inventive spirit. The round barn was a pioneering example of functionalism in American architectural design. The efficiency of the building soon became obvious and many versions of the building, using a wide choice of materials, were erected by people outside the sect. While some of them were years ahead of their time in moving hay and silage, the difficult and expensive construction undoubtedly prevented them from becoming more popular.

Eventually there were a number of specialized buildings that became common in the areas where they were needed. The root cellar for storing fruits and vegetables was usually built into a bank to take advantage of the uniformly cool soil temperature. It was undoubtedly the forerunner of the potato storages of New England.

Tobacco curing barns were of various designs necessary to meet the needs of the curing process. In the Southeast they were rather small, high buildings with provisions for a fire to flue-cure the bright leaf tobacco. A lean-to often covered the wood storage area. Air drying of cigar tobacco in the North called for a much longer curing period and therefore larger sheds. The vertical siding was designed so that alternate boards either swung out at the bottom or were hinged at the side to provide maximum ventilation.

Figure 1-10.   Flue curing tobacco barn of the Southeast.

Figure 1-11.   Air curing tobacco shed of Connecticut and Massachusetts.

Other small buildings, important to the business or the quality of farm life, included smoke and ice houses, corn cribs, spring houses, forges and several others.

CHANGES IN AGRICULTURE

The continued change in North American agriculture has influenced the design of farm buildings to a considerable extent. Mechanization and improved cultural practices have increased crop production. Improved breeding, feeding, and health care have similarly increased animal production. These developments have required larger buildings designed for the specific needs of the enterprise housed.

Competition for quality farm labor has boosted wages and fringe benefits while working conditions are influenced by new safety laws. This means that modern buildings must be designed for maximum efficiency, comfort, and safety.

The last few decades have witnessed the shift from the small multipurpose farm with a barn housing cows, horses, sheep, pigs, and chickens plus hay and grain, to large single enterprise operations. The farmyard flock has been replaced by modern cage laying units housing 40–100,000 birds; fruits and vegetables are harvested by machines to be handled in bulk and stored in modern environmentally controlled storages; and far greater use is being made of on-farm grain storage incorporating sophisticated drying and handling systems. These are just three examples of the influence that a changing agriculture has had on farm building requirements. However, that influence extends to the housing needs of practically every farm enterprise in the United States and Canada today.

REAL VALUE

It has been estimated that early barns had an average life of nearly 50 years. Actually, with a good foundation and proper roof maintenance, many barns have lasted much longer than that. But the real value of a barn built years ago needs to be determined. As a result of their long life, many old barns, though obsolete, have continued to be used simply because they seem "too good to be abandoned." These barns, designed in years past for far different conditions, are inflexible and inefficient for today's operations. While remodeling is a possibility, in many cases it would not only be expensive but would produce questionable results.

Thus it becomes necessary to assess the real value of an old building for the present enterprise and decide whether it is satisfactory in its present condition or whether it should be remodeled, added to, or abandoned and replaced. The following outlines will serve to systematically analyze a situation and help in making such a decision. The next chapter discusses a number of ways to analyze the influence that the choice of housing has on the economic success of an enterprise.

HOW BUILDINGS INFLUENCE AN ENTERPRISE

Farm buildings represent a production or a storage cost. And just as a return from feed or labor costs is expected, a benefit from a building investment also should be anticipated.

There are at least five benefits that a building should provide:

- Facilities for an efficient operation
- An environment providing healthful and sanitary conditions
- Comfortable surroundings for both stock and workers
- Safe conditions for both stock and workers
- Desirable conditions for production or storage

DESIGN CHARACTERISTICS OF BUILDINGS

A number of factors must be considered in planning a building to obtain the greatest number of benefits at a reasonable cost. Some of these design factors are:

1.   The functional requirements for the enterprise, such as space, temperature, light, physical protection, sanitation, and safety.

2.   The efficiency of the system, including mechanization, centralized operation, circular travel, and bulk handling of materials.

3.   A structural design that is adequate for the loads to which the building will be subjected, one in which both original cost and maintenance costs are reasonable, and one which will provide the desired length of life.

4.   The suitability of materials, including such characteristics as durability, fire resistance, cost, upkeep, ease of cleaning, insulating value, and appearance.

5.   Economy of construction. Costs are reduced by choosing module dimensions, standard size materials and components, and prefabricated subassemblies.

6. Flexibility of design that will allow production methods for the proposed enterprise to be altered or a completely new enterprise to be established with minimum expense and effort. Examples of planned flexibility include such features as large doors, level floors, truss construction, and a large electrical service designed to allow the addition of several circuits.

PROBLEMS

1.1 Make a list of the major changes in agriculture in your state over the past two decades and describe how those changes have affected farm building requirements and design.

1.2 Determine the five most important agricultural enterprises in your state based on total annual income. For each of these, list the major building requirements.

REFERENCES

Arthur, Eric and Dudley Witney. *The Barn*. Greenwich, Conn.. New York Graphic Society, Ltd., 1972.

Fitchen, John. *The New World Dutch Barn*. Syracuse, NY: Syracuse University Press, 1968.

Gray, Harold E. *Farm Service Buildings*. New York: McGraw-Hill, 1955.

Sloane, Eric. *An Age of Barns*. New York: Funk & Wagnalls, 1966.

Welsch, Roger L. *Sod Walls, The Story of the Nebraska Sod House*. Broken Bow, Nebr.: Purcells, Inc., 1968.

Chapter Two

Economic Feasibility

When constructing an agricultural building the expense must be justified. As mentioned previously, the use of a building results in an annual production or storage cost to the enterprise. In fact, it can be thought of as an item of production equipment. While there are no hard and fast rules concerning how much annual cost can be justified to house an enterprise, some effort should be made to estimate the cost and determine the feasibility of the related investment.

APPROACHES

Several approaches have been used for determining the economic feasibility of a farm building. Three of them are (1) the *present practice theory* in which a building similar to others already existing in the area is assumed to be justifiable, (2) a *percentage of gross income* which is considered a reasonable amount to allow for annual building cost, and (3) a *residual after cost theory* in which the building cost is provided for after all other costs have been deducted from gross income.

The first of these methods is likely to emphasize what the average farmer is doing or more likely has done in the past. It isn't necessarily correct for the present or the future. Also an attractive building or system may actually have resulted in over-investment, thus making it a questionable example to follow. The second and third suggestions relate building cost allotments to gross income. They imply that high income-producing enterprises can and perhaps should be housed in more expensive facilities. Typical values used for the percentage of gross income method are: dairy, 11 percent; beef and poultry, 9 percent, and sheep, 8 percent. This method does not take into account the value of labor, the cost of which may justify a larger investment due to improved labor efficiency.

Two additional approaches for determining economic feasibility involve partial budgeting. The first of these shows the *profit potential* and the second estimates the minimum possible *payback period* for the building. However, before investigating these approaches, it is important to review some of the costs involved in owning a building.

Building Costs

Most costs of owning a building are considered to be fixed costs because they occur quite independently of the building's use. There are five categories of fixed costs: depreciation, interest, repairs, taxes and insurance (sometimes referred to as the "DIRTI FIVE"). Of these costs, only repairs may be somewhat related to the degree of use. But even then weather-related deterioration of such things as paint and roofing must be attended to even when a building stands idle. Consequently repairs are ordinarily considered a fixed cost.

An examination of each of these costs follows:

Depreciation This is a noncash expense which provides a means of spreading the original cost of a building over the expected life of the building. There are at least two reasons for distributing the cost in this way: first, the cost of an expensive building must be distributed over several years to justify the expense to the enterprise housed; second, in filing a federal tax return the cost of a building must be shown on a depreciation schedule. It cannot be taken as an ordinary business expense. In fact, even a new roof must be depreciated instead of being charged as an expense. While there are several ways of calculating depreciation, the one most commonly used for buildings is the straight line method; i.e., an equal amount is allowed for depreciation annually throughout the life of the building.

Interest Interest may be either a cash or noncash expense. If the building is financed, the interest charge is a very real cash payout. However, even if the building is free of debt, an interest charge should be made against the owner's equity. If the owner did not have money tied up in the building, it could be earning interest in a bank.

Repairs These hardly need to be explained. General deterioration due to weathering, plus wear and damage, will require continual repair to such things as paint, roofing, windows, doors, etc.

Taxes   Taxes are universally levied against real property although the amount varies considerably from place to place.

Insurance   Insurance is considered a necessity by most owners. But even if commercial coverage is not purchased, a charge should be included because, in effect, the owner is self-insuring the property.

A variety of circumstances produces a rather sizable range in these five fixed costs. The following examples are given as a percentage of the *original* cost or value of a farm building:

	Low	Average	High
Depreciation	2½ (40 yr)	5 (20 yr)	10 (10 yr)
Interest*	2½	3	4
Repairs	1	2	2½
Taxes	1½	2	2½
Insurance	½	1	1
Annual Cost	8%	13%	20%

* Rate divided by two as the average value of the building over its life is one half of the original value.

This wide range of annual costs (8 to 20 percent) results primarily from the length of the depreciation period chosen.

The Internal Revenue Service will probably not allow less than 20 years and prefers 30 years for depreciating a farm building. However, any period may be chosen for farm planning purposes. If during this period of rapidly changing economic conditions the depreciation can be completed in a reasonably short time, then much of the risk of a large investment is removed.

Partial Budgeting

Partial budgeting, in which variable factors are considered while omitting those factors that remain constant, can be useful in determining either the *profit potential* or the *payback period* which may result from the construction of a new housing system for an enterprise.

Profit potential (the prospects of increasing profits by a change in the housing system) will be illustrated by using a partial budget and the economic base of an existing structure. From that base, any additional investment to improve the facilities must be proven feasible by either *increasing returns* or *decreasing costs*. Increased returns with minimal increase in costs may result from increased production or improved product quality. Reduced costs with little change in income may result from improved labor efficiency, better feed conversion, or improved animal health.

The following assumptions illustrate this method: A dairyman has a 50-cow herd housed in a stanchion barn. He is interested in expansion and needs to decide whether he should abandon his present facilities, with a resulting small salvage value, and build a new free-stall and parlor system, or whether he should expand his present stanchion barn. Because of the flexibility of other enterprises on the farm he can make available whatever labor is required.

Although many degrees of basic condition and usefulness could exist, we will assume that the building is reasonably efficient and equipped with a pipeline milker and gutter cleaner. Only a minimal breakdown of barn, milking, and manure equipment costs is undertaken. It is assumed, however, that the daily labor requirements for each 10 cows is 1.6 man hours for a stanchion barn and 1.14 man hours for a free-stall system.

Following is a comparison of the cost of expansion to handle 100 milking cows. While the cost of the new free-stall system is greater, labor savings show it produces an increase in net profit of $3,057 over an expansion of the stanchion barn. While the stanchion barn may be used for other purposes if the free-stall barn is built, there is the possibility that high taxation will make it of questionable economic value.

Costs incurred from enlarging existing barn:

Annual cost of original barn, addition to barn, milk and manure equipment	$13,600*
Total annual cost of labor to care for the dairy herd (16 man hours × 365 days × $3.25/hr)	$18,980

Cost incurred from constructing a new free-stall system:

Annual cost of new free-stall barn, parlor, milk and manure equipment	$15,200**
Extra feed required resulting from lower temperature	800
	$16,000
Total annual cost of labor to care for the dairy herd (11.4 man hours × 365 days × $3.25/hr)	$13,523

*Estimated as follows:

Existing barn	$500 × 50 cows = $ 25,000
Addition	1350 × 50 cows = 67,500
Milk and manure equipment	= 12,115
	$104,615 × 13% = $13,600

** Estimated as follows:

Cost of barn	$1,000 × 100 cows = $100,000
Parlor and equipment	= 13,925
Manure equipment	= 3,000
	$116,925 × 13% = $15,200

Summary

Annual cost (Housing)

New free-stall barn	$16,000
Enlarged stanchion barn	13,600

Net change + $ 2,400   Net added cost   + $2,400

Annual costs (Labor)

Stanchion barn	$18,980
Free-stall barn	13,523

Net change — $ 5,457   Net reduced cost — $5,457

Total reduction in cost $3,057

It must be kept in mind that this is only an example and that every farm presents its own unique situation that must be analyzed using the best information available at the time.

The payback period may also be illustrated by using partial budgeting. The payback period is an estimate of the number of years in which the margin over all other costs equals the original cost of the building. Having determined a reasonable estimate of this period of time, a decision may be made on the basis of the confidence in the future of the enterprise to be housed.

The following partial budgets for a 100-cow dairy enterprise show the effects of three levels of building investment on the length of the payback period. All values are on a per-cow basis.

Investment:

Building (only variable shown)	$ 800	$1,000	$1,200
Cow	600	600	600
Machinery	500	500	500
Land (two acres per cow)	800	800	800
Total	$2,700	$2,900	$3,100

Interest and operating costs:

Silage (16 tons)	$ 240	$ 240	$ 240
Grain (2½ tons)	320	320	320
Miscellaneous	50	50	50
Fixed costs (cow, machinery, land)	295	295	295
Labor (60 hrs @ $3.25)	195	195	195
Interest (8% on one half of investment)	108	116	124
Total	$1,208	$1,216	$1,224

Gross income:

Milk (13,500 lbs @ $9.60 cwt + 1 calf @ $30)	$1,326

Margin for building expenses:

Gross income	$1,326	$1,326	$1,326
Interest and operating expenses	1,208	1,216	1,224
Margin	$ 118	$ 110	$ 102

Annual building cost as a percent of original building cost:

Repairs	2½%
Taxes	2½%
Insurance	1%
	6%

Original investment:	$800	$1,000	$1,200
Annual building cost as percent	.06	.06	.06
Annual building cost	$ 48	$ 60	$ 72

Margin for payback:

Margin for building expense	$118	$ 110	$ 102
Repairs, taxes, insurance	40	60	72
Margin	$ 70	$ 50	$ 30

Years to pay for building:	$800/$70	$1,000/$50	$1,200/$30
Years to pay back:	11.43	20	40

It is logical to conclude that if all income and expenses shown can reasonably be expected to remain in the same ratio for some time to come, the $800 investment and the associated 11.4 year payback period seems a very good arrangement. The 20-year period resulting from the $1,000 investment might also seem reasonable. However, the 40-year period associated with the $1,200 investment involves a considerable risk in a rapidly changing agricultural economy.

In summary it must be emphasized that the budgets illustrated are only examples. Every farm is an individual situation and all costs should be carefully estimated for the particular farm being considered. The opportunity to keep farm building costs low is desirable but not at the expense of poor labor efficiency, low production, or reduced quality of products stored. The possibility for a rapid payback period greatly reduces the risk of a new investment. But remember, the conclusions that are drawn can be no better than the information used in budget calculations.

The previous examples of methods for determining the feasibility of investing in a new structure involve relatively simple calculations. A more sophisticated analysis may be made with the aid of linear programing which makes it possible to maximize profits potential while considering a wide range of variables. The Agricultural Extension Service or private consultants may have access to the computer services needed to solve a linear program.

PROBLEMS

2.1   It is desirable to appraise the future prospects of any enterprise to be served by a new or expanded building. Agriculture is changing at such a rapid rate that a thorough study of the prospects for making the building pay off is essential. List some sources of information on the following subjects:

(a)   Trends in farm production and prices

(b)   Management systems for an enterprise

(c)   Building plans for one or more management systems

(d)   Basic materials, prefabricated units, and manufactured buildings

2.2   Assume that a father and son partnership is being formed. They want to increase the size of the business from a two- to a three-man operation. Choose a livestock enterprise and assume that it has been operating in buildings which have provided a minimum of controlled environment. Develop a partial budget to compare the relative merits of expanding along the present lines of operation compared to constructing a new housing system including a maximum of confinement and controlled environment. Assume that crop production is not a limiting factor and that full utilization of three workers is desired.

Chapter Three

Farmstead Planning

Planning is the first and most important step in designing a farmstead. While it costs very little to change a plan on paper, the expense of an alteration to a finished building can be prohibitive and a poorly conceived arrangement of buildings can diminish profits far into the future. Since the construction of a new farmstead is a long term project, good planning can hardly be overemphasized.

Only a few years ago most planning involved expansion or replacement of some parts of an existing farmstead. Today, however, the trend to larger farms requiring more space for larger buildings has greatly increased the frequency of constructing a completely new farmstead on a new site. The discussion that follows assumes such a situation. Most of the factors also apply to expansion or replacement plans, although such a situation is often more difficult to control. By long-range planning with gradual change, the efficiency of an existing farmstead may be materially improved.

Every farmstead is unique. The various factors must be evaluated and reasonable compromises made. An example of such a compromise might be the distance between the home and a large free-stall dairy barn. Convenience and efficiency might indicate very close proximity. Fire safety might indicate a minimum of 100 feet (30 m). Freedom from offensive odors might suggest several hundred feet. The compromise would be something in between—perhaps 200 feet (60 m). Conflicting factors are common and require subjective judgment. Careful planning with the very best information available will help to attain desirable compromises.

SELECTING A SITE

Certain factors which significantly influenced the selection of a farmstead site in the recent past have relatively less importance today. The location of the farmstead in relation to the fields, for instance, once was of prime consideration. Today large farms require considerable travel at best and most equipment is designed for efficient road speeds. So while this aspect may call for some deliberation, it is of secondary importance. Likewise, with modern snow removal equipment, distance from the road is of less concern. In some cases, farm practices, such as the use of large irrigation systems, may influence the choice of a farmstead site. Nevertheless, there are several critical factors to consider in any farmstead development.

Drainage This is the most important consideration in selecting a site for a farmstead. Adequate surface and subsurface drainage will insure all-weather driveways and dry foundations and will prevent local flooding. Well drained soil is essential for satisfactory operation of septic tank drainage fields and for the removal of feedlot runoff and other wastes. Fractured or limestone geologic formations may present as serious a problem as poorly drained soils because pollution may be carried underground for long distances.

Waste Management   If the farmstead is to house a major livestock enterprise, one of the prime considerations is waste management. The ability to handle waste without serious problems is essential. If drainage and other factors are to be adequate for a livestock enterprise, all or most of the following questions should be answered affirmatively before a site can be considered satisfactory.

1. Can the site conform with all state and local environmental regulations? Additional regulations that may be issued in the future should also be anticipated.

2. Is the topography satisfactory for the required storage and drainage of manure and effluent produced at the farmstead?

3. Is there sufficient area to store and dispose of effluent from stables and yards without polluting a stream, river, or lake?

4. Are prevailing wind directions, air drainage, and distances such that the farm home and neighboring farms will not be bothered by odors?

Water An adequate supply of good quality water is nearly as important as the possibility for good waste management. While water may reasonably be piped for some distance, it is advisable to insure a satisfactory water source early in the site selection process.

There are a number of other factors of varying importance to be considered.

Utilities and Services   These include telephone, electrical service, school bus, feed delivery, product pickup, snow removal, road maintenance and the possibility for adequate access drives and turnaround areas.

Soil, particularly around the house, should be well drained and rich enough to provide landscaping, gardens, play areas and a septic tank drainage field.

Orientation   Orientation on a gentle southerly slope may be desirable for air drainage and maximum sunshine. However, prevailing winds should also be taken into account and natural barriers used where possible. While much of the eastern half of the United States experiences westerly winds in the winter and the southern half of the country receives southerly winds in the summer, there is considerable local variation and information should be obtained from the nearest weather station.

Expansion   Is there room for expansion? Any plans for farmstead development should anticipate growth in the enterprise and the layout should facilitate expansion of buildings and services. Increased production volume requires more than additional or larger buildings; expansion of all facilities from machinery inventories to utilities and drainage fields may become necessary. It is wise to look for twice as much area as that required initially and, in developing a layout, recognize the full impact of increasing production volume in the future.

Other considerations in selecting a site are the proximity of housing developments, other commercial or industrial enterprises, and airports.

BUILDING ARRANGEMENT

The arrangement of facilities for maximum efficiency of operation should be the prime concern in farmstead planning. Proper arrangement increases efficiency by reducing walking distances to a minimum and providing adequate driveways and turn-arounds. It can also minimize the negative and utilize the positive effects of climatic elements (sun, wind, rain, and snow) and will in turn be influenced by drainage, slope, and other topographic features. Finally, fire protection, safety, and security are all influenced by the farmstead layout.

When a site has been selected, a large-scale map should be drawn and all major details indicated. These should include contour lines, the direction of north, the direction of prevailing winds and the general slope, existing roads, and natural wind barriers and waterways. Using model cutouts drawn to the same scale as the map, buildings then can be arranged and rearranged until a satisfactory layout is designed.

An operation center should be located for a starting point. Generally this will be the farm home which is likely to house the office and phone, and perhaps a CB base station. It should be situated at least 100 feet (30 m) from the road and located so that the flow of traffic to and from the farmstead may be observed from inside. It should also be oriented to make maximum use of sunlight and to take advantage of the best possible view.

The remaining buildings can then be arranged in relation to the operating center. There are a number of factors to be considered, the priority of which will vary with the enterprise.

Slope   Buildings should be located on relatively high ground with surface drainage directed away from foundations. When constructing a building on an area that slopes, some cutting and filling will be required. Costs may be kept to a minimum if the structure is carefully positioned and planned at an elevation that allows the volume of cut soil to just equal the fill soil required.

Drainage   Assuming that drainage was found to be adequate in the original selection of the site, buildings should be arranged to take the greatest advantage of the natural conditions.

Prevailing winds   Winds can blow from all directions, but the prevailing summer breezes and winter winds need to be considered in farmstead planning. As a general rule, winter winds sweep in from the north or northwest while summer breezes blow from the south, southwest, west, southeast, or east. Local conditions may further alter wind patterns, and information on prevailing winds for a given locality should be obtained from the local weather station.

The arrangement of buildings shown in Figure 3-1 should take advantage of the cooling effects of summer breezes and minimize the discomfort caused by cold winter winds. Open-front buildings faced away from the prevailing winter wind will usually benefit from the cooling summer currents.

Winds carry odors, dust, and noise, and prudent arrangement of buildings will use the wind to carry these away from the living center. Livestock yards and buildings should be located down wind from the farm home and from neighbors.

Buildings lined up at right angles to the wind rather than parallel

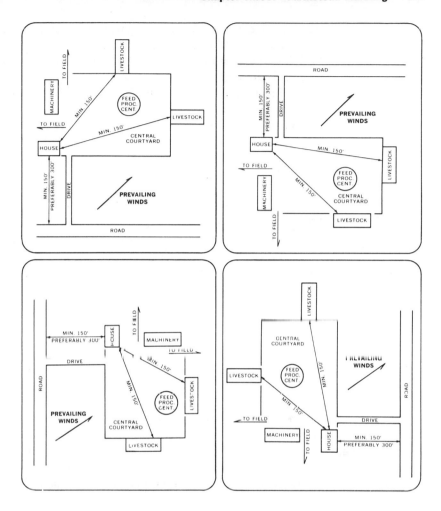

Figure 3-1. Farmstead and road relationships. (*Courtesy* Granite City Steel Division of National Steel Corporation)

are less subject to the spread of fire. In areas with appreciable snowfall, care should be taken to arrange buildings and fences to reduce to a minimum the drifting of snow into yards, drives, and open-front buildings.

Sun Open-front buildings, stock yards and solar heated facilities should be arranged so that in winter they receive the full benefit of sunlight throughout the day. Tall buildings, such as tower silos, should be located so they do not cast a shadow on feedlots.

Distances Labor efficiency is improved by reducing travel to a minimum. Buildings between which there will be the most travel should be located close together. If separate feed storage structures are used, locate them as close as possible to where the feed will be used. Arrange buildings in relation to drive and yard to allow easy maneuvering of large vehicles and equipment.

The distance between buildings usually is determined by a compromise involving efficiency, fire safety, odor control, and the space available. Fifty to 100 feet (15 to 30 m) is usually considered a minimum safe distance between buildings or groups of buildings. This minimizes the risk of fire spread and permits access for fighting fire. It is advisable to check with an insurance company before starting construction.

Guidelines for distances between buildings can be useful. One method for designing a layout is to divide the map of the farmstead site into concentric zones 100 feet (30 m) wide with the farm home at the center. This facilitates using the recommended distances to locate specific buildings (Figure 3-2). Zone 1 encompasses the family living area and should be protected from noise, odors, dust, and hazards to children. Machinery and supply storages and the farm shop may be located about 100 feet (30 m) from the house in zone 2 where they are easily accessible and, being relatively quiet and odor free, do not create a nuisance. Sheep, and young animals that need supervision but do not develop heavy odors and waste, can be located within 200 to 300 feet (60 to 90 m). In this same area, zone 3, dust-producing feed and grain storages are located a suitable distance from the house and at the same time close to the livestock units they are to serve. Hog facilities and large animal units should be located 300 feet (90 m) or more from the center. This not only reduces the danger of odors reaching the home but also places the unit which is most likely to be expanded in an area where space will be available. These recommendations are for a large scale enterprise; some adjustments would be made for smaller operations.

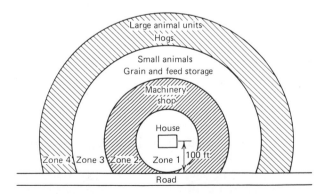

Figure 3-2. Farmstead planning zones. Each activity zone is 100 ft (30 m) wide. A visual aid for locating buildings and activities on a farmstead layout plan.

DRIVES, TURNAROUNDS, AND PARKING AREAS

Drives define the plan of circulation on the farm, directing traffic to service areas and parking. The layout of drives should allow space for vehicles to safely travel, maneuver, and park. It should also provide convenient parking for family and guests, and, in cold regions, space for disposing of plowed snow.

Drives that will be carrying large equipment, and on which cars may meet, should be a minimum of 16 feet (5 m) wide. In addition there should be several feet of clearance on either side to accommodate machinery over-hang, drainage and snow accumulation. The drive should be in view of the house or operations center and terminate in a turnaround with a minimum diameter of 110 feet (33 m). A small building, perhaps the fuel and lubricant storage, may be located in the center of the turnaround. Ordinarily, a U-shaped drive is not recommended. However, if the length is not great and the whole drive is visible from the house, it may be the most satisfactory design.

Branch drives may be as little as 8 feet (2.5 m) wide in straight areas, but should be wider on curves. A centerline radius of 25 feet (8 m) should be adequate for the curves.

Parking areas   Parking areas should be provided near the home and, if in a different location, the farm office. If the house is designed with front and back doors about equidistant from the parking area, then one area should be enough. Otherwise two areas are desirable.

YARD LIGHTING

Automatically controlled yard lights are a desirable feature of the farmstead. They help to prevent accidents by improving visibility, allowing a quick nighttime check of the farmstead from the house, and helping to discourage theft and vandalism. Mercury vapor and metal halide lamps have greater efficiency and longer life than incandescent lamps. Fluorescent lamps are not generally satisfactory for outdoor use because they fail to start under cold or damp conditions.

WIND AND SNOW CONTROL

Winter winds create a chill factor that causes a much greater stress on livestock than extreme cold alone. In addition, uncontrolled drifting snow can fill drives, yards, and even open-sided buildings. Also, extreme accumulations on roofs may cause structural failure.

In the north central states and Canadian plains provinces, tree wind-breaks or shelterbelts are commonly planted to reduce wind velocities and to control snow accumulations. From 6 to 12 rows are usually planted on the north and west sides of the farmstead. The shelter belts may be 125 to 150 feet (38 to 45 m) wide and offer wind protection for a distance equivalent to 10 times the tree height. Snow will accumulate for 50 to 100 feet (15 to 30 m) on the lee side of the shelterbelt (Figures 3-3 and 3-4).

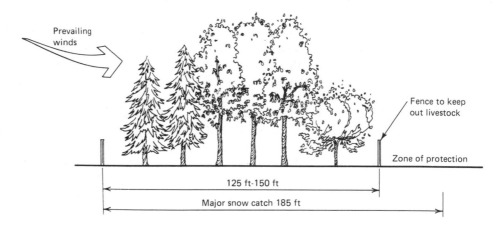

Figure 3-3.   Shelter belt for protection from wind and snow. The zone of major protection is approximately ten times the height of the trees.

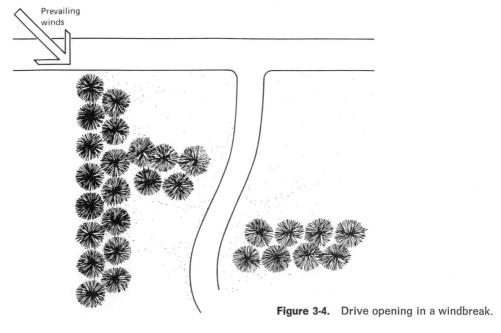

Figure 3-4.   Drive opening in a windbreak.

In other areas, and also while the trees are still small, fences are an effective way of controlling wind and snow (Figure 3-5). Slat fences, either vertical or horizontal, with a density of 75 to 85 percent will trap most of the snow in an area on the downwind side equal in width to four to five times the fence height. A fence of this type also offers good wind protection. Obviously these fences should be installed far enough from buildings or yards to allow the snow to accumulate in an unused area. The yard fence may be of solid construction, thus causing much of the remaining snow to accumulate on the windward side of the fence (outside of the yard).

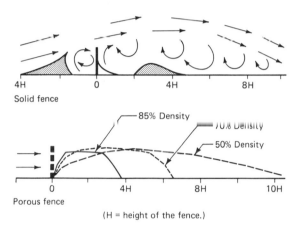

Figure 3-5. Snow drifting about solid and porous fences. (From *Snow and Wind Control for Farmstead and Feedlot*, Canada Department of Agriculture Bulletin #1461)

Fences should be attached to open-front buildings, somewhat back from the front and the same distance from the building. This produces a swirl chamber that dumps the snow outside rather than inside the building (Figure 3-6). Note also that buildings too closely connected may cause air currents that dump snow inside open fronts.

Almost any open-front building with its back to the wind, regardless of roof shape, is likely to have some snow accumulation just inside the open front. It has been found that a 6- to 8-inch (150- to 200-mm) slot at the rear eaves will prevent much of this.

Finally, do not forget the aesthetics of the total farmstead layout. Is the arrangement attractive? Is the home oriented to take advantage of natural views or landscaped areas? Aesthetics certainly can influence pride of ownership and the quality of life even though farm income is not increased.

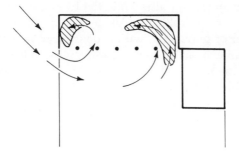

(a) Fence in line with end of building and attached building at right
     end cause air currents that carry snow into shed.

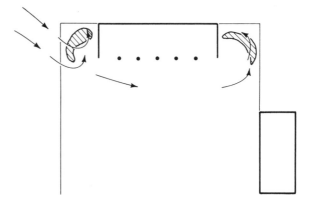

(b)   Fence and building moved away from shed as shown reduces
      likelihood of snow in open shed.

Figure 3-6. Building and fence location relative to snow accumulation in open-sided buildings. (From *Snow and Wind Control for Farmstead and Feedlot,* Canada Department of Agriculture Bulletin #1461)

The following check list may help to avoid the omission of factors that should be considered in choosing a site and planning a farmstead:

General

Zoning law clearance	Cutting and filling required
Title with no encumbrance	Prevailing wind
Environmental clearance	Soil quality
Good drainage	Electricity
Good water supply	Telephone
Space adequate for initial and expansion needs	School bus
	Road maintenance
Slope of land	Central to crop land

<table>
<tr><td align="center">Home</td><td align="center">Layout</td></tr>
</table>

Home	*Layout*
View	Spacing for fire safety and freedom from odors
Near driveway	
Good water supply	Silos and feed storage located to allow for barn expansion
Septic tank and drainage field	
Garden	Driveway width and location
Play area	Turnaround diameter
Garage	Farm pond possibilities
Wind protection	Wind and snow control
Parking space	Full use of sunshine

PROBLEMS

3.1   Prepare a map of an existing farmstead showing all details required to make an analysis of the layout. Using the checklist in the chapter, note the desirable features and those that could be improved.

3.2   With a separate map or overlay, show how housing facilities could be expanded and how other changes might be made in the farmstead layout to improve the efficiency and safety of the farmstead or to reduce the pollution potential.

3.3   Assuming that topography is not a limitation, lay out a new farmstead for a fruit farm that will sell at retail a part of the production at the storage. Assume that the farmstead will be located west of the highway and that the home and other supporting structures, as well as a storage and sales room, will be constructed.

REFERENCES

Midwest Plan Service. *Farmstead Planning Handbook.* Ames, Iowa: Midwest Plan Service, 1977.

Canada Department of Agriculture. *Snow and Wind Control for Farmstead and Feedlot* (Bulletin 1461). Canada Department of Agriculture, Ottawa, Canada.

Midwest Plan Service. *Structures and Environment Handbook.* Ames, Iowa: Midwest Plan Service, 1977.

Chapter Four

Wood

From the time of the earliest settlers wood has been a popular building material in the United States and Canada and has numerous applications in the construction of agricultural buildings today. It has some advantages over other materials and several disadvantages as well. It is easy to work, has some insulating value, and is light in weight in relation to its strength. On the other hand, wood is subject to damage by insects, moisture, and fire.

In order to select lumber for a particular job, the specific requirements for the job must first be determined and then the lumber selected that has the combination of qualities that will best meet those requirements. In order to make a wise selection, one must understand the general characteristics of wood as well as the differences relating to species, moisture content, and quality, and be able to relate those properties to a particular use. This chapter will deal with these characteristics as they relate to the use of wood for construction.

CLASSIFICATION OF WOOD

All woods native to the United States and Canada are classified as either hardwood or softwood. Hardwoods are obtained from deciduous trees (those that lose their leaves in autumn). Softwoods are obtained from coniferous or needle-bearing trees. There is no relationship to the actual hardness. For example, willow is classified as hardwood but actually is quite soft. Yellow pine, on the other hand, is classified as softwood but is very hard.

WOOD CHARACTERISTICS

Strength   The strength of wood is its ability to resist breaking when loaded. The strength in bending is particularly important for applications such as rafters, floor joists, and beams. The heavier, higher density species have the greatest strength. However, any member may have a reduced strength because of knots, crossgrain or other defects. The strength of wood is indicated by its safe fiber stress in pounds per square inch (kPa). A high moisture content reduces strength thus requiring lower design values.

Stiffness   The stiffness of wood is its ability to resist deflection or bending when loaded. Like strength, it is an important characteristic for such members as studs, joists and beams. Stiffness is necessary to prevent a gradual deflection in members which are loaded continuously over long periods of time. In general, the strongest species are also the stiffest. However, there are exceptions such as western hemlock and sitka spruce which are noted for their stiffness although they are only of medium strength. The stiffness of wood is indicated by its modulus of elasticity in pounds per square inch (MPa).

Hardness   Hardness is the property of wood that resists denting, scratching, and wear. Hardness is a desirable characteristic for flooring and stair treads. Bearing blocks used at the top of posts must be hard in order to avoid crushing. Hard species are difficult to work with and are subject to splitting when nailed. For such things as cabinets and furniture, hard wood is desirable because it will resist scratches and produce a high polish.

Toughness   The ability of a wood to withstand shock-loading is spoken of as toughness. Even when loaded to the breaking point, members made from a tough specie resist separation. Joists and beams under drive floors that will carry trucks and tractors need the property of toughness.

Dimensional stability   All wood will shrink or swell with a change in moisture level. However, those species that show the greatest stability and least change are desirable for use with materials that are themselves stable. The frame for a plastered house should be stable to avoid cracks. The best quality flooring is made from woods that exhibit little shrinking and swelling.

Resistance to warping   Warping is the characteristic bowing, twisting, or cupping displayed by some woods. While warping is affected by

Table 4-1   Classification of Woods According to Properties
Ranked A, B or C (A is highest or desirable)

Kind of Wood	Bending Strength	Strength as a Post	Hardness	Toughness	Freedom from Warping	Nail Holding	Paint Holding	Decay Resistance	Ease of Working	Freedom from Odor	Typical Use
Hardwoods											
Ash, white	A	A	A	A	B	A	C	C	C	A	Implements, containers
Aspen	C	C	C	C	B	C	A	C	A	A	Boxes, lumber, pulp
Birch	A	B	B	A	B	A	B	C	C	A	Flooring, furniture
Cherry	A	A	B	B	A	A	B	C	B	B	Furniture, woodenware
Cottonwood	C	C	C	C	C	C	A	C	B	B	Pulpwood, containers
Elm	A	A	A	A	B	A	C	C	C	A	Furniture, containers
Hickory	A	A	A	A	B	A	C	C	C	B	Handles, athletic equipment
Locust	A	A	A	A	B	A	C	A	C	B	Poles, posts
Maple, hard	A	B	A	A	B	A	B	C	C	A	Flooring, furniture
Oak, red	A	B	A	A	B	A	C	C	C	B	Flooring, furniture
Oak, white	A	B	A	A	B	A	C	A	C	B	Furniture, cooperage
Poplar	B	B	C	B	A	B	A	C	A	A	Furniture, plywood
Walnut	A	A	B	A	A	A	C	B	B	A	Furniture, gunstocks
Softwoods											
Cedar, eastern red	B	B	B	B	A	B	A	A	B	C	Posts, paneling, chests
Cedar, western red	C	B	C	C	A	C	A	A	A	C	Shingles, siding, poles
Fir, Douglas	A	A	B	B	B	A	B	B	B	A	Construction, plywood
Fir, white	B	B	C	C	B	C	C	C	B	A	Light construction, containers
Hemlock, eastern	B	B	B	B	B	B	B	C	B	A	Construction, containers
Hemlock, western	B	B	B	B	B	B	B	C	C	A	Construction, pulp
Larch, western	A	A	B	B	B	A	C	B	A	C	Construction, poles
Pine, Idaho white	B	B	C	C	A	C	A	C	B	C	Millwork, construction
Pine, lodgepole	B	B	C	C	B	B	B	C	A	C	Poles, lumber, ties
Pine, eastern white	C	C	C	C	A	B	A	C	A	C	Millwork, furniture
Pine, ponderosa	C	C	C	C	A	B	B	C	A	C	Millwork, construction
Pine, sugar	C	C	C	C	A	C	A	C	A	C	Millwork, patterns
Pine, yellow southern	A	A	B	B	B	A	C	B	B	C	Construction, poles, siding
Redwood	B	A	B	B	A	B	A	A	A	A	Siding, tanks, millwork
Spruce, eastern	B	B	C	C	A	B	B	B	B	A	Construction, pulpwood
Spruce, Englemann	C	C	C	C	A	B	C	C	C	A	Light construction, poles
Spruce, sitka	B	B	C	B	A	B	B	C	B	A	Construction, millwork

From Selection and Use of Wood Products for Home and Farm Building, USDA, Forest Service, Agriculture Information Bulletin N. 311.

the method of sawing, different species vary considerably in their natural tendency to warp. Warping is objectionable because it causes waste, poor fitting, and a generally undesirable appearance.

Nail holding The ability to hold nails is closely related to density. While harder woods hold nails better, they are also prone to splitting which can seriously reduce their holding value. Preboring a hole 75 percent of the nail diameter, the use of smaller nails, or the use of blunt-pointed nails are methods used to reduce the incidence of splitting. Since nailing is the most commonly used fastening method for wood members, good nail holding properties are essential in agricultural construction.

Ease of working Softer species that have a uniform grain are easiest to work and generally are more resistant to splitting. Wood that is easy to work increases labor efficiency and helps insure uniformity in the strength of nailed joints.

Paint holding ability Species that have a uniform grain and exhibit little swelling and shrinkage are likely to hold paint well. Edge grain ordinarily holds paint better than flat grain. Softwood species in particular should be free of knots and excessive pitch if they are to be painted. Regardless of specie, paint holding properties are affected by moisture in the wood as well as exposure to sun and rain.

Decay resistance Some species have a high natural resistance to decay. However, for any given specie, the heartwood (darker, center area of a tree) is likely to be much more resistant than the sapwood (lighter colored, outer area of the tree made up of active living cells). Almost any wood that continuously has below 20 percent or more than 35 percent moisture content is not likely to decay. Varying moisture in the 21 to 25 percent range is likely to cause decay in any but the most resistant species. Construction members that come in contact with the ground should be selected for decay resistance, or better still, they should be made of pressure-preservative treated wood.

Grain Some woods are chosen for a particular application because of the appearance of their grain. Naturally finished furniture, wall paneling and siding are typical examples.

Odor A few woods, such as cedar, may be selected for a particular application because they have a pronounced odor. Others may be selected because they are free of odor and taste. This would be a consideration in the construction of certain types of food storage buildings. Apples in storage, for example, may absorb odors and flavor from a specie that has a strong scent.

Defects in Wood

Defects in wood may be either natural or caused by the type of milling and curing.

Decay   Decay results from moisture levels of 21 to 25 percent in the presence of air. Obviously decay reduces the strength of the wood and spoils its appearance.

Knots   If tight and small, knots may be of little consequence. However, if they are large, loose, or missing, they seriously reduce the strength and appearance value of the piece.

Wane   This refers to an area on a piece of wood that either has exposed bark or an area where the bark has dropped off. The principal objection to wane is the appearance, although the strength may be affected in some cases.

Checks   Checks are cracks *across* the growth rings that occur during curing. They reduce strength and increase the likelihood of splitting due to nailing near the end of a piece.

Shakes   Cracks *along* the growth rings are called shakes, but they produce the same results as checks.

Pitch pockets   These are found in some softwood species. The pocket, hole, or crack, with a pitch accumulation, is almost impossible to paint or varnish satisfactorily.

Crossgrain   Crossgrain results from sawing crooked logs. It may seriously reduce the strength of the piece.

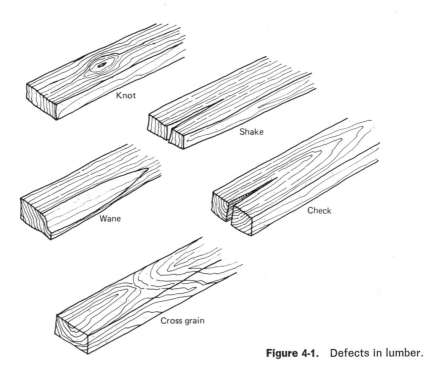

Figure 4-1.   Defects in lumber.

Warping This may not always be classified as a defect but can certainly reduce the usefulness of lumber. It is caused by unequal shrinkage as the lumber is cured and results in bowing, twisting, cupping, etc. Warping is much more prevalent in some species than others and will be worse for a given specie if the lumber has been slash sawn and not "stuck" well while curing. To insure as equal drying as possible during air curing, a pile will have one inch strips "stuck" between each layer to let the air circulate freely.

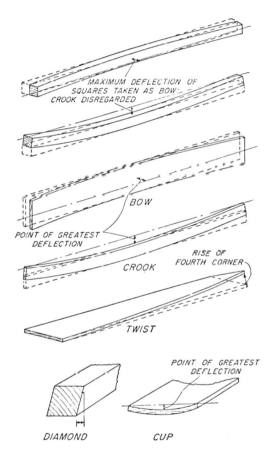

Figure 4-2. Various kinds of warp. (From *Handbook 72,* U.S. Department of Agriculture)

Shrinking and Swelling

Besides its effect on warping, excessive shrinking and swelling can present other problems. It may result in paint failure, cause cracks in floors or paneling, and in some cases is severe enough in a roof deck to cause asphalt roof coverings to buckle and become uneven. Wood shrinks the most tangentially, that is at right angles to the growth rings. It shrinks about a half to two-thirds as much radially, that is parallel with the growth rings, and very little along its length.

LUMBER FROM LOGS

The rate at which a tree grows varies with the season. Rapid spring growth is followed by slower summer growth and eventual dormancy in the winter. The resulting growth rings of alternate low and high density produce the grain found in lumber.

The appearance of the grain and its effect on warping, shrinkage and swelling, paint holding, and wear resistance is largely determined by the method in which the log is sawed into lumber. If the log is *slash sawed* (simply sawed from one side of the log to the other) there will be variations ranging from all flat grain to all edge grain with most pieces having some of each. This is the easiest, least wasteful, and least expensive method and produces the widest boards. However, the boards are very likely to warp as they dry. *Quarter sawing* refers to the two or three methods used to saw a log in such a way that a predominately edge grain is obtained throughout the width of the board. Quarter-sawed lumber is less likely to split, warp, or shrink excessively. It also holds paint better and wears well if used for flooring.

Commercial vs Native Lumber

Most commercial lumber that is available in lumber yards is softwood and is graded under the American Softwood Lumber Standard. Particularly in the eastern United States and Canada, a number of native woods may be purchased from local sawmills. The quality and seasoning vary greatly, and finish is to order. The cost of this lumber, often used rough-cut, is somewhat less than yard lumber. Many species are satisfactory for boards and some for light framing.

American Softwood Lumber Standard

The U.S. Department of Commerce publishes voluntary standards for softwood lumber. The latest revision provides for standardization in terminology, classification, size, and grading provisions.

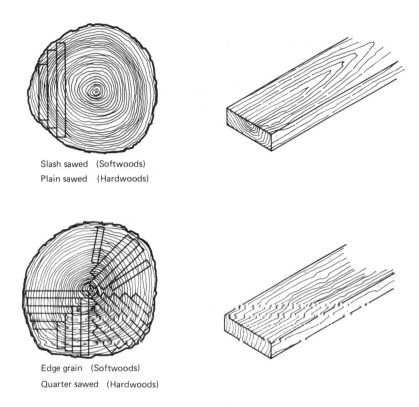

Slash sawed   (Softwoods)
Plain sawed   (Hardwoods)

Edge grain   (Softwoods)
Quarter sawed   (Hardwoods)

Figure 4-3.   Methods of sawing logs into lumber.

The standard classifies lumber according to use:

Factory and shop lumber   This lumber is graded on the basis of what usable material can be cut from the piece.

Structural lumber   Large-sized joists, beams, and posts are classified as structural lumber.

Yard lumber   Most commonly found in retail lumber yards, yard lumber is graded on the basis of the use of the entire piece.

Boards   Boards are less than 2 inches thick and 2 inches or more in width.

Dimension lumber   Dimension lumber is 2 inches to 4 inches thick and 2 inches or more in width.

Timbers   These are 5 inches or more in their least dimension.

Grade Examples

There are six U.S. agencies plus the NLGA (National Lumber Grades Aunthority), a Canadian agency, that have established, under the provisions of the American Softwood Lumber Standard, grades for lumber which have been approved by the Board of Review of the ASLS Committee. The yard lumber class may be broken down into *finish lumber, boards* and *framing.* The first two are graded on the basis of appearance, while the framing is graded on the basis of strength. A typical grading system is shown in Table 4-2. Figure 4-4 A and B shows the interpretation of a grade stamp and two typical stamps.

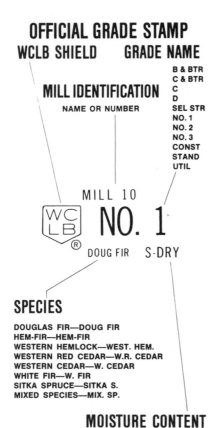

Figure 4-4(a). Interpretation of a grade stamp. (*Courtesy* West Coast Lumber Inspection Bureau)

Figure 4-4(b). Typical grade stamps. (*Courtesy* Western Wood Products Association and Southern Pine Inspection Bureau)

Table 4-2 Grades of Lumber

Classification	Grades	Description and Use
DIMENSION 2" to 5" thick 2" or more wide	*Structural Light Framing* (2"-4" thick, 2"-4" wide) Select Structural	For engineered application where higher bending strength ratios are needed. Use where high strength and stiffness and good appearance are needed.
	No. 1	Use about the same as SEL STR, slightly lower in quality.
	No. 2	Recommended for most general construction.
	No. 3	Appropriate for use in general construction where appearance is not generally a factor.
	Light Framing (2"-4" thick, 2"-4" wide) Construction	Provides good appearance at lower design levels where high strength and high appearance are not needed. Recommended and widely used for general construction.
	Standard	Customarily used for the same purposes or in conjunction with Construction grade; a little lower in quality.
	Utility	Used for studding, blocking, plates, bracing and rafters where a combination of good strength and economical construction is desired.
	Economy (2"-4" thick, 2" and wider)	Suitable or crating, bracing, and temporary construction.
	Studs (2"-4" thick, 2"-6" wide) Stud	Only one grade. Suitable or all stud uses including use in load bearing walls.
	Structural Joists & Planks (2"-4" thick, 5" and wider) Select Structural	For engineering applications requiring lumber 5" and wider.
	No. 1	Recommended for use where both high strength and stiffness and good appearance are required.
	No. 2	About the same as SEL STR, somewhat lower in quality. Recommended for most general construction use.
	No. 3	Appropriate for use in general construction where appearance is not a factor.

Table 4-2—continued

Classification	Grades	Description and Use
DIMENSION	*Appearance Framing* (2"–4" thick, 2" and wider)	
	A	For exposed use in housing and light construction where knotty type lumber of high strength and finest appearance is required. Only one grade.
POSTS AND TIMBERS	Select Structural	Used for columns, posts, and struts in heavy construction such as warehouses and docks where superior strength is required.
5"x5" and larger Width not more than 2" greater than thickness	No. 1 Structural	Use the same as SEL STR where appearance is less exacting, but where high strength is required. Slightly lower quality.
	Standard	Recommended for general construction.
	Utility	Recommended for rough general construction.
BOARDS	Select Merchantable	Primarily for use in housing and light construction where it is exposed as paneling, shelving and other uses where a knotty type of lumber with finest appearance is required.
Up to 1½" thick 2" and wider	Construction	Recommended for subfloors, roof and wall sheathing, concrete forms.
	Standard	Used more widely than other grades for general construction. Used for same purposes as Construction, lower in quality.
	Utility	Combines usefulness and low cost for general construction.
	Economy	Suitable for low grade sheathing, crating, bracing, and temporary construction.
FINISH	C and BTR	Graded for appearance. Highest type product produced from the clear section of the log. Recommended for interior trim and cabinet work with a natural finish.
2" and thinner 2" and wider	D	Suitable where requirements for finishing are less exacting; paint finish.

(Extracted from Standard Grading Rules for West Coast Lumber)

Lumber Finish

After sawing, and before further finishing, lumber is referred to as *rough-cut*. Most lumber is planed for better appearance and easier working. It is then referred to as *dressed* or *surfaced*. The degree of dressing is often indicated by abbreviations such as S2E if two edges are planed or S4S if all four surfaces are finished.

In addition, lumber may be *worked*. Lumber with a tongue and groove is referred to as *matched* or T & G. Lumber that is rabbeted on both edges to provide a close-fitting lapped joint is referred to as *ship-lap*. If a shape or molded form is cut into the surface, it is referred to as *patterned* lumber. Some worked and molding cross section shapes are shown in Figure 4-5.

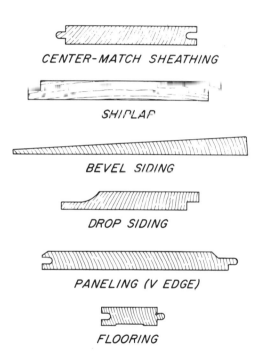

CENTER-MATCH SHEATHING

SHIPLAP

BEVEL SIDING

DROP SIDING

PANELING (V EDGE)

FLOORING

Figure 4-5. Typical patterns of lumber. (*Agricultural Information Bulletin 311*, U.S. Department of Agriculture)

Lumber Size

Lumber is spoken of and sold on the basis of *nominal* size. However, the actual size of dressed lumber is appreciably smaller than the nominal size.

In order to improve the standardization of actual sizes, the American Softwood Lumber Standard defines *dry* and *green* lumber and the minimum sizes for each category. Dry lumber has been dried or seasoned to 19 percent or less moisture content. Green lumber is that with a moisture content in excess of 19 percent.

Table 4-3 gives the normal and actual measurements for dressed boards and dimension lumber.

Table 4-3   Nominal and Actual Sizes of Dressed Lumber

Nominal Size		Minimum Dressed Size of S4S			
inches	millimeters	inches		millimeters	
		Dry	Green	Dry	Green
1	19	¾	25/32	19.05	19.84
1¼		1	1-1/32		
2	38	1½	1-9/16	38.10	39.69
3	64	2½	2-9/16	63.50	65.09
4	89	3½	3-9/16	88.90	90.49
6	140	5½	5⅝	139.70	142.87
8	184	7¼	7½	184.15	190.50
10	235	9¼	9½	234.95	241.03
12	286	11¼	11½	285.75	292.10
14	337	13¼	13½	336.55	342.90

Lumber Measurement

The unit of measure used for lumber is the board foot. One board foot is a volume of any shape that is equal to a piece 1 foot long, 1 foot wide and 1 inch thick. Board measure is always calculated with nominal sizes.

A rule of thumb that is useful in calculating board feet starts with the number of pieces, the width in inches, the thickness in inches and the length in feet. Look for the number 12 and cancel it to 1. The product of the remaining numbers is the board feet.

For example:

12 pcs—2″x8″x10′, 12/12=1, 1x2x8x10=160 board feet

In determining the quantity of lumber to cover a surface such as a roof deck or subfloor, the measurements will be in square feet. Because the actual size of the lumber is less than the nominal size, it is necessary to order more board feet than the square feet of surface to be covered. The following rules of thumb may be used.

- Rough-cut—Order 10 percent extra.
- Dressed, S4S—For sizes over 4 inches, order 10 percent extra; for 4-inch width, order 15 percent extra.
- Tongue and groove—For sizes over 4 inches, order 20 percent extra; for 4-inch width, order 30 percent extra.

Very little waste is assumed with these rules. Consequently an additional amount may need to be ordered to account for waste.

An extra 5 percent in addition to the above quantities will be needed if the lumber is to be installed diagonally.

For example: a shed roof, 16x32 feet, is to be decked with 1″x8″ T & G boards. The board feet required would be 16x32=512 square feet + 20 percent; 512x1.20=615 board feet to order.

Preserving Lumber

The best way to preserve wood is to keep it dry, well ventilated and sufficiently above the ground to discourage termites. Where it is necessary to have wood exposed to the weather or have it in contact with the ground, there are a number of effective commercial wood preservatives. Pressure treatment by a wood treating company insures deep penetration of the preservative and therefore the greatest protection. Some preservatives may be brushed on by the user with a ¼- to ½-inch penetration. While this is helpful, it is not as satisfactory as the pressure process.

Coal tar creosote This is excellent for protecting lumber and poles that will be in continuous contact with the ground. Creosote is dark in color, produces unpleasant fumes that are harmful to plants, and the treated wood cannot be painted. Wood that is freshly treated with creosote is easily ignited and produces a dense smoke. Fortunately, this characteristic decreases with time.

Pentachlorophenol Pentachlorophenol is a preservative that is dissolved in either volatile or heavier oils which may be applied by pressure treatment or by brush. The pressure treatment is much more effective. If volatile oils are used, the wood may be painted after several days. While penta-treated wood is less toxic to plants than creosote, there is still a possibility for damage from the carrier oil or from slight leaching. Other materials should be used if there is any chance of the treated wood coming in contact with the plants. It should be noted that plastic films may be damaged.

There is some indication that wood treated with penta and still bleeding to any extent may present a health hazard to animals. While it may not be the penta itself, but minute quantities of dioxins that are produced in the manufacturing process, it seems advisable to avoid using penta-treated lumber in feed bunks, hay racks, or in any place where the feed is in direct contact with the wood. This would also apply to bunker silos unless they are lined with plastic before filling. Existing feed bunks or silos can be lined with plywood after thorough cleaning. Penta-treated poles, stall gutters, posts, and outside gates and posts probably do not present a hazard. It is unnecessary and undesirable to use penta-treated wood for stall dividers.

Copper naphthenate This is available in volatile oils at 2 to 10 percent concentrations. It will provide limited protection of plant structures when brushed on by the user. It is not commonly available as commercial pressure-treated lumber. There may be some plant damage during the first season.

Waterborne salt-type preservatives These are essentially nontoxic to plants and are recommended for use on flats and benches where plants will come in contact with the treated wood. These include ammonical copper arsenite (ACA), chromated copper arsenate (CCA) Types I and II, and fluor chrome arsenate phenol (FCAP). The CCA Type II and the FCAP are most commonly used for pressure treated material, although they may not be a stock item and may have to be ordered. The CCA is suitable for both above ground and ground contact applications, while the FCAP is more subject to leaching and is most suitable for above ground use. All of the waterborne preservatives leave a suitable surface for painting or gluing.

Fire Retardant Treatments

The pressure treatment of lumber or plywood with certain inorganic salts, such as polybrominated biphenyls, can greatly reduce the possibility for the wood to support combustion. In case of fire, noncombustible gases and water vapor that tend to reduce the flammability of the wood are released. Unfortunately, PBB presents a health hazard to livestock, people and wildlife. The lumber should not be used in any location where animals can come in contact with it.

Fiber stress design values (the allowable strength), for fire retardant treated material should be reduced by 10 percent.

PROBLEMS

4.1   Prepare a list of the species of wood that are available from local lumber yards or that are grown and sawed locally. Note the particular applications or uses for each specie.

4.2   Using a detailed plan for a small building, develop a bill of materials for all of the lumber needed, including the size of lumber for each part, the length and number of pieces required for each part and finally, a summary showing the order and the total board measure. Save this information for related problems in later chapters.

4.3   A single-pitch shed roof 26 by 36 feet (8 by 11 m) is to be covered with 8-inch (184-mm) tongue and groove roofers. Determine the size of the order assuming minimal waste.

4.4   Calculate the total board measure for the following:

30 — 2″ x 4″ x 12′ (38 x 89 x 3658 mm)

16 — 2″ x 6″ x 10′ (38 x 140 x 3048 mm)

12 — 2″ x 8″ x 14′ (38 x 184 x 4267 mm)

REFERENCES

Anderson, LeRoy O. *Selection and Use of Wood Products for Home and Farm Building.* U.S. Department of Agriculture Forest Service, Agricultural Information Bulletin 311. Madison, Wis., 1967.

Duncan, G A. and J.N. Walker. *Preservative Treatment of Greenhouse Wood.* Lexington: University of Kentucky.

Forest Products Laboratory. *Wood Handbook.* U.S. Department of Agriculture Handbook No. 72, 1955.

Midwest Plan Service. *Structures and Environment Handbook.* Ames, Iowa: Midwest Plan Service, 1977.

National Forest Products Association. *National Design Specification for Wood Construction.* Washington, D.C.: National Forest Products Association, 1977.

Shull, Lee R. *Wood Preservatives Should be Used With Caution.* Hoard's Dairyman, Vol. 122, no. 17, 1977.

U.S. Department of Agriculture. *Gardening for Food and Fun* (U.S. Department of Agriculture Yearbook of Agriculture), 1977.

U.S. Department of Agriculture. *Preservative Treatment of Fence Posts and Farm Timbers.* U.S. Department of Agriculture Farmers Bulletin 2049, 1956.

Chapter Five

Plywood

Plywood is a useful building material manufactured by laminating wood veneers together under great pressure. Strength and rigidity are obtained by alternating the direction of the grain in each layer. Although the layers usually consist of single veneers which have been peeled from logs, they also are made by laminating *two veneers* with their grain parallel.

Most plywood is produced in 4 by 8 foot (1200 by 2400 mm) panels. However, other sizes are available on special order. From three to seven layers are used to produce panels ranging from 3/16 inch (4.8 mm) up to 1⅛ inches (28.6 mm) in thickness. The common thicknesses used for sheathing grade panels are ⅜, ½, and ¾ inches (9, 12, and 18 mm).

The American Plywood Association, which represents manufacturers of more than 80 percent of the U.S. production, has initiated a voluntary product standard for construction and industrial plywood (U.S. Product Standard PS 1-74, 1974). The purpose of the standard is "to provide a basis for common understanding among producers, distributors and users." It covers such subjects as wood species, grading, glue, construction, moisture content, dimensions and tolerances. Although the U.S. National Bureau of Standards publishes the standard, it has no regulatory authority. Building specifications, codes, sales contracts, and advertising tend to make its provisions effective. Any discussion about plywood must by necessity be based largely on this standard along with engineering and technical data presented in numerous APA publications.

CLASSIFICATION

Plywood is classified in a number of ways including moisture resistance, strength, and veneer grade.

Type

Plywood is classified as *interior* or *exterior* on the basis of the type of adhesive and veneer grade. Exterior type is made with 100 percent waterproof glue. Generally the interior plys, and in some cases surface veneers, are of higher grade than those used for the interior type. A number of interior type panels are manufactured with exterior glue and are considered satisfactory for protected agricultural applications.

Grade

There are a number of grades based on the appearance and defects in the veneers. The grades, with some but not all of their characteristics, follow. A is so free of defects and has so few repairs that it is suitable for a natural finish and is often used for cabinet work. A grade is smooth, free of knots, and paintable, although a limited number of repairs may be present. Patches may be of the "boat," "router" or "sled" type and small cracks may be repaired by filling. B grade is also smooth and generally suitable for painting. However, sound, tight knots may be found along with varying numbers of repairs. Minor sanding defects, holes up to 1/16 inch (1.5 mm) and splits up to 1/32 inch (1 mm) are also allowed in this grade. C grade allows 1½-inch (38-mm) tight knots, 1-inch (25-mm) knot holes and occasional 1½-inch (38-mm) knot holes. Splits of up to ⅜ inch (9.5 mm) of any length are permitted if they taper to 1/16 inch (1.5 mm) or ½ inch (13 mm) for half the panel length. Repairs may be of either wood or synthetic material and are restricted in size but not in number. Sanding defects that do not impair strength or serviceability are permitted. *C-plugged* is a repaired C grade that limits defects to ¼ by ½ inch (6 by 13 mm) and splits to ⅛ inch (3 mm) so that the panel is suitable for use as underlayment for nonrigid floor covering materials. D grade veneers may have any number of repairs, worm or borer holes, and sanding defects that do not seriously affect the strength or serviceability of the panel. Tight knots and knot holes up to 2½ inches (64 mm) and an occasional 3-inch (76-mm) knot are allowed as long as the aggregate width does not exceed 10 inches (250 mm) out of the 48-inch (1200-mm) panel. Up to 1-inch (25-mm) splits are allowed, but they must taper to 1/16 inch (1.5 mm) at one end.

Limited quantities of "white pocket," a decay that occurs in living conifers, are allowed in veneers.

Almost any combination of the foregoing grades is available as face and back surfaces for panels. In buying plywood for appearance, attention should be paid to the surface veneer grade (A-A where both sides will show, A-D where only one side will show). If the plywood is to be used in any location where high moisture may occur, an exterior panel should be selected.

In contrast, by far the greatest quantity of plywood used in agriculture consists of grades engineered to the needs of construction applications.

Group

There are approximately 70 species of logs peeled for use as plywood. Since these vary considerably in strength and stiffness they are divided into five groups for use in the engineered grades. The lower the number the greater the strength.

Engineered Grades

The engineered grades include C-D Interior with exterior glue (often called CDX), Structural I and II C-D Interior, Structural I and II C-C Exterior, and C-C Exterior. Structural I and II grades are made with exterior glue. Structural I is made from Group 1 species, while Structural II is limited to Group 1, 2, or 3 species. Only Structural I and II C-C Exterior and C-C Exterior are fully exterior type and suitable for high moisture applications.

Identification Index

The unsanded engineered grades of ⅞ inch (22 mm) or less in thickness carry an identification index consisting of a fraction, the numerator of which indicates the safe spacing of roof supports for the panel, while the demoninator indicates the safe spacing of floor supports for the panel. For example, a 48/24 means that a 48-inch (1200-mm) span on a roof deck or a 24-inch (600-mm) span on a subfloor is acceptable. A 24/0 means a 24-inch (600-mm) roof span is satisfactory, but the panel is not recommended for subflooring. These values are based on a 35-pound per square foot (1676 Pa) roof load and a 100-pound per square foot (4788 Pa) floor load. The floor load limitation is a deflection of 1/360 of the span. Due to differences in strength of species in the groups, the same identification index may be found on panels of differing thicknesses.

Structural panels made of Group 2 species may sometimes be given the same identification index as Group 1, but only when the panels have been manufactured to an increased thickness specification. In some cases this variation in thickness may be objectionable. Therefore it is desirable to specify thickness as well as the identification index when ordering.

Table 5-1 shows the identification indexes for unsanded, engineered grade panels.

Table 5-1   Identification Indexes for Unsanded Plywood Grades

Thickness (inch)	C-D INT—APA C-C EXT—APA		
	Group 1 & Structural I	Group 2 or 3 & Structural II	Group 4
5/16	20/0	16/0	12/0
3/8	24/0	20/0	16/0
1/2	32/16	24/0	24/0
5/8	42/20	32/16	30/12
3/4	48/24	42/20	36/16
7/8	—	40/24	42/20

(From Plywood Agricultural Construction Guide, 1976.)

Figure 5-1 shows four typical APA grade trademarks along with an explanation of each term shown.

Identification Index for Agriculture

The acceptability of identification index values by local building codes should be verified before designs for homes or public buildings are finalized. In the case of agricultural buildings, it is often possible to design for greater allowable deflections or on the basis of strength alone. APA publishes a family of curves (Plywood Agricultural Construction Guide, 1976) allowing one to determine the safe load for a range of spans with a deflection of 1/180 or 1/240 of the span or for strength alone. Table 5-2 provides values extracted from these curves.

Specialty Panels

There are dozens of combinations of grade, size, type, thickness, and group, many but not all of which are found in the marketplace. In addition, there are some specialty plywoods which are produced for specific applications. A brief description of several of these follows.

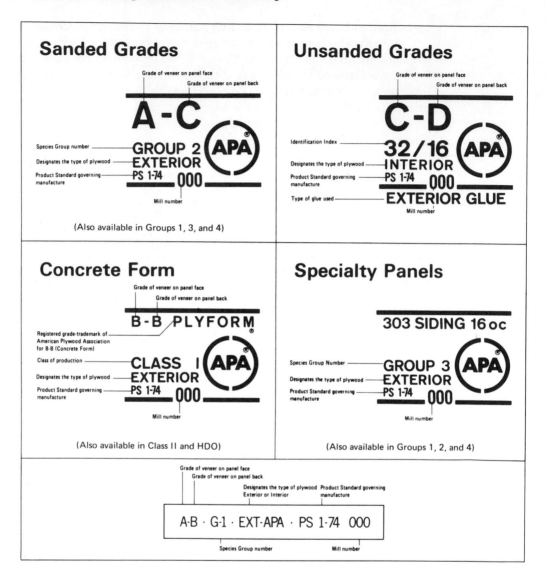

Figure 5-1. Typical grade-trademarks of the American Plywood Association.

2-4-1 The numerals 2-4-1 denote a combination subfloor and underlayment panel for use with supports that are 4 foot (1200 mm) o.c. (on center). These 4- by 8-foot (1200 by 2400 mm), interior type, tongue-and-groove panels are 1⅛ inches (28.6 mm) thick and have a C-plugged face.

Table 5-2   Allowable Panel Loads Determined by Strength
(Face grain perpendicular to framing, continuous over 3 spans,
C-D unsanded panels)

| Identi-fication Index | lb/sq ft | | | | Pascals | | Strength Parallel to |
	Span 12 in.	16 in.	24 in.	48 in.	400 mm	600 mm	Framing
24/0	220	120	54	—	5 746	2 586	21%
32/16	335	185	80	—	8 858	3 830	23%
42/20	475	290	125	30	13 885	5 985	25%
48/24	675	380	165	40	18 194	7 900	48%

Adjustment factors:

3 spans related to 1, (32 in. & under)	0.80
2 spans related to 1, (over 32 in.)	1.00
Over 16% moisture	0.71
C-C exterior unsanded	1.17

(From Plywood Agricultural Construction Guide, 1976.)

Plyform   Plyform is manufactured especially for use in building concrete forms. It is a sanded panel that has a B veneer on both sides and is edge-sealed and mill-oiled at the factory. It comes in Class 1 with Group 1 species face veneers and Class 2 with faces of either Group 1 or 2 species.

MDO and HDO   These are the designations for medium density overlay and high density overlay. The surface is a hard, semiopaque, resin-impregnated fiber overlay that is heat-fused to both panel faces. It is highly abrasion resistant. The MDO makes an excellent base for paint while the HDO ordinarily does not need to be painted. The overlays are suitable for cabinets, countertops, concrete forms, and are often the base for reflective road signs.

303 siding   This siding is available in many textures and finishes including MDO. The grade stamp indicates the specie group as well as the recommended stud spacing. The 303 siding panels may be installed over sheathing or directly to studs for greater economy. Texture 1-11 panels, now included in the 303 category, are available as ⅝-inch (16-mm) exterior, sanded or unsanded, with ¼-inch (6-mm) grooves giving the appearance of vertical siding. Texture 1-11 is also available with an MDO finish.

Marine plywood   Marine plywood is made only from Douglas fir or western larch and has solid-jointed core construction. Although it is made only with A, B, or overlay veneers, it is no more resistant to moisture damage than any other exterior-type plywood.

APPLICATION RECOMMENDATIONS

1. Exterior type plywood (C-C is the minimum grade) should always be chosen if moisture levels are likely to exceed 16 percent either continuously or intermittently. In continuously dry applications, the less expensive C-D Structural grades with exterior glue are satisfactory.

2. For greatest strength and stiffness, plywood should be installed with the face grain perpendicular to the framing.

Table 5-3   Plywood Grades for Agricultural Applications

	Use these terms when you specify	Description and Most Common Uses	Typical Grade-trademarks	Veneer Grade			Most Common Thicknesses (inch) (3)					
				Face	Back	Inner Plies	1/4	5/16	3/8	1/2	5/8	3/4
APPEARANCE (1)	A-A EXT-APA (2) (4)	Use where the appearance of both sides is important. Fences, built-ins, signs, cabinets, commercial refrigerators, tanks and ducts	A A G3 EXT APA PS 1 74	A	A	C	■		■	■	■	■
	A-B EXT-APA (2) (4)	For use similar to A-A EXT panels but where the appearance of one side is less important	A B G1 EXT APA PS 1 74	A	B	C	■		■	■	■	■
	A-C EXT-APA (2) (4)	Exterior use where the appearance of only one side is important. Sidings, soffits, fences, structural uses, truck lining and farm buildings. Tanks, commercial refrigerators	A-C GROUP 2 EXTERIOR PS 1 000	A	C	C	■		■	■	■	■
	B-B EXT-APA (2) (4)	An outdoor utility panel with solid paintable faces for uses where higher quality is not necessary	BB G1 EXT APA PS 1 74	B	B	C	■		■	■	■	■
	B-C EXT-APA (2) (4)	An outdoor utility panel for farm service and work buildings, truck linings, containers, tanks, agricultural equipment	B-C GROUP 3 EXTERIOR PS 1 000	B	C	C	■		■	■	■	■
ENGINEERED	C-D INT-APA w/ext glue (2)	A utility panel for use where exposure to weather and moisture will be limited	C-D 32/16 INTERIOR PS 1 000 EXTERIOR GLUE	C	D	D	■	■	■	■	■	■
	C-C EXT-APA (2)	Unsanded grade with waterproof bond for subflooring and roof decking, siding on service and farm buildings. Backing, crating, pallets and pallet bins	C-C 32/16 EXTERIOR PS 1 000	C	C	C	■	■	■	■	■	■
	C-C PLUGGED EXT-APA (2)	For refrigerated or controlled atmosphere rooms. Also for pallets, fruit pallet bins, tanks, truck floors and linings. Touch-sanded	C C PLUGGED GROUP 4 EXTERIOR PS 1 000	C Plgd	C	C	■	■	■	■	■	■
	STRUCTURAL I & II C-D INT & C-C EXT-APA	For engineered applications in farm construction. Unsanded. For species requirements see (4)	STRUCTURAL C-C 32/16 EXTERIOR PS 1 000	C	C or D	C or D		■	■	■	■	■
SPECIALTY	HDO EXT-APA (2) (4)	Exterior type High Density Overlay plywood with hard, semi-opaque resin-fiber overlay. Abrasion resistant. Painting not ordinarily required. For concrete forms, signs, acid tanks, cabinets, counter tops and farm equipment	HDO A A G1 EXT APA PS 1 74	A or B	A or B	C (5)	■		■	■	■	■
	MDO EXT-APA (2) (4)	Exterior type Medium Density Overlay with smooth opaque resin-fiber overlay heat-fused to one- or both panel faces. Ideal base for paint. Highly recommended for siding and other outdoor applications. Also good for built-ins and signs	MDO BB G4 EXT APA PS 1 74	B	B or C	C	■		■	■	■	■
	303 SIDING EXT-APA inc. Texture 1-11 (2) (7)	Grade designation covers proprietary plywood products for exterior siding, fencing, etc., with special surface treatment such as V-groove, channel groove, striated, brushed, rough-sawn	303 SIDING 16 S/W GROUP EXTERIOR PS 1 000	(6) C	C	C			■	■	■	
	PLYRON EXT-APA (2)	Exterior panel surfaced both sides with hardboard for use in exterior applications. Faces are tempered, smooth or screened	PLYRON EXT APA PS 1 74			C				■	■	■

Notes:

(1) Sanded both sides except where decorative or other surfaces specified
(2) Available in Group 1, 2, 3, 4 or 5 unless otherwise noted
(3) Standard 4 - 8 panel sizes, other sizes available
(4) Also available in STRUCTURAL I (all plies limited to Group 1 species) and II (limited to Groups 1, 2 and 3)

(5) Or C Plugged
(6) C or better for 5-plies, C Plugged or better for 3-ply panels
(7) Stud spacing is shown on grade stamp

(*Courtesy* American Plywood Association)

3. Plywood roof decking marked with an identification index may be installed with an unsupported edge equal to the roof portion of the index up to 24 inches (600 mm). Spans of 32 to 48 inches (800 to 1200 mm) require a "plyclip" or blocking between supports. Spans of more than 48 inches (1200 mm) require two plyclips.

4. Texture 1-11 or other panels applied vertically on studs spaced 48 inches (1200 mm) apart should be supported with cross blocks at 32-inch (800-mm) intervals (Figure 5-2).

Table 5-4 Minimum Recommendations for Single-Wall Construction

Stud Spacing	Utility Buildings Panel Thickness		Premium Construction Panel Thickness		Nail Spacing	
	Vertical in.	Horizontal in.	Vertical in.	Horizontal in.	Edges in.	Inter- mediate in.
16 in. (400 mm)	5/16	1/4	3/8	3/8	6	12
24 in. (600 mm)	3/8	5/16	1/2	3/8	6	12
32 in. (800 mm)	—	3/8	—	1/2	6	12
40 in. (1200 mm)	1/2 '	1/2	3/4 *	5/8	6	12

* Use cross blocking 4 ft (1200 mm) o.c. between frames
(From Plywood Agricultural Construction Guide, 1976.)

5. When plywood siding is used on pole buildings, nailing-girts may be spaced 32 inches (800 mm) o.c. However, if the building is to be insulated, a 24-inch (600-mm) spacing will usually be more convenient.

6. When ceiling joists are spaced up to 24 inches (600 mm) o.c., 3/8-inch (9-mm) plywood may be installed, face grain perpendicular to the joists, without noticeable sag if nothing more than insulation is supported. However, blocking at the edges will provide a more dust-free installation and should be used on spans of more than 24 inches (600 mm).

7. Plywood is subject to some swelling and shrinking. Consequently it is recommended that 1/16-inch (1.5-mm) spaces be left between the ends of the panels and 1/8-inch (3-mm) spaces between the edges. These values should be doubled under high moisture conditions. Panel size tolerances run plus zero, minus 1/16 inch (1.5 mm), which helps to facilitate the end and edge spacing during installation.

8.   The general recommendation for nail spacing is 6 inches (150 mm) along the edge and 12 inches (300 mm) at intermediate supports except that with spans of 48 inches (1200 mm), spacing is 6 inches (150 mm) at all supports. Common, galvanized, or ring-shank nails may be used. Recommended nail sizes are:

- Panels up to ½ inch (12 mm)—6d nails
- ⅝ to ⅞ inch (15-21 mm)—8d nails
- 1 inch (25 mm)—10d nails

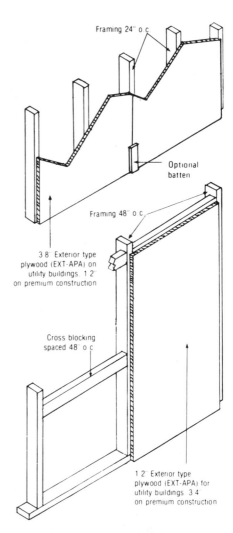

Figure 5-2. Typical wall installation. (*Courtesy* American Plywood Association)

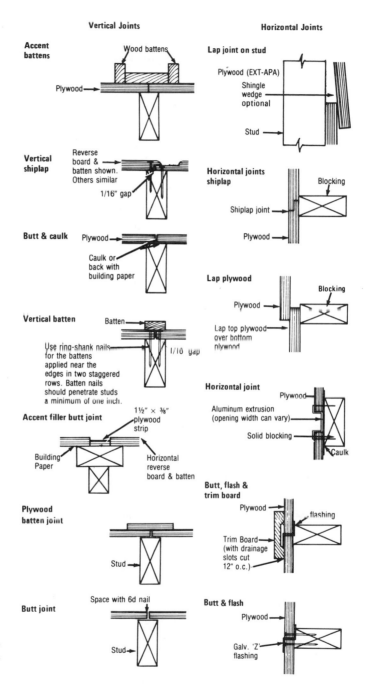

Figure 5-3. Plywood joint details. (*Courtesy* American Plywood Association)

GRAIN BINS

Plywood is an excellent material from which to construct grain storages. The floor load may be determined by multiplying the depth times the weight per unit volume, as given in Table 9-4.

The pressure on bin walls, however, is more difficult to obtain. Nevertheless, a good estimate may be made by using Figure 5-4 and Table 5-5. The equivalent bin diameter needed in Figure 5-4 is one of the following:

- Diameter of a round bin
- Width of a bin more than 1.5 times as long as wide
- Equivalent diameter $= 4 \times$ floor area/perimeter when length is less than 1.5 times width

Using the grain depth and the equivalent diameter, find the pressure zone on Figure 5-4. Using that pressure zone, the identification index of a suitable plywood and the maximum support spacing may be found.

Table 5-5   Plywood and Support Spacing for Bin Walls

Pressure (1) Zone	Identification (2) Index	Thickness of A-C EXT Group 1 (inch) (3) (4)	Support Spacing (inches)	Approximate Pressure lb/sq ft
11	48/24	3/4	32	80
9	42/20	5/8	24	115
8	48/24	3/4	24	145
7	32/16	1/2	16	165
6	24/0	3/8	12	195
5	42/20	5/8	16	255
4	32/16	1/2	12	295
3	48/24	3/4	16	325
2	42/20	5/8	12	450
1	48/24	3/4	12	575

(1) Special design is required for bin sizes where no number is shown.
(2) Any sheathing grade may be used for dry conditions (moisture content less than 16%). Where moisture content is 16% or more, plywood must be C-C EXT, and continuous over three or more spans.
(3) For each step the group number of sanded plywood departs from Group 1, take one step down to the next smaller zone number. For example, if Group 3 plywood is used, and the applicable figure shows Zone 11, use the plywood and support spacing shown for Zone 9.
(4) Where moisture content is 16% or more, plywood must be continuous over three or more spans.
(From Plywood Agricultural Construction Guide, 1976.)

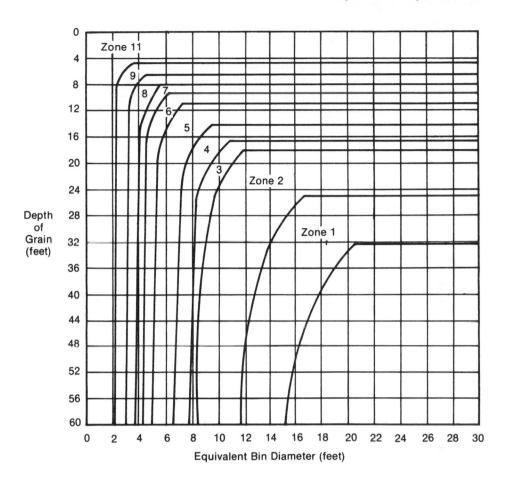

Figure 5-4. Bin pressure zones for shelled corn, wheat, flaxseed, and rye. (*Courtesy* American Plywood Association)

PRESSURE-TREATED PLYWOOD

Plywood may be pressure treated with wood preservatives to increase the resistance to decay and insect attack. Oil-borne creosote, oil or gas-borne pentachlorophenol, or water-borne salts are all satisfactory for agricultural purposes. Salt-preservative-treated plywood is readily paintable after drying. As there may be some roughening of the surface during treatment, the MDO panels give the best results when painting is required. Ordinarily the painting of creosote or oil-borne penta-treated plywood is not recommended. A more complete discussion of wood preservatives, including certain risks to plants and animals, is found in Chapter 4.

FINISHING PLYWOOD

Special primers are available for plywood. They are recommended to help prevent the hairline checking that often develops in plywood over long periods of time. The MDO surface on plywood is an excellent base for painting and avoids the checking completely.

Exterior plywood, used outside, can be stained, painted, or left to weather. Painting or staining does not materially increase the life of the plywood but is used instead to produce a desired appearance. A penetrating stain will leave no surface film and will weather gradually. When paint is to be applied, it is very important to prime and paint the edge of the panels, as any moisture entering the end grain moves along readily and can cause paint failure and checking. Edge priming and painting may be most easily accomplished while the plywood is still in the pile.

FIRE-RETARDANT PLYWOOD

Fire-retardant treated plywood is available and has a flame spread of 25 or less. The material used as a retardant tends to be toxic to animals and humans.

PROBLEMS

5.1   Give the specifications for plywood panels that would be appropriate for each of the following applications:

    a. Sheathing for a home   e. Roof deck for a barn
    b. Cupboard doors for a home   f. Siding for a barn
    c. Underlayment for vinyl tiles   g. Wall panelling for a home
    d. Fruit pallet boxes   h. Walls in a CA storage

5.2   Five grade-stamps are shown in Figure 5-1. List the items shown on each stamp and explain briefly but explicitly what information is indicated by each.

5.3   Trusses are to be spaced 48 inches (1200 mm) o.c. on a shed. Give the specifications for a suitable panel to use for the roof deck.

5.4   A grain bin is to be built 12 feet (3600 mm) square to store dry, shelled corn to a maximum depth of 10 feet (3000 mm). Determine a suitable plywood panel and safe support spacing for the bin.

REFERENCES

American Plywood Association. *Guide to Plywood Grades.* Tacoma, Wash.: American Plywood Association, 1977.

American Plywood Association. *Plywood Agricultural Construction Guide.* Tacoma, Wash.: American Plywood Association, 1976.

American Plywood Association. *Plywood Siding.* Tacoma, Wash.: American Plywood Association, 1977.

American Plywood Association. *Pressure Preserved Plywood.* Tacoma, Wash.: American Plywood Association, 1974.

National Bureau of Standards, Products Standards Section, *U.S. Product Standard PS 1-74 for Construction and Industrial Plywood with Typical Grade-Trademarks.* Reprinted by American Plywood Association, Tacoma, Wash., 1974.

Chapter Six

Wood Fasteners

A primary objective in fabricating wood structures is to design joints that approximate the strength of the members to be joined. When this is accomplished, a safe, economical structure results. The fact that this is not always achieved is shown by the fact that a large proportion of wooden building failures result from inadequate joint design or assembly. Member breakage often results from the crash rather than being the cause of the failure.

Farm buildings still stand today in which the framing timbers were fastened together without a nail. The wall frames were assembled on the ground with a mortise-and-tenon joint (an extension of one piece of wood fitted into the socket of another) and secured with a wooden peg. Then with the help of neighboring farmers using metal tipped poles, the "broadside" was pushed to an upright position. The strength and durability of this type of fastening is demonstrated by the survival of these early buildings. But the time required to construct and fit such a joint became prohibitive in the early 19th century when cut iron nails came into use followed by steel wire nails around 1875. Bolts were introduced about the same time as the early nails but have never been used as extensively since they are not as simple to use. Timber connectors that significantly increase structural strength were introduced in 1930 and more recently glue has been developed to make prefabricated joints readily available.

NAILS

Nails are the most frequently used connector for wood construction. In addition to the common wire nail shown in Figure 6-1, there are literally dozens of special purpose nails, including the hardened-steel threaded-shank nails used in heavy construction, and various types used to secure wall panels, roofing, flooring, and trim. Figure 6-2 illustrates the wide variety.

The most frequently used nails for frame construction and wood trim include the following:

Common wire nails   These are used for framing where there will be considerable lateral load.

Spikes   Spikes parallel the length of a number of the sizes of common nails. However, their larger diameter gives them greater holding power where they can be used without splitting the wood.

Box nails   Smaller in diameter than common nails, box nails are used for installing sheathing or roof decks. Although their holding power is less, they also reduce the danger of splitting.

Casing and finishing nails   These are smaller in both diameter and head size than common nails of the same pennyweight. The small head may be countersunk and covered for a neat appearance.

Nail Size

Nails are sized in pennyweight (d) which is related to their length. Diameters for each size vary with the type of nail. Nail sizes and a suggested nailing schedule are shown in Figure 6-1.

Safe Lateral Loads for Nails[1]

The following formula may be used to obtain the safe lateral load for a common wire nail:

$$P = K D^{3/2}$$ Where:

P = the safe load in pounds per nail

K = a constant varying with wood specie

D = diameter of the nail in inches

---

[1] Much of the material on load design for nails, bolts, and metal connectors is taken from National Design Specification for Wood Construction, 1977.

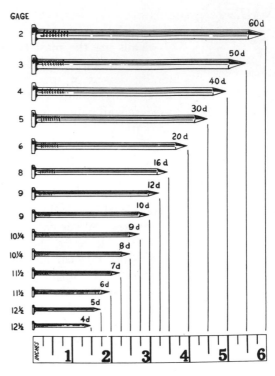

Recommended Nailing Schedule
Using Common Nails

Joist to sill or girder, toe nail	3-8d
Bridging to joist, toe nail each end	2-8d
Ledger strip	3-16d at each joist
1" x 6" subfloor or less to each joist, face nail	2-8d
Over 1" x 6" subfloor to each joist, face nail	3-8d
2" subfloor to joist or girder, blind and face nail	2-16d
Sole plate to joist or blocking, face nail	16d @ 16" oc
Top plate to stud, end nail	2-16d
Stud to sole plate, toe nail	4-8d
Doubled studs, face nail	16d @ 24" oc
Doubled top plates, face nail	16d @ 16" oc
Top plates, laps and intersections, face nail	2-16d
Continuous header, two pieces	16d @ 16" oc along each edge
Ceiling joists to plate, toe nail	3-8d
Continuous header to stud, toe nail	4-8d
Ceiling joists, laps over partitions, face nail	3-16d
Ceiling joists to parallel rafters, face nail	3-16d
Rafter to plate, toe nail	3-8d
1-inch brace to each stud and plate, face nail	2-8d
1" x 8" sheathing or less to each bearing, face nail	2-8d
Over 1" x 8" sheathing to each bearing, face nail	3-8d
Built-up corner studs	16d @ 24" oc
Built-up girders and beams	20d @ 32" oc along each edge

Figure 6-1. Sizes of common wire nails. (*Courtesy* National Forest Products Association)

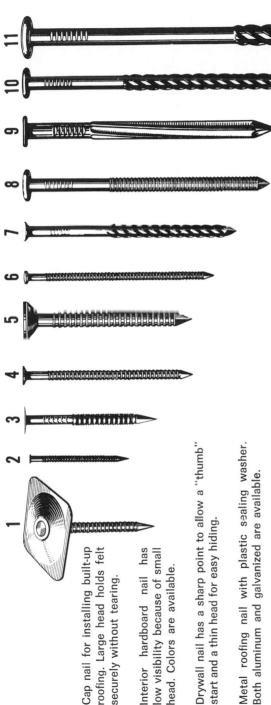

1. Cap nail for installing built-up roofing. Large head holds felt securely without tearing.

2. Interior hardboard nail has low visibility because of small head. Colors are available.

3. Drywall nail has a sharp point to allow a "thumb" start and a thin head for easy hiding.

4. Metal roofing nail with plastic sealing washer. Both aluminum and galvanized are available.

5. Underlayment floor nail holds securely and prevents nail heads from showing through tile.

6. Wood shingle face-nail used for installing shingles on side walls. Prevents curling and wind damage.

7. Flooring nail hardened for driving through hard woods. Safety goggles are required when driving hardened nails.

8. Common nail with annular thread for general use.

9. Masonry nail hardened for driving into bricks and concrete blocks. Goggles are required.

10. Trussed rafter nail hardened and especially designed for truss construction. Goggles required.

11. Pole type construction nail hardened and of slimmer gauge to reduce splitting while increasing structural strength.

Figure 6-2. Special purpose nails. All of these nails are designed to have superior holding strength in addition to their other features. (*Courtesy* Independent Nail, Inc.)

Table 6-1 divides the most common woods into four groups and provides a value for K for each group.

Table 6-1   Woods Grouped for Fastening Design

Grouping	Specie	For nails K	Specific Gravity G	$G^{5/2}$
Group I	Ash, white		0.62	0.302
	Birch, sweet and yellow		0.66	0.354
		2040		
	Hickory		0.75	0.487
	Maple, sugar		0.66	0.354
	Oak, red and white		0.67	0.367
Group II	Douglas fir, Larch	1650	0.51	0.185
	Pine, southern		0.55	0.225
Group III	Redwood, dense		0.42	0.114
	Hemlock		0.43	0.122
	Spruce, eastern and sitka	1350	0.43	0.122
	Pine, northern		0.46	0.141
	Pine, red, sugar and ponderosa		0.42	0.114
	Pine, lodgepole		0.44	0.128
Group IV	Balsam fir		0.38	0.089
	Redwood, open grain		0.37	0.084
		1080		
	Cedar		0.31	0.053
	Spruce, Englemann		0.36	0.078
	Pine, Idaho white		0.40	0.101

(Extracted from National Design Specification for Wood Construction, 1977.)

Table 6-2 gives information and safe lateral values for various sizes of common and threaded steel nails using the above formula as a basis.

To illustrate how to find the safe lateral load for a nail, assume a 10d nail used with Douglas fir. From Table 6-1, K for Douglas fir is 1650. From Table 6-2, D for a 10d nail is 0.148.

$$P = K D^{3/2}$$

$$P = 1650 \times 0.148^{\,3/2}$$

$$P = 94 \, lb$$

There are a number of conditions associated with the use of the formula and the values given in Table 6-2.

1.   Values assume that the nails are driven at approximately right angles into the side grain of seasoned wood with 19 percent or less

Table 6-2 Lateral Load Design Values for Nails

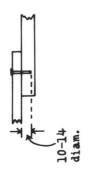

10–14 diam.

	6d	8d	10 & 12d	16d	20d	30d	40d
Length—inches	2	2½	3 3¼	3½	4	4½	5
Diameter—inches	0.113	0.131	0.148	0.162	0.192	0.207	0.225
Group I Species							
Penetration*	1.13	1.31	1.48	1.62	1.92	2.07	2.25
Safe Load, pounds	77	97	116	133	172	192	218
Group II Species							
Penetration	1.24	1.44	1.63	1.78	2.11	2.28	2.48
Safe Load, pounds	63	78	94	108	139	155	176
Group III Species							
Penetration	1.47	1.70	1.92	2.11	2.50	2.69	2.93
Safe Load, pounds	51	64	77	88	114	127	144
Group IV Species							
Penetration	1.58	1.83	2.07	2.27	2.69	2.90	3.15
Safe Load, pounds	41	51	61	70	91	102	115

* Penetration refers to the distance the nail must penetrate the member receiving the point.
For sizes 8d through 20d, threaded, hardened-steel nails have equal load values. Penetration values are slightly less because of smaller diameters. Sizes 20d through 60d threaded, hardened-steel nails have the same load value as a 20d common nail.
Multiply penetration by 25.4 to obtain millimeters.
Multiply safe load by 4.45 to obtain newtons of force.
(Extracted from National Design Specification for Wood Construction, 1977.)

moisture, except that toe-nails should be started at a point approximately one-third the length of the nail from the end of the piece and be driven at an angle of approximately 30 degrees with the piece.

2.   The minimum amount of penetration given in the table varies with the group and is based on 10 diameters in Group I, 11 diameters in Group II, 13 in Group III and 14 in Group IV. Straight-line interpolation to zero may be used for lesser penetrations into the piece receiving the point, except that nothing less than one-third the table value is acceptable.

3.   When more than one nail is used, the sum of the value for single nails may be used if the following factors are observed: 1½-inch (38-mm) edge distance, spacings of 1 inch (25 mm) across grain, 2½ inches (64 mm) parallel to the grain, 2¼-inch (57-mm) end distance in tension members.

4.   For lateral loads on end-nailed joints, use 67 percent of values in Table 6-2.

5.   For lateral loads on unseasoned wood that will remain wet or will be loaded before seasoning, use 75 percent of the values in Table 6-2.

6.   Values for double shear joints—three members—may be increased as follows:

> (a) If each side member is not less than one third of the thickness of the center member, add 33 percent.
> (b) If three members are equal in thickness, add 67 percent.
> (c) If side members are at least ⅜ inch (10 mm) thick and nails up to 12d in size are used and clinched, double the value.

7.   With properly designed metal side plates, add 25 percent.

8.   Values for nails used to install large panels for sheathing, flooring, or roof decks may be increased 30 percent.

9.   Lateral load design values for toe-nailed joints should not exceed 83 percent of the table value.

10.   When using prebored guide holes of up to 0.9 of the diameter of the nail for Group I species, or 0.75 of the nail diameter for Groups II, III, and IV, do not reduce table values.

11. Values for nails used with kiln-dried, fire-retardant treated woods should be reduced by 10 percent.

12. Clinching nails that protrude through joint members will effectively maintain the normal joint strength and may increase the lateral resistance as much as 50 percent.

Safe Withdrawal Loads for Nails

The following formula may be used to obtain the safe withdrawal load for common nails:

$$p = 1380 \, G^{5/2} \, D \qquad \text{where:}$$

p = the safe load in pounds per inch of penetration in members receiving the point

G = the specific gravity (see Table 6-1)

D = the diameter of the nail (see Table 6-2)

Table 6 3 gives safe withdrawal design values for various sized common and threaded steel nails.

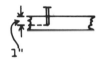

Table 6-3   Withdrawal Load Design Values for Nails
Pounds per inch of penetration

Size	Common and Threaded				Common Only		
	6d	8d	10, 12d	16d	20d	30d	40d
G							
0.75	76	88	99	109	129	139	151
0.66	55	64	72	79	94	101	110
0.62	47	55	62	68	80	86	94
0.55	35	41	46	50	59	64	70
0.51	29	34	38	42	49	53	58
0.46	22	26	29	32	38	41	45
0.44	20	23	26	29	34	37	40
0.42	18	21	23	26	30	33	35
0.40	16	18	21	23	27	29	31
0.38	14	16	18	20	24	25	28
0.36	12	14	16	17	21	22	24
0.31	8	10	11	12	14	15	17

Values for threaded nails, sizes 30d to 60d, are the same as 20d common.
Multiply safe load values by 175 to obtain newtons per meter.
(Extracted from National Design Specification for Wood Construction, 1977.)

There are a number of conditions associated with the use of the formula for safe load in withdrawal and the values given in Table 6-3:

1. Values apply to nails driven into side grain for either seasoned or unseasoned wood.

2. When a nail is driven into wood parallel to the grain, the holding power may be reduced as much as 50 percent. For this reason nails driven into end grain should not be loaded in withdrawal.

3. Values for toe-nailed joints may be taken at 67 percent.

4. Values for nails used with kiln-dried, fire-retardant treated wood should be reduced by 10 percent.

BOLTS

When loads on wood connections are particularly heavy, bolted joints may be advisable. Table 6-4 gives brief information for designing bolted joints. More complete information may be found in National Design Specification for Wood Construction, 1977.

There are a number of conditions associated with the use of the values in Table 6-4:

1. The values apply to one bolt in double shear in seasoned wood at 19 percent or less moisture.

2. Additional bolts multiply the load values if they are installed center to center as follows:

   (a) Parallel grain loading of bolts in rows requires the bolts to be four diameters apart in the row and in rows one and one-half diameters apart.
   (b) End distance in tension requires seven diameters for softwoods and five for hardwoods. End distance in compression requires four diameters.
   (c) Edge distance requires one and one-half diameters.
   (d) Loading of bolts perpendicular to the grain requires the bolts to be in rows up to five diameters apart in the member loaded with the grain. End distance requires at least four diameters.

3. When side members are less than one-half the thickness of the

Table 6-4   Safe Load Design Value for Bolts

Safe load in pounds for a double-shear joint (three members) in which the thickness of each side member is equal to or greater than one-half the main (center) member. P = parallel to grain. Q = perpendicular to grain.

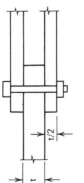

Length of bolt in main member	Diameter of bolt (in.)	Diameter of bolt (mm.)	White Ash Hickory P	White Ash Hickory Q	Douglas Fir Southern Pine P	Douglas Fir Southern Pine Q	Beech, Birch Maple P	Beech, Birch Maple Q	Red and White Oak P	Red and White Oak Q	Hemlock Northern Pine P	Hemlock Northern Pine Q	Western Pines P	Western Pines Q
1½ (38mm)	½	12	1,080	780	940	430	900	430	830	650	750	300	630	190
	5/8	16	1,360	880	1,180	490	1,130	540	1,050	730	930	340	790	240
	¾	20	1,630	980	1,420	540	1,360	640	1,260	820	1,120	370	950	240
2 (51mm)	½	12	1,340	1,040	1,170	570	1,120	640	1,040	870	990	400	840	250
	5/8	16	1,790	1,170	1,550	650	1,490	720	1,380	980	1,240	450	1,050	290
	¾	20	2,170	1,300	1,890	720	1,810	840	1,680	1,090	1,490	500	1,260	320
3 (76mm)	½	12	1,460	1,460	1,270	860	1,220	830	1,130	1,130	1,280	590	1,080	330
	5/8	16	2,260	1,760	1,960	970	1,880	1,090	1,740	1,470	1,800	670	1,530	430
	¾	20	3,020	1,950	2,630	1,080	2,520	1,220	2,340	1,630	2,230	750	1,890	480
3½ (89mm)	½	12	1,460	1,460	1,270	980	1,220	570	1,130	1,130	1,280	690	1,080	480
	5/8	16	2,280	2,020	1,980	1,130	1,900	1,250	1,760	1,690	1,970	780	1,670	500
	¾	20	3,220	2,280	2,800	1,260	2,690	1,410	2,440	1,910	2,540	870	2,150	560

Multiply values by 4.448 to obtain newtons.
(Extracted from National Design Specification for Wood Construction 1977.)

Table 6-5 Safe Load Design Values for Split-Ring Connectors

Safe load in pounds per ring when installed in single shear on a surface parallel with the grain in seasoned wood of 1½ inches or more in thickness. P = parallel with grain. Q = perpendicular to the grain.

Ring Diam. in.	Ring Diam. mm.	Bolt Diam. in.	Bolt Diam. mm.	Faces per Piece	Loading	Minimum Edge Distance, Inches Unloaded	Minimum Edge Distance, Inches Loaded	Minimum End Distance, Inches Tension	Minimum End Distance, Inches Compression	Wood Group I	Wood Group II	Wood Group III	Wood Group IV
2½	64	½	12	1	P	1¾	—	5½	4	3,160	2,730	2,290	1,960
					Q	1¾	1¾	5½	5½	1,900	1,620	1,350	1,160
					Q	1¾	2¾	5½	5½	2,280	1,940	1,620	1,390
2½	64	½	12	2	P	1¾	—	5½	4	2,430	2,100	1,760	1,510
					Q	1¾	1¾	5½	5½	1,460	1,250	1,040	890
					Q	1¾	2¾	5½	5½	1,750	1,500	1,250	1,070
4	100	¾	20	1	P	2¾	—	7	5½	6,020	5,160	4,280	3,710
					Q	2¾	2¾	7	7	3,490	2,990	2,490	2,150
					Q	2¾	3¾	7	7	4,180	3,590	2,990	2,580
4	100	¾	20	2	P	2¾	—	7	5½	4,110	3,520	2,940	2,540
					Q	2¾	2¾	7	7	2,480	2,040	1,700	1,470
					Q	2¾	3¾	7	7	2,980	2,450	2,040	1,760

Multiply load value by 4.448 to obtain newtons.
(Extracted from National Design Specification for Wood Construction, 1977.)

center member, a thickness value for the center member is used which is equal to twice the thickness of the thinnest side member.

4. For a two-member joint, use one-half the table value for a thickness equal to twice the thinnest of the two members or one-half the table value for the thicker member whichever is least. (See National Design Specification for Wood Construction, 1977, for design of more complex joints.)

RING CONNECTORS AND SHEAR PLATES

A steel ring connector installed concentrically with a bolt in a wood-to-wood joint can increase the strength of that joint considerably over the bolt alone. A tool is used to cut an accurate groove into each of the wood surfaces to be joined, spreading the shear forces over a greater area of the wood. Steel or malleable iron shear plates are also available that transfer the force from wood to bolt and back to the wood again.

Tables 6-5 and 6-6 give details for the design of single split-ring connections for single shear joints in seasoned wood that will remain dry in service.

The design of joints using these connectors at some angle to the grain is an involved process that is covered in detail, along with more complete design tables, in National Design Specification for Wood Construction, 1977.

Table 6-6 Spacing of Split-Ring Connectors Center to Center

Ring Diameter in.	Type of Loading	Spacing Parallel to Grain in.	Spacing Perpendicular to Grain in.
2½	Parallel	6¾	3½
	Perpendicular	3½	4½
4	Parallel	9	5
	Perpendicular	5	6

Multiply inches by 25.4 to obtain millimeters.
(Extracted from National Design Specification for Wood Construction, 1977.)

FRAMING ANCHORS

Framing anchors are available in a wide variety of configurations to aid in increasing the strength of connections of structural members in building frames. Several applications are shown in Figures 6-3, 6-4, and 6-5 along with safe working loads for Group I and II woods in the direction indicated on the diagrams. The special nails supplied with the anchors are required.

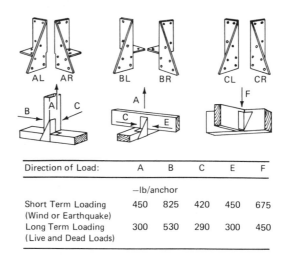

Direction of Load:	A	B	C	E	F
	—lb/anchor				
Short Term Loading (Wind or Earthquake)	450	825	420	450	675
Long Term Loading (Live and Dead Loads)	300	530	290	300	450

Figure 6-3. Safe working values for framing anchors, lbs/anchor. Multiply working value by 4.448 to obtain newtons. (*Courtesy* Timber Engineering Company)

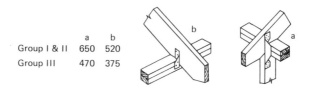

	a	b
Group I & II	650	520
Group III	470	375

Figure 6-4. Safe uplift values for rafter anchors, lbs/anchor. Multiply working value by 4.448 to obtain newtons. (*Courtesy* Timber Engineering Company)

Plywood and other panel sheathing materials offer an alternative to anchors in some locations. Properly nailed to sill, stud, and plate, panels provide excellent strength and bracing.

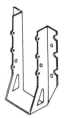

Recommended Joist or Beam Size	Steel Ga.	Height	Seat Width	Seat Depth	Recommended Safe Working Values
2x4	18	3-1/4"	1-5/8"	2"	400 lbs.
2x6-8	18	5-1/4"	1-5/8"	2"	900 lbs.
2x8-10-12	18	7"	1-5/8"	2"	1000 lbs.
2x10-12-14	18	8-1/2"	1-5/8"	2-3/4"	1200 lbs.
(2) 2x6-8	16	5-1/4"	3-1/4"	2-3/4"	1700 lbs.
(2) 2x8-10-12	16	7"	3-1/4"	2-3/4"	2200 lbs.
(2) 2x10-12-14	16	8-1/2"	3-1/4"	2-3/4"	2800 lbs.
3x6-8	16	5-1/4"	2-5/8"	2-3/4"	1700 lbs.
2x10-12-14	16	8-1/2"	2-5/8"	2-3/4"	2800 lbs.
4x6-8	16	5-1/4"	3-5/8"	2-3/4"	1700 lbs.
4x10-12-14	16	8-1/2"	3-5/8"	2-3/4"	2800 lbs.

Figure 6-5. Safe working values for joist hangers, lb/ hanger. Multiply working value by 4.448 to obtain newtons. (*Courtesy* Timber Engineering Company)

GUSSET PLATES

While nailed or nailed and glued joints using plywood gussets are popular, there is increasing use of predrilled flat and deformed metal plate connectors. They are available in a large number of sizes and configurations. Most of them speed up the prefabrication of trusses and other structural components to a considerable extent.

Allowable design stresses for plate connectors are determined by tests with seasoned lumber. The least of the following two observations is chosen:

1. The load at which wood-to-wood slip of 0.03 inches occurs divided by 1.6 or,

2. The utlimate load divided by 3.

The value obtained from these tests is subject to adjustment for duration, unseasoned wood (reduced 20 percent) and fire-retardant treated wood (reduced 10 percent if kiln dried). Since there is a great variety of plate connectors used, the design value for a specific connector should be obtained from the manufacturer.

STRESSES AT AN ANGLE TO THE GRAIN

When bolted or ring connector joints are loaded at an angle between 0 and 90 degrees to the grain, a corrected safe compression stress value may be obtained by the use of the Hankinson formula. (Figure 6-6)

$$N = \frac{P \ Q}{P \ Sin^2\theta + Q \ Cos^2\theta} \qquad \text{where}$$

N = allowable stress at angle θ with the grain

P = allowable compressive stress parallel to grain

Q = allowable compressive stress perpendicular to grain

θ = angle of stress with grain

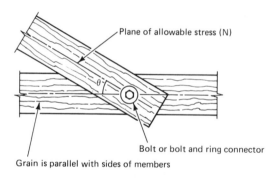

Figure 6-6. Stresses at an angle to the grain.

From Table 6-5, a 2½-inch ring in a two-member joint made with Type I wood shows values for P = 3160 and Q = 1900. The safe load value may be found for a 45-degree angle as follows:

$$Sin \ 45° = Cos \ 45° = 0.707$$

$$N = \frac{3160 \times 1900}{3160 \times .707^2 + 1900 \times .707^2}$$

$$N = 2374 \text{ pounds}$$

DURATION OF LOAD

All of the design values for nails, bolts, and connectors have been based on a normal duration of loading period of 10 years. As shown in Figure 6-7, permanent design loads should be reduced to 90 percent while loads with a duration of less than 10 years may be increased in relation to time.

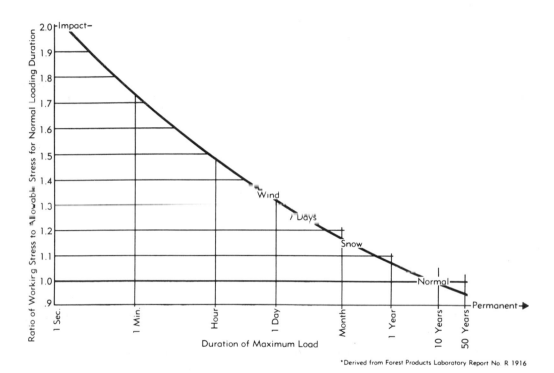

*Derived from Forest Products Laboratory Report No. R 1916

Figure 6-7. Adjustment of working stress to duration of load. (*Courtesy* National Forest Products Association)

GLUED JOINTS

Arched rafters, trusses, beams, posts, and other prefabricated parts of buildings can be made particularly strong and rigid by the use of glue.

However, glue is best used in the controlled conditions of a factory. Surfaces must fit together with close tolerances. In most cases, only a limited temperature range is permitted for using the glue and the spread must be accurate. Finally, the proper pressure must be applied to the joint during curing. Poor procedures cause serious weaknesses to occur.

Joints designed for adequate strength when nailed alone may be given additional rigidity by using glue with the nails.

If it is decided to perform gluing operations at the construction site, there are several factors to consider. Wood should be clean and free of oily deposits and both surfaces to be glued should be dry (15 percent moisture or less) and equal in moisture level. Surfaces should be milled accurately to insure a close fit. Preservative-treated wood may need to be resurfaced before gluing to remove any surface coating.

One of three types of glue is usually chosen for construction work. *Resorcinol* glue is waterproof and should be used when moisture levels may be high. It is relatively expensive, has a short working life, and needs close-fitting surfaces since the glue does not fill well.

Casein glue with a mold inhibitor is highly moisture resistant, and fills well in imperfectly fitting joints. It is workable at temperatures as low as 40°F, but with a considerably extended curing time. Woods that tend to be naturally oily may be sponged with a dilute solution of caustic soda an hour before gluing. This treatment, plus the naturally alkaline characteristics of the casein glue, provides the most satisfactory bond for naturally oily woods.

Plastic resin (urea-formaldehyde) glue provides strong, moisture resistant joints with a light colored glue-line. The glue has a working life in excess of eight hours.

Gluing Procedure

Directions supplied by the manufacturer should be followed in all cases. When working with glue, the room temperature should be approximately 70°F (21°C). Assuming a butt joint with a plywood gusset, coat both surfaces with a uniform layer of glue; align the pieces carefully and then apply pressure with nails spaced to give a nail for each 8 to 9 square inches (5000 to 5800 mm²).

Three other adhesives used in home construction are *contact cement*, used to apply plastic laminates to wood; *panel adhesives*, used for installing wall panels to masonry, rigid insulation, or wood framing; and *epoxies* that adhere to a wide range of materials, including metal. The epoxies are too expensive for more than limited use.

PROBLEMS

6.1   The lower chord (tension member) of a truss is subjected to a maximum tension load of 500 pounds (2224 N). The 2- by 4-inch (38 by 89 mm) chord is spliced together using 1-inch (19 mm) splice plates on each side of the chord. If western hemlock lumber is used for all members, determine the size and number of nails required to make the joint structurally sound.

6.2 Assuming the same loading and materials, how many bolts would be needed if one 2- by 4-inch (38 by 89 mm) plate was used on just one side?

6.3 A 2- by 12-inch (38 by 286 mm) joist is attached to a 2- by 6-inch (38 by 140 mm) stud with one 2½-inch (63.5-mm) ring connector. What is the maximum safe load on the joint if both members are Douglas fir?

6.4 Two members in the supporting structure for a feed bin are connected with a 2½-inch (63.5-mm) ring connector. The maximum angle of the stress with the grain is 30 degrees. Assuming that a lap joint and Type II lumber are used, what is the maximum safe load that may be imposed on the joint?

REFERENCES

American Society for Testing and Materials. *Standard Methods of Testing Metal Fasteners in Wood.* Book of American Society for Testing and Materials Standards, Part 16, 1971.

Forest Products Laboratory. *Wood Handbook.* U.S. Department of Agriculture Handbook No. 72, 1955.

Independent Nail Corporation. *Advertising Brochure.* Bridgewater, Mass., 1977.

Midwest Plan Service. *Structures and Environment Handbook.* Ames, Iowa: Midwest Plan Service, 1977.

National Forest Products Association. *Manual for House Framing.* Washington, D.C.: National Forest Products Association, 1961.

National Forest Products Association. *National Design Specification for Wood Construction.* Washington, D.C.: National Forest Products Association, 1977.

Timber Engineering Company. *Structural Wood Fasteners.* Washington, D.C.: Timber Engineering Company, 1976.

Chapter Seven

Concrete and Masonry Construction

Concrete has several properties that make it eminently suited for a wide variety of agricultural uses. When first mixed it is plastic, and may be formed into almost any shape required. When properly cured, it provides a hard, sanitary surface with an attractive appearance. It is durable, noncombustible, resistant to termites and rodents and is maintenance free. When made with a rich mixture it can be virtually waterproof. Concrete is strong in compression and, with the incorporation of steel reinforcing, can withstand bending and tensile forces as well.

Concrete is made by mixing portland cement with water, a fine aggregate (sand) and a coarse aggregate (gravel*, crushed rock, crushed slag, etc.). The cement and water form a paste which, during mixing, coats the aggregate. Within two to three hours a chemical action known as hydration causes the paste to harden, binding the sand and rock particles into a dense, homogeneous, rock-like mass.

The name portland refers to the type of cement which is universally produced by all manufacturers. Natural cements have been used since the time of the Roman Empire. However, in the mid-18th Century, it was found that burning and grinding impure limestone produced a superior natural cement. In 1824 Joseph Aspdin, an Englishman, patented a process in which he calcined a mixture of limestone and clay (Giese,

---

* *Gravel* refers to small stones of varying sizes without sand. Bank-run gravel contains sand, small and large stones.

1948). He called the resulting powder "portland cement" because when it hardened in water it resembled the stone found in quarries on the Isle of Portland.

About the same time natural cement rocks were discovered and used in a similar way in the eastern United States. However, it was 50 years before true portland cement was being manufactured in a plant near Allentown, Pennsylvania. Today portland cement is a carefully controlled mixture of lime, silica, alumina, and iron oxide burned and ground into a fine powder. Tremendous quantities are used in all phases of the construction industry.

Portland cement is available in five types as designated by the American Society for Testing and Materials (ASTM) (Portland Cement Association, 1952).

Type I   Normal portland cement is a general purpose cement suitable for most farm and general construction work.

Type II   Modified portland cement is a low heat-producing cement that may be specified for very large concrete structures.

Type III   This is spoken of as high-early-strength cement. Because of extremely fine grinding it hydrates more rapidly and gains strength sooner. It may be specified for cold weather application or when a load must be supported as early as possible.

Type IV   Low heat portland cement has a still lower heat of hydration than Type II and is intended for use only in large masses of concrete such as large gravity dams.

Type V   Sulfate-resistant portland cement is a special cement that resists damage due to the high sulfate content of water. It is also used in construction that is subjected to severe sulfate action.

White portland cement is used for producing white concrete or tinted concrete when color pigment is added. Color may be added to normal portland cement, but the full coloring value of pigments can be obtained only with white portland cement.

MAKING QUALITY CONCRETE

Although much of the concrete used in agricultural construction is delivered to the site "ready-mixed" or "transit-mixed," ready to be placed in the forms, it is important to understand what makes good quality concrete. This will help in ordering and using ready-mixed material or, when necessary, mixing on the job. No other building material depends so much on the user for its success. The use of good quality materials, accurate proportioning, and careful control in all operations are essential to the production of good quality concrete. Any lapse in quality control during any phase of these operations can destroy the inherent performance of quality concrete.

1. Selecting Proper Ingredients

Quality control begins with the careful selection of cement, water, and aggregates.

Cement   Normal portland cement is suitable for most farm and general construction work. For on-the-job mixing, cement is sold in sacks, each sack containing 94 pounds or 1 cubic foot. Where SI units are used, sacks weigh 40 kilograms. Cement tends to absorb moisture which gradually reduces its strength, but if kept dry, it will retain its quality indefinitely. Dry storage is therefore essential. Cement containing lumps that cannot be easily broken up should not be used.

Cement is available with an air-entraining additive which causes millions of microscopic air bubbles to form throughout the cement mixture. The resulting tiny voids increase the resistance of the concrete to scaling due to freezing and thawing and to the action of deicing salt. Although the strength of concrete made with air-entraining cement is somewhat less than that made with standard cement, it should be used for all yards, drives and structures exposed to freezing and thawing because of its resistance to weather.

Water   Water for making concrete should be clear, free of acids, alkalies, oil, and organic matter. In short—it should be fit to drink. In some areas the sulfate content of the water may make it unsuitable for use with normal cement, in which case sulphate-resistant cement should be used.

Aggregates   Both the cost and quality of the concrete are affected by the kind of aggregate selected. Small aggregate is that which will pass through a ¼-inch (6-mm) mesh screen. Larger material is referred to as coarse aggregate. Aggregates used for concrete should be clean, hard, and strong. Sharp, rough or flat aggregates make excellent concrete, but require more cement-water paste. Concrete can be no stronger than the aggregate used. Easily fractured material or any flaky surface layers will severely reduce the strength of the final product. Excessive amounts of silt will prevent a secure bond between the paste and aggregate and will likewise reduce the durability of the concrete.

Bank-run gravel is a natural mixture of sand and stones. The character of bank-run gravel varies widely according to the locality in which it is found and often contains an excessive amount of silt and organic matter. If concrete is mixed from unwashed and ungraded materials such as bank-run gravel, the following two tests will check the suitability of the material.

Silt test Two inches (50 mm) of aggregate and 6 inches (150 mm) of water are shaken vigorously in a glass jar. If, after standing for an hour, more than ⅛ inch (3 mm) of silt has settled at the top of the aggregate, the aggregate should either be abandoned or washed.

Organic matter test One-half pint (250 mL) of water and ½ pint (250 mL) of aggregate are stirred with 1 teaspoonful (6 g) of lye (sodium hydroxide). If after three to four hours the water is clear, the aggregate is suitable. Even if the water is a light straw color, it is suitable for all but those jobs requiring great durability. A dark straw color indicates too much organic matter for most jobs. (Note: Lye is injurious to the skin and eyes. Use it with caution.)

2. *Proportioning Materials*

The considerations governing the design of concrete mixes are strength and durability, economy of materials, and workability during placing. Correct proportioning of materials will achieve a proper balance among these essentials.

Designing a concrete mix consists of selecting the water-cement ratio which will produce concrete of the required strength and durability, and finding the most suitable combination of aggregates which will give proper workability when mixed with the cement and water in this ratio.

Water-cement ratio The key element in producing good concrete is the ratio of water to cement. This is commonly expressed as the ratio of the volume of water to a sack of cement. The strength of concrete is directly proportionate to the amount of cement used. For given materials and handling, the lower the water-cement ratio, the stronger the concrete. Figure 7-1 shows that the strength of concrete develops over a long period of time, but the relative strength at any one time is always related to this water-cement ratio as long as the cement-aggregate ratio remains the same.

Figure 7-2 illustrates two factors. First, as the maximum size of coarse aggregate used increases, the yield of concrete per sack of cement also increases. Within the limits of the thickness of section of the finished concrete, the use of larger aggregate will reduce costs. Secondly, for any

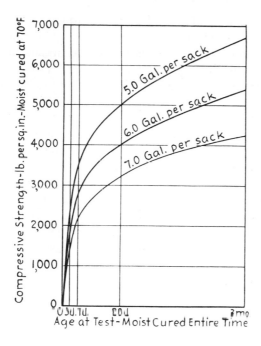

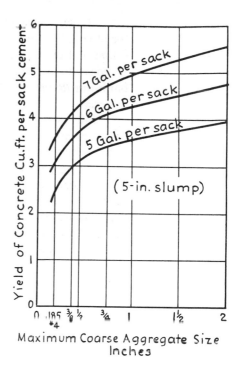

Figure 7-1. The effect of the quantity of water on the strength of concrete.

Figure 7-2. Volume of concrete (cubic feet) produced from one sack of portland cement (using various sizes of coarse aggregate and 5 gallons, 6 gallons, and 7 gallons of water per sack of cement). (From Giese, 1948)

one maximum size of coarse aggregate used, increasing the water per sack of cement allows the use of more aggregate. While this reduces the strength and durability of the concrete, it also increases the yield. For construction in which lower strength and less durable concrete is satisfactory, more sand and gravel may be used with the same quantity of cement with a resulting saving in cost.

The water-cement ratio not only affects strength. Durability, watertightness, and resistance to freeze-thaw action are all controlled by the amount of water used per sack of cement in forming the paste.

It is important to bear these facts in mind when selecting a concrete mix for a specific job. For example, footings and below-grade walls are not exposed to severe weather conditions. Structural strength is the

sole requirement in selecting the mix. On the other hand, exterior walls, floors, and partitions are exposed to abrasion, animal manure, corrosive moisture, and freezing and thawing. Exposure and durability are the prime concerns. Table 7-3 gives the suggested ratios for various jobs. Concrete structures that must be waterproof should be made with a mixture not exceeding 6 gallons (21.2 L) of water per sack of cement. Care should be taken not to use too much aggregate, as a fully plastic and workable mixture that can be placed without any voids is essential. Six gallons of water per sack is also recommended for resistance to freeze-thaw action.

Combination of aggregates   The use of well graded aggregates will produce an economical mixture requiring the least amount of cement for the job. "Well graded" in this case means a variety of materials ranging from fine sand, to coarse sand, small stones, and aggregate as large as is suitable for the particular job. The economy and quality results from each succeedingly smaller size filling in the spaces between the larger particles as shown in Figure 7-3. It is necessary for good quality concrete to have the cement-water paste coat all the surfaces and to fill all the voids not occupied by fine sand. If only coarse aggregate were used, the cement-water paste would have to fill in all the large voids. If only fine aggregate were used, the cement-water paste would have to coat much more surface

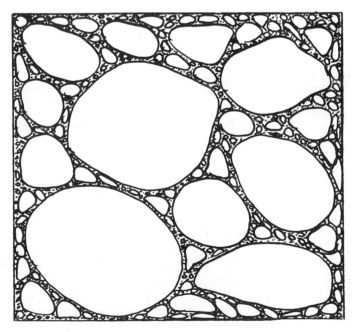

Figure 7-3. Well graded aggregates fit together so perfectly that a minimum of cement-water paste is required.

area. Since the cement is the most expensive ingredient in the mix, the importance of the proper ratio of sizes cannot be overemphasized.

The mixture of fine and coarse aggregates as taken from a gravel bank does not usually make good quality concrete unless it is first screened to separate the fine aggregate from the coarse and then recombined in the correct proportions. Most gravel banks contain an excess of sand in proportion to coarse material. Use of this ungraded bank-run gravel does not result in the most economical concrete, largely because the excess of fines requires more cement paste than would otherwise be necessary to produce concrete of a given quality.

For the sake of economy, coarse aggregate should be graded up to the largest size suitable for the job. This may be illustrated by thinking of an apple. Whole, it has a certain volume and surface. Cut into quarters, it will have the same total volume but considerably more surface. Large-size aggregate will fill more volume in relation to the amount of surface area that must be covered with cement-water paste. The maximum size of aggregate that can be used depends on the shape and size of the concrete structure and the distribution of reinforcing steel. The maximum size should not exceed one-fifth the minimum dimension of the member, or three-fourths of the clear spacing between reinforcing rods.

Not only does the coarse aggregate affect quality and economy of concrete, but the grading of sand particles also influences workability, quality, and economy. The suitability of sand for concrete may be determined with a sieve analysis. The standard sieves used are numbered 4, 8, 16, 30, 50, and 100, each with square openings. The recommended range of particle size for well graded sand to be used for concrete is given in Table 7-1.

Table 7-1   Desirable Range of Sand Particle Size

Sieve size	Percent retained (cumulative)
No. 4	0–5
No. 8	10–20
No. 16	20–40
No. 30	40–70
No. 50	70–88
No. 100	92–98

(From Portland Cement Association, 1952)

Where washed materials are used, it may be found that much of the very fine material has been undesirably removed.

Suggested ratios may need to be adjusted to obtain the best concrete. Too much coarse aggregate will be difficult to work and result in a rough, porous concrete. Too little coarse aggregate will be easy to work, but the low yield of concrete makes it uneconomical. Figure 7-4 A, B, and C illustrate these characteristics.

(a) This mix is *too sandy* because it contains too much sand and not enough coarse aggregate. It would place and finish easily, but would not be economical, and would be very likely to crack.

(b) A *workable mix* contains the correct amount of cement paste, sand, and coarse aggregate. With light trowelling, all spaces between coarse aggregate particles are filled with sand and cement paste.

(c) This mix is *too stony* because it contains too much coarse aggregate and not enough sand. It would be difficult to place and finish properly and would result in honeycomb and porous concrete.

Figure 7-4. Proportioning aggregates for economy and ease of working.

Slump test Mixtures of plastic consistency are required for most concrete. However, a much stiffer mix will be suitable for a flat surface such as a floor or driveway than for a thin, heavily-reinforced member. The consistency of a trial batch may be measured with a slump test.

An open-ended cone 12 inches (305 mm) high, 4 inches (102 mm) in diameter at the top and 8 inches (203 mm) at the bottom is set on a flat surface and filled with concrete. A rod is used to insure that the concrete is well compacted. The cone is then lifted off and set next to the concrete. The rod is laid across the top of the cone and the distance down to the concrete is measured. A 2- to 4-inch (51 to 102 mm) slump is satisfactory for most agricultural construction. Figure 7-5 A and B shows the extremes that might be found with a slump test.

(a) This mix is *too stiff* because it contains too much sand and coarse aggregate. It would be difficult to place and finish properly.

(b) This mix is *too wet* because it contains too little sand and coarse aggregate for the amount of cement paste. Such a mix would not be economical or durable and would have a strong tendency to crack.

Figure 7-5.   Extremes found in slump test.

Table 7-2 provides suggested ratios of water, cement, and aggregate for various jobs. Note that the water used is reduced when sand is damp, wet, or very wet. To determine the amount of water in the sand, a small amount of sand is squeezed in the hand as shown in Figure 7-6, and then the hand is opened, palm up. Damp sand will fall apart; wet sand will form a ball; very wet sand will glisten and leave the hand wet.

Table 7-2 Trial Mixes Made with Separate Aggregates

Kind of Work	Water-cement ratio required	Maximum size of Aggregate	Suggested ratio by mass (weight) * Cement-sand-gravel	Reduce water by percent given if sand is:		
				Damp**	Wet	Very wet
Concrete subjected to severe wear, weather, or weak acid and alkali solutions	5 gal/sack	3/4"–19mm 1½"–38mm	1–1.9–2.3 1–1.7–3.1	10%	20%	30%
Floors (such as home, basement, dairy barn), driveways, walks, septic tanks, storage tanks, structural beams, columns and slabs	6 gal/sack	3/4"–19mm 1½"–38mm	1–2.5–2.8 1–2.2–3.7	8%	17%	25%
Foundation walls, footings, mass concrete, etc.	7 gal/sack	3/4"–19mm 1½"–38mm	1–3.1–3.3 1–2.8–4.2	11%	21%	32%

* Based on sand of medium fineness.
** See Figure 6-6 A, B and C for a description of moisture content in sand.
(From Geise, 1948.)

(a) *Wet sand*, which describes most sands, forms a ball when squeezed in your hand, but leaves no noticeable moisture on the palm.

(b) *Damp sand* falls apart when you try to squeeze it into a ball in your hand.

(c) *Very wet sand*, which describes sand exposed to a recent rain, forms a ball if squeezed in your hand and leaves moisture on the palm.

Figure 7-6.   Moisture test for sand.

Table 7-3 provides a guide for ordering ready-mixed concrete for various types of work.

Table 7-3 A Guide for Ordering Ready-Mixed Concrete

Specifications for medium consistency concrete with a 3 in. (76 mm) slump	When using 1½-in. (38 mm) maximum size aggregate			When using ¾-in. (19 mm) maximum size aggregate		
	Severe exposure (garbage feeding floors, floors in dairy plants)	Normal exposure (paved barn-yards, floors for farm buildings, sidewalks)	Mild exposure (building footings, foundations, concrete improvements in mild climates)	Severe exposure (mangers for silage feeding, manure pits)	Normal exposure (reinforced concrete walls, beams, tanks, foundations)	Mild exposure (concrete improvements in mild climates)
Cement content						
Minimum number of 94 lb sacks per cubic yard OR	7	6	5	7¾	6½	5½
40 kg sacks per cubic meter	10.0	8.5	7.●	11.0	9.0	8.0
Water content						
Maximum number of gal/94 lb sack OR	5	6	7	5	6	7
L/40kg sack	17.7	21.2	24.3	17.7	21.2	24.8

Order air-entrained concrete for all concrete exposed to freezing and thawing and salt action. For 1½ in. (38 mm) maximum size aggregate, specify 4 to 6 percent air content. For ¾ and 1 in. (19 and 25 mm) maximum size, specify 5 to 7 percent air content. (From Giese, 1948.)

3. *Calculating the Amount of Materials Required*

The grading and size of the aggregate as well as the moisture content of the sand will affect the proportions and amounts required. Consequently, the most accurate way to determine the volume of concrete from a mixture of ingredients is with a trial batch. However, when a trial-mix ratio by mass (weight) is given, as in Table 7-2, the volume to be expected from a trial batch may be calculated with the absolute volume method.

$$\text{Absolute Volume} = \frac{\text{Mass of loose material}}{\text{Specific gravity} \times \text{unit mass of water}}$$

The specific gravity for cement may be taken as 3.15 and for aggregate as 2.65. The sum of the absolute volumes of cement, sand, and coarse aggregate, plus the water, will equal the volume of the concrete.

	Customary	SI Unit
Mass of 1 sack cement	94 lb	40 kg
Volume of 1 sack cement	1 cu ft	0.0262 m³
Mass of a 1 sack volume of water	62.4 lb	26.5 kg

As an example of the use of this method, take the first ratio listed in Table 7-2:
Water—5 gal/sack of cement and cement, sand, and gravel 1-1.9-2.3 by mass (weight).
To determine the volume of a one-sack batch:

$$
\begin{aligned}
\text{Water—5 gal/(7.5 gal/cu ft)} &= 0.67 \text{ cu ft} \\
\text{Cement—94 lb/(3.15} \times \text{62.4 lb/cu ft)} &= 0.48 \text{ cu ft} \\
\text{Sand—94} \times 1.9/(2.65 \times 62.4) &= 1.08 \text{ cu ft} \\
\text{Gravel—94} \times 2.3/(2.65 \times 62.4) &= \underline{1.31} \text{ cu ft} \\
&\quad\ 3.54 \text{ cu ft}
\end{aligned}
$$

Thus 3.54 cubic feet of volume would be filled by each sack-batch of concrete. To make 1 cubic yard of concrete would require 27/3.54 or 7.63 sack-batches consisting of:

$$
\begin{aligned}
\text{Cement} &= 7.63 \text{ sacks} \\
\text{Sand}\quad 7.63 \times 1.9 \times 94 &= 1363 \text{ lb} \\
\text{Gravel}\ 7.63 \times 2.3 \times 94 &= 1650 \text{ lb} \\
\text{Water}\ 7.63 \times 5 \text{ gal} &= 38 \text{ gal}
\end{aligned}
$$

A satisfactory estimate for the volume of the materials required for a job may be made with the following formula:

$$C = 40^*/(c + s + g) \quad S = C \times s/27^{**} \quad G = C \times g/27^{**} \qquad \text{where:}$$

C = Sacks of cement per cu yd (m^3) of concrete
c = proportion of cement in mix
s = proportion of sand in mix
g = proportion of gravel in mix
S = cu yd (m^3) of sand per cu yd (m^3) of concrete
G = cu yd (m^3) of gravel per cu yd (m^3) of concrete

For example, suppose a job will require 5 cubic yards of concrete. Determine the quantity of materials to order when a 1–2–3 ratio by volume of cement, sand, and gravel will be used.

C = $40/(1 + 2 + 3) = 6.67$ sacks of cement/cu yd concrete
S = $6.67 \times 2/27$ $= .49$ cu yd sand/cu yd concrete
G = $6.67 \times 3/27$ $= .74$ cu yd gravel/cu yd concrete

For the job:

$5 \times 6.67 = 33.4$ or 34 sacks of cement
$5 \times .49 \ = 2.45$ or 3 cu yd of sand
$5 \times .74 \ = 3.7$ or 4 cu yd of gravel

Inasmuch as they are inexpensive, the aggregates are rounded up to the nearest cubic yard. Leftover cement that is undamaged and not opened may be returned.

In measuring the materials during the mixing operation, nothing is as accurate as weighing. This is particularly true with sand where a change of 2 percent in moisture causes a similar change in weight required. However, that same 2 percent change might result in a 10 percent change in the volume required because of the bulking characteristic of damp sand.

4. Mixing

Thorough mixing of concrete is essential to obtain a plastic and workable mixture. In using a power mixer at the site, it is desirable to put the materials in the mixer in the following order: the measured quantity of water, a little aggregate, the measured amount of cement,

---

* Use 56 with SI Units
** Use 38 with SI Units

and then the balance of the aggregate for the desired consistency. *More water should not be added at any time.*

If a small amount of concrete for an odd job must be mixed by hand, the usual procedure is as follows: spread the measured amount of sand on a flat, watertight surface and distribute the required amount of cement over it evenly. Use a shovel to turn the cement and sand over until a uniform color indicates they are thoroughly mixed. Spread out this mixture and add the measured coarse aggregate in a layer over the top. Again turn with a shovel until the coarse aggregate is evenly distributed. At least three turnings are necessary. Form a hollow in the center of this mixture and slowly add the measured water, while at the same time turning the material towards the center. Continue mixing in this manner until all ingredients are thoroughly and uniformly combined and the desired workability and smoothness is obtained.

Ready-mixed concrete is almost always well mixed when it arrives on the job. The driver should not be asked nor allowed to dilute the mix with water to get it to flow more easily.

5. *Forms*

Forms should be ready and in place before the concrete is mixed or before the ready-mix arrives. They may be made of any of several materials including plywood, steel, or the roofers or sheathing to be used on the building. The forms should be clean, tight, and rigid, and tied together with form ties to prevent bulging. They must also be tied down to prevent floating. It should be remembered that concrete has a density of nearly three times that of water. Thus wood forms will readily float unless they are well anchored. Wood forms should be oiled with form oil or used crankcase oil prior to placement of the concrete to facilitate removal, and to give a better surface to the concrete. Earth forms should be firm and smooth.

In warm weather, forms may be removed from footings or foundations in 24 hours. However, concrete which is supported by forms, such as floor slabs or beams, may need four to five days of curing before it is safe to remove them.

6. *Placing the Concrete*

Before placing the concrete, the job site must be properly prepared. Subgrades should be uniformly graded and compacted. If the supporting earth is extremely dry, it should be dampened to prevent absorption of the mixing water from the concrete. Steel reinforcement rods, if needed, should be in place.

Concrete placement should be done when the plastic mixture has a mushy, not soupy, texture. To prevent segregation of the aggregates, it is important not to "flow" the concrete any more than necessary. It is equally important not to drop the concrete more than 3 feet (1 m). Chutes are recommended when concrete is dropped more than 3 to 4 feet. In deep forms it is desirable to place the concrete in 6- to 12-inch (150 to 300 mm) layers. Spading and tamping, or vibrating with a mechanical vibrator to remove all entrapped air pockets is essential for a dense, smooth job. But again, too much will cause segregation.

7. Finishing

Immediately after the concrete is in place, it is struck off with a straight edge, usually a 2- by 4-inch or 2- by 6-inch board. This is called *screeding* and removes all humps and hollows, leaving an even surface. In screeding, the use of short strokes avoids tearing the surface. Soon after screeding, the surface may be floated, that is, smoothed somewhat with a flat wooden float about 6 inches by 2 feet (150 mm by 1 m) in size and equipped with a long handle. The surface should not be worked again until the concrete has begun to set and the free water has disappeared from the surface.

The type of finish depends on the tool used. A wood or magnesium float will leave a sand finish. Brooming or scoring will produce an anti-skid surface. A steel trowel leaves a smooth, dense surface. The timing of steel troweling is critical. If done prematurely, it brings a mixture of water, cement and fine sand to the surface, resulting in a surface that will flake or develop numerous fine cracks. Regardless of the type of finish, the surface should not be overworked, and dry cement or water should never be added to the surface during working.

Slabs poured over polyethylene film are slow to reach working condition. It is desirable to pour the concrete in the afternoon for finishing the following morning. Unvented oil heaters in rooms where concrete is being poured should be avoided as the CO_2 will cause the surface to powder.

Exposed concrete walls may be improved in appearance by first saturating the surface and then brushing on a grout made of one part cement to one and one-half to two parts of sand. The surface is then vigorously scoured with a wood or cork float. A rubber float may then be used to remove excess grout, and after drying, the surface is rubbed with burlap to remove all signs of the grout. Moist curing is continued for at least two days.

8. *Curing*

Fresh concrete develops 70 percent of its potential strength and durability during the first seven days of curing. During this critical period the concrete must be protected from freezing and excessive heat, and kept continually damp. Cured in this way, concrete will be as much as 50 percent stronger than that which is allowed to dry out quickly. Damp sand or moist straw is commonly used to protect the newly placed concrete and should be kept wet by sprinkling. Covering the concrete surface with plastic film or other watertight material to seal in the moisture is another satisfactory method.

Curing at 70 to 80°F (21 to 27°C) is optimum but not essential. As temperatures decrease, hardening gradually takes place more slowly until at 32°F (0°C) it ceases altogether. If freezing takes place during the first 24 hours, permanent injury to the concrete is almost certain.

Cold weather curing   If concrete must be placed in cold weather, the ground first must be thawed. The freshly mixed concrete should be between 50 and 70°F (10 and 21°C) when it is placed in the forms. To achieve this, the mix water can be heated as high as 150°F (65°C) and when air temperatures are below 30°F (−1°C) it may be necessary to heat the aggregate as well. As soon as the concrete is placed, it should be covered and maintained at 50°F (10°C) for seven days.

Type III high-early strength cement is often used for winter concrete work because it sets more rapidly than Type I portland cement. When Type I portland cement is used in cold weather, replacing two to four percent of the cement with calcium chloride will hasten setting but will have little effect on the freezing point. Calcium chloride should not be used in concrete that will have aluminum conduit imbedded within it.

Hot weather curing   During hot, dry weather special precautions must be taken to keep the concrete moist and cool. Concrete placed in the late afternoon takes advantage of the cooler evening temperatures. The subgrade and wood forms should be dampened so they will not absorb water from the mix. After placing, the concrete must be kept constantly wet to avoid alternate wetting and drying during the curing period. Water not only acts as a curing agent, but also cools the cement. Satisfactory curing conditions can also be maintained by directing a fine spray of water directly on the concrete as soon as it has set firmly enough to avoid damage from the spray.

Reinforced Concrete

Although concrete has a high compressive strength, it has relatively low tensile strength. To compensate for this weakness, steel reinforcing rods are imbedded in the tensile area of the concrete. Reinforced concrete structures are more rigid than steel and are virtually fireproof. Reinforcement of floor slabs poured on grade also reduces the chance of cracking due to changes in temperature. The design of reinforced concrete structures is a complex subject. However, a brief discussion appears in Chapter 11.

CONCRETE MASONRY

Walls constructed with stones, bricks, tile, cinder blocks, or concrete blocks bonded together with cement mortar are described as masonry construction. This type of construction is popular because it is durable, fire resistant, low in maintenance, and attractive in appearance. It is not affected by high humidity, termites, or most agricultural products and wastes. However, because it is more porous and more subject to cracking than concrete, it is difficult to make it watertight.

Concrete Masonry Units

Of the above mentioned masonry units, the concrete block is by far the most common for agricultural use, resulting no doubt from the fact that it is the least expensive "in place." These blocks come in a number of different shapes and sizes. Some of the more common types along with their nominal sizes and typical use are shown in Table 7-4.

Actual sizes are three-eighths of an inch (10 mm) less than nominal in each dimension. However, when laid in place with mortar, the length and height should equal the nominal dimensions.

Several of the blocks are also available in 12-inch (300-mm) widths where greater wall loads are expected or where greater lateral stability is required, although less common, 6-inch (150-mm) and 10-inch (250-mm) blocks are available in some localities. Lightweight aggregate (cinder) blocks are available in several of these sizes. They are not quite as strong and are likely to be slightly more expensive.

Table 7-4   Masonry Units

Key to fig. 7-7	Block	Nominal Size		Typical Use
		inches	millimeters	
A	Stretcher	8x8x16	200x200x400	For the bulk of the wall
B	Corner block	8x8x16	200x200x400	Has square end for corner
C	Half block	8x8x8	200x200x200	Used in alternate rows at openings
D	Sash block	8x8x16	200x200x400	Has vertical groove in end for metal sash
E	Jamb block	8x8x16	200x200x400	Has a 2"x4" piece cut out at one end for a door jamb or wooden window sash
F	Bull nose	8x8x16	200x200x400	Has one rounded corner for smooth wall openings
G	Partition	4x8x16	100x200x400	For inside walls subject to small loads

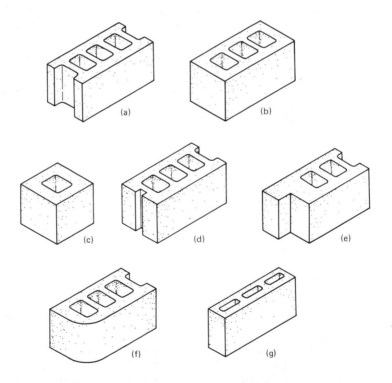

Figure 7-7.   Shapes of concrete masonry units.

Dimensioning Block Walls

In designing a building to be constructed of concrete masonry units, it is desirable to make all dimensions divisible by 8 inches (200 mm). This will allow construction without the need to cut blocks, an economy of both materials and labor. Cut pieces of block also detract from the appearance of the wall.

Block walls have limited lateral strength which determines the recommended unsupported length and height. Eight-inch (200-mm) blocks may be used in walls up to 12 feet (3.6 m) high if no more than 7 feet (2 m) is below grade in well-drained soil. Higher walls should be constructed with 12-inch (300-mm) blocks although the top 12 feet (3.6 m) may be of 8-inch (200-mm) units. No block wall should be more than 35 feet (10 m) high.

Lateral Support and Control Joints

Because high-roof barns cause large, horizontal thrusts to the walls long barn walls should be stiffened at regular intervals. Lateral bracing, either with cross walls or pilasters should be provided each 12 feet (3.6 m) or less in an 8-inch (200-mm) block wall and each 18 feet (5.6 m) or less in a 12-inch (300-mm) block wall. A pilaster is built as an integral part of the wall by turning two 8-inch blocks crosswise to the wall on alternate courses as illustrated in Figure 7-8. The pilaster

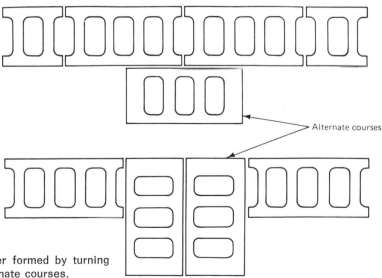

Alternate courses

Figure 7-8. Pilaster formed by turning two blocks in alternate courses.

should be built on the side opposite the expected lateral force, e.g., inside of basement walls, on the outside of storage buildings. In the side walls of long barns, stresses may develop that tend to cause cracks near doors and windows. To relieve the stresses due to expansion and contraction, control joints should be placed in above-grade walls at major openings and, on unbroken sections, at intervals no more than two and one-half times the wall height. The wall must be keyed together at the control joint so that lateral strength is not sacrificed. The vertical joints are filled with a nonhardening mastic to allow for expansion and contraction and to make it watertight. Figure 7-9 shows three methods of constructing control joints to maintain stiffness in the wall.

(a) Michigan-type control joint

(b) Control joint with two jamb blocks

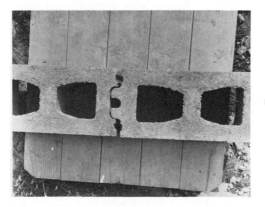

(c) Special units for tongue-and-groove control joint

Figure 7-9.   Three methods of constructing control joints.

Lintels and Sills

Lintels are reinforced concrete beams used over doors, windows, and other openings. Precast units are available from block suppliers in lengths to bear 8 inches (200 mm) into the wall on each side of the opening. They may be split into two 3⅝-inch (90-mm) wide units for easier handling.

Concrete sills below windows prevent water from seeping into the cores of the block. Water running off the windows is directed away from the wall to prevent streaking. Sills may be precast or cast on the site.

Roof Anchorage

A farm building is no stronger than its weakest connection. Often this is where the roof is anchored to the wall. This joint is subject to severe strain during high winds. A rigid connection between the roof and the wall furnishes lateral support to the walls and prevents high winds from lifting off the roof.

To anchor the roof, ½-inch (12-mm) by 18-inch (450-mm) bolts are inserted into the core of every third block, extending down through two courses. The core area containing the bolts should be filled with concrete to insure good anchorage. After the concrete has hardened, the roof plate is placed and fastened securely to the wall. Rafters and trusses can then be attached to the plate with framing anchors. In high wind areas, local codes may require anchorage to more layers of the wall or all the way to the footing.

Mortar

Mortar bonds the concrete blocks together to form a wall, but the quality of a masonry wall can be no better than that of the mortar with which it is laid. Therefore, the selection and mixing of the ingredients is of prime importance.

Masonry cement is widely used for preparing mortar. It contains lime or an air-entraining agent that helps to make it plastic and workable and reduces the possibility of weather damage. However, if a wall is likely to be subjected to extremely heavy loads or water pressure, violent winds, or severe frost action, it is advisable to substitute 50 percent portland cement in the mix. Usual proportions are:

Normal conditions   1:2¼-3 of masonry cement to loose damp sand
Conditions requiring extra strength   1:1:4½-6 of masonry cement to portland cement to sand

Sufficient water is added to obtain a workable mortar.

For face shell joints, of either 8- or 12-inch (200-300 mm) blocks, approximately 2.3 cubic feet (0.064 m³) of mortar will be needed for 100 blocks. A cubic foot of mortar requires one-third sack of mortar cement and 1 cubic foot of sand.

Figure 7-10 illustrates several of the steps in masonry construction.

1 SET BATTER BOARDS AT SAME ELEVATION –

A hose with glass tubes in each end may be used to do this.

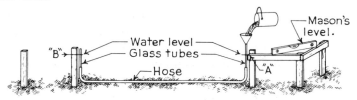

1. Set batter boards at one corner as at right.
2. Place hose as shown.
3. Fill with water until water level is at top of batter board "A".
4. Mark water level at opposite end "B" and set board to mark.

2 LAY OUT BUILDING FIRST

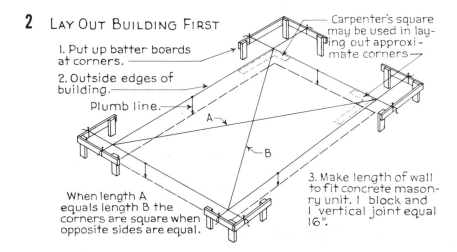

1. Put up batter boards at corners.
2. Outside edges of building.
Plumb line.
Carpenter's square may be used in laying out approximate corners
When length A equals length B the corners are square when opposite sides are equal.
3. Make length of wall to fit concrete masonry unit. 1 block and 1 vertical joint equal 16".

Figure 7-10.   Steps in masonry construction.

3 ADEQUATE FOOTINGS ESSENTIAL

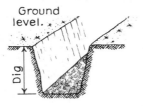
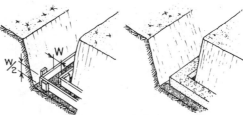

1. Dig trench down to firm soil below frost.

2. Make bottom of trench flat and level.

3. Forms to make footings proper size.

   W = Twice masonry wall thickness.

4. Fill with 1:2¾:4 concrete.

5. Remove form after concrete hardens.

6. Sweep off top of footing before laying concrete masonry.

4 START LAYING BLOCK AT CORNERS

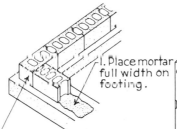
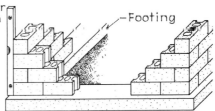

4. Make height of wall to fit concrete masonry unit. 1 block and 1 horizontal joint equal 8".

1. Place mortar full width on footing.

2. Use corner block with one flat end at corners.

3. Mortar placed on face shells only for succeeding courses.

5. Build corners up using mason's level to keep plumb and straight.

5 BUILD WALL BETWEEN CORNERS

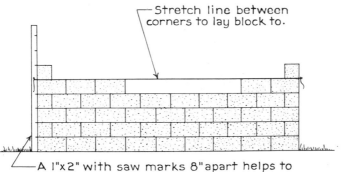

Stretch line between corners to lay block to.

A 1"x2" with saw marks 8"apart helps to space courses at corners.

Mortar joints are ⅜" thick.

Block should be dry when laid in wall.

Figure 7-10 (continued)

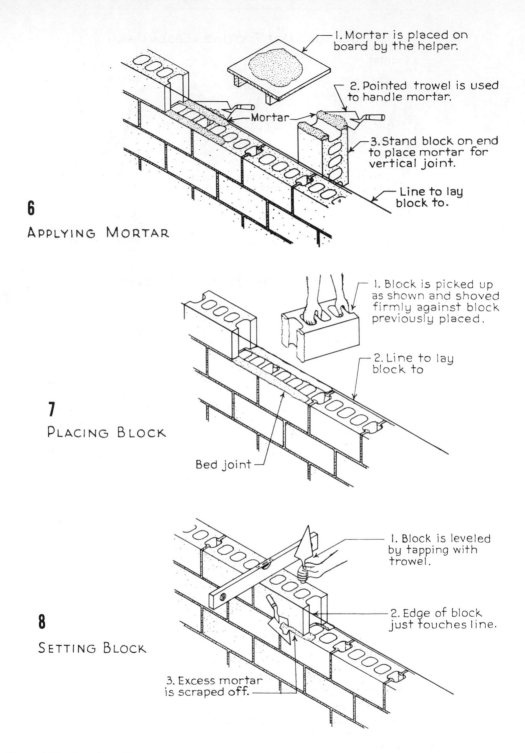

6

APPLYING MORTAR

1. Mortar is placed on board by the helper.

2. Pointed trowel is used to handle mortar.

Mortar

3. Stand block on end to place mortar for vertical joint.

Line to lay block to.

7

PLACING BLOCK

1. Block is picked up as shown and shoved firmly against block previously placed.

2. Line to lay block to

Bed joint

8

SETTING BLOCK

1. Block is leveled by tapping with trowel.

2. Edge of block just touches line.

3. Excess mortar is scraped off.

Figure 7-10   (continued)

9 Joints are Tooled after Mortar has Become Quite Stiff

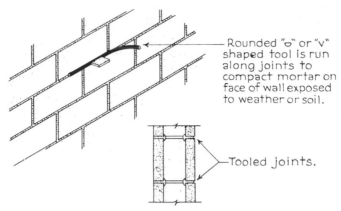

Rounded "o" or "v" shaped tool is run along joints to compact mortar on face of wall exposed to weather or soil.

—Tooled joints.

Figure 7-10 (continued)

Laying Block Walls

Blocks should be well cured and dry before use. After delivery on the job, the blocks should be stored on a dry base, covered and not wetted prior to laying them in a wall. Cracking in the wall results from the shrinkage that occurs when damp blocks dry out. The wall should be started on a good concrete footing installed on firm, undisturbed, well-compacted soil. In laying masonry walls, mortar is placed between the ends of adjoining blocks (butt joints) and between the courses of adjoining blocks (bed joints). The first course of blocks is laid in a full mortar bedding placed on the footing. Succeeding courses are laid with *face shell* joints (mortar along the edges of the blocks only). All the joints should be tooled to compress the mortar, leaving it neat and compact. Tooling the joints on both sides of the wall enhances its appearance and improves its watertightness. Improperly filled and tooled joints are often the cause of water leakage through a masonry wall. In contrast to masonry blocks, bricks should be damp when they are laid to prevent too rapid removal of moisture from the mortar.

Surface Bonding

Surface bonding is a system of constructing masonry walls without the use of mortar joints. The blocks are simply stacked up on a carefully leveled first course and then the surface bonding material is applied to both sides of the wall. The finished wall is generally stronger than a wall laid up with mortar in the usual way and less skilled labor is needed for the construction. The hard double surface is virtually waterproof. Either smooth or textured surfaces are possible and color may be added if desired, thus eliminating any further finishing.

The most important requirement before starting the first course of blocks is a concrete foundation that is level and smooth. The base layer of blocks is laid in a bed of mortar using great care so that the succeeding courses can be built accurately and rapidly into a straight, plumb, and level wall. To avoid settling, the mortar should be allowed to set up before stacking additional courses.

Inasmuch as there are no mortar joints, it is desirable to use special full-size blocks with ground surfaces. Where these are not available, it must be remembered that standard blocks are ⅜ inch (10 mm) undersize in each direction and produce walls with nonmodular dimensions that make it difficult to install windows and doors. The full-size ground surface blocks are not only more convenient to work with but also produce a wall with considerably more compressive strength.

It is also important to have high quality blocks of uniform size. If the units vary in size, they must be shimmed with sheet metal or mortar (never wood) to make them plumb. Rough blocks should be smoothed at the top and bottom by scraping two units together to remove excess materials and burrs.

Once the wall is in place the bonding mix is applied to both sides of the wall with a trowel or with specialized spray equipment.

The ingredients for home-mixed surface bonding are portland cement (preferably white portland cement), hydrated lime, calcium chloride, calcium stearate, and fiberglass. These can be purchased from building material dealers, agricultural chemical dealers, and chemical distributors.

Commercial premixes are also available in bags ranging from 25 to 80 pounds (11-36 kg), and offer several advantages. While the commercial premixes may run as much as three times the cost of the ingredients for home mixing, they are accurately proportioned and eliminate most of the labor of mixing. They also eliminate the need to locate ingredients, some of which are sold only in large quantities.

Although this is a relatively new method of construction, general approval has been given by several code agencies (Owens-Corning Fiberglas Corporation, 1977).

TILT-UP CONCRETE

Tilt-up concrete is a system of constructing durable, maintenance-free buildings that can be erected quickly with little labor and equipment. Concrete panels are cast in a horizontal position and then raised to a vertical position. After carefully plumbing and bracing, columns are cast between the panels to stabilize them and form the wall of the building.

Simple pier foundations are used for some low-cost buildings, but a continuous foundation is preferred. This allows the wall panels to bear uniformly on the footing. It also helps to control rodents and undermining caused by erosion.

Tilt-up panels may be cast either on a previously placed concrete floor or on a carefully prepared bed of sand; the methods work equally well. In either case a sheet of 4 mil polyethylene film is spread over the surface before casting is begun to prevent bonding with the wall panel.

To form the panels, two-by-fours are set on edge and fastened together to the desired panel size. The panels need reinforcement to withstand the stresses of tilting into place. A typical design is shown in Figure 7-11 in which five No. 3 bars are spaced equally in each direction starting 3 inches (75 mm) from the edge. The horizontal bars are allowed to extend 2 inches (50 mm) so that they may anchor the panel to the column. Bolts must also be cast in the panel in such a way that the tilting frame may be attached for the erecting operation. Reinforcing bars are cast in the footings that extend up through the columns. Three No. 4 bars are used with 8- by 8-foot (2.4- by 2.4-mm) panels or three No. 6 bars with 10- by 10-foot (3- by 3-m) panels. The three bars are spaced 6 inches (150 mm) apart in a triangular position as shown in Figure 7-11.

Once the panels have been cast to size and cured for five days, a tilting frame is attached and a tractor used to tilt the panel into position.

Tilt-up concrete is especially suitable in construction where temperature control is not essential, as in a machinery shed. However, insulated panels may be cast for tilting up where it is necessary to maintain a more uniform temperature. Perhaps the most practical application of tilt-up concrete is in the construction of horizontal silos, either above grade or below. It is also an ideal way to construct windbreaks for feed-lots and barnyards.

PROBLEMS

If possible mix, weigh, and cast three trial batches of concrete. Cure in water for a week and then compare their relative strength. Suggested ratios by weight:

	Water		Cement		Sand		Pea gravel
1.	1.25	:	2	:	6.2	:	5.8
2.	.9	:	2	:	3.8	:	4.3
3.	.9	:	2	:	6.2	:	—

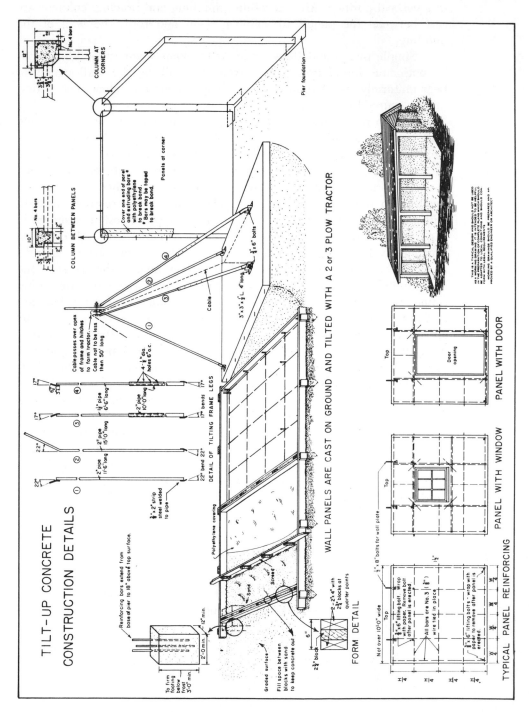

Figure 7-11. Tilt-up concrete construction details. (*Courtesy Portland Cement Association*)

7.1 a. What is the effect of using more water per sack of cement on the amount of concrete obtained per sack?

b. what is the effect of using sand only and very small aggregate on the amount of concrete obtained per sack of cement?

c. Why is it sometimes more expensive to use free bank-run gravel to make concrete instead of purchased sand and gravel?

d. What is the comparative strength of the three samples? What factor causes the greatest difference in these samples?

7.2 Using the same plan assigned for Problem 4.2, determine the total amount of concrete to be ordered for a monolithic foundation. Calculate separately the amounts required for the footings, foundations, and any piers needed. List the specifications for the concrete to be ordered and indicate the total amount to be ordered from the transit-mix company.

7.3 For the same plan used in the previous problem, plan a masonry block wall. Determine the amount of concrete required for footings and for piers. Also determine the number of blocks of suitable width needed to construct the foundation walls.

7.4 Compare the cost of materials required in Problems 7.2 and 7.3. Compare the labor and other material costs to put each of the two alternatives in place.

REFERENCES

Giese, Henry. *A Practical Course in Concrete.* Chicago, Ill.: Portland Cement Association, 1948.

Haynes, B.C. Jr., and Simons, J.W. *Construction with Surface Bonding.* U.S. Department of Agriculture Agricultural Research Service Information Bulletin 374. Washington, D.C., 1974.

Portland Cement Association. *Concrete Construction Practices.* Skokie, Ill.: Portland Cement Association, 1974.

Portland Cement Association. *Concrete Improvements on Farm and Ranch.* Chicago, Ill.: Portland Cement Association, 1963.

Portland Cement Association. *Control Tests for Quality Concrete.* Skokie, Ill.: Portland Cement Association, 1967.

Portland Cement Association. *Design and Control of Concrete Mixtures.* 10th edition. Chicago, Ill.: Portland Cement Association, 1952.

Owens-Corning Fiberglas Corporation. *BlocBond Construction Techniques.* Toledo, Ohio: Owens-Corning Fiberglas Corporation, 1977.

Chapter Eight

Manufactured Building Materials and Paints

MATERIALS

There is an ever increasing number of manufactured building materials available, most with characteristics that make them suitable for a few rather specific applications. They may be superior in insulating value, fire resistance, ease of cleaning, and resistance to weathering, or they may be prefinished to provide an attractive and durable appearance.

Building Boards

Gypsum boards   Gypsum boards consist of a noncombustible core of gypsum with paper facings on front, back, and along edges. They may be used to construct durable, fire resistant, and economical walls and ceilings in buildings. With proper design they also contribute to the isolation of sound. They are not particularly resistant to rupture from heavy blows.

Although gypsum boards do not have a low coefficient of heat transfer, they have a high resistance to the spread of fire. This results from the fact that gypsum ($CaSO_4 \cdot 2H_2O$) contains about 21 percent water in combined form. In the presence of high temperature due to fire, the gypsum is subjected to very slow calcination as the moisture is driven off in vapor form. Since the temperature beyond the plane of calcination does not rise much above 212°F (100°C), there is little chance for the fire to spread until the calcination process is complete. With 21 percent of the substance being driven off, there is a tendency for the board to shrink and crack. Type X gypsum board, available in ½- and ⅝-inch (13–16 mm) thicknesses, has improved fire resistance due to additives that reduce the shrinking and cracking. When Type X board is applied to a partition in a single layer on each face of load-bearing, wood framing members, the ⅝-inch (16-mm) thickness provides at least a one hour fire rating and the ½-inch (13-mm) thickness a three-quarter hour rating.

Regular gypsum board is available in thicknesses ranging from ¼ inch (6.3 mm) to 1 inch (25 mm). However, the three most commonly available are three-eighths of an inch (9.5 mm), used as a single layer in economy construction, or more commonly, double layer for quality construction; ½ inch (13 mm), generally used as a single layer; five-eighths of an inch (16 mm), used either as a single or double layer where additional fire or sound resistance is required.

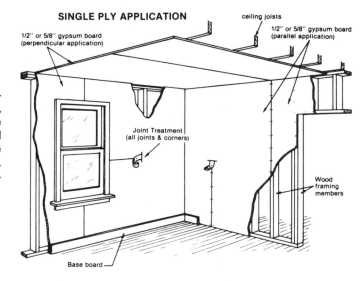

Figure 8-1. Wood stud framing should provide a firm, level, plumb, and even base for single-ply gypsum board application. All joints are treated before decorating. (*Courtesy* Gypsum Association)

SINGLE PLY APPLICATION

1/2" or 5/8" gypsum board (perpendicular application)

ceiling joists

1/2" or 5/8" gypsum board (parallel application)

Joint Treatment (all joints & corners)

Wood framing members

Base board

Standard sizes are 4 feet (1200 mm) wide and 8, 10, 12, or 14 feet (2400, 3000, 3600 or 4200 mm) long. Other sizes may be ordered from the manufacturer.

In addition to regular and Type X, there are a number of other types of gypsum board available. Those most significant for agricultural construction include the water-resistant type and gypsum sheathing. The water-resistant type has both a water-resistant core and a water-repellant, paper facing. It is used as a base for various finish surfaces in bath, kitchen, and laundry areas. It is available as regular and Type X in ½-

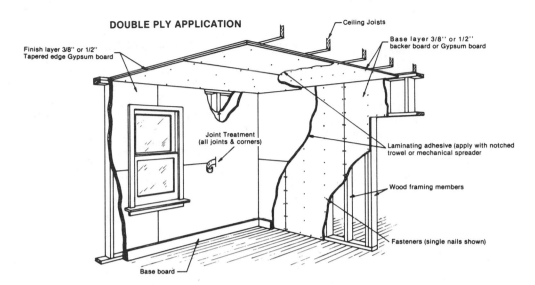

DOUBLE PLY APPLICATION

Finish layer 3/8'' or 1/2'' Tapered edge Gypsum board

Ceiling Joists

Base layer 3/8'' or 1/2'' backer board or Gypsum board

Joint Treatment (all joints & corners)

Laminating adhesive (apply with notched trowel or mechanical spreader)

Wood framing members

Fasteners (single nails shown)

Base board

Figure 8-2. Double layer multi-ply system has laminated surface layer of gypsum board and base layer of gypsum backing board for greater fire resistance (*Courtesy* Gypsum Association)

and ⅝-inch (13 and 16 mm) thicknesses. Gypsum sheathing is available in 2- and 4-foot (600 and 1200 mm) widths and ½- and ⅝-inch (13 and 16 mm) thicknesses. A water-repellant facing paper is used. It has a bracing effect and can be used under various surface materials that may be attached through the sheathing directly to the framing members.

By far the greatest quantity of gypsum board is used for interior walls in homes and public buildings. The most common edge is tapered to allow the installation of reinforcing tape and joint treatment compound, producing a nearly invisible, permanent joint between two gypsum boards. The boards may be installed either vertically or horizontally on wood or metal studs. The horizontal position usually results in the shortest and least noticeable joints. Specially designed ring shank nails or screws are used for wood studs and self-tapping screws for metal studs. The use of adhesives can reduce the number of nails or screws by 50 percent. The adhesive alone may be used to attach the boards to above-grade masonry or concrete that is dry, smooth, clean, and flat. When panels are nailed only, the nails should be spaced 7 inches (175 mm) along ceiling supports or 8 inches (200 mm) along studs. Nailing, started near the center of a board, progresses outward to the edges. Nails that miss the support should be removed and those that are accidentally driven too deeply should be supplemented with another nail 2 inches (50 mm) away.

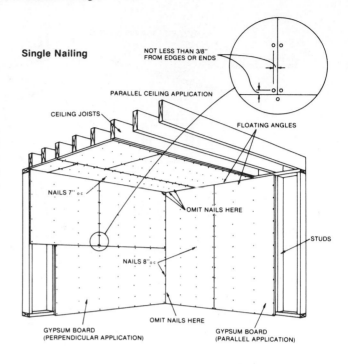

Single Nailing

Figure 8-3. Floating angle construction helps eliminate nail popping and corner cracking. Fasteners at the intersection of walls or ceilings are omitted. (*Courtesy* Gypsum Association)

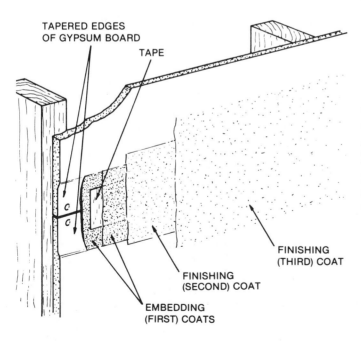

Figure 8-4. Reinforcing joints with tape prevents cracks from appearing at filled gypsum board joints. The joint fill and first coat may be joint compound or all-purpose compound. The second and third coats should be finishing compound or all-purpose compound. (*Courtesy* Gypsum Association)

The chances for cracking in the corner will be reduced by leaving the edge of one of the two boards that meet in a corner unnailed.

Table 8-1   Maximum Frame Spacing for Single-Ply Gypsum Board

Location	Thickness		Application	Spacing	
	Inches	mm		Inches	mm
Ceilings	3/8	9.5	Perpendicular	16	400
	1/2	12.7	Perpendicular	16	400
	5/8 *	16.0	Parallel	16	400
	1/2 *	12.7	Perpendicular	24	600
	5/8	16.0	Perpendicular	24	600
Walls	3/8	9.5	Perpendicular or Parallel	16	400
	1/2	12.7	Perpendicular or Parallel	24	600
	5/8	16.0	Perpendicular or Parallel	24	600

* Only 5/8-inch boards should be used, and then perpendicular to joists, when a water-base texture finish is to be sprayed on.
(From Gypsum Association, 1977)

Asbestos-cement board   This is a hard, durable, water-resistant, noncombustible material composed of portland cement, reinforced with asbestos fibers. A-C board is commonly available in 4- by 8-foot (1200 by 2400-mm) sheets in 1/8-, 1/4-, and 3/8-inch (3, 6, and 9.5 mm) thicknesses. It is rather heavy to work with and driving nails near the edges may cause some cracking. The 3/8-in (9.5-mm) thickness must be drilled. The material may be cut with a carburundum-tipped saw or by scoring and breaking over an edge. Asbestos-cement board is available in two types. *F* is somewhat stronger, smoother and more flexible than type *U*. Either type is suitable for both interior and exterior applications.

For interior walls that are not subject to rough treatment (e.g., milkroom walls), 1/4-inch (6-mm) sheets may be installed directly to studs spaced 16 inches (400 mm) on center. All edges must be supported, and if the walls are to be hosed down, the edges should be bedded in caulking compound. When the wall may be subject to contact by large animals, it is necessary to back up the A-C board with plywood or lumber.

For exterior walls, horizontal joints may be lapped 1½ inches (38 mm) or protected with a metal Z flashing. Vertical joints are usually protected with 3-inch (76-mm) battens. Water-repellent, but not vapor-proof, paper should be used under both the sheets and the battens.

Nails for installing A-C board should be corrosion-resistant, threaded, and as slim as possible. Hardened nails are easier to drive. Nails should be spaced 8 inches (200 mm) along all edges and 16 inches (400 mm) along intermediate supports.

Hardboards   These are produced by pressing wood fiber mats at high pressure and temperature until the natural lignin in the fibers binds them together into a hard, permanent board that is more dense than the wood from which it was made. Hardboards are available as either standard (Type 1) or tempered (Type 2). The tempered is oil treated to make it highly water resistant.

Probably the greatest use for hardboards is in the form of the nearly unlimited choice of decorative panels available for finishing walls. Those that are at least ¼ inch (6 mm) thick may be placed directly on studs 16 inches (400 mm) on center. Thinner panels should be backed up with plywood, gypsum board or rigid insulation. Contact adhesives, with a minimum of nailing, provide a rapid method of application with few nailheads to mar the appearance. While it is unnecessary, the blemish-free surface of the unfinished hardboards may be readily painted. The boards are easy to cut and nail, but a carbide saw is advisable. Hardboards are commonly available in thicknesses of ⅛, ¼, and ⅜ of an inch (3, 6 and 9.5 mm) and in sheets 4 feet (1200 mm) wide and 6 to 16 feet (1800 to 4800 mm) long. The sheets are more flexible than plywood and may be used to form curved surfaces with as little as a 12-inch (300-mm) radius. Manufacturer's recommendations should be followed both in procedure and in the minimum radius attempted. Hardboard underlayment is sanded on one side to aid in obtaining a good bond with the finish material. It is often used to bring finish floors level where different floor covering materials are used in the same area. When nailed to the recommended specifications of 4 inches (100 mm) along the edges and 8 inches (200 mm) along intermediate supports, considerable bracing effect is obtained.

Particleboard   Particleboard is formed of wood chips bonded together with synthetic resin to produce a uniform, smooth, and dimensionally stable panel with excellent glue-bond characteristics. Although particleboard may be used as sheathing, subfloor, and underlayment, much of it is used as core stock by manufacturers of furniture, cabinets, countertops and wall paneling. Most particleboard is intended for interior use, although a phenolic bonded type is available for exterior use. There is a wide range of densities, thicknesses, and panel sizes. For building purposes, the 4- by 8-foot (1200- by 2400- mm) size in either ⅜- or ¾ -inch (9.5- or 19-mm) thickness is most common.

Plastic laminates   Surfaced with melamine, these are available in numerous patterns, both smooth and textured. They are commonly used in homes for surfaces of countertops and tables and for cabinet facings. Because of their hard, smooth, waterproof finish, they are also suitable for wall or work surfaces in agricultural buildings where ease of cleaning is a primary factor.

Fiberglass reinforced plastic paneling   This paneling, often used in the food processing industries for years, is now becoming popular on the farm for surfaces that are subject to impact, wear, and frequent cleaning. It is available either laminated to plywood or as a flat panel for installation on walls or ceiling. The laminated version is available in 4- by 8-foot (1200- by 2400-mm) and 4- by 10-foot (1200- by 3000-mm) panels from ¼ to ¾ inches (6–19 mm) thick. Using a carbide-tip saw for cutting, the material is installed in the same manner as ordinary plywood, and a good quality caulking compound is used to seal the joints.

The flat panel material comes in thicknesses of 0.09 to 0.17 of an inch (2.3–4.3 mm) in regular sheets of 4 by 8 feet (1200 by 2400 mm) and 4 by 10 foot (1200 by 3000 mm). In addition, panels are available in widths up to 8⅓ feet (2542 mm) and 40 feet (12 m) or longer in length. This is of particular advantage in milking parlors or milkrooms where a minimum number of joints is desirable. A silicone sealant is recommended for the joints in this type of installation. Finally, a fire-retardant version with a Class A flame spread rating of 15 may be obtained where that is required.

Solid plastic panels   Solid plastic panels that meet U.S. Food and Drug Administration and Public Health standards for clean room applications are available. The 4- by 8-foot (1200- by 2400-mm) size in ¼ -inch (6-mm) thickness may be installed directly on studs 16 inches (400 mm) on center. Although first cost is high, it should offer a long life and an easily-cleaned surface.

Insulating fiberboards   These are usually too thin to be of much value as insulation and too soft to have very much strength or resistance to rupture. However, when used as sheathing and nailed as directed, there is a good bracing effect and some insulating value. The finish siding material must be fastened through the board directly to the framing. One manufacturer is producing an insulating board from recycled wood-fiber material which is resistant to weathering and is suitable for either exterior or interior wall and ceiling surfaces. It is available with a natural gray surface or prime-coated, ready for finish-painting. The material is easily cut and handled. However, due to considerable dimensional change with changing moisture conditions, it must be installed with edge gaps as specified by the manufacturer. For exposed exterior applications, the gaps should be caulked and covered with a batten. Instructions call for spacing nails 6 inches (150 mm) along all edges and 10 inches (250 mm) along intermediate supports which are spaced 16 inches (400 mm) on center. Insulating boards are available in thicknesses of 15/32 to 29/32 of an inch (12 to 24 mm) and in sizes ranging from ceiling tiles up to 4- by 14-foot (1200- by 4200-mm) panels.

Plastic-coated insulation boards   As shown in Figure 8-5, these provide a smooth, easily-cleaned surface with very low permeability. If the surface is to be hosed down, the joints must be sealed with tape. These panels may only be installed in areas where they are not subject to physical damage. The core may be of low-cost fiber material or of polyurethane. While the polyurethane is a considerably better thermal insulator, because of its burning characteristics local code restrictions may require that it be covered with some other surface material.

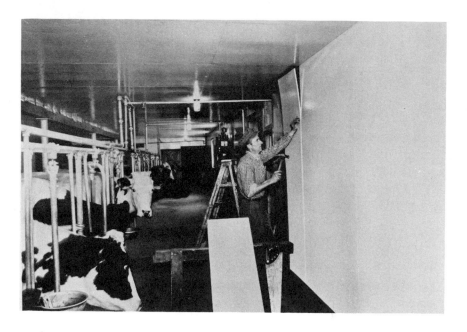

Figure 8-5.   Polyethylene coated fiber board provides an easily cleaned surface. (*Courtesy* of the Homasote Company)

Siding Materials

There is a wide range of siding materials available for farm buildings and homes. They vary in appearance, initial cost, frequency and cost of maintenance, resistance to physical damage, vapor permeability, and bracing effect. Because of the expected long life of most of the materials, it is essential to consider all factors carefully before making a choice.

Wood shingles and shakes   Whether painted, stained or left natural, these provide an attractive and durable siding. They may be dipped in paint before installation to provide increased protection from moisture. Shingles are usually sawed from either cedar or redwood. Shakes are split or made to appear split from the log. Shingle grades include No. 1, which will be 100 percent heartwood, edge grain and clear; No. 2, which will be clear for 12 inches (300 mm) from the butt; and Nos. 3 and 4, which will have some flat grain and sapwood as well as increasing numbers of defects. Any amount up to just under half the length of the shingle may be exposed to the weather. Shingles may be applied with an uneven butt line and a noticeable side gap, giving a patterned appearance, or they may be lined up carefully and installed with a minimal side gap, giving almost the same appearance as beveled wood siding. Shingles may be *squared* and *rebutted*, that is, cut so the sides are parallel with each other and perpendicular to the butt when they are to be installed with a minimal side gap.

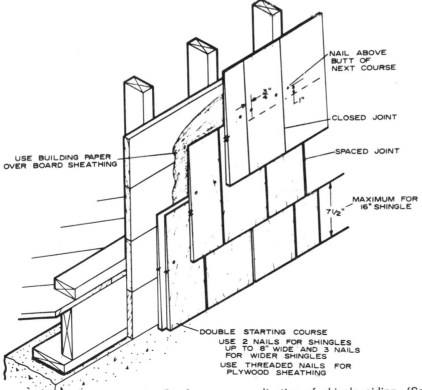

Figure 8-6. Single course application of shingle siding. (Source: USDA Forest Service)

Bevel siding or clapboards   Milled from pine, redwood, or cedar, these have been used as an attractive siding for generations. They may be left natural, stained or painted. Although failure to install a good vapor seal and to properly caulk around windows and doors has often caused premature paint failure, with proper attention to moisture control, paint life can be satisfactory. Figure 8-7 illustrates the proper layout of the siding around a window. A minimum of 1 inch (25 mm) of vertical overlap should be allowed.

Vertical wood siding   Left natural, stained or painted, vertical wood siding can provide good service and an attractive appearance. Moisture is less likely to be a problem than with horizontal siding. There are examples of unpainted vertical siding that are in excess of 150 years old, weathered very thin, but still with no signs of rot. Figure 8-8 shows three styles of vertical siding. It is important to nail the boards and battens as shown in the figure so that shrinking and swelling will not split the boards.

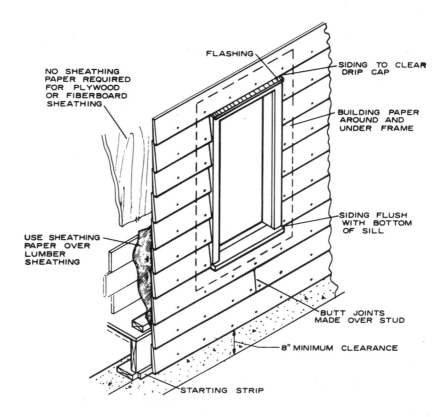

Figure 8-7.   Application of bevel siding to coincide with window sill and drip cap. (Source: USDA Forest Service)

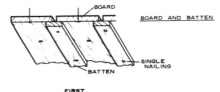

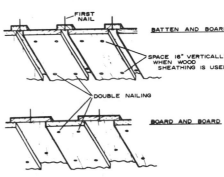

Figure 8-8. Application of vertical wood siding. (Source: USDA Forest Service)

Plywood siding   Designated as 303 siding by the American Plywood Association, plywood siding is available in many different patterns. Plywood provides a siding that is durable, gives good bracing effect, and requires little maintenance. One of the 303 sidings, Texture 1-11, has vertical grooves cut in either sanded or unsanded panels. One of the least expensive siding materials, it is suitable for many farm buildings as well as homes. The APA 303 grade stamp indicates the maximum stud-spacing for panels installed with the face grain vertical. This applies both for panels installed over sheathing or directly to the studs. The suggested nail size is 6d for ½ inch (13 mm) or less and 8d for thicker panels, with the nails spaced 6 inches (150 mm) along the edges and 12 inches (300 mm) along intermediate supports.

Metal siding   This siding, made from aluminum or galvanized steel, provides an attractive finish for agricultural buildings with either wood or steel frames. Either material is available in painted or unpainted sheets with a variety of rib designs and widths. Typically, aluminum, as well as some steel sidings, carries a 20 to 30 year guarantee against leaking due to corrosion. The steel has the advantage of greater strength and dent resistance along with a lower coefficient of expansion which helps to reduce hole enlargement around the nails. Aluminum is available in 0.016- to 0.024-inch (0.4- to 0.6-mm) thicknesses while steel comes in 26 (the heaviest), 28, and 29 gauge. The thickness does not appreciably affect the life of either material, but it does influence the spacing of supports. Figure 8-9 provides some typical procedures used in installing metal siding and roofing. Panels are easily handled and may be installed rapidly.

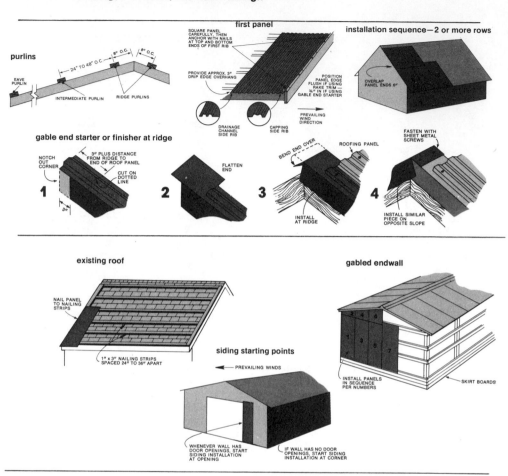

Figure 8-9.   Installing metal roofing and siding. (*Courtesy* INRYCO, Inc.)

Manufactured sidings   Using a variety of prefinished materials these sidings are rapidly gaining in popularity. Painted aluminum, solid vinyl, vinyl-coated hardboard, or plywood and asbestos-cement are among the most common. They not only are attractive, but the promise of little or no maintenance tends to offset any greater initial cost. It is significant that most of them are excellent vapor barriers. Therefore the vapor barrier near the inside surface of the wall must have a very low vapor permeability and must be installed very carefully if moisture is to be prevented from accumulating within the wall cavity.

Masonry construction   Although usually more costly to build, masonry is popular in some areas of the country. It is attractive, low in maintenance, and not subject to rot or termite damage. Frame construction with masonry veneer is much more common in colder climates because of the ease of installing the necessary insulation. The surface bonding technique described in Chapter 6 may increase the popularity of masonry construction.

Roofing Materials

A roofing material should be carefully chosen to ensure a type suitable for the roof pitch, the type of roof deck, and for the desired life. The lowest first cost may not necessarily be the most economical over the life of the building. Most roofing materials are sold by the square. One square covers 100 square feet of roof surface.

Referring to Figure 13-3, which identifies the various parts of a gable roof, one sees that the pitch of a roof is equal to the rise divided by twice the run. On even-pitch buildings, the rise divided by the span would be equally satisfactory. A 24-foot (7.3-m) wide building with a 6-foot (1800-mm) rise has a one-quarter pitch. This same pitch is often indicated by an inverted right triangle dimensioned 6:12 (50:100).

Wood shingles   Wood shingles produce an attractive roof with a

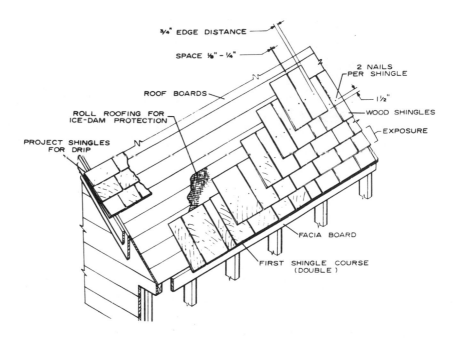

Figure 8-10.   Installing wood shingles on a solid roof deck. (Source: USDA Forest Service)

long life. They may be installed on a tight roof deck. However, it is more economical to install them on a slatted deck with the slats spaced equal to the shingle exposure. Providing the attic is well ventilated, the slatted deck will increase shingle life. For 16-inch (400-mm) shingles, the exposure of the butt to the weather is usually 5 inches (125 mm). As mentioned under the section on siding, shingles come in four grades. Because of the high labor costs involved, it is not practical to use any but the No. 1 grade for a permanent building.

Asphalt materials   These require a solid roof deck in all cases except the corrugated type. The weight per square of the saturated roofing is a reasonable measure of the durability of the material.

Figure 8-11. One of many new textures available in asphalt shingles. (*Courtesy* Asphalt Roofing Manufacturers Association)

Felts are used to construct a built-up covering on a flat roof deck. A low pitch of 0.5 to 0.75:12 is desirable, to provide adequate drainage but it is also the maximum pitch. On greater pitches, the roof tends to creep in hot weather. Felts are available in 15- and 30-pound (6.8- and 13.6-kg) weights. They are installed three to five layers thick with hot asphalt as the material binding the layers together.

Roll roofing is the least expensive asphalt material, but it also has the shortest life. It is available in rolls of 45 to 105 pounds (20 to 48 kg) covering one square. Roll roofing is suitable for a minimum pitch of 3:12 when a 2-inch (51-mm) overlap is secured with exposed nails. A 2:12 pitch is satisfactory when the nails are concealed and the overlap is sealed down with asphalt cement.

Double coverage roll roofing has a considerably longer life than ordinary roll roofing. It may be used on a pitch as low as 1:12. Available in weights of 55 to 70 pounds (25 to 32 kg) per square, it combines blind nailing with cementing to provide the double coverage. A square requires two rolls plus 2 gallons (7.6 L) of asphalt cement.

Shingles are available in many styles and colors. They are the most popular roofing for homes in much of the temperate climate areas of the United States and Canada. Qualities weighing from 205 to 390 pounds (93 to 177 kg) per square are common, and depending on the weight, there are usually two to four bundles per square. Shingles are satisfactory for use on a roof with at least a 4:12 pitch. However, if it becomes necessary to use shingles on a lower pitch, roll roofing should be installed first.

Asphalt shingles carry an Underwriters Laboratories' label indicating the degree of resistance to fire. Most carry a Class C rating which is effective against light exposure to fire, but a few carry a Class A label indicating effectiveness against severe exposure to fire. The Underwriters Laboratories' label for wind resistance indicates the ability to withstand a 60-mph (100 km/h) wind for two hours. Strip shingles carrying the UL label have factory-applied adhesive which is activated by the sun's heat to form a wind resistant bond. Methods of application of asphalt shingles are shown in Figures 8-12, 8-13 and 8-14.

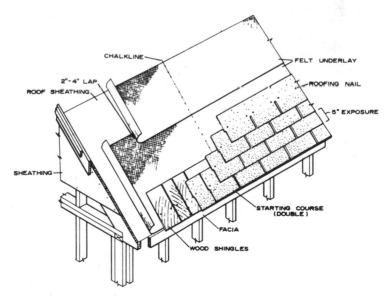

Figure 8-12. Application of asphalt shingles on a plywood roof deck. (Source: USDA Forest Service)

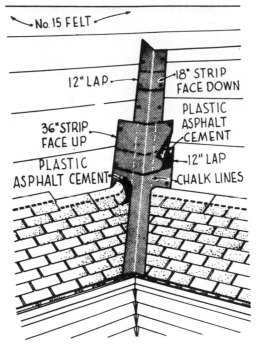

No. 15 FELT

12" LAP

18" STRIP FACE DOWN

36" STRIP FACE UP

PLASTIC ASPHALT CEMENT

PLASTIC ASPHALT CEMENT

12" LAP

CHALK LINES

Figure 8-13. Roll roofing used for an open valley. (*Courtesy* Asphalt Roofing Manufacturers Association)

36" ROLL ROOFING 50# OR HEAVIER

EACH STRIP TO EXTEND AT LEAST 12" BEYOND CENTER OF VALLEY

6" MIN

EXTRA NAIL IN END OF STRIP

Figure 8-14. A woven valley. (*Courtesy* Asphalt Roofing Manufacturers Association)

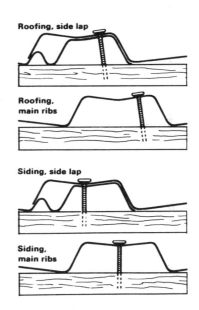

Roofing, side lap

Roofing, main ribs

Siding, side lap

Siding, main ribs

Figure 8-15. Metal roofing side lap showing anti-siphon design and proper nailing. (*Courtesy* Granite City Steel Division of National Steel Corporation)

Corrugated asphalt roofing is available in several colors either with or without a mineral surface. The material is not affected by dust or fumes from fertilizers or animal wastes and it may be installed on an open roof deck of at least 3:12 pitch in the same manner as metal roofing. It is probably a little less subject to condensation on the underside of an open roof deck than are metals. In addition, it is flexible enough to be curved around a 15-foot (4.5-m) radius. Like most asphalt products, it carries the UL Class C fire rating. It also carries a 25-year guarantee against leaks. The necessary accessories, including translucent PVC panels, are available.

Steel roofing   Steel roofing is a popular material for farm buildings but is considered too noisy to be desirable for homes. It is suitable for use on open roof decks of at least 3:12 pitch. Steel is available in three gauges: 26 (the heaviest), 28, and 29. The gauge has little effect on durability and a high-tensile strength 29-gauge provides as strong a sheet as an annealed 26-gauge. Sheets are available in several rib designs, each of which will affect the panel strength. Consequently it is important to follow the manufacturer's specifications on purlin spacing.

Steel roofing is galvanized to reduce corrosion by coating the surface with a thin layer of zinc. The thickness of the zinc in the coating, once listed as 1.25 ounces, is now designated G-90 by the American Society for Testing and Materials. For increased durability of unpainted roofing, a 2-ounce coating is available. This indicates 1 ounce per square foot on each side of the sheet. Metallic zinc dust in an oil, alkyd, or phenolic base is recommended as a prime coat when painting steel roofing. Galvanized roofing is also available with factory-applied paint coatings that improve appearance and durability.

Steel roofing is installed with galvanized ring shank nails that come with either a neoprene or lead washer. For metal framing, self-tapping screws with a sealing washer are used. Aluminum nails or paint should never be used with galvanized roofing as the resulting electrolytic action will soon cause corrosion.

Aluminum roofing   Also popular for farm buildings, aluminum roofing is light in weight, naturally corrosion resistant, and easy to install on open roof decks of at least 3:12 pitch. It is available in sheets similar to galvanized steel roofing except that the sheets are typically wider and come in lengths up to 30 feet (9.14 m). It also comes in rolls and in 4-foot (1200-mm) wide sheets backed with foam insulation. Although the long sheets speed installation and reduce the number of joints, the high coefficient of expansion of aluminum may cause the enlargement of nail holes. A 24-foot sheet of aluminum expands one-quarter inch (6 mm) with a temperature rise of 80°F (45°C). Aluminum roofing generally carries a 20- to 30-year guarantee against corrosion. Aluminum nails with neoprene washers are used for installing the sheets on purlins. Approximately 100 nails per square are required. Although the span between purlins is related to the thickness of the sheets chosen, which may range from 0.016 to 0.032 of an inch (0.4 to 0.8 mm), the alloy and temper of the metal greatly influences the strength and stiffness. Consequently it is important to follow the manufacturer's instruction in matching the type of sheet to the purlin spacing. Embossing the sheets not only reduces glare from sunshine but also slightly increases the stiffness. If there is a possibility that the aluminum roofing or siding will come in direct contact with a steel frame, it must be protected from electrolytic action by paint or a layer of heavy builder's felt. Stainless steel self-tapping screws should be used to be compatible with both metals.

Asbestos-cement roofing   This is available in corrugated panels and as shingles. The shingles provide a durable and attractive roof surface. However, they are difficult to repair or replace in case of damage. The corrugated panels are available in two qualities, either 2 or 4 pounds per square foot (9.8 or 19.5 kg/m^2). Although they are resistant to almost any atmosphere and have a long life expectancy, the panels are very heavy to handle during installation and their weight may increase the strength requirements for roof framing.

Corrugated roofing, whether asphalt, steel, aluminum, or asbestos-cement may be installed on an open roof deck. The savings in materials and labor partially offset the extra cost of these materials over some other types. In most cases the supplier will have fiberglass-reinforced or PVC panels with the same rib design allowing a few of the regular roofing panels to be replaced by the translucent panels to provide light for the building.

Slate or tile roofing   These materials are seldom used on agricultural buildings. Although very durable and attractive, their extra weight requires a stronger roof frame and they may be difficult to repair or replace in case of damage. In addition, the original cost is likely to be substantially higher than for most other materials.

Table 8-2   Nails Required for Roofing

Roofing materials	Type of Nail	Length		Lbs/Square	
		New Roofing	Over Old Roofing	New Roofing	Over Old Roofing
Wood shingles	Galvanized	1½"	2"	3½-4½	4½-6½
Asphalt shingles	Galvanized	1¼"	1¾"	1⅞	2¼
Galvanized steel	Galvanived L-H	1¾"	2-2½"	1½	
Aluminum	Aluminum Neo	1¾"	2-2½"	100 nails/square	

PAINTS AND CAULKS FOR AGRICULTURAL USE

Paints and stains are applied to exterior wood surfaces primarily for the attractive appearance they provide. Although there are differences of opinion about the economic value of painting the exterior of farm buildings, most people will agree that there is an aesthetic value to a neat appearing, well-painted farmstead. Although paint offers wood surfaces limited protection against moisture and sunshine, there is no guarantee that moisture will not penetrate through cracks and other defects in the paint or permeate from within the building and cause considerable deterioration.

On the other hand, corrosion-prone metal surfaces can be provided considerable protection with quality paint carefully applied. Some factory-applied finishes last for up to 20 years or more while painting surfaces in place offers protection for a shorter period.

There are many types of surface coverings manufactured from an even greater number of ingredients and formulated in an infinite number of ways. A brief description of some of the more common coverings and the materials from which they are made will precede a chart which can then be used for the selection of a suitable material for a specific application.

Caulking and Sealing Materials

The success of a paint job is often related to how well cracks and joints are sealed prior to painting. In turn, the quality of the sealing is often determined largely by the kind and quality of the materials used. Table 8-3 lists some of the more common caulking and sealing compounds with some of their characteristics and applications.

Types of Surface Coatings

Paints Paints consist of a hiding pigment, and a resin which serves as a binder to hold the pigment together and to form a protective surface. The binder may be a vegetable oil or a synthetic resin. Paint may be thinned with an organic solvent, in which case it is called a solvent or reduced paint, or with water, in which case it is usually called a latex paint. Most solvent type paints harden by oxidation while the latex paints harden, as the water evaporates, by the coalescing of the resins in the binder.

A third type of paint hardens by the curing action of its resins. This type usually comes in two parts that must be mixed immediately before

Table 8-3   Caulks and Sealers

Type	Applications	Ease of Use	Surface Preparation	Life Expectancy	Can be Painted	Cost Comparison	Comments
Oil-base	Interior or exterior No movement	Easy	Primed	1-7 years	Yes	Low	Hardens and cracks
Acrylic-latex	Interior or exterior No movement	Very easy	Clean and dry Best primed	5-10 years	Yes	Low-med.	Dries rapidly
Butyl rubber	Interior or exterior	Easy	Clean and dry	10 years +	After 7 days	Low-med.	Adheres well Shrinks
Polysulfide rubber	Interior or exterior Tolerates movement	Difficult	Primed	20 years +	1-2 weeks	High	May be toxic
Silicone rubber	Interior or exterior Tolerates movement	Medium	Primed	20 years +	Read directions	High	Good on metal
Polybutene	Temporary sealing	Easy	Best primed	20 years +	Yes	Medium	Low adhesion Never hardens
Neoprene rubber	Sealing metal outdoors	Difficult	Clean and dry	15-20 years	Yes	Medium	Slow curing
Urethane	Interior or exterior	Easy	Clean and dry	20 years +	Yes	Medium	Available in pour form for horizontal cracks

using. The "pot life" for this type of paint may be just a few hours.

Varnish Varnish is a single-element coating consisting only of the resin and, unlike paint, has no pigments. Its sole purpose is to protect a surface without hiding its natural beauty. Varnishes provide a treatment of protective finish that is used for either interior or exterior surfaces. However, varnishes are not always suitable for exterior use since they are usually subject to deterioration from the ultraviolet rays of the sun. A number of different resins are used and both solvent- and water-thinned varnishes are available.

Stains Stains are intermediate between paints and varnishes. They contain coloring pigments, often transparent rather than opaque, but not enough to hide the wood grain in most cases. Some stains penetrate more deeply into the wood than paint or varnish. Most do not leave a surface film and therefore are not subject to peeling or cracking.

Lacquers Lacquers are rapid-drying coverings that harden by the evaporation of the solvent. They produce a glossy surface that is some-what less durable than varnish. Lacquers are commonly used in factory-coated building materials.

Primers and Topcoats

Most paint systems consist of a primer coat and one or more top or finish coats. The primer seals the original surface and provides a uniform, nonporous, dull surface on which to apply the top coat.

The top coat provides most of the protection against weathering, chemicals, dirt, and staining. Top coats are available in three different finishes: gloss, semigloss, and flat. The gloss finish has the least pigment and does not cover imperfections well, but usually has the hardest, smoothest, and most easily-cleaned surface. Flat finish paints contain the highest pigment-to-binder ratio and provide the most opaque covering. They have the best surface for repainting. Semigloss paints fall between the other two in most characteristics.

Binders Used in Paints

Oil Oil-based paints have largely been replaced by alkyd-based or latex-based paints which are superior in most characteristics. However, linseed oil paints continue to be sold for use on houses and barns.

Alkyds Alkyds are produced by the reaction of plant oils with certain alcohols. They have a wide range of desirable characteristics and have largely replaced oil paints. Alkyds are classified as long-oil, medium-oil, and short-oil. Long-oil alkyds are used extensively as house paints because they are easy to spread and they penetrate sufficiently to adhere well. Medium-oils are the base for gloss and semigloss enamels. The short-oil alkyds are used primarily for factory-applied finishes.

Alkyd-based paints are used for both interior and exterior wood surfaces as well as for metal. They are *not* recommended for fresh plaster or concrete surfaces as they do not tolerate the alkaline conditions.

Epoxies   Although epoxy paints offer a wide range of surface characteristics, the types used in agriculture produce a hard, smooth, easily-cleaned surface. The high cost of epoxy paints is balanced by the durability and superior performance under adverse conditions such as those existing on milking parlor walls and the inside walls of concrete silos. When used for exterior application, there is apt to be considerable chalking which may or may not be desirable.

Latex (acrylics and vinyls)   Polyvinyl acetate and acrylics are the most important of the resins thinned with water. Paints manufactured with these resins are used extensively for both interior and exterior application. They are easy to apply because of thixotropic additives which give enough body to cause the paint to adhere to the brush without dripping and to the painted surface without sagging. At the same time, the pressure of the brush causes it to thin out for easy spreading. Latex paints offer good color retention and resistance to blistering, the latter resulting from a rather high permeability to water vapor. They may be applied on damp, but not wet, surfaces and are easily cleaned from brushes and rollers with soap and water.

Inorganic vehicles   These binders are used primarily with zinc dust as a metal primer.

Phenolic resins   Phenolics were among the first synthetic resins used. Originally based on tung oil, their prices became excessive until other sources were developed. Phenolic resins are used in exterior varnishes and as a base for aluminum paint.

Rubber-based resins   These are distinguished from rubber-based latex in that they are solvent rather than water-reduced binders. They are used extensively on masonry surfaces, particularly swimming pools, because of their very low permeability to water and water vapor.

Silicone resins   Silicone resins are used in high temperature paints which will withstand more than 1,000°F (540°C). Furthermore, they are very resistant to oxidation and are mixed with other resins to produce long-lasting, weather-resistant paints. Many of the silicone mixtures are used by manufacturers in finishes guaranteed for up to 20 years. They are not widely available to the public.

Urethanes   Urethanes are similar to, but more complex than alkyds, and often exhibit superior wear, hardness, and solvent-resistant characteristics. They are used in both pigmented and clear finishes for both interior and exterior applications.

Pigments

Pigments are used to hide or color an underlying surface or to serve some chemical purpose such as corrosion resistance or ultraviolet absorption.

Titanium dioxide   Titanium dioxide has such superior hiding power that, although its cost per pound is high, it offers the least expensive hiding power per unit of area.

Zinc oxide   Zinc oxide is used to provide a harder, and more chalk-resistant film. It is also mildew resistant, adds brilliance to white paints and helps retain color integrity in colored paints by absorbing ultraviolet rays.

Lead pigments   These have been banned by law from use in either interior or exterior house paint. Even though they were useful pigments, the danger they pose to health has resulted in a nationwide ban.

Extender pigments   Extender pigments, such as calcium carbonate, clay, and talc do not add significant hiding power, but they do add necessary bulk and other desirable characteristics that improve coating performance. They also reduce cost as compared to using the hiding pigments alone.

Colored pigments   These are almost always used in very small quantities and are too numerous to cover individually. It is significant that tinted or colored paints almost invariably outlast the same formulation in white.

Solvents and Additives

Solvents are necessary to thin the resins so they can be spread or sprayed on a surface. Manufactured hydrocarbons such as *benzene, toluene* and *xylene* along with derivatives of petroleum such as *naphthas* and *mineral spirits* are used as solvents for oil- and alkyd-base paints and varnishes. High cost and strong odor have reduced the use of *turpentine.* *Esters* and *glycols* are used primarily as lacquer solvents. However, they are also used to some extent in urethanes and in small quantities in most latex paints to improve coalescence of the resins at the instant the water evaporates. *Alcohol* is used for thinning shellac and *glycol ethers* are used to a limited extent for epoxies. Lastly, *water* is the solvent for latex paints, and its low cost, safety, and freedom from odor have all contributed to the great popularity of latex paints.

A number of additives are used in small percentages to improve spreading properties and the storing and mixing qualities of paints.

Table 8-4 lists a number of more common paints that have application in agriculture along with information concerning their use.

Table 8-4   Paint and Stain Selection Chart

Type of Paint	Applications	Advantages	Disadvantages
Linseed oil paint	Wood buildings Exterior metal	Easy to apply Flexible Adhesive	Slow drying Soft Low water resistance
Alkyd-base paint	Interior or exterior wood and metal	Easy to apply Low cost Durable	Low water resistance
Latex, exterior paint	Wood, masonry, primed metal	Easy to use Water cleanup Blister resistant	Freezes Low heat resistance
Latex, trim paint	Door and window trim	Less chalking	Higher cost
Latex, interior paint	Interior wood, plaster, drywall, and masonry	Easy to use Water cleanup Nonflammable	Freezes Low heat resistance
Epoxy paint	Interior wood, masonry	Water resistant Easy to clean Smooth	Difficult to apply Expensive
Aluminum paint	New metal Old metal over primer	Weather resistant	
Zinc primer	Rust inhibitive primer	Durable Sacrificial corrosion inhibiting	High cost Must be top coated
Barn paint	Smooth or rough wood	Durable Inexpensive Covers well	
Asphalt coating	Roof coating	Heavy cover Low cost	Hot unless aluminum pigmented
Urethane varnish	Interior wood floors Exterior wood floors	Hard, durable inside	Only fair ultraviolet tolerance
Water-repellent preservative	Exterior wood	Penetrates Preserves Repels moisture	

Silicone sealer	Masonry	Repels water for several years	Can't be painted for several years
Stains, semi-transparent (latex or oil)	Unfinished wood	No failure except normal wear	Won't cover other finishes
Stains, opaque (latex or oil)	Finished or unfinished wood	Resists peeling	May not cover old finishes well

Painting New Wood Surfaces

In addition to the composition and quality of the paint used, the appearance and durability of the paint applied to a building are influenced by the care taken during application. The following steps are recommended:

1. Seal all joints and around all door and window trim. Nailheads should be primed with an alkyd primer if latex paint is used as a first coat.

2. The use of a water-repellant wood preservative (WRP) will help to repel water and prevent damage to wood that paint by itself cannot prevent. It is essential that the WRP dry for two days or more in good drying weather before proceeding with painting.

3. Apply the primer recommended for the paint used. This is usually and alkyd-based paint. When latex paint is used, the wood may be damp. In all other cases the wood should be dry before painting begins.

4. Apply two top coats as directed by the manufacturer for maximum durability. Latex paint should not be applied in direct sunlight, on a windy day, or when the temperature will drop below 50°F (10°C) before the paint is dry.

Repainting Wood Surfaces

1. Repaint after original paint has weathered considerably and has worn thin, but if possible, before there is excessive failure by cracking and peeling.

2.   All loose paint should be removed with a scraper and the edges sanded to blend or eliminate the delineating edges of the paint failure.

3.   Bare spots are treated as new wood by first using a WRP and then spot priming.

4.   If there are signs of mildew or excessive chalking, the surface should be thoroughly washed with trisodium phosphate or a strong detergent mixed with 8 ounces (¼ L) of bleach in a gallon (4 L) of water. After washing, the surface should be thoroughly rinsed and painted immediately with a latex paint or as soon as the surface is completely dry if an alkyd paint is used.

5.   Latex paint does not adhere well to a chalky surface. An alkyd primer may be necessary if the surface cannot be cleaned of all loose material.

6.   Two coats of finish paint will increase paint life considerably.

Painting Metal Surfaces

1.   The surface must be cleaned and free of any oil, wax, loose paint, or corrosion.

2.   A metal primer should be applied before the top coat. If corrosion is present or if the surface is galvanized, a metallic zinc powder primer is advisable. Paint adheres to galvanized surfaces best after three to four years of weathering.

PROBLEMS

8.1   Following is a list of locations where surfacing materials are required. Choose one or more materials that would be satisfactory for each and give supporting reasons.
   a. Milkroom walls and ceiling
   b. Milking parlor walls
   c. Siding for a cold free stall barn
   d. Greenhouse covering for bedding plants
   e. Inside walls of an apple storage
   f. Walls and ceiling in a cage laying-house
   g. Walls for a roadside produce market
   h. Inside walls for a home

    i. Outside wall covering for a home
    j. Inside walls for a ski lodge
    k. Outside wall covering for a ski lodge
    l. Wall covering for a machinery shed

8.2 Choose a finishing material for each of the following situations. Give brief reasons for your choice.
    a. Plywood siding on a barn
    b. Galvanized steel roof just starting to rust
    c. Smooth-finish roll roofing on a poultry house
    d. A home sided with wood shingles
    e. Wood trim on a brick home
    f. Plywood walls in a milking parlor

REFERENCES

American Plywood Association. *Plywood Siding.* Tacoma, Washington: American Plywood Association, 1974

Asphalt Roofing Manufacturers Association. *Manufacture, Selection and Application of Asphalt Roofing and Siding Products.* New York: Asphalt Roofing Manufacturers Association, 1974.

Callender, J. H., ed. *Time-Saver Standards, a Handbook of Architectural Design.* New York: McGraw-Hill, 1966.

Fabral Corporation. *Galvanized Steel-Aluminum Roofing and Siding Systems.* Lancaster, Pa.: Fabral Corporation, 1970.

Gypsum Association. *Gypsum in the Age of Man.* Evanston, Ill.: Gypsum Association, 1974.

Gypsum Association. *Using Gypsum Board for Walls and Ceilings.* Evanston, Ill.: Gypsum Association, 1977.

Onduline U.S.A., Inc. *Installation Instructions—Performance Data— Specifications.* Fredericksburg, Va.: Onduline U.S.A., Inc., 1977.

Chapter Nine

Loads on Buildings

Before a building can be designed with adequate strength characteristics, the loads to which it will be subjected must be determined. To do this, the designer should understand the nature and significance of the various types of loads that act on farm buildings and then relate this information to all decisions on design, materials, and construction methods. Not all loads can be predicted with complete accuracy, but with proper use of the information available, sufficiently accurate estimates can be made to insure adequate design.

TYPES OF LOADS

Loads are commonly classified as:

Dead loads, which include the weight of all of the materials used in constructing the building, such as concrete in footings and foundation, lumber, and other material used in the frame and roof. Dead loads are an integral part of the structure, permanent and stationary.

Snow and wind loads, which must be estimated on the basis of meteorological records for the area as well as the use to which the building will be put.

Live loads, which include the weight of stored products, equipment, livestock, and vehicles. These are often the most difficult to estimate as they are frequently intermittent and may cause stresses to be applied in an unpredictable manner. Live loads also include the forces of nature such as snow load, wind and earthquake, although they are generally treated separately.

Dead Loads

The dead load for a building or portion of a building may be estimated by making a bill of materials and then determining the force by using values given in Table 9-2. The force in SI units should be in newtons. Multiply kilograms by 9.8 to get newtons.

Snow Loads

Snow and wind loads must be estimated on the basis of the probability of occurrence of snow or wind storms of a given intensity. The *mean recurrence interval* is the number of years on the average between which storms of a given intensity will occur. The probability that a storm will occur in any one year is the reciprocal of the recurrence interval.

The recurrence interval chosen depends on the use and occupancy of the building. Three classes are assigned as follows (American Society of Agricultural Engineers, 1077).

Class A   100-year interval—large permanent buildings in which failure would cause an unusually high hazard to life and property.

Class B   50-year interval—private dwellings and smaller buildings occupied by the public.

Class C   25-year interval—buildings with no human occupants or in which people work for relatively short periods of time. Most farm buildings other than the home fall into this class.

Maps, such as shown in Figure 9-1, have been developed from weather records and are useful in determining snow-load design values. Figure 9-1 shows the seasonal snow pack for a 25-year recurrence interval. At any given time during the winter season, these values may be increased appreciably by the occurrence of a storm. However, the values found on the map may be assumed to be satisfactory design values based on two factors: (1) a safety factor in excess of 2.5 is usually used for building materials and connections, and (2) the snow load is of short duration, in which case a 10 percent overload is acceptable. Figure 9-2 shows maps for regional areas. Comparing them to the national maps will illustrate the importance of using local or regional data when it is available.

If a building is exposed to normal winds and not subjected to unusual drifting on roof surfaces, the snow load may be taken as:

$L = 0.6(\cos p)S$ Where: Customary   SI

L = load on horizontal projected area of the roof   lb/sq ft   kg/m²

0.6 = estimated part of snow pack that occurs as a load on a flat roof   —   —

p = the pitch angle of the roof   degrees   degrees

S = snow pack value from figure 9-1 or 9-2   lb/sq ft   kg/m²

$$kg/m^2 = lb/sq\ ft \times 4.88$$

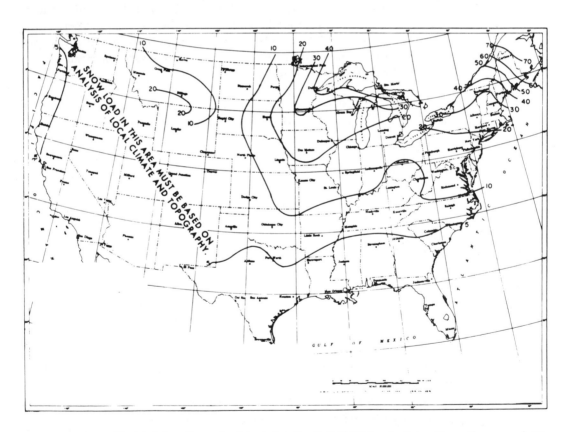

Figure 9-1a. Snow load map for the United States in lb/sq ft. on the ground, 25-year mean recurrence interval. (*Agricultural Engineers Yearbook,* 1977)

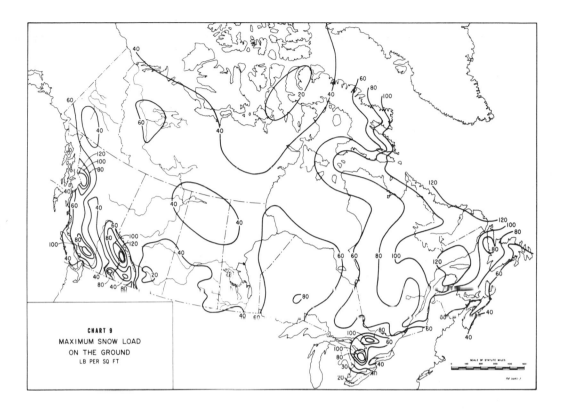

Figure 9-1b. Snow load map for Canada. (*Courtesy* National Research Council Canada, Associate Committee on the National Building Code)

Snow load values for roof shapes subject to drifting (sawtooth, valleys, levels lower than roof above) should be increased according to the best prediction of maximum snow depth.

Trusses should be designed to withstand the snow load as an unbalanced load on each slope independently.

Local snow conditions that are known to differ from the values on the map should always be considered.

It has been suggested by Theakston (1975) that it is possible to make accurate predictions of the areas where snow will be deposited on a roof by the use of laboratory analysis with a "snow simulator." This information allows for increasing design values in some areas of a roof for added safety, while reductions may be made in other areas of the roof for economy.

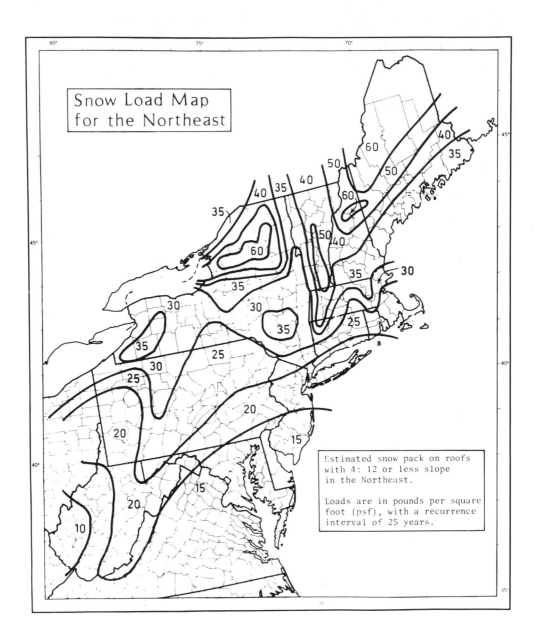

Figure 9-2. (a) Snow load map for the northeast. (*Courtesy* Northeast Regional Agricultural Engineering Service)

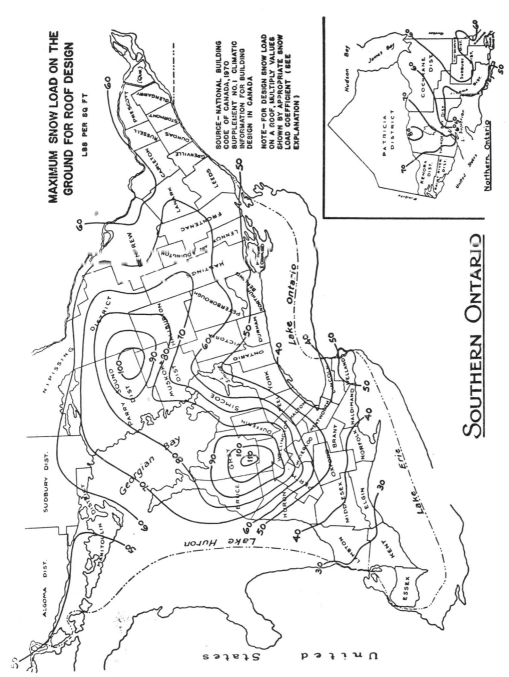

Figure 9-2. (b) Snow load map for Ontario (*Courtesy* National Research Council Canada, Associate Committee on the National Building Code)

Wind Loads

Wind forces may often prove to be the most critical loads imposed on agricultural buildings, especially in areas where high winds occur frequently. When the wind strikes a building, it exerts a considerable force on both the wall and roof surfaces which must be withstood by the frame of the building. Failure to take this into account has caused great damage to farm buildings. Adequate bracing and the use of strong fasteners or anchors at critical joints is a necessary precaution against wind damage. It will be noted in Table 9-1 that many forces imposed by the wind are negative, or lifting forces, and these must be resisted by solid foundations and secure fasteners.

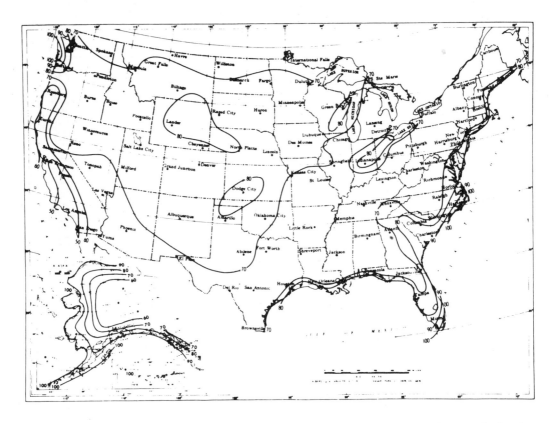

Figure 9-3. Annual extreme fastest-mile wind velocity in MPH at 30 ft. height, 25-year mean recurrence interval (*Agricultural Engineers Yearbook,* 1977)

Data on extreme wind velocities have been obtained from weather records and are shown in Figure 9-3. Wind pressures on buildings may be

Table 9-1 Wind Pressure Coefficients for Class C Buildings
Gable Type—Completely Enclosed
H = average height to eaves, W = total width of building

H/W	Windward Wall Coef	Windward Roof Coef Roof Slope				Leeward Roof Coef	Leeward Wall Coef
		1:12	3:12	5:12	7:12		
0.15	0.70	—0.51	—0.20	0.05	0.19	—0.5	—0.4
0.20	0.70	—0.60	—0.27	0.05	0.19	—0.5	—0.4
0.30	0.70	—0.60	—0.41	0.01	0.16	—0.5	—0.4
0.50	0.70	—0.60	—0.60	—0.29	0.00	—0.5	—0.4

Negative values indicate suction or lifting forces.
(From American Society of Agricultural Engineers, 1977)

estimated with the following formula (American Society of Agricultural Engineers, 1977):

$$q = 0.00256 \ V^2 \ k \qquad \text{Where:}$$

q — wind pressure, lb/sq ft ($\times$ 47.9 = Pa)

V = 25 year wind in mph

$k = (h/30)^{0.286}$

h = height to eave of building, except if the height from the eave to the top of the building is greater than height to the eave; then h is the mid-elevation of the roof. All heights are in feet from the average grade.

30 = height at which velocities are reported

The design pressures established for various surfaces of buildings are related to the shape of the building and to whether it is open or enclosed. They may be obtained by multiplying q by the appropriate coefficients found in Table 9-1.

For gable-roof buildings that are open on both sides, the following coefficients may be used:

Roof Slopes	30° (7:12) or more	Less than 30°
Windward slope	+0.8	+0.6
Leeward slope	—0.8	—0.6

The corrected wind pressures act at right angles to the roof or wall surface. The end walls of buildings may be considered subject to the same pressures as the sides.

From the coefficients given above, it should be noted that it is imperative to design roof frame connections so that they are adequate for the negative or lifting forces that may occur. Coefficient values as great as —1.2 are produced by some arched and gambrel roof shapes.

Combined Loads

It is highly unlikely that maximum snow and wind loads will occur simultaneously. Consequently, the dead load plus the snow load and the dead load plus the wind load may be calculated, and the greater of the two combinations used for determining the final roof frame design. Any live loads that will be supported by the roof framing must also be included.

Table 9-2   Weights of Building Materials

Material		Weight (Mass)			
		Customary lb/cu ft	SI kg/m³	Customary lb/sq ft	SI kg/m²
Concrete		150	2432		
Steel		490	7943		
Oak 1″ (19 mm)		45	729	3.5	17.1
Yellow pine 1″ (19 mm)		39	632	3.0	14.6
Douglas fir 1″ (19 mm)		34	551	2.5	12.2
Soft pine 1″ (19 mm)		30	486	2.2	11
Plywood ⅜″ (9 mm)				1.1	5.4
½″ (12 mm)				1.5	7.3
⅝″ (15 mm)				1.8	8.8
Aluminum roofing (0.024)				0.4	1.9
Galvanized roofing (28 gauge)				0.8	3.9
Asphalt shingles				2.2-3.2	11-16
Asphalt selvage roll				1.5	7.3
Asphalt roll roofing				0.5-1	2.4-4.8
Wood shingles				2.0	9.8
Concrete block wall	4″ (100 mm)			30	145
	8″ (200 mm)			57	275
	12″ (300 mm)			80	390
Brick walls	4″ (100 mm)			37	180
	8″ (200 mm)			79	385
Glass blocks				20	98

In designing the building frame below the roof, the maximum roof load plus any lateral or vertical live loads must be considered along with the dead loads. Dead loads may be estimated from the weights of various building materials given in Table 9-2.

Live Loads

Table 9-3 provides design load values for some livestock and other enterprises for solid, suspended floors and slotted floors.

Table 9-4 provides several design factors for a number of farm products.

Table 9-3 Live Design Loads

		Solid Floors		Slotted Floors			
		lb/sq ft	kg/m²	lb/sq ft	kg/m²	lb/ft of slat	kg/m
Cattle	Tie stalls	70	342				
	Loose housing	80	390	100	448	250	372
	Young stock (400 lb) (180 kg)	50	244	50	244	150	223
Sheep		30	146	50	244	120	179
Horses		100	488				
Swine	To 200 lb (90 kg)			50	244	100	149
	400 lb (180 kg)			65	317	150	223
Poultry	Floor management	40	195				
	Cage management	Obtain from manufacturer					
Greenhouse		50	244				
Maintenance shop		70	342				
Machinery storage		150	732	minimum, but perhaps much greater depending on weight per wheel for vehicles			

(From American Society of Agricultural Engineers, 1977)

Table 9-4   Product Storage Information

Product	Angle of Repose		Weight (Mass)		EFD*
	Emptying	Filling	lb/cu ft	lb/bu	lb/cu ft
Barley	28	16	39	48	15
Corn, shelled	27	16	45	56	18
Oats	32	18	26	32	11
Rice (paddy)	36	20	36	45	11
Rye	26	17	45	56	18
Soybeans	29	16	48	60	16
Wheat	27	16	48	60	19
Apples				54/box	
Beans, dry			48	60	
Corn, ear			28	35	
Hay, loose			4-5		
chopped			8-10		
baled			12-15		
Peanuts, unshelled			13.6	17	
Potatoes				60	
Silage			30-40		

* Derived from Rankin's equation for effective fluid density (EFD):

$$EFD = w \tan^2(45° - a/2)$$ Where: w = bulk density
a = emptying angle of repose

PRESSURES EXERTED BY FLUIDS

A liquid, being a true fluid, exerts a force against any surface with which it is in contact. The force it exerts per unit area is defined as pressure. In an open tank, the pressure increases uniformly from the top of the liquid to the bottom. The pressure exerted at a given level will be equal in all directions and normal to all surfaces.

The *pressure* exerted by a liquid at any depth may be found by the formula:

$p = dh$	Where:		*Customary*	*SI*
p = pressure			lb/sq ft	kg/m²
d = density of liquid			lb/cu ft	kg/m³
h = depth of liquid			ft	m

SI conversion, $Pa = kg/m^2 \times 9.8$

For water, $d = 62.4 \text{ lb/cu ft} = 1013 \text{ kg/m}^3$

The *force* exerted by a liquid on the surface area at any depth may be found by the formula:

F = pA	Where:	*Customary*	*SI*
F = force		lb	kg
p = pressure		lb/sq ft	kg/m²
A = area		sq ft	m²

SI conversion, $N = kg \times 9.8$

For example, a drum 2 feet in diameter and 3 feet high is filled with water. The pressure at the bottom is: p = dh

$$p = 62.4 \times 3$$

$$p = 187.2 \text{ lb/sq ft}$$

The force at the bottom of the drum us:

$$F = pA$$

$$F = 187.2 \times 1^2 \times 3.14$$

$$F = 588 \text{ lb}$$

Note that if a 10-foot length of 1-inch pipe is installed on top of the drum and filled with water, the pressure becomes:

$$p = 62.4 \times 13$$

$$p = 811.2 \text{ lb/sq ft}$$

Likewise the force becomes proportionally greater.

This leads to the next assertion: Neither the cross section area of the column nor the volume of the liquid affects the pressure; only the depth and density have an effect.

The lateral force of a liquid against a vertical section of wall may be found by the formula:

$P = \dfrac{dh^2}{2}$	Where:	*Customary*	*SI*
P = horizontal force against a section of wall		lb/ft	kg/m
d = density of liquid		lb/cu ft	kg/m³
h = depth of liquid		ft	m

SI conversion, $N = kg \times 9.8$

As shown in Figure 9-4 the centroid of this force is two-thirds below the surface of the fluid. The horizontal dimension (the distance it extends from the wall) of the liquid has no effect on the pressure on the wall.

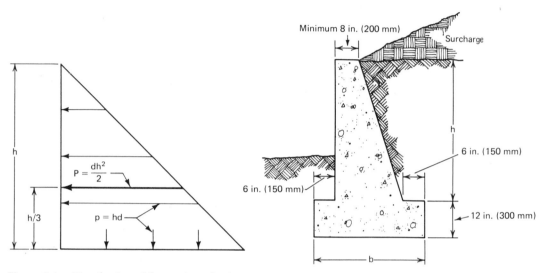

Figure 9-4.   Distribution of forces by a fluid.

Figure 9-5.   Dimensions of a concrete gravity retaining wall.

LATERAL GRAIN AND SOIL PRESSURES

The pressures exerted by granular materials, such as grain or soil, are more complex than those exerted by fluids because of the friction of the particles moving against one another. These materials may be referred to as semifluid. Table 9-4 lists *fluid equivalent* values that may be used with the fluid equations to obtain approximate values for shallow bins.

These values (d) may be used to find the lateral force (P) against a bin wall with a depth of grain (h) using $P = dh^2/2$. This is suitable only for bins in which (h) is no greater than the width or diameter. SI conversions: $Pa = 47.88 \times lb/sq\,ft$, $kg/m^2 = 4.88 \times lb/sq\,ft$.

The pressure of soil against walls varies greatly with depth, type of soil, and moisture content. It is always desirable to provide drainage behind retaining walls, underground tanks, and building foundations that are below grade. The reason for this is illustrated by the values in Table 9-5 which lists fluid equivalent values for liquid manure and soils with differing degrees of drainage.

Table 9-5   Loads Against Walls—Fluid Equivalent
(Tank or Foundation Walls)

		Customary lb/cu ft	SI kg/m³
Manure	Outward, if above ground	60	961
Manure	Either direction on partition	60	961
Soil	Inward, well drained	15	240
Soil	Inward, fair drainage	30	481
Soil	Inward, high water table	60	961
Soil	Inward, saturated fine sand	110	1762

If vehicles drive within 5 feet (1.5 m) of the wall, a 100 lb/sq ft (4.8 kPa) uniform surcharge load is added.

(From Midwest Plan Service, 1977)

For example, assume a storage tank extends 5 feet into the ground and is moderately well drained. Find the total force on each foot of length of the wall.

$$P = \frac{dh^2}{2}$$

$$P = 30 \times 5 \times 5/2$$

$$P = 375 \text{ lb}$$

Figure 9-5 depicts the cross section of a concrete retaining wall and Table 9-6 lists the dimensions that are recommended for several heights. The soil that slopes up and away from the back of the wall is referred to as the surcharge. It causes an additional force on the wall and requires a larger footing for stability.

Table 9-6   Recommended Dimensions for Retaining Walls

Height of Wall (h)		Width of Footing (b)			
		Without Surcharge		With Surcharge	
Customary ft	SI m	Customary ft	SI m	Customary ft	SI m
3	0.9	2¼	0.7	2½	0.8
4	1.2	2½	0.8	3	0.9
6	1.8	3⅓	1.0	4	1.2
8	2.4	4¼	1.3	5½	1.7
10	3.0	5¼	1.6	7	2.1

PROBLEMS

9.1   Apple boxes are 17 inches long, 13 inches wide and 11 inches high (432 x 330 x 279 mm). What is the load per unit area on the floor when boxes are piled 12 high? The mass of each box is 54 pounds (24.5 kg).

9.2   A barn floor was originally designed to support a depth of 16 feet (5 m) of loose hay. What depth of baled hay would impose a similar load?

9.3   A farm pond has been constructed with a deep spillway 6.5 feet (2 m) wide which is closed off with planks dropped into guides cast in the concrete at either end. What is the total uniform load on the 12-inch (300-mm) plank in the lowest position when the water is 5 feet (1.5 m) deep at the bottom of the spillway (bottom edge of the plank)?

9.4   Determine the dead, snow, and live loads to be carried by the foundation and/or pier footings for the plan used in problems 4.2 and 7.2.

REFERENCES

American Society of Agricultural Engineers. *Agricultural Engineers Yearbook.* St. Joseph, Mich.: American Society of Agricultural Engineers, 1977.

Housing and Home Finance Agency. *Snow Load Studies.* Housing Research Paper 19. Washington, D.C.: Housing and Home Finance Agency, 1952.

Irish, W.W., et al. *Pole and Post Building Construction.* Ithaca, N.Y.: Northeast Regional Agricultural Engineering Service, 1977.

Midwest Plan Service. *Structures and Environment Handbook.* Ames, Iowa: Midwest Plan Service, 1977.

Theakston, F.H. *Snow Loads on Roofs of Farm Buildings.* Paper No. 75-4067. St. Joseph, Mich.: American Society of Agricultural Engineers, 1975.

Chapter Ten

Building Foundations and Floors

FOUNDATIONS

A well designed and constructed foundation is essential for the structural integrity of a building. The foundation must resist and distribute the forces acting on it so that any movement will be small and uniform. Properly built footings and foundations keep buildings plumb, free of cracks, and in the case of a below grade basement, free of leaks.

The most important loads acting on a foundation are:

1. The dead weight of the building, the contents of the building, and the snow load, all acting in a vertical direction.

2. Wind loads that impose lateral or lifting forces.

3. Horizontal forces from soil, water or stored products.

4. Uneven soil forces caused by nonuniform and variable moisture levels as well as frost action.

Each of these forces must be considered in footing and foundation design.

Footings

A footing is the enlarged base for a foundation. It increases the bearing area between the foundation and the underlying soil, thus reducing the unit pressure to a safe level. The size of the footing will depend on the weight imposed by the building and the safe bearing capacity of the soil.

Soil Bearing

The soil on which a footing is installed should be undisturbed, level, and smooth. When construction in a filled area is unavoidable, special precautions are required. The best solution is to extend the foundation so that the footing is on undisturbed soil. Alternatives are to let the filled soil settle for a year or to compact the soil thoroughly and then use larger footings to reduce the unit load on the soil.

The bearing capacity of soils varies with type and moisture. Typical load-carrying capacities are shown in Table 10-1.

Table 10-1   Soil Load-Carrying Capacities

Type of soil	lb/sq ft	kilopascals
Soft clay or sandy loam	2,000	96
Firm clay or fine sand	4,000	192
Dry clay or compact fine sand	6,000	288
Loose gravel or compact coarse sand	8,000	383
Compact sand and gravel mixture	12,000	575

If there are doubts about the bearing capacity of the soil, it is good policy and not expensive to simply assume a lower safe-bearing value and increase the footing size. In the design of a large building that will impose a heavy load on a foundation, soil-bearing tests may be required before the footing size is determined.

Frost Action

A combination of below freezing temperature and moisture can cause the soil to heave or expand, only to settle again as the temperature rises. This situation is unsatisfactory for supporting a building foundation because the freezing is seldom uniform in all areas. The result will be uneven lifting and settling, cracking of the foundation, and a building that is out of plumb. To avoid frost heave problems, the footing for the foundation should be located below the maximum penetration of frost.

Table 10-2 provides recommended footing depths for various temperature zones. Local conditions and the inside temperature of the building
will influence the depth actually chosen. If, to avoid frost damage, an
appreciably deeper foundation is required than for other considerations,
a column-and-beam design may be more economical. In that case, the
column footings extend below frost level, while a beam rests on the
columns just above the soil surface. If the use of the building requires a
rodent-proof joining of the wall and ground, the beam may be designed
at least 12 inches (300 mm) below and 8 inches (200 mm) above grade.
There should be 6 to 8 inches (150-200 mm) of uniform size gravel below
the beam to prevent frost heaving.

Table 10-2   Suggested Footing Depths

Average January Temperature*		Light Buildings		Heavy Buildings	
Deg. F	Deg. C	inches	mm	inches	mm
<25	−4	24-48	600-1200	36-60	900-1500
25-35	−4-2	18-36	450-900	30-48	750-1200
35-50	2-10	12-24	300-600	18-36	450-900

* See isotherm map, Figure 16-7.

Foundation Footings

Regardless of the material used for a foundation, a continuous
footing cast of concrete is desirable. The width of the footing depends
on the soil-bearing capacity and the load that it must carry. Having
determined the width of the footing by dividing the load per unit of
length by the soil-bearing capacity, the thickness of the footing for a
wall or pier can be found in Figure 10-1. Wall and pier footings should
have a depth equal to two times the distance from the wall to the edge of
the footing, while a wood or metal column footing-depth should equal
one and one-half times the distance from the column to the edge of the
footing.

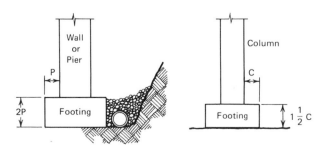

Figure 10-1.   Footing proportions.

It is good practice to install a footing even for a lightly-loaded building that does not appear to need one because it provides a level surface on which to install the foundation forms and helps to insure a plumb wall. When the load does not require a footing, a rule of thumb that is frequently used calls for making the footing as deep as the wall is thick and twice as wide.

Figure 10-2 illustrates the distribution of dead loads and snow loads on various portions of the building footings. Each of the piers will carry one-eighth of the total load. The one-half total load on the foundation at the rear of the building will be distributed uniformly.

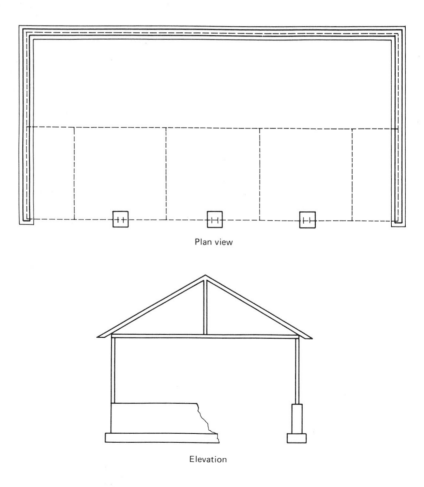

Plan view

Elevation

Figure 10-2. The division of loads on various areas of the foundation and piers.

If a wall footing is to be installed that has appreciably more area than is required to support the load, then it is desirable to design any column footing to have approximately the same area per unit of load. Any settling that occurs should then be equal in all locations. For the same reason, if a foundation is partly on bedrock and partly on soil, the part on soil should be twice as wide as would otherwise be indicated.

All foundations, piers, and columns should be loaded as nearly as possible along their central axis to prevent any tipping action.

If a building is constructed on sloping land, the footing may need to be stepped down with the grade. In such a situation, the horizontal length of each step should be at least double the height of the step and each section of footing should be tied to the adjacent wall with reinforcing rods. It should be emphasized that each section of the footing should be bearing on ground that has been carefully leveled. Figure 10-3 illustrates a stepped footing.

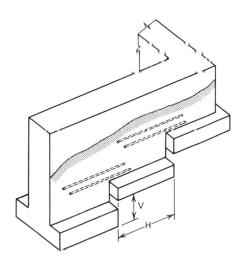

Figure 10-3. Stepped footing, showing location of reinforcing rod. A relation of H = 2V should exist.

Lateral Pressure on Foundations

Lateral pressure from soils and liquids is discussed in Chapter 9 in the section regarding loads. While in some cases it may be desirable to estimate the soil pressures more accurately, in most cases it will be satisfactory to assume a lateral force of 60 pounds per square foot (2.8 kPa) for a wall without drainage and 30 pounds per square foot (1.4 kPa) for a wall with drainage (Midwest Plan Service, 1977).

To illustrate a method for finding a safe footing size, assume the following.

A gable roof building 24 by 48 feet is supported by a foundation in the rear and three piers in the front. The total load above the piers and foundation is 60,000 pounds. The soil at the building site is soft clay. The foundation wall is 4 feet high and 8 inches thick. The piers are 1 foot square and 4 feet high.

1. From Table 9-2 the weight of concrete is 150 lb/cu ft.

2. Figure 10-2 shows that the rear foundation supports one-half of the the load, or 60,000/2 = 30,000 lb.

3. The wall weighs $4 \times .67 \times 48 \times 150 = 19,300$ lbs.

4. The total weight per foot of length is $(30,000 + 19,300)/48 = 1,027$ lbs.

5. Table 10-1 lists soft clay having a bearing capacity of 2,000 lb/sq ft.

6. The required footing width is $1,027/2,000 = .51$ ft.

7. While this value indicates that no footing is required to support the load, it is recommended that one be used as a desirable construction practice. Use this rule of thumb: 8 inches thick, 16 inches wide.

8. Figure 10-2 shows that each pier supports $\frac{1}{8}$ of the building load: 60,000/8 = 7,500 lbs.

9. A pier weighs $1 \times 1 \times 4 \times 150 = 600$ lbs.

10. Arbitrarily try a pier footing of $2 \times 2 \times 1 \times 150 = 600$ lbs.

11. The required footing area is: $(7,500 + 600 + 600)/2,000 = 4.35$ sq ft.

12. The estimated size of 2 by 2 feet is too small. Try 2.25 feet square.

13. The new footing weight is $2.25 \times 2.25 \times 1.25 \times 150 = 949$ lbs.

14. The new required footing area is $(7,500 + 600 + 949)/2,000 = 4.5$ sq ft.

15. Being somewhat under the 5 square feet actual size, it is satisfactory.

The end foundations, while supporting only a minimal load, would be constructed with the same dimensions as the rear foundation.

Types of Foundations

In areas which are subject to little or no ground frost, a floating **slab foundation** consisting of a concrete floor in which the outer 6 inches (150 mm) is thickened to at least 12 inches (300 mm) below grade is simple and economical to construct for small buildings.

A **curtain wall foundation,** Figure 10-4, with soil filled against both sides to within a foot or two of its top is commonly used for agricultural buildings which have their first floor at just above grade level. The typical wall is built 8 to 10 inches thick without reinforcing. A much thinner wall could easily support the vertical load but would need to be reinforced near the top and bottom with #4 bars. The additional labor in placing the bars and concrete, plus the possibly higher cost for concrete with smaller size aggregate that would be needed, tend to make the cost for either wall about the same. If a minimum thickness curtain wall is installed where the grade is different on the two sides, it may need to be supported by buttresses or by tying into the floor.

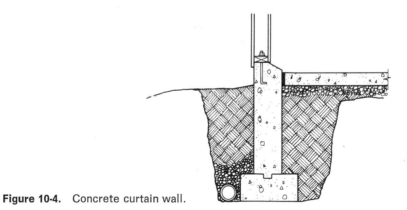

Figure 10-4. Concrete curtain wall.

Masonry blocks of 8-, 10-, or 12-inch (200-, 250-, or 300-mm) width may be used for a foundation (Figure 10-5). However, they are neither as strong nor as watertight as poured concrete foundations. While the labor and materials for form work are saved, the cost of blocks and the labor of placing them often equals or even exceeds the cost of a concrete wall. When a block foundation is chosen, the first course should be set in a full bed of mortar on a concrete footing. A block wall can be made quite watertight by:

1.   Using a rich mortar and tooling it carefully.

2.   Plastering the surface and then applying a commercial sealer.

3.   Installing a footing drain with a foot of gravel over it.

4.   Backfilling carefully and sloping the fill away from the wall.

For lightweight construction, piers may be used in place of a continuous foundation with a resulting saving in cost of materials and labor. However, it is difficult to get a tight fit between the ground and the side of the building. It may also be necessary to design sills as weight-bearing beams.

Treated wood and **plywood** may be used for a foundation as shown in Figure 10-6. Crushed stone, with an assumed safe-bearing strength of 3,000 pounds per square foot (144 kPa) may be used as a base on which to install a footing plate of pressure-treated wood. A treated sill and studs are installed above the footing plate and treated plywood is nailed to the outside of the studs. The foundation is made waterproof by the installation of a mastic and polyethylene barrier on the outside of the plywood below grade. This type of construction may be used for curtain walls, for low walls with a crawl space, or for full basement walls. The principal advantages include the reduced labor required for installation and the ease with which insulation may be installed.

Footing Drains

High water levels on the outside of a wall can produce lateral pressures that endanger the wall and greatly increase the possibility of water leaks into a basement. In areas where there is sufficient slope so that a drainage line can be brought to grade in a reasonable distance, it is desirable to install a continuous drain around the outside of the foundation footing. This will help to maintain stable conditions in the soil that supports the building, to reduce the possibility of frost damage, and perhaps most important in buildings with basements, it will help to prevent leakage problems.

The drain should be at a level below the concrete floor but not below the level of the bottom of the footing. In some soils that are subject to easy separation, it is best to place the drain 4 inches (100 mm) above

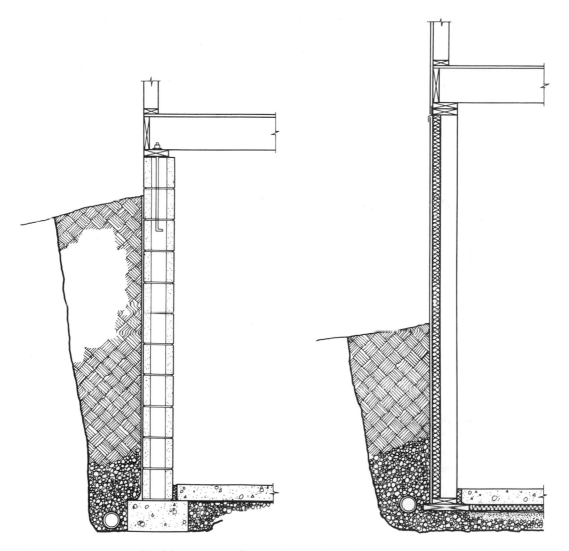

Figure 10-5.   Concrete block basement wall.   **Figure 10-6.**   Preservative treated wood foundation.

the bottom of the footing to prevent flowing ground water from washing out the fine material under the footings. In most cases 4-inch (100-mm) land tile, or perforated plastic or asphalt-fiber drainage pipe should be satisfactory. In a few cases where gravelly soils are known to carry large quantities of ground water, 6-inch (150-mm) drains may be required. (Figure 10-1).

The drains should be installed with little or no gradient. This will help maintain a level ground water table at all points along the foundation footing while still keeping the drain line below the floor and above the bottom of the footing.

In areas of flat topography, the construction of a basement foundation may leave little choice but to end the footing and floor drains in a sump that can be pumped automatically.

In back-filling around a foundation wall, 1 to 2 feet (300-600 mm) of fine stone should be placed over the drain followed by soil that is graded to slope away from the foundation. The cost of footing drains is small in comparison to the total cost of the building, and they should not be omitted even when the location appears to be quite dry.

Pole Building Support

Footings for the base of the poles in pole buildings are important for stability and reasonable life. Concrete pads under each pole should be sized to adequately support both the dead load of the building as well as the expected snow load. Inasmuch as pole buildings are comparatively light and do not have a heavy foundation, it is important to protect the building from wind damage by anchoring the base of each pole. This may be done by running a rod through the pole a few inches above the base and then pouring a concrete collar at least 12 inches (300 mm) in diameter around the base of the pole. Another method is to drive eight to sixteen 20d nails half their length into the base of the pole before pouring the concrete collar. A third alternative is to spike pieces of treated wood twice the pole diameter in length to the sides of the pole near the base. The soil is then well compacted above the wooden crosspieces to securely anchor the pole. The three alternatives suggested are shown in Figure 10-7.

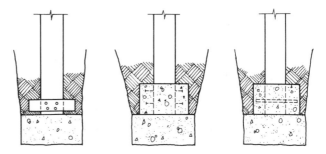

Figure 10-7. Methods of anchoring poles.

CONCRETE FLOORS

Concrete floors are used in almost all farm buildings. They are hard, strong, and durable and make an effective barrier against rodents. Concrete floors are especially valuable in buildings housing livestock and poultry because they are easy to clean and can be readily sanitized.

The type of construction varies with the use of the building. The floors of some buildings, such as grain storages, need to be protected from ground moisture only, while other floors need to be well insulated. For example, insulation helps to prevent heat loss in a farrowing house or freezing of the soil under a low-temperature storage building. Other buildings, such as machinery sheds, need only a smooth, durable surface.

The subgrade is prepared by removing all top soil and debris and then filling with at least 6 inches (150 mm) of gravel. If the area is well drained, bank-run gravel should be satisfactory. However, if the subgrade is damp, a single size of graded stones between ½ and 2 inches (13 and 50 mm) should be used in order to break any capillary action. When there is a high water table, there is a possibility for ground water to accumulate under the floor, and it is advisable to install drain lines in the gravel fill to remove any free water. The fill should be placed in 6-inch (150-mm) layers and each layer thoroughly compacted with tampers, rollers, or vibrators.

If it is particularly important to have a dry floor, such as in a grain storage, a vapor seal of 4 to 6 mil polyethylene plastic with well-lapped joints should be installed on top of the fill. A thin layer of stiff concrete or grout spread evenly under the plastic sheet will help avoid puncturing during placement of the concrete. Figure 10-8B illustrates this type of construction.

For a warm, dry floor, such as is required in a farm home, more complete insulation is necessary to reduce heat loss to the ground. A 1-inch (25-mm) thick layer of rigid waterproof insulation, such as expanded polystyrene, is placed on top of the grout. Details of this construction are shown in Figure 10-8C.

Floors usually have a slab thickness of 4 inches (89 mm) for ordinary usage, and 6 inches (140 mm) when subjected to heavy loads such as tractors and trucks. Two-by-four-inch (38 x 89 mm) or 2-by-6-inch (38 x 140 mm) forms are used depending on the load requirements of the building. The forms should be securely staked in place and oiled for easy removal.

A strip of rigid insulating material should be installed along the base of the wall before placing the concrete. This serves as a heat barrier and also allows the concrete to expand and contract with temperature changes. Also, in the case of large areas, the concrete should be cast in 10- to 15-foot (3- to 5-m) strips to allow for expansion. A tapered

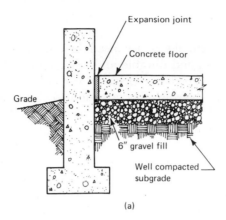

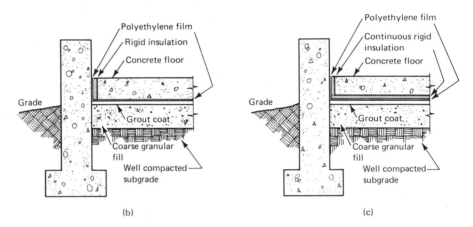

Figure 10-8. Concrete floor construction: (a) floor slab on gravel fill with no provision for heat or moisture barrier; (b) moisture-proof floor; (c) insulated floor.

wood strip along one side of the form provides a "key" to keep adjacent slabs in alignment. However, it is best to put a piece of asphalt paper or polyethylene in the joint to prevent bonding. A groover may be used to cut control joints across the strips. These grooves should be one-fifth the thickness of the slab and spaced 10 to 15 feet (3 to 5 m) apart.

Concrete used for floors should have relatively small sized coarse aggregate, one to one and one-half inches (25 to 40 mm), and be mixed relatively stiff. Once in place and thoroughly spaded to eliminate cavities, it may be struck off with a screed board. A nonslip surface for livestock may be obtained by dragging a stable broom over the wet concrete. Using a wood float leaves the surface level but gritty. A smooth surface is possible by using a steel trowel after the watery sheen has disappeared from the surface of the concrete.

As soon as the concrete has set, it should be kept wet for several days. A good method is to spread a layer of sand over the concrete and wet it down well. A film of polyethylene is also effective and labor efficient.

Slotted Floors

In recent years slotted floors have become increasingly popular in housing for several types of livestock. It is generally conceded that the use of slotted floors has made confinement housing for swine an economically viable system.

Regardless of whether manure is stored in a pit under the floor, drained, or scraped away, the slotted floor provides a very efficient method of removing the manure from under the animals. The slotted floor has a number of other advantages. It permits greater animal density and at the same time the animals remain cleaner. There is less moisture to be removed by the ventilation system. Where supplemental heat is needed, the amount of heat required is less than in buildings with conventional floor construction. In solid-floor barns, free stalls or bedded rest areas have been commonly used to provide clean resting areas for the animals. The slotted floor, on the other hand, will usually remain clean enough to make stalls unnecessary.

But slotted floors have some drawbacks too. The original cost is high when compared with a solid floor. However, this added cost can eventually be recouped by the greater number of animals housed and by the saving in labor. In the past, slotted floors have tended to cause some problems with animals slipping, but there have been recent improvements in surface textures that promise to alleviate the difficulty.

Materials Concrete has been far and away the most popular material for making slats. Concrete slats are hard, durable, easy to clean, and relatively free of slipping problems, but they are the heaviest to handle and require the strongest supports.

Wood slats are inexpensive and lighter to handle, but they are less durable and subject to warping which in turn leaves unequal spacing.

Expanded metal has been satisfactory for small animals up to 50 pounds (22 kg) but has failed when subjected to the weight of larger animals.

Steel slats must be protected from corrosion to insure a satisfactory life. Aluminum slats are much more corrosion resistant, lighter in weight, and easier to install, but they are also considerably more expensive. Some metal floor units are formed so that short slots are staggered and spaced between the supports, a design that resists plugging and keeps the floor drier and cleaner. Extruded plastic and fiberglass slats also show promise although they tend to be slippery.

Concrete slat design   Concrete slats can be purchased precast or they may be cast on the job either in forms on the ground or in place. While form construction is more difficult in place, the problem of lifting the heavy slats during installation is avoided and the top reinforcing bar may be eliminated. The specifications for concrete to be used in casting slats is given in Table 10-3.

Table 10-3   Concrete Specifications for Slats

	Customary	SI Metric
Air entrainment	7%	7%
Cement	7¾ sack/cu yd	11 sacks/m³
Water	5 gal/sack	17.7 L/sack
Aggregate	¾ in. max. diameter	20 mm max. diameter
Slump	2-3 in.	50-75 mm
28 day strength	3600 lb/sq in.	25 MPa

Design loads and slat dimensions are given in Table 10-4. The reinforcing bar recommended in the table is placed 1¼ inches (32 mm) above the bottom of the slat. If the slat will be handled after casting, a No. 3 reinforcing bar is placed three-quarters of an inch (19 mm) below the top surface.

Recommendations for finishing and curing include:

1. Finish the surface with a wooden float in all cases except for a farrowing house where a steel float should be used.

2. Leave a slight crown for good drainage.

3. Use an edging tool to produce a slightly rounded edge.

4. Keep the slats wet for at least a week for proper curing.

Table 10-4 Design Loads and Slat Dimensions

Animal	Load per Unit				Span						
	Length		Area		4 ft (1.2 m)		6 ft (1.8 m)		8 ft (2.4 m)		
					B&D* inch Bar#	B&D* mm Bar#	B&D* inch Bar#	B&D* mm Bar#	B&D* inch Bar#	B&D* mm Bar#	
	lb ft	kg m	lb sq ft	kg m²							
Dairy cow	250	373	100	489	4x4 #4	100x100 15M	4x5 #5	100x125 15M	4x7 #5	100x175 15M	
Calves and Swine to 400 lb (180 kg)	150	224	50	245	4x4 #3	100x100 10M	4x5 #4	100x125 15M	4x6 #5	100x150 15M	
Sheep and Swine to 200 lb (90 kg)	120	179	50	245	4x4 #3	100x100 10M	4x4 #4	100x100 15M	4x5 #5	100x125 15M	
Swine 50 lb (23 kg)	50	75	35	171	4x4 #3	100x100 10M	4x4 #3	100x100 10M	4x4 #4	100x100 15M	
All slats to be lifted—top bar					#3	10M	#3	10M	#3	10M	

* B&D = Top breadth and depth. The bottom breadth is 1 inch (25 mm) less in all cases.

PROBLEMS

10.1   A 20-x-30 foot (6 x 9 m) pole shed is supported by 8 poles. The total dead load of the building is 3,960 lb (1800 kg). Assume the building is located in the central Middlesex District of Ontario. The 5:12 pitch gable roof has a total area of 720 square feet. (67 m²). Determine the design snow load. Combine the snow and dead loads and then determine the size of pad that should be installed under each pole.

10.2   Using the total load value found for Problem 9.4, Chapter 9, design safe footings for the building using local soil conditions.

10.3   Design the slotted floor for a dairy herd replacement barn which has a slotted area 12 feet (3.66 m) wide and 100 feet (30 m) long. Give the specifications for the slats and indicate the load per foot (m) on a central supporting member.

REFERENCES

Callender, J.H., ed. *Time-Saver Standards, a Handbook of Architectural Design.* New York: McGraw-Hill, 1966.

Baumeister, Theodore, ed. *Marks' Standard Handbook for Mechanical Engineers.* 7th edition. New York: McGraw-Hill, 1967.

Gray, H.E. *Farm Service Buildings.* New York: McGraw-Hill, 1955.

Lytle, R.J. *Farm Builder's Handbook.* Farmington, Mich.: Structures Publishing Company. 1973.

Midwest Plan Service. *Structures and Environment Handbook.* Ames, Iowa: Midwest Plan Service, 1977.

Chapter Eleven

Beam and Column Design

Beams and columns are the structural members of a building frame. They must be carefully designed to carry the loads to which they will be subjected. A *beam* is a structural member which is subjected to loads that are primarily perpendicular to the long axis. Beams such as floor joists are ordinarily installed horizontally, but they may be inclined as in the case of a rafter, or installed as a wall stud in a vertical position where they are subjected to the lateral load of stored grain.

A *column* is a structural member which is subjected to loads that are primarily parallel to the long axis. Ordinarily columns are installed vertically, such as a post under a beam. However, members subjected to similar compressive forces are also found at various angles in trusses and other structures.

LOADS AND REACTIONS

Structural members are subjected to the loads of snow, wind, stored products or equipment, and other components of the building. The forces that resist the loads are called *reactions*. If the reactions just balance the loads, the structural member is said to be in *static equilibrium*.

In discussing forces and reactions a few constraints will be assumed. All beams will be treated as planar members, that is, all forces will be in only one plane. However, forces may or may not be concurrent, that is, passing through a common point, and they may or may not be parallel.

While forces may act in any direction, it is common practice to resolve all forces into horizontal (x) and vertical (y) components. It is then easier to combine them to find a state of equilibrium. Forces may act along a line and tend to cause displacement along that line or they may act in such a way that they tend to cause rotation about a point or axis. A rotational force is called a *moment*. The moment is due to a force acting at a perpendicular distance from the axis.

When a beam remains stationary and is in equilibrium, the sum of all the horizontal forces acting on the beam is equal to zero, the sum of all the vertical forces is equal to zero, and the sum of all the moments acting about a point is equal to zero. Any of the following combinations of equations expresses a state of equilibrium:

$$\Sigma F_x = 0 \qquad \Sigma F_x = 0 \qquad \Sigma F_y = 0 \qquad \Sigma M_a = 0$$
$$\Sigma F_y = 0 \quad or \quad \Sigma M_a = 0 \quad or \quad \Sigma M_a = 0 \quad or \quad \Sigma M_b = 0$$
$$\Sigma M_a = 0 \qquad \Sigma M_b = 0 \qquad \Sigma M_b = 0 \qquad \Sigma M_c = 0$$

For the purpose of making a stress analysis, upward forces, forces to the right and clockwise moments will be considered positive; downward forces, forces to the left and counterclockwise moments will be considered negative.

An example will illustrate the resolution of an angled force into the x and y components and the determination of the reactions (Figure 11-1).

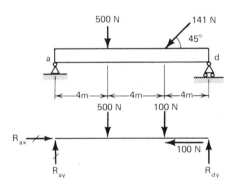

$$C_x = \cos 45° \times 141$$
$$= 0.707 \times 141$$
$$= 100 \text{ N}$$

$$C_y = \sin 45° \times 141$$
$$= 0.707 \times 141$$
$$= 100 \text{ N}$$

Figure 11-1. Force reactions.

$$\Sigma F_x = 0, \xrightarrow{+}, \ R_{ax} - 100 = 0, \ R_{ax} = 100 \text{ N}$$

$$\Sigma M_d = 0, +\circlearrowleft, \ (R_{ay} \times 12) - (500 \times 8) - (100 \times 4) = 0$$
$$R_{ay} = (4000 + 400)/12 = 366.67 \text{ N}$$

$$\Sigma M_a = 0, +\circlearrowright, \ (500 \times 4) + (100 \times 800) - (R_{dy} \times 12) = 0$$
$$R_{dy} = (2000 + 800)/12 = 233.33 \text{ N}$$

$$\Sigma F_y = 0, +\uparrow, \ 366.67 - 500 - 100 + 233.33 = 0$$

Occasionally members may have some special configuration or connection which will require *equations of condition*. For example, in Figure 11-2, assuming that the two members are connected by a frictionless hinge at b, the equation of condition would indicate that $\Sigma M_b = 0$. This is true regardless of whether the moment is determined from the left or the right.

$\Sigma M_a = 0, + \circlearrowleft$, $(200 \times 4) + (300 \times 15) - (R_{cy} \times 20) = 0$
$R_{cy} = (800 + 4500)/20 = 265$ N

$\Sigma M_c = 0, + \circlearrowleft$, $(R_{ay} \times 20) - (200 \times 16) - (300 \times 5) = 0$
$R_{ay} = (3200 + 1500)/20 = 235$ N

$\Sigma F_y = 0, + \uparrow$, $235 - 200 - 300 + 265 = 0$

$\Sigma M_b = 0, + \circlearrowleft$, $(235 \times 10) - (200 \times 6) - (R_{ax} \times 10) = 0$
$R_{ax} = (2350 - 1200)/10 = 115$ N $^+$

$\Sigma M_b = 0, + \circlearrowleft$, $(R_{cx} \times 10) + (300 \times 5) - (265 \times 10) = 0$
$R_{cx} = (-1500 + 2650)/10 = 115$ N $^+$

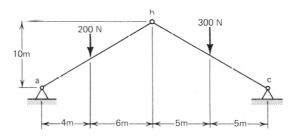

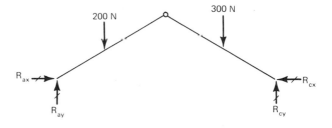

Figure 11-2. Equation of condition.

In analyzing the stresses in objects, it is often convenient to use free-body diagrams. A *free-body diagram* shows all of the forces acting on a body or member. If a body as a whole is in equilibrium, then it may be assumed that a cut at any desired point in the body will result in two members that are still in equilibrium. The solution for maximum bending moment using Figure 11-3 will illustrate the use of free-body diagrams.

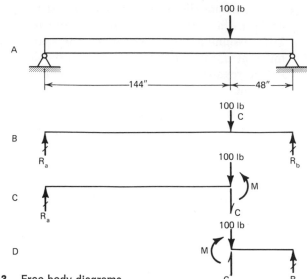

Figure 11-3.   Free body diagrams.

Maximum Bending Moment

The external forces acting on a beam that tend to bend or break that beam produce a bending moment. Although the magnitude of the moment varies throughout the length of the beam, it is the *maximum bending moment* (BM) that must be considered in designing a beam to safely resist the bending forces to which it is subjected.

The steps in finding the maximum bending moment include:

- Determining the reactions at the supports.
- Drawing a shear diagram to locate the maximum bending moment.
- Calculating the maximum bending moment.

Having determined the reactions described above, the *shear diagram* may be drawn. The diagram consists of a base line which represents both the length of the beam and the axis of zero shear. The vertical forces are represented by the displacement of the shear line from the zero axis. The *shear force* at any point is determined by the algebraic sum of all of the forces to the left of that point. Starting at the left end, the reactions and load forces are drawn in proper direction and magnitude. The point at which the shear line crosses the zero axis will indicate the point on the length of the beam at which the maximum bending moment occurs. The bending moment is then calculated for that location.

Referring to Figure 11-3B, the reactions at either end of the beam may be found as follows:

$\Sigma M_a = 0, (100 \times 144) - (R_b \times 192) = 0$

$R_b = 14400/192$

$R_b = \textbf{75 lb}$

$\Sigma M_b = 0, (100 \times 48) - (R_a \times 192) = 0$

$R_a = 4800/192$

$R_a = \textbf{25 lb}$

Next the shear diagram is constructed starting with the 25-pound reaction at the left end. Since that is a concentrated force and there are no other forces between it and the 100-pound load, the shear is represented by a horizontal line. At the point of the 100-pound load force, the shear line drops vertically to 75 pounds below the axis. From there it is horizontal to the right end. The 75-pound reaction returns vertically to the zero axis. The fact that the shear line terminates at the zero axis is a check on the accuracy of the line. The shear line crosses the zero axis 144 inches from the left end. This indicates the location of the maximum bending moment.

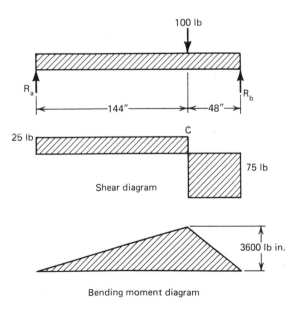

Figure 11-4. Shear and bending moment diagram.

The bending moment around the point of zero shear (C) may be determined from either end of the beam. Usually the side having the fewest forces is chosen for simplicity. Using Figure 11-3C:

$$\Sigma M_c \text{ (left)}, +\curvearrowright, = BM = 25 \times 144 = 3,600 \text{ lb in.}$$

As a check, the moment around point C from the right end may be calculated. Using Figure 11-3D:

$$\Sigma M_c \text{ (right)}, -\curvearrowleft, = BM = -(75 \times 48) = -3,600 \text{ lb in.}$$

The sum of all of the moments around point C is equal to zero.

$$\Sigma M_c = (25 \times 144) - (75 \times 48) = 0$$

The maximum bending moment for the beam is determined in pound-inches because the beam cross section dimensions are in inches and the strength characteristics of the beam material are in pounds per square inch. The corresponding SI units are newtons, meters, and pascals.

Bending moment equations may be derived from the equations used in analyzing the free-body diagrams. In Figure 11-5, a simple beam with a load concentrated at the center is shown. The bending moment equation may be derived as follows:

$$M_c = R_b \times L/2; \text{ however, } R_b = W/2; \text{ therefore}$$
$$M_c = W/2 \times L/2 = WL/4$$

The bending moment is WL/4. Similar derivations, although often much more complex, may be made for beams with many combinations of support and loading.

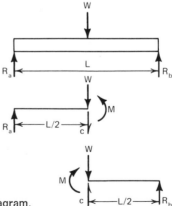

Figure 11-5.   Free body diagram.

When designing the beams for agricultural buildings it is often necessary to make an assumption about the type of loading to which a beam will be subjected. In Figure 11-6, the bending moment equations are given for seven commonly assumed situations.

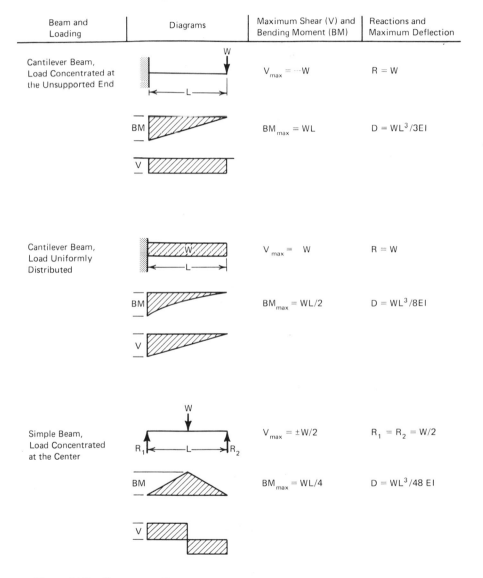

Beam and Loading	Diagrams	Maximum Shear (V) and Bending Moment (BM)	Reactions and Maximum Deflection
Cantilever Beam, Load Concentrated at the Unsupported End		$V_{max} = \cdots W$	$R = W$
		$BM_{max} = WL$	$D = WL^3/3EI$
Cantilever Beam, Load Uniformly Distributed		$V_{max} = W$	$R = W$
		$BM_{max} = WL/2$	$D = WL^3/8EI$
Simple Beam, Load Concentrated at the Center		$V_{max} = \pm W/2$	$R_1 = R_2 = W/2$
		$BM_{max} = WL/4$	$D = WL^3/48\,EI$

Figure 11-6.   Beam equations.

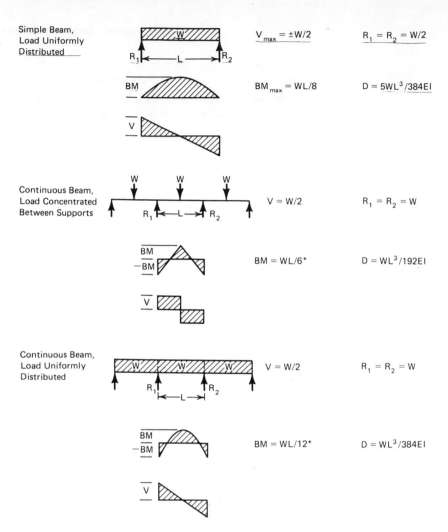

Simple Beam,
Load Uniformly
Distributed

$V_{max} = \pm W/2$

$R_1 = R_2 = W/2$

BM

$BM_{max} = WL/8$

$D = 5WL^3/384EI$

V

Continuous Beam,
Load Concentrated
Between Supports

$V = W/2$

$R_1 = R_2 = W$

BM
−BM

$BM = WL/6*$

$D = WL^3/192EI$

V

Continuous Beam,
Load Uniformly
Distributed

$V = W/2$

$R_1 = R_2 = W$

BM
−BM

$BM = WL/12*$

$D = WL^3/384EI$

V

*Continuously loaded beams present varying moment equations depending
on the number of supports. The equations listed here are conservative
estimates for all except the two end sections. It is best to treat the end
sections as simple beams.

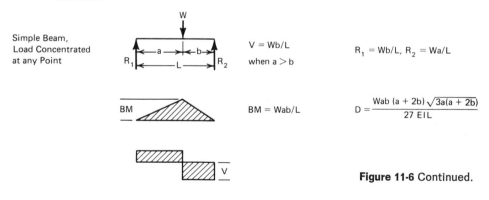

Simple Beam,
Load Concentrated
at any Point

$V = Wb/L$
when $a > b$

$R_1 = Wb/L,\ R_2 = Wa/L$

BM

$BM = Wab/L$

$$D = \frac{Wab\,(a + 2b)\sqrt{3a(a + 2b)}}{27\ EIL}$$

V

Figure 11-6 Continued.

Fiber Stress

Beams and columns are subject to failure in one or more ways, depending on the material from which they are made and the type of loading to which they are subjected. The unit force within a body which tends to resist deformation is called *stress*. It may be tensile, compressive, shearing or flexural. The *safe fiber stress* of a material in pounds per square inch (kPa) is a measure of the strength characteristics of the material that resist failure in each of the following ways:

1. Fiber stress in *bending* is the result of loading that tends to cause bending or breaking of a beam. In most cases this is the critical stress factor on beams in farm buildings.

2. Fiber stress in *horizontal shear* is the result of loading that tends to cause parallel fibers to slip in relation to each other, much as slipping would occur between a number of thin wooden strips laid one on top of another, supported at the ends, and loaded at the center. Horizontal shear is most significant in short, very heavily loaded beams.

3. Fiber stress in *compression perpendicular to the grain* occurs at points of concentrated loading where the force tends to crush across the grain. This is most likely to be critical at points where beams and joists are supported.

4. Fiber stress in *compression parallel to grain* occurs at the ends of members subjected to column loading and tends to crush parallel with the grain. This is most likely to be critical when heavily loaded short columns are bearing against a metal plate.

5. Fiber stress in *tension* occurs in members subjected to tensile loads. This is most likely to be critical in collar beams and tension members in trusses.

Some representative values for safe fiber stress in lumber are given in Table 11-1.

Table 11-1 Design Values for Visually Graded Structural Lumber* ***

Species and Grade	Size inches	Extreme Fiber in Bending		Tension Parallel to Grain	Horizontal Shear	Comp. Perpendicular to Grain	Comp. Parallel to Grain	Modulus Elast. $\times 10^6$
		Single	Repetitive					
Douglas Fir, Western [1,2**]								
Construction	2 to 4 thick 4 wide	1,050	1,200	625	95	385	1,150	1.5
Standard		600	675	350	95	385	925	1.5
Utility		275	325	175	95	385	600	1.5
No. 1	2 to 4 thick 5 & wider	1,500	1,750	1,000	95	385	1,250	1.8
No. 2		1,250	1,450	650	95	385	1,050	1.7
No. 3		725	850	375	95	385	675	1.5
Southern Pine [3]								
Construction	2 to 4 thick 4 wide	1,000	1,150	600	100	405	1,100	1.4
Standard		575	675	350	90	405	900	1.4
Utility		275	300	150	90	405	575	1.4
No. 1	2 to 4 thick 5 & wider	1,450	1,700	975	90	405	1,250	1.7
No. 2		1,200	1,400	625	90	405	1,000	1.6
No. 3		700	800	350	90	405	625	1.4
Spruce-Pine-Fir, Canada [4]								
Construction	2 to 4 thick 4 wide	725	850	425	70	265	775	1.2
Standard		400	475	225	70	265	650	1.2
Utility		175	225	100	70	265	425	1.2
No. 1	2 to 4 thick 5 & wider	1,050	1,200	700	70	265	875	1.5
No. 2		875	1,000	450	70	265	725	1.3
No. 3		500	575	275	70	265	450	1.2

| Species and Grade | Size inches | Extreme Fiber in Bending | | Tension Parallel to Grain | Horizontal Shear | Comp. Perpendicular to Grain | Comp. Parallel to Grain | Modulus Elast. $\times 10^6$ |
		Single	Repetitive					
Mountain Hemlock[6] Hem-Fir[2]								
Construction	2 to 4	825	975	500	75	245	900	1.0
Standard	thick	475	550	275	75	245	725	1.0
Utility	4 wide	225	250	125	75	245	475	1.0
No. 1	2 to 4	1,200	1,400	800	75	245	1,000	1.3
No. 2	thick	1,000	1,150	525	75	245	825	1.1
No. 3	5 & wider	575	675	300	75	245	525	1.0
Northern Pine[5,6]								
Construction	2 to 4	825	950	475	70	280	875	1.1
Standard	thick	450	525	275	70	280	725	1.1
Utility	4 wide	225	250	125	70	280	475	1.1
No. 1	2 to 4	1,200	1,400	800	70	280	975	1.4
No. 2	thick	950	1,100	525	70	280	825	1.3
No. 3	5 & wider	575	650	300	70	280	525	1.1

Design Values in Pounds Per Square Inch

* Used at 19% maximum moisture content.
** The reference numbers relate to the following grade agencies:
1. West Coast Lumber Inspection Bureau
2. Western Wood Products Association
3. Southern Pine Inspection Bureau
4. National Lumber Grades Authority (Canada)
5. Northeastern Lumber Manufacturers Association, Inc.
6. Northern Hardwood and Pine Manufacturers Association, Inc.
*** Conversion to SI units, 1 lb/sq in. = 6.89 kPa; dimension equivalents 2 in. = 38 mm, 4 in. = 89 mm, and 5 in. = 114 mm.

Section Modulus

The ability of a beam to resist a bending moment depends not only on its safe fiber stress, but also on its section modulus (S) which is a cubic measurement based on shape, dimensions, and position of installation. For a rectangular cross section beam the equation is $S = 1/6\ bd^2$, where b is the breadth and d is the depth as installed. Other section moduli may be found in Figure 11-7 or an engineering handbook.

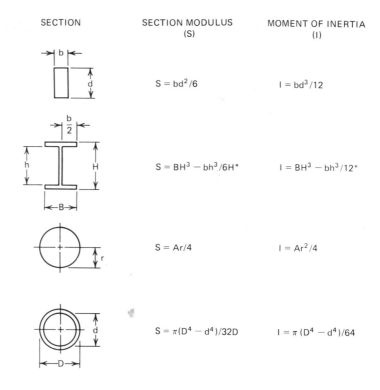

SECTION	SECTION MODULUS (S)	MOMENT OF INERTIA (I)
	$S = bd^2/6$	$I = bd^3/12$
	$S = BH^3 - bh^3/6H^*$	$I = BH^3 - bh^3/12^*$
	$S = Ar/4$	$I = Ar^2/4$
	$S = \pi(D^4 - d^4)/32D$	$I = \pi(D^4 - d^4)/64$

*Values for steel I beams will be found in a steel handbook. These equations provide an approximation.

Figure 11-7. Section modulus (S) and moment of inertia (I) for some common shapes.

Note that the section modulus of a rectangular beam, and thus its carrying capacity, is greatly affected by whether it is installed flat or on edge. For example, a 2- by 8-inch member installed on edge has an

S = 21.33 (S = 2 × 8 × 8/6), while it is only 5.33 (S = 8 × 2 × 2/6) when installed in a flat position.

Safe Bending Moment

The *actual* bending moment (BM) on a beam depends on the beam length, how it is loaded and how it is supported. The *safe* bending moment (BM_s) for a beam depends on the safe fiber stress (f) of the beam material and the section modulus (S) as installed as shown in the expression $BM_s = fS$.

However, the bending moment will be related to the load (W) and the length (L) in some manner as shown in Figure 11-6. Thus the correct WL relationship may be substituted for the bending moment. It is then possible to determine the missing parameters. Given a safe bending moment (BM_s), safe values for beam length and loading may be found. Given an actual bending moment (BM), the required fiber stress and section modulus for the beam may be found.

For example, a simple beam is 10 feet long, has a safe fiber stress of 1,200 pounds per square inch and is installed on edge. The beam, a nominal 2 by 6 inches in size, is actually 1½ by 5½ inches. The safe, uniformly distributed load may be found as follows:

$$
\begin{aligned}
\text{BM} &= \text{WL}/8, \text{ thus WL}/8 = \text{fS} \\
\text{S} &= 1/6\,\text{bd}^2 = 1/6 \times 1.5 \times 5.5 \times 5.5 = 7.56 \text{ in.}^3 \\
\text{fS} &= 1,200 \times 7.56 = 9,072 \text{ in. lb} = \text{WL}/8 \\
\text{WL} &= 9,072 \times 8 = 72,576 \text{ in. lb} \\
\text{L} &= 10 \times 12 = 120 \text{ in.} \\
\text{W} &= 72,576/\text{L} = 72,576/120 = 605 \text{ lb total load} \\
\text{w} &= 605/10 - 60.5 \text{ lb/ft safe load (load/unit of length)}
\end{aligned}
$$

Note that it is essential to use actual and not nominal sizes when calculating section modulus. Had the nominal size been used in the above example, the section modulus would have been 12 and the safe load 96 pounds per foot.

Although it is necessary to use equations to design beams involving unusual shapes or loadings, in many cases rectangular wooden beams with symmetrical loading are involved, in which case Table 11-2 may be used as a simplified means of designing a safe beam. The values given in the table are for *simple* beams with a *uniformly distributed* load. However, conversion to other types of beams and loadings can be accomplished by using the multipliers given with the table.

Table 11-2   Safe Bending Loads for Wood Beams

Length	Size	bd ft	1000 lb/sq in. No. 1 Eastern White Pine		1200 lb/sq in. No. 1 Northern Hemlock		1500 lb/sq in. No. 1 Douglas Fir	
			lbs/ft	Total lbs	lbs/ft	Total lbs	lbs/ft	Total lbs
4	2x4	2⅔	128	510	154	612	192	765
6	2x4	4	57	341	68	409	86	511
	2x6	6	140	840	168	1,010	210	1,260
8	2x4	5⅓	32	255	38	306	48	382
	2x6	8	79	630	95	756	118	945
	2x8	10⅔	136	1,090	163	1,310	204	1,635
10	2x4	6⅔	20	204	24	245	30	306
	2x6	10	51	505	61	606	77	756
	2x8	13⅓	87	873	105	1,050	130	1,310
	2x10	16⅔	143	1,427	172	1,710	214	2,140
12	2x4	8	14	170	17	210	21	255
	2x6	12	35	420	42	504	52	630
	2x8	16	61	727	73	872	92	1,090
	2x10	20	99	1,190	119	1,430	148	1,785
	2x12	24	147	1,760	177	2,230	220	2,640
14	2x6	14	26	360	31	432	39	540
	2x8	18⅔	45	624	54	748	67	935
	2x10	23⅓	73	1,020	88	1,222	110	1,530
	2x12	28	107	1,500	129	1,800	168	2,250
16	2x6	16	20	317	24	380	30	475
	2x8	21⅓	34	546	41	655	51	820
	2x10	26⅔	56	892	67	1,070	84	1,344
	2x12	32	83	1,320	100	1,585	125	1,980
	2x14	37⅓	114	1,830	137	2,195	171	2,740
18	2x8	24	27	485	32	582	41	726
	2x10	30	44	793	53	950	66	1,337
	2x12	36	65	1,172	78	1,405	98	1,760
	2x14	43	90	1,625	108	1,950	135	2,435

(Instructions for Use)

The values in the table are for *simple* beams with *uniformly distributed* loads. To find safe-load values for other types of beams or for concentrated loads, multiply the table value as follows:

Cantilever, concentrated load, table value × 0.125
Cantilever, distributed load,   table value × 0.25
Simple, concentrated load,   table value × 0.50
Continuous, concentrated load, table value × 0.75
Continuous, distributed load,   table value × 1.50

All values shown in the table are for S4S lumber. Table values may be multiplied by 1.1 for rough sawed lumber.

All values in the table are for a single member. Table values may be multiplied by 1.15 for repetitive use.

The following conversions to SI units may be used:

Multiply lb/ft by 14.6 to get N/m
Multiply lb by 4.45 to get N

Equivalents: ft	m	in.	mm
4	1.2	2	38
6	1.8	4	89
8	2.4	6	140
10	3.0	8	184
12	3.7	10	235
16	4.9	12	286
18	5.5	14	337

Deflection in Members

While most agricultural buildings are designed to be safe from failure due to expected loading, there are cases, such as farm homes, where maximum deflection (elastic bending) of members becomes an additional factor. Excessive deflection can cause uneven floors, cracks in wall and ceiling panels and a feeling of excessive vibration from active loads on a floor.

Two factors that are used in determining deflection are *modulus of elasticity* and *moment of inertia*. The modulus of elasticity (E) is a measure of the stiffness of the material. It is the ratio of the stress, pounds per square inch (Pa), divided by the strain (deformation), inch/inch (m/m), within the elastic limit of that material. The unit of the modulus of elasticity is pounds per square inch (mPa or GPa).

The *moment of inertia* (I) is a measure of the effect of the cross-sectional shape on a beam's resistance to a bending moment. The magnitude of the moment also varies with the cross-sectional area of the beam. The usual units are inches^4 (m^4).

A number of methods for computing deflection may be found in structural analysis texts. In view of the relatively few cases of agricultural structures in which deflection must be considered, the study of deflection will be limited to inclusion of the formulae for the seven beams shown in Figure 11-6.

Horizontal Shear

The horizontal shear force on a rectangular beam may be determined with the equation:

$$h = 3R/2bd \qquad \text{Where:}$$

Customary		*SI*
h = the horizontal shear, lb/ sq in.		(Pa)
R = end reaction at a post, lb		(N)
b = breadth of beam, in.		(m)
d = depth of beam, in.		(m)

The value for h should not exceed the safe fiber stress allowed for the specie. Excessive horizontal shear loads usually do not occur except in very short and very heavily loaded beams. Using the same information given for the safe bending moment example, it will be noted that horizontal shear is below the allowable stress found in Table 11-1.

$$R = w/2 = 960/2 = 480 \, lb$$

$$h = 3R/2bd = 3 \times 480/1.5 \times 5.5 \times 6 = 87 \, lb/sq \, in. \text{ horizontal shear}$$

Most species listed in Table 11-1 with a bending stress of 1,200 pounds per square inch have a value for horizontal shear of 90 to 95 pounds per square inch.

Safe Loads in Compression

The safe load in compression, either parallel or perpendicular to the grain, may be found by dividing the load at a supporting point by the actual area of contact at that point. The value obtained may then be compared with safe values for the specie or material.

Safe Loads in Tension

While safe loads in tension on wooden members are often limited by the connectors used, it is also desirable to determine the fiber stress in tension by dividing the load by the cross section area. The stress may then be compared to the safe values found in Table 11-1.

Columns

The formulas used for determining the safe loads on solid wood columns are based on pin-end (hinged) conditions. However, they may also be applied to square-end conditions. One of the factors affecting the design of columns is the slenderness ratio (l/d), where (l) is the unsupported length of the column. If the column has intermediate lateral support, such as is shown in Figure 11-8, the l/d ratio is the greater of l_1/d_1 or l_2/d_2.

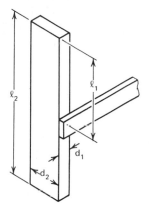

Figure 11-8. Slenderness ratio.

The factors determining the safe load on a column are the cross section area and the adjusted safe fiber stress for the column. Given these two factors, the following formula may be used:

$$C - F_c A \qquad \text{Where.}$$

$\qquad$ C = total safe axial load for the column in lbs

$\qquad$ A = cross section area in sq in.

$\qquad$ F_c = the adjusted safe fiber stress in lb/sq in.

The factors determining the adjusted safe fiber stress (F_c) are the safe fiber stress of the specie in compression parallel with the grain (f_c) and the slenderness ratio. One of the following three formulas, chosen on the basis of the l/d ratio, is used to find F_c. However, the l/d ratio must not exceed 50.

1. Short columns, when $l/d < 11$,
   $$F_c = f_c$$

2. Intermediate columns, when $11 < l/d < K$,
   $$K = 0.671 \sqrt{E/f_c} \qquad \text{when } E = \text{modulus of elasticity in} \\ \text{lb/sq in.}$$
   $$F_c = f_c [1 - 1/3((l/d)/K)^4]$$

3. Long columns, when $l/d \geqslant K$,
   $$F_c = 0.30E/(l/d)^2$$

   Examples: Given, E = 1,400,000 lb/ sq in., f_c = 1,000 lb/ sq in. and dimensions are full size.

1. A 3.5-ft x 4-in x 4-in. column
    $l/d = 42/4 = 10.5$, $l/d < 11$, use the first formula
    $F_c = f_c = 1,000$ lb/sq in.
    $C = F_c A$
    $= 1,000 \times 4 \times 4 = 16,000$ lb total safe load

2. A 6-ft x 4-in. x 4-in. column
    $l/d = 72/4 = 18$
    $K = 0.671 \sqrt{E/f_c}$
    $K = 0.671 \sqrt{1,400,000/1,000}$
    $= 25$
    $11 < l/d < K$, $11 < 18 < 24$, use the second formula
    $F_c = f_c [1 - 1/3 ((l/d)/K)^4]$
    $= 1,000 [1 - 1/3 (18/25)^4]$
    $= 910$ lb/sq in.
    $C = F_c A$
    $= 910 \times 4 \times 4 = 14,560$ lb total safe load

3. A 6-ft x 2-in. x 4-in. column   ($K = 25$ as determined in part 2)
    $l/d = 72/2 = 36$; $11 < l/d > K$, $11 < 36 > 25$, use the third formula
    $F_c = 0.30E/(l/d)^2$
    $= 0.3 \times 1,400,000/36^2$
    $= 324$ lb/sq in.
    $C = F_c A$
    $= 324 \times 2 \times 4$
    $= 2,592$ lb total safe load

The safe load on a column of round cross section may be assumed to be the same as on a square column of equal cross-sectional area when they are both the same specie and grade.

For convenience, safe load values for selected wood columns may be taken from Table 11-3, and safe load values for standard heavyweight concrete-filled columns may be taken from Table 11-4.

Table 11-3 Safe Loads on Solid Wood Columns in Pounds

The values in the table show safe loads for columns both in bending and in compression *parallel* to the grain. The safe load against the beam, *perpendicular* to the grain, should be checked and an appropriate hardwood bearing block or steel plate used on top of the column if more bearing area is needed to protect the beam.

To simplify the table, the following varieties are classified as Type A: white ash, beach, birch, Douglas fir (#1), hickory, maple, oak, southern yellow pine

(#1). Those classified as Type B are California redwood (#2), hemlock, eastern spruce (#1), western pines (#1).

Type A woods are considered to have a minimum modulus of elasticity of 1,500,000 lbs/sq in. and a strength in compression parallel with the grain of 1,000 lbs/sq in., while Type B woods are considered to have a minimum modulus of elasticity of 1,062,000 lbs/sq in. and a strength in compression parallel with the grain of 700 lbs/sq in.

The safe load in compression perpendicular to the grain for beams made of Type A woods may be taken as 400 lb/sq in. and for Type B woods, 300 lb/sq in. Oak and hickory may be taken at 600 lb/sq in. and 720 lb/sq in. respectively. These species make good bearing blocks.

Length of Column feet	Nominal Size inches	S4S			Rough Cut		
		End Area	Type A	Type B	End Area	Type A	Type B
4	2x4	5.25	2,305	1,633	5.89	3,033	2,150
	4x4	12.25	11,932	8,367	13.14	12,837	9,001
6	2x4	5.25	1,024	725	5.89	1,349	954
	4x4	12.25	10,645	7,473	13.14	11,644	8,176
8	4x4	12.25	7,327	5,187	13.14	8,431	5,966
	4x6	19.25	11,514	8,142	20.39	13,082	9,257
	6x6	30.25	28,193	19,772	31.64	29,678	20,806
10	4x4	12.25	4,692	3,320	13.14	5,401	3,824
	4x6	19.25	7,373	5,217	20.39	8,380	5,933
	6x6	30.25	25,234	17,756	31.64	26,862	18,857
	8x8	52.56	49,669	34,847	54.39	51,616	36,168
12	4x4	12.25	3,259	2,303	13.14	3,745	2,654
	4x6	19.25	5,121	3,619	20.39	5,811	4,119
	6x6	30.25	19,874	14,066	31.64	21,705	15,357
	8x8	52.56	46,574	32,692	54.39	48,625	34,122

Conversion to SI units: 1 lb = 4.45 N, 1 ft = 0.305 m
Size equivalents are: 2 in = 38 mm, 4 in. = 89 mm, 6 in. =140 mm, 8 in. = 184 mm

Table 11-4A Safe Concentric Loads on Concrete Filled Columns

Size			Load (thousands of lb)				
Diameter inches	Weight lb/ft	Section Area sq. in.	Length (feet)				
			6	8	10	12	14
3½	15	9.62	45	40	33	26	—
4	20	12.57	58	53	47	39	30
4½	24	15.90	72	67	61	54	45
5	29	19.65	87	82	76	69	61

Table 11-4B   Safe Concentric Loads on Concrete Filled Columns

Size			Load (thousands of newtons)				
				Length (meters)			
Diameter mm	Weight kg/m	Section Area mm²	1.83	2.44	3.05	3.66	4.27
89	22.4	6 205	200	178	147	116	—
102	29.8	8 108	258	236	209	173	133
114	35.8	10 256	320	298	271	240	200
127	43.2	12 674	387	365	338	307	271

REINFORCED CONCRETE

Because ordinary concrete has very little tensile strength, it is necessary to use steel reinforcing imbedded in that portion of a beam, slab, or column that will be subjected to a high tensile force.

Reinforcing steel   Reinforcing steel consists of either deformed (rough surface) bars or welded wire mesh. Bar sizes and specifications are shown in Table 11-5. Reinforcing steel should be clean and free of both rust and oil.

Table 11-5   Characteristics of Round Reinforcing Bars

No.	Diameter inches	mm	Area sq inch	mm²	Perimeter inches	mm	Safe Bonding Stress lb/sq inch*** 2,500	3,000	3,500**
2*	0.250	6.35	0.05	32.	0.786	19.96	160	160	160
3	0.375	9.53	0.11	71.	1.178	29.92	500	500	500
4	0.500	12.70	0.20	129.	1.571	39.90	480	500	500
5	0.625	15.88	0.31	200.	1.963	48.86	384	421	454
6	0.750	19.05	0.44	284.	2.356	59.84	320	351	379
7	0.875	22.23	0.60	387.	2.749	69.82	274	301	325
8	1.000	25.40	0.79	510.	3.142	79.80	240	263	284

* No. 2 bars are not deformed, all others are deformed
** Lb/sq in. compressive strength of concrete
*** May be converted to kPa by multiplying by 6.89

Concrete   Good quality concrete with the correct size aggregate is essential for constructing reinforced structures. Usually not more than 6 gallons (21.25 L) of water per sack are used with enough aggregate to produce a medium slump concrete. Maximum aggregate size may be limited by the spacing of the reinforcing bars.

Before a reinforced concrete structure is designed, it is advisable to become acquainted with local code requirements so that all aspects of the design may be in compliance.

Although some short cuts and rules-of-thumb are used in the discussion that follows, the results of calculations should comply with standards established by the American Concrete Institute (American Concrete Institute, 1963).

Reinforced concrete may be designed either for working stress or ultimate strength. The values and methods suggested here are for working stress. For example, the three 28-day compressive strength values given in Table 11-6 are about 40 percent below generally measured compressive strength values for the corresponding water-cement ratios (Portland Cement Association, 1952). A tensile strength of 20,000 pounds per square inch (137.8 MPa) is assumed for bars. This is well below the yield strength of most reinforcing steels. It is best, however, to determine the working stress for the bars to be used for a particular job.

Table 11-6 Allowable Water-Cement Ratios and Shear Stresses for Concrete

Compressive Strength after 28 days	lb/sq in.	2,500	3,000	3,500
	MPa	17.2	20.7	24.1
Non-air-entrained concrete	gal/sack**	7¼	6½	5¾
	L/sack***	26	23	20
Air-entrained concrete	gal/sack**	6¼	5¼	4½
	L/sack***	22	19	16
Maximum allowable Shear Stress*	lb/sq in.	55	60	65
	kPa	379	413	448

* No web reinforcement. With properly combined stirrups and bent bars, the values may be increased by a factor of 4.5. Consult a handbook for stirrup design.
** Customary sack has a mass of 94 pounds.
*** SI sack has a mass of 40kg.

Beams

Beams have their main reinforcement in one direction in order to resist the bending moment. *One-way slabs* are similar to shallow beams, although they will carry cross reinforcing to distribute the effects of temperature changes and nonuniform loads. They will ordinarily be supported continuously along the sides that are perpendicular to the main reinforcing. *Two-way slabs*, either square or rectangular in shape, have reinforcing designed to withstand bending moments in both directions. They will ordinarily be supported on all four sides. *Flat slabs* or *flat plates* are those that are supported directly by columns. They are also reinforced to withstand a bending moment in each direction. Both two-way and flat slabs are highly indeterminate and require much more sophisticated analysis than one-way slabs or beams. Only one-way slabs and rectangular beams that are cast integrally with a slab will be discussed here.

Design Procedure for a One-Way Slab or Beam

1.   The following rules of thumb may be used to determine trial dimensions for the member:

For floors, d= span/2

For beams, d = span

For floor and beams, D = d + d′

For floors, design based on b = 12 in.

For beams, b = d/2 (approximate)   Where:

$\quad$ d = depth from top surface to center of main reinforcing bar in *inches*

span = length in *feet*

$\quad$ b = breadth of member in *inches*

$\quad$ d′ = bottom of member to center of main bar

$\quad$ D = total depth of member in inches

Look ahead to procedure Step 4 where a value for d′ may be determined from the required covering of the bars.

2.   The methods used to determine loads for wood beams and the bending moment equations found in Figure 11-6 may be used. Be sure to include the weight of the member. Concrete weighs 150 pounds per cubic foot.

3.   The total cross section area of reinforcing bars required may be found with:

$\quad$ A_s = BM/0.86 f_sd   Where:

$\quad$ A_s = cross section area of bars, sq in.
BM = maximum bending moment
$\quad$ f_s = working tensile strength of steel, lb/sq in.

d $=$ depth of slab or beam, top surface to center of bar, in.

4.   Having chosen a size from Table 11-5, the required spacing for the bars may be determined. The clearance between bars should be equal to the diameter of the bar, one and one-third the maximum aggregate diameter or 1 inch (25 mm), whichever is largest. The bars should be covered with concrete as follows:

	(To center of bars)
Concrete on ground	3½ in. (89 mm)
Exposed to weather, less than No. 5 bar	2 in. (51 mm)
Exposed to weather, No. 5 bar and up	2½ in. (64 mm)
Not exposed to weather, slabs and walls	1½ in. (38 mm)
Not exposed to weather, beams and walls	2 in. (51 mm)

5.   Check for shear. Failure in this respect may cause a crack from near the top of the end diagonally toward the bottom of the beam.

$$V = W/2, \quad v = V/bd \qquad \text{Where:}$$

v — shear in lb/sq in. of cross section area

V $=$ total shear, lb

W $=$ total load on member, lb

Note the maximum allowable shear from Table 11-6. If the maximum allowable shear is exceeded, either the member may be made deeper or stirrups may be used to reinforce the web. Consult a reinforced concrete handbook for stirrup design. A girder which is not cast integrally with a slab will require web reinforcement.

6.   Check for bonding between bar and concrete. Plain bars must be hooked at the ends.

$$u = V/0.86 \, \Sigma_o d \qquad \text{Where:}$$

u $=$ bonding stress in lb/sq in. of bar surface area

Σ_o $=$ sum of the perimeters of the bars, in.

Note the maximum safe bonding stress in Table 11-5. If bonding is inadequate, a larger number of smaller size bars will increase the safe bonding stress.

7.   Check for minimum safe bearing area at supports.

$$B = V/0.25f_c \qquad \text{Where:}$$

B $=$ safe bearing area in sq in.

f_c $=$ design compressive strength of concrete from Table 11-5

8. Bars may be bent and placed as shown in Figure 11-9.

9.   Cross bars are needed for one-way slabs to distribute temperature and concentrated loads. Use bars of the same size as the main reinforcing and space them five times the member depth or 18 inches (457 mm), whichever is smaller.

10.   When bars must be overlapped, the distance in inches should be 12, or three times the size number, whichever is larger. For example, No. 5 should overlap 15 inches. Welded wire mesh is overlapped the larger of one mesh or 6 inches (150 mm).

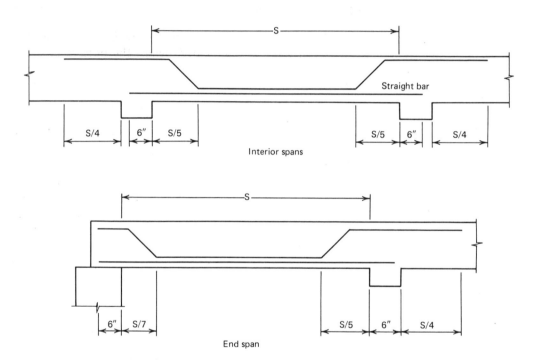

Figure 11-9.   Shapes of reinforcing bars. Alternate bars are bent.

Concrete Columns

Reinforced concrete columns are not often required in agricultural construction unless a high degree of fire resistance is needed. Piers of lengths up to four times the least diameter do not require reinforcing. Columns of lengths up to 11 times the least dimension can be reinforced with a bar in each corner embedded at least 1½ inches (38 mm) from each surface. The minimum area for each bar may be found by:

$$A_s = 0.01a_c/4 \qquad \text{Where:}$$

$$a_c = \text{cross section area of column, sq in.}$$

The corner bars are held in place with No. 3 bars formed into squares and installed 12 inches (305 mm) on center.

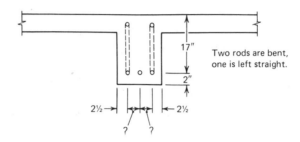

17″

Two rods are bent, one is left straight.

2″

2½   2½

?   ?

Figure 11-10. Beam cross section showing location of reinforcing bars.

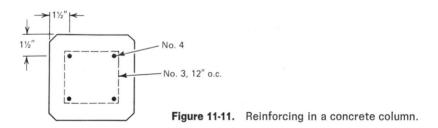

1½″

1½″

No. 4

No. 3, 12″ o.c.

Figure 11-11.   Reinforcing in a concrete column.

Example of Reinforced Concrete Design

Given a floor panel 18 by 24 feet with a uniform 32-pound per square foot dead load above the floor and a 50-pound per square foot live load. The floor will be carried on four 18-foot beams, giving a 7-foot clear span to each slab. The beams will be carried on girders which in turn are supported by columns 24 feet on center.
Design:
   A.   A 1 ft section of the slab
   B.   An 18 ft section of beam (17 ft clear span)
   C.   A column (8 ft unsupported length)

The panel may be assumed to be an interior section and all members are continuous. The girder may be assumed to weigh 225 lb/ft.

A.   1.   d $=$ span/2 $= 7/2 = 3\frac{1}{2}$ in.
D $=$ d $+$ d$'$ $= 3\frac{1}{2} + 1\frac{1}{2} = 5$ in.
b $= 12$ in.
Weight of slab $=$ $(5 \times 12 \times 12/1{,}728)\ 150 = 0.42$ cu ft $\times$ $150 = 62.5$ lb/ft

2.   w $= 32 + 50 + 62.5 = 144.5$ lb/ft of slab

3.   For an interior span continuous beam, the

W $=$ w $\times$ L (ft) $= 1\ 44.5 \times 7 = 1011.5$ lb
BM $=$ WL/12 $= 1011.5 \times 84$ (in.)/12 $= 7080.5$ in.lb

4.   A$_s$ $=$ BM/0.86 f$_s$d $= 7080.5/0.86 \times 20{,}000 \times 3.5 = 0.118$ in.^{2}

Bar spacing $=$ bar area /A$_s$ $\times$ 12 $= (0.11/0.118) \times 12 = 11.22$ in. o.c. (Area of No. 3 bar $= 0.11$ sq in.)

5.   Aggregate can easily be 1 in. maximum diameter

6.   Check shear stress.

V $=$ W/2 $= 1{,}011.5/2 = 506$ lb

v $=$ V/bd $= 506/12 \times 3.5 = 12.05$ lb/sq in.

The stress is well below the maximum of 55 shown in Table 11.5.

7.   Check bonding.

12/11.25 $= 1.07$ bars per foot
Σ_o $= 1.07 \times 1.178 = 1.257$ in. for a No. 3 bar
u $=$ V/0.86Σ_od
    $= 506/0.86 \times 1.257 \times 3.5$
    $= 133.7$ lb/sq in.

The bonding stress is well under the 500 shown in Table 11-5.

8.   Bearing area required.

B $=$ V/0.25 f$_c$ $= 506/.25 \times 2{,}500 = 0.81$ sq in.

9.   Bar positions are shown in Figure 11-8.

10.   Temperature and shrinkage bars. Spacing 5d or 18 in.

$5 \times 3.5 = 17.5$ in., choose 18 in. o.c.

Use same size (No. 3) bars as used for main reinforcing. Place bars just under main bars.

B.   1.   d $=$ span $= 17$ in.

D $=$ d $+$ d$'$ $= 17 + 2 = 19$ in.

b $=$ d/2 $= 17/2 = 8\frac{1}{2}$, use 9 in.

2. W $=$ (178 $+$ 1,012) $\times$ 17 $=$ 20,230 lb
3. BM $=$ WL/12 $=$ 20,230 $\times$ 17 $\times$ 12/12 $=$ 343,910 in. lb
4. $A_s =$ BM/0.86f_sd $=$ 343,910/(0.86 $\times$ 20,000 $\times$ 17) $=$ 1.176 sq in. of bar cross section.
   Choose 3 No. 6 bars @ 0.44 sq in. $=$ 1.32 sq in. total
   Space bars 2½, 2, 2, 2½ in.
5. Coarse aggregate may be ¾-⅞ in. maximum diameter.
6. Check shear stress.

$$V = W/2 = 20{,}230/2 = 10{,}115 \text{ lb}$$

$$v = V/bd = 10{,}115/9 \times 19 = 59.2$$

This is over the safe stress for 3,000 lb/sq in. concrete found in Table 11-6. Stirrups should be used.

7. Check bonding.

$$\Sigma_o = 3 \times 2.356 = 7.068 \text{ in.}$$

$$u = V/0.86 \, \Sigma_o d$$

$$u = 10{,}115/ \, 0.86 \times 7.068 \times 17 = 97.9 \text{ lb/sq in.}$$

This is well under the 351 lb/sq in. found in Table 11-5.

8. Bearing area required.

$$B = V/ \, 0.25f_c$$

$$B = 10{,}115/0.25 \times 2{,}500 = 16.2 \text{ sq in. minimum}$$

9. Bar positions are shown in Figure 11-9.

C. 1. The total weight on a column is one-fourth the total weight from each of four 18-by-24-ft sections. Therefore the total weight from one section may be used.

Weight of 3 slabs and beams $=$ 3 $\times$ 20,230 $=$ 60,690
Weight of 24 ft of girder $\quad = 24 \times \quad 225 = \underline{\quad 5{,}400}$
$\overline{\hphantom{xxxxxxxxx} 66{,}090 \text{ lb}}$

2. Column cross section area determined by compressive strength
   $=$ 66,090/3,000 $=$ 22 sq in., $\sqrt{22}$ $=$ 4.7 in. sq
3. Column side determined by maximum slenderness ratio (l/d) of 11.
   96/11 $=$ 8.73 in. per side; use 9 in.
4. $A_s =$ 0.01 a_c/4 $=$ 0.01 $\times$ 81/4 $=$ 0.2 sq in./bar
5. Use a No. 4 bar (0.2 sq in.) in each corner, embedded 1½ in. from each side. Use No. 3 bars, 12 in. o.c., to form 6 in. squares to support No. 4 bars.

PROBLEMS

11.1   What size and grade of joist is required to support a uniform load of 55 pounds per foot (82 kg/m) with a 10-foot (3 m) span?

11.2   If the same load was concentrated at the center of the beam, what size and grade would be required?

11.3   Find the total safe uniform load for a simple beam that is 2 by 6 inches (38 x 140 mm) and spans 13 feet (4 m). The piece is set on edge and has a safe fiber stress in bending of 1,300 pounds per square inch (8957 kPa).

11.4   What size column would be required to support a 14,000 pound (6364 kg) load when the length is 6 feet (1.8 m)? What kind of bearing plate, if any, is needed? Assume a Type A wood beam is supported.

11.5   Repeat Problem 11.4 using a load of 5,000 pounds (2273 kg) and a length of 12 feet (3.7 m). Assume a Type A wood beam is supported.

11.6   The joists for a storage floor are spaced 2 feet (600 mm) apart, and are supported on girders that are 12 feet (3600 mm) apart. The girders are supported by posts spaced 10 feet (3000 mm) apart. The posts are 8 feet (2400 mm) long. The flooring load is assumed to be 3 pounds per square foot (14.7 kg/m²) and the product load 75 pounds per square foot (366 kg/m²). The joists are just 12 feet (3600 mm) long, but the girder may be considered a *continuous* beam.
Find the following: (Assume S4S material throughout)
(a) The load per foot on the joist, including an estimated weight for the joist.
(b) The size, grade, and kind of wood that would be satisfactory for the joist.
(c) The load on the girder. (Remember that joists extend on both sides of the girder. Include an estimated weight for the girder. The load directly over the post does not have to be included in determining the size of girder needed; that is, a pair of joists are located directly over the posts [columns].)
(d) The size, grade, number of pieces, and kind of wood that would be satisfactory for the girder. Assume the girder is a *continuous* beam.

(e) A size, grade and kind of wood that is satisfactory for posts.

(f) The size and kind of bearing plate to go on top of the post, if one is necessary.

11.7   Design a concrete slab bridge to span 4 feet (1.2 m) over a drainage ditch. The bridge is 10 feet (3 m) wide and is subjected to maximum loads of 2,000 pounds per foot of width (2982 kg/m) at the center of the 4-foot (1.2-m) span.

REFERENCES

American Concrete Institute. *Building Code Requirements for Reinforced Concrete.* ACI 318-63. American Concrete Institute, 1963.

Baumeister, Theo., ed. *Marks' Standard Handbook for Mechanical Engineers,* 7th edition. New York: McGraw-Hill, 1967.

Boyd, James S. *Practical Farm Buildings.* Danville, Ill.: The Interstate Printers and Publishers, Inc., 1973.

Callender, John H. *Time-Saver Standards, A Handbook of Architectural Design.* New York: McGraw-Hill, 1966.

National Forest Products Association. *National Design Specifications for Wood Construction.* Washington, D.C.: National Forest Products Association, 1977.

Perry, Robert H., ed. *Engineering Manual.* New York: McGraw-Hill, 1967.

Portland Cement Association. *A Design Manual for Concrete Farm Floors.* Skokie, Ill.: Portland Cement Association, 1954.

Portland Cement Association. *Design and Control of Concrete Mixtures.* Skokie, Ill.: Portland Cement Association, 1952.

Wilbur, J.B., and Norris, C.H. *Elementary Structural Analysis.* New York: McGraw-Hill, 1948.

Chapter Twelve

Building Frames

The structural members of the main frame in a building provide support for all of the loads that may be imposed on the building. The frame must not only be strong enough to support vertical loads, but it must be anchored, braced, and fastened together to withstand forces from any direction. Many failures in buildings have occurred because of inadequate bracing or joint strength. Rather than being the cause of the structural failure, members frequently fail as a result of a building collapse.

TYPES OF FRAMES

The type of frame chosen for a building will depend on floor and wall loads, the clear span required, and the type of interior and exterior wall coverings desired. In some cases it is difficult to distinguish between the main wall frame and the roof frame, while in others there is a distinct difference.

Timber frames Timber frames constructed of heavy structural members, spaced well apart, were popular in the 19th century, primarily because much less sawing of timbers was necessary. That they were well designed and durable is evident today by the number of old barns still standing. More efficient methods of using wood are employed in most present-day frames.

Platform or western frames These frames (Figure 12-1) are used extensively in home building and in farm buildings subjected to heavy floor loads. In general, each succeeding group of members rests on top of the previous one. There are no open flues or passages within the walls from floor to floor through which fire may travel.

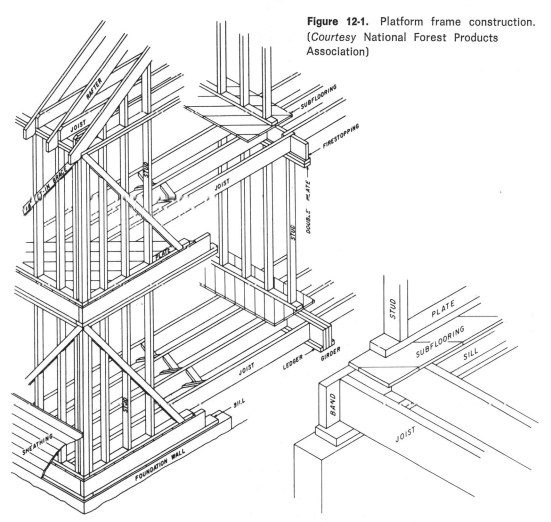

Figure 12-1. Platform frame construction. (*Courtesy* National Forest Products Association)

Balloon frames Balloon frames (Figure 12-2) have vertical members that extend from base to roof, thus tying the building together and making it more wind resistant. Since some weight-bearing members are supported by ribbons attached to the sides of vertical members, the weight-bearing capacity is usually less than with a platform frame. Firestops may need to be installed between the wall studs.

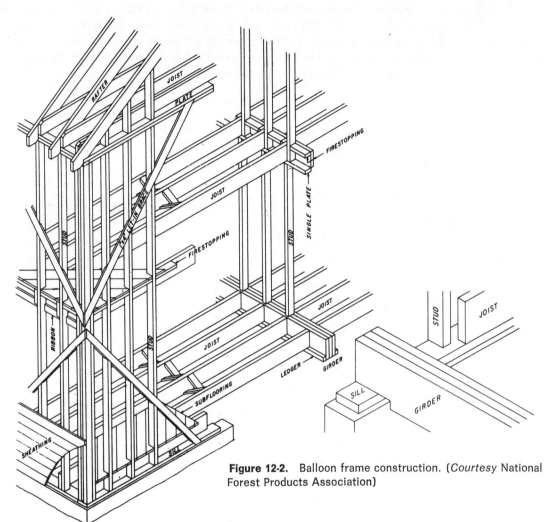

Figure 12-2. Balloon frame construction. (*Courtesy* National Forest Products Association)

Pole frames   Pole frames (Figures 12-3 and 12-4) are simple, fast to construct, and usually less expensive because of minimal foundation cost. Frame members are often overlapped which reduces cutting and improves the strength of the joints. One or more sides may be left open. Pole buildings are usually limited to a single story and are commonly used where insulation is not needed.

Rigid frames   These frames (Figures 12-5 and 12-6), may be fabricated from either steel or wood. Many manufacturers of steel buildings make use of either solid-web or open-web rigid frames to produce a simple, low-pitch building with maximum interior clearance. Rigid frames fabricated from wood include glued laminated rafters for Gothic arch roofs and medium-pitch frames made with dimension lumber and nailed

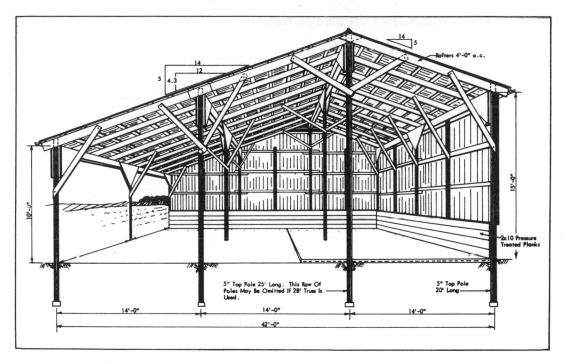

Figure 12-3. Pole building with interior poles. (*Courtesy* Midwest Plan Service)

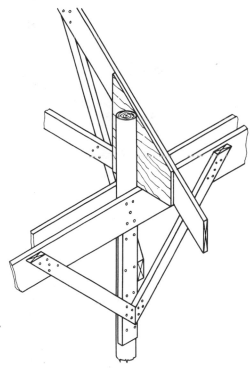

Figure 12-4. Bracing detail.

plywood gussets. Cost of these frames is comparable to other types offering clear spans of equal length.

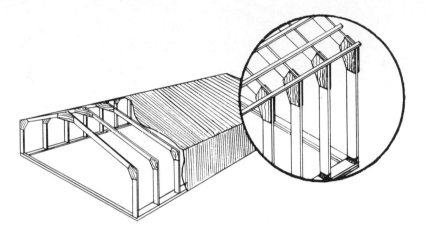

Figure 12-5.   Rigid frame of wood and plywood.

Figure 12-6.   Rigid frame of steel. (*Courtesy* Armco Steel Corporation)

FRAMING COMPONENTS

Sills   Sills are the horizontal wood members laid on the foundation, usually 2 inches (38 mm) thick and from 4 to 12 inches (89 to 286 mm) wide depending on stud size and whether or not joists rest on the sill. If joist loads are heavy, a wide sill may be necessary to get adequate bearing surface between the joist and sill.

Sills should be anchored to the foundation to reduce the possibility of wind damage. The following anchor design is recommended:

Single story buildings	½ in. (14 mm) bolts, 6 ft (2 m) o.c.
	or
	⅝ in. (16 mm) bolts, 8 ft (2.5 m) o.c.
Two or three stories	⅝ in. (16 mm) bolts, 6 ft (2 m) o.c.

All bolts should reach at least 12 inches (300 mm) into concrete walls, 16 to 18 inches (400 to 450 mm) into piers and from 2 blocks to 2 feet (600 mm) in masonry walls. In high wind areas, masonry walls should be avoided altogether or should be tied all the way to the footing. In all cases, large washers should be used on the bolts.

Sills that are used on piers must be designed for beam loads.

Joists These extend from sill to girder on the first floor and from plate to plate on subsequent floors. They are usually made of 2-inch (38-mm) dimension lumber with the depth and spacing determined by the load. In homes, the choice might be made on the basis of deflection in order to keep vibration to a minimum. In most agricultural buildings, the design would be based on strength. With platform frames, the floor will be installed on the joists and a *shoe* on which to install the studs put around the perimeter.

Bridging Bridging consists of wood or metal bracing between joists as shown in Figures 12-1 and 12-7. Installed at the center of the joist span, bridging helps distribute concentrated loads and reduces vibration by increasing the rigidity of the joists.

Girders Girders support the interior ends of first-floor joists. When made of wood, they are frequently "built up" of two or more pieces as shown in Figure 12-8. Figures 12-8, 12-9 and 12-10 show typical joining of joists and both wood and steel girders.

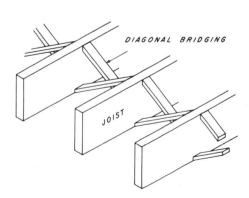

Figure 12-7. Bridging.

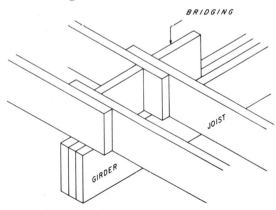

Figure 12-8. A built-up girder. (*Courtesy* National Forest Products Association)

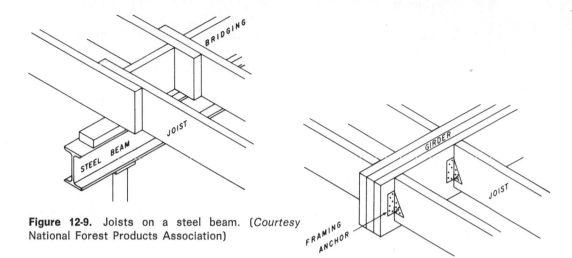

Figure 12-9. Joists on a steel beam. (*Courtesy* National Forest Products Association)

Figure 12-10. Joist connections. (*Courtesy* National Forest Products Association)

Studs   Studs are the upright wall members, usually spaced 16 inches (400 mm) or 24 inches (600 mm) apart to provide a modular spacing that conforms well with common building materials. While the smaller spacing has been most common in home construction, with slightly thicker wall coverings, the larger spacing is satisfactory. A wider stud used with the larger spacing also allows additional insulation to be installed. The width of the stud used depends on the height of the building and floor loads supported by the studs along with wind and product loads that impose forces perpendicular to the wall. While 2- by 4-inch (38 x 89 mm) studs are common in single-story buildings, 2- by 6-inch (38 x 140 mm) studs are often required for multistory buildings.

Plates   Plates are the horizontal members on top of the studs and provide rigidity and strength to the wall, particularly in resisting loads perpendicular to the wall. In addition, the plate must be wide enough to provide adequate bearing surface for joists or rafters. Vertical plates or headers as shown in Figure 12-11, are required to span openings such as doors or windows. They are often used in addition to the regular horizontal plates which are still needed to resist horizontal forces.

Rafters   The roof framing members are known as rafters and are usually spaced to modular dimensions of 16 inches, 2 feet or 4 feet (400, 600 or 1200 mm) on center. Rafter size is influenced by length, intermediate supports, spacing, and expected roof and ceiling loads. Intermediate supports are called *purlins*.

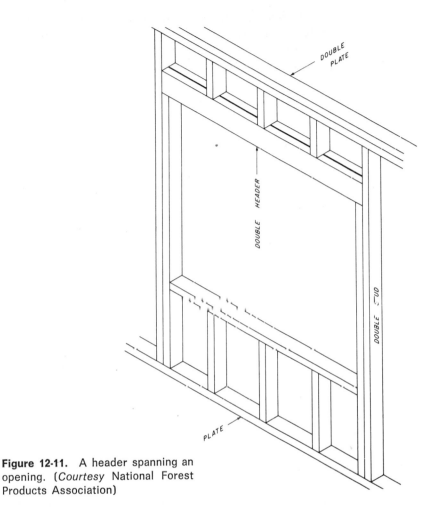

Figure 12-11. A header spanning an opening. (*Courtesy* National Forest Products Association)

FRAMING CONNECTIONS WITH STUD CONSTRUCTION

The traditional method of fastening studs to sills, plate to studs, and rafters or joists to plate is by toe-nailing or end-nailing. These provide satisfactory rigidity in most cases but do not give very high ultimate strength. The use of metal straps and gussets in addition to the toe-nailing will improve the strength. Commercial fasteners, used according to recommendations, provide both adequate rigidity and strength.

One of the easiest ways to achieve superior strength and rigidity, as well as bracing effect, is through the use of plywood or large size building boards nailed according to the manufacturer's recommendations.

Rafters and trusses may be anchored by nailing them to the side of studs, using wooden or metal ties to the studs or commercial fasteners. Toe-nailing alone is risky, particularly where spans are long and rafter spacing is 2 feet (600 mm) or more.

Bracing

The importance of adequate bracing in a building cannot be over emphasized. Along with inadequate fastening at joints, lack of bracing is a major cause of structural failure.

While it is impossible to generalize all bracing requirements, the important locations for bracing can be suggested.

Lateral bracing   Lateral bracing in a wall may be obtained by a brace that is "let" into notches in the studs, in both directions, at each corner as shown in Figure 12-2. However, diagonal wood sheathing or fiberboard sheathing will provide better bracing while properly nailed plywood sheathing is best.

Knee braces   Knee braces should be installed between columns and beams or joists at each column position. If interior walls are more than 36 feet (11 m) apart, it is desirable to install knee braces between the side wall and joists or rafters on 12-foot (3.6-m) spacings. Knee braces should be a minimum of 4 feet (1.2 m) long and made of 2- by 4-inch (38- x 89-mm) or 2- by 6-inch (38- x 140-mm) lumber. Plywood roof decks and sheathing installed as recommended by APA will materially increase the rigidity of a building and allow the omission of knee braces if the building is not more than 80 feet (25 m) long or has partitions no more than 80 feet (25 m) apart.

Truss bracing   Truss bracing to a side wall may be overlooked because the truss itself is such a well-braced unit. However, the truss offers no bracing to the wall until it is securely fastened and braced to the wall. Unless there are interior walls, knee braces should be no more than 12 feet (3.6 m) apart and should be long enough to extend from a point at least one-third of the way along the rafter to 3 feet (1 m) down on the wall member. Trusses should also be braced in relation to each other in order to prevent a "domino" type of collapse.

End bracing   End bracing of buildings that have more than 18 feet (6 m) of width without an inner partition or 8 feet (2.4 m) of height without a floor is desirable. In connection with this bracing, horizontal plate members should be used in order to withstand the wind loads against the end of the building.

Pole Building Framing

Pole spacing is influenced by pole diameter, building height and wind load but should not ordinarily be more than 16 feet (5 m) on center.

Table 12-1 Spacing of Pressure Treated Douglas Fir or Southern Pine Poles

Top Diameter		Wind Load		Effective Building Height							
inches	mm	psf	kPa	feet 9	m 2.75	feet 12	m 3.67	feet 15	m 4.5	feet 19	m 5.8
6.7	170	10	69	16	4.8	16	4.8	16	4.8	16	4.8
		12	83	16	4.8	16	4.8	16	4.8	14	4.8
		15	103	16	4.8	16	4.8	14	4.2	11	3.4
		20	138	16	4.8	14	4.2	10	3.0	8	2.4
6.0	150	10	69	16	4.8	16	4.8	16	4.9	13	4.0
		12	83	16	4.8	16	4.8	13	4.0	11	3.4
		15	103	16	4.8	14	4.2	11	3.4	9	2.7
		20	138	10	4.0	10	3.0	8	2.4	—	—
5.4	137	10	69	16	4.8	16	4.8	12	3.6	10	3.0
		12	83	16	4.8	13	4.0	10	3.0	8	2.4
		15	103	16	4.8	10	3.0	8	2.4	6	1.8
		20	138	12	3.6	8	2.4				

Wind loads may be calculated from information in Chapter 9.

Pole embedment should be 4 feet (1.2 m) in firm soil and 5 feet (1.5 m) in soft soil but always below the frost line. Pads and anchors for poles are discussed in Chapter 10.

Figure 12-4 illustrates the details of girder and truss connections at a pole, including the recommended bracing. A girder support block, secured to the pole with an adequate number of nails, is required in most cases in order to have safe support for the girders. In pole construction, knee braces are advised at every weight-bearing pole. They should be installed in both directions as shown in Figures 12-3 and 12-4. An alternative to knee braces is the *diaphragm effect* obtained by the installation of metal roofing and siding as follows (Hausmann and Esmay, 1975). Trusses or rafters should be no more than 4 feet (1.2 m) on center and 2- by 4-inch (38- x 89-mm) purlins no more than 2 feet (600 mm) on center. The metal roofing is then installed on the purlins with screws placed 12 inches (300 mm) apart in the flats (not the ridges) of the roofing. Similar methods are used for the siding. It is not advisable to install insulation board between the metal panels and the framing.

PROBLEMS

12.1   Give examples in which the choice of each of the following frame types would be suitable:
   a. Balloon frame
   b. Pole frame
   c. Platform frame
   d. Rigid frame

12.2   A pole building is to be constructed in central Iowa. The dimensions are 36 by 48 feet (11 x 14.6 m) with a 12-foot (3.7-m) eave height. The roof slope is 4:12 and the building will be enclosed and designed with knee braces. The soil conditions are soft. Determine a safe pole spacing, pole diameter, and pole embedment.

REFERENCES

American Plywood Association. *Plywood Rigid Frame Design Manual.* Tacoma, Wash.: American Plywood Association, 1962.

Armco Steel Corporation. *Armco Building Systems.* Middletown, Ohio: Armco Steel Corporation, 1977.

Hausmann, C.T., and Esmay, M.L. *Pole Barn Wind Resistance Design Using Diaphragm Action.* Paper No. 75-4035. St. Joseph, Mich.: American Society of Agricultural Engineers, 1975.

Irish, W.W., et al. *Pole and Post Building Construction.* Ithaca, N.Y.: Northeast Regional Agricultural Engineering Service, 1977.

Midwest Plan Service. *Structures and Environment Handbook.* Ames, Iowa: Midwest Plan Service, 1977.

National Forest Products Association. *Manual for House Framing.* Washington, D.C.: National Forest Products Association, 1961.

Chapter Thirteen

Roof Framing

It is important to design a roof frame to withstand the live loads expected in the particular climatic area and the dead load imposed by the framing, roof deck, and roofing material. Careful fitting is important as the angle cuts tend to magnify measurement errors. Poorly-fitted joints will result in reduced rigidity of the roof frame.

COMMON ROOF SHAPES

Flat roofs (A)   These are simple to construct with clear spans of 16 to 18 feet (5 m) using roof joists. Greater spans are possible by using flat trusses. Being flat, they require a "built-up" asphalt roof covering which may be more expensive than some other types.

Shed roofs (B)   Shed roofs are inexpensive and, like a flat roof, can have clear spans of 16 to 18 feet (5 m) without resorting to truss construction. A less expensive roof covering may be used.

Gable roofs (C)   These are medium in cost, easy to construct, and probably the most common style found on barns. Depending on the pitch, several different roof coverings are satisfactory. A medium-pitch gable roof is one of the most wind-resistant shapes available. Clear spans of up to 24 to 26 feet (7–8 m) are feasible with plain rafters, while trusses may be used for greater widths.

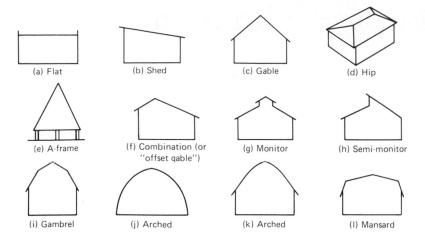

Figure 13-1.   Roof shapes.

Hip roofs (D)   Hip roofs are most often chosen for their appearance. The framing and roofing are more complicated and expensive, and attic ventilation is more difficult than with a gable roof.

A-frame roofs (E)   These are somewhat of an architectural novelty. Because of their shape, outside maintenance is largely retricted to roof covering while at the same time usable floor space is partially restricted by the sloping walls. Snow loads seldom present a problem.

Combination roofs (F)   Sometimes called "offset gable," these roofs are often used on buildings that are open on one side. Depending on the requirements, the high side may be left open to provide maximum clearance or the low side may be left open for maximum weather protection.

Monitor or semimonitor roofs (G-H)   Although more expensive to construct, these may be chosen if a considerable amount of natural light is required near the center of the building. In widths up to 36 feet (11 m), ventilation is adversely affected, while in buildings of 70 feet or more it may be enhanced.

Gambrel roofs (I)   Barns with gambrel roofs came into use to provide greater storage space than was easily obtainable with gable roofs. They tend to be expensive, have uneven roof deterioration, and are subject to greater wind forces than most other shapes.

Arched roofs (J-K)   Arched roofs may vary in shape from semicircular to high Gothic. The choice of shape and height depends largely on the space required. These roof shapes became popular with the advent of commercially-available, glue-laminated rafters. Many of them have replaced gambrel-roof barns because of lighter weight and lower cost

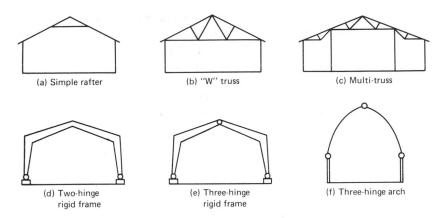

(a) Simple rafter   (b) "W" truss   (c) Multi-truss

(d) Two-hinge   (e) Three-hinge   (f) Three-hinge arch
rigid frame   rigid frame

Figure 13-2.   Roof frames.

of construction, while still offering large storage volume. Deterioration tends to be uneven on these roofs.

Mansard roofs (L)   Mansard roofs are chosen primarily for their appearance. The low pitches commonly used in the center area may present some problems with leakage.

COMMON RAFTERS

The parts of a common rafter, extending from the plate to the ridge, are shown in Figure 13-3. Note that when a rafter extends outside of the plate, as in the figure, the length of the rafter is measured along a *workline* parallel to the edge of the rafter and extending from the outer edge of the plate to the center of the ridge. All measurements are made in relation to this line and not the edges of the rafter.

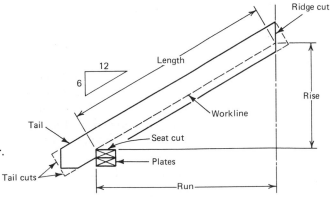

Figure 13-3.   Parts of a common rafter.

The *run* of a rafter is the horizontal distance from the outside edge of the plate to a vertical (plumb) line dropped from the center of the ridge.

The *rise* is the vertical distance from the top of the plate to the intersection of the ridge-cut with the workline.

The *pitch* of the roof may be expressed either with an inverted right triangle showing the ratio of rise to run or it may be described with a fraction. The formula for the pitch fraction is:

$$\text{Pitch} = \text{rise}/(2 \times \text{run})$$

Note that with an even-pitch gable roof, the span equals the run multiplied by two. However, on shed or combination roofs with unequal pitches, rafters for each pitch are designed separately and the equation should be used as shown.

For Figure 13-3 the pitch fraction would be:

$$\text{Pitch} = \text{rise}/(2 \times \text{run}) = 6/(2 \times 12) = \tfrac{1}{4}$$

Other pitch relationships are:

$$3 : 12 = \tfrac{1}{8} \qquad\qquad 8 : 12 = \tfrac{1}{3}$$
$$4 : 12 = 1/6 \qquad\qquad 12 : 12 = \tfrac{1}{2}$$

There are at least four ways to determine the length of a common rafter:

1. By taking the square root of the sum of the rise squared plus the run squared.

2. By using tables on a rafter square.

3. By scaling with the aid of a steel square.

4. By stepping off the length with a steel square.

It is desirable to determine the length of the rafter to the nearest eighth of an inch (5 m) to insure a good fit. The first method, particularly with the aid of a pocket calculator, gives this precision. The fourth method provides a rough check of the accuracy of the first and also determines the angle of the ridge and seat cuts.

Briefly, the procedure for determining the length and the cuts for a common rafter with a one-quarter pitch (6:12) is:

1. Find the rise and the run from the building print or with the pitch equation.

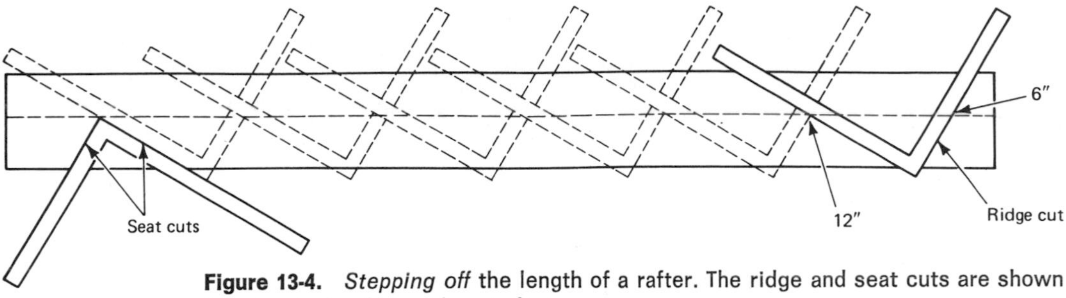

Figure 13-4. *Stepping off* the length of a rafter. The ridge and seat cuts are shown for a ¼ pitch rafter with a six-foot run.

2. Decide on the depth of the seat cut and draw the workline. For low pitches, the seat cut often is deep enough so that the seat covers the plate. However, if there is to be a rafter tail, an extension beyond the plate, there must be sufficient material left to be of adequate strength.

3 Place the square on the workline near the ridge end of the rafter as shown in Figure 13-4. In this case, that will be 6 inches on the tongue and 12 inches on the blade. Use the outside scales. Mark the ridge cut. Also mark the intersection of the workline with the 12-inch point on the blade of the square. Continue to place the square on the workline and mark the intersections for as many times as there are feet of run. Figure 13-4 shows six feet of run. The last mark should be the horizontal side of the seat cut. The millimeter values on a pitch triangle may be used in a similar manner.

4. Calculate the rafter length and measure from the ridge cut to the seat cut along the workline. Make any necessary corrections in length.

5. Complete the seat-cut lines. Make both seat and ridge cuts. Cut out a second rafter and try the pair for fit.

6. If a ridge board is to be used, remove one-half the thickness of the board from each ridge cut.

7. Sometimes the remainder of a piece of dimension lumber from which a rafter can be cut will provide an adequate rafter tail. If not, then either a tail must be nailed to the rafter, or a longer piece of lumber selected for the rafter.

Figure 13-5 shows examples of hip, valley, and jack rafters. A good carpentry book may be consulted to obtain a method for designing these rafters.

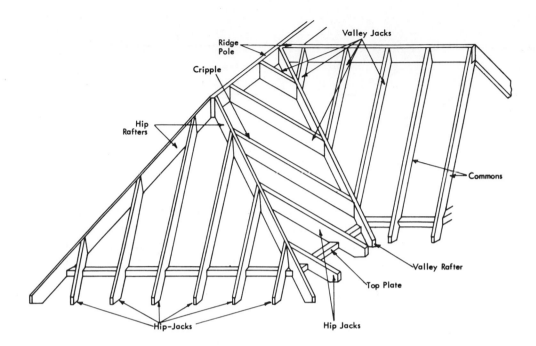

Figure 13-5.   Types of rafters (*Courtesy* Midwest Plan Service)

ROOF LOADS

Chapter 9 (Loads on Buildings) covers in detail the types of loads to which roofs are subjected. The dead loads from the framing, roof deck, and roofing are easily estimated. The live loads from snow and wind are much more difficult to predict. Not only do they differ greatly from one area to another, but data may be based on a 25- or 50-year mean recurrence interval. In choosing a design load it is necessary to comply with any code regulations and also desirable to obtain storm data for the local area. A final decision may be influenced by the hazard to life and property resulting from a roof failure.

TRUSSES

A truss is a structure composed of members assembled to form one or more connected triangles, thus producing a rigid frame capable of supporting a heavy load over a considerable span. The most commonly used wood trusses for agricultural construction are pitch designs with spans ranging from 24 to 60 feet (7–18 m). For spans of more than 50 to 60 feet (15–18 m) the use of multiple trusses will be more economical. Several designs are shown in Figure 13-6. Figure 13-7 illustrates a complete truss design.

The *king post* truss is simple and economical for relatively short spans. The "W" *type* is suitable for spans of up to about 40 feet (12 m), while the *Belgian* truss might be chosen for longer spans requiring a pitched roof. The *sissors* truss is recommended when a high ceiling clearance is required and the *flat* truss for very long spans. Flat metal trusses are often used as joists or carrying beams.

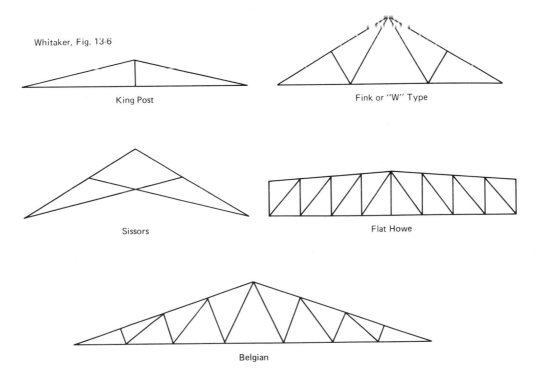

Whitaker, Fig. 13-6

King Post

Fink or "W" Type

Sissors

Flat Howe

Belgian

Figure 13-6. Types of trusses.

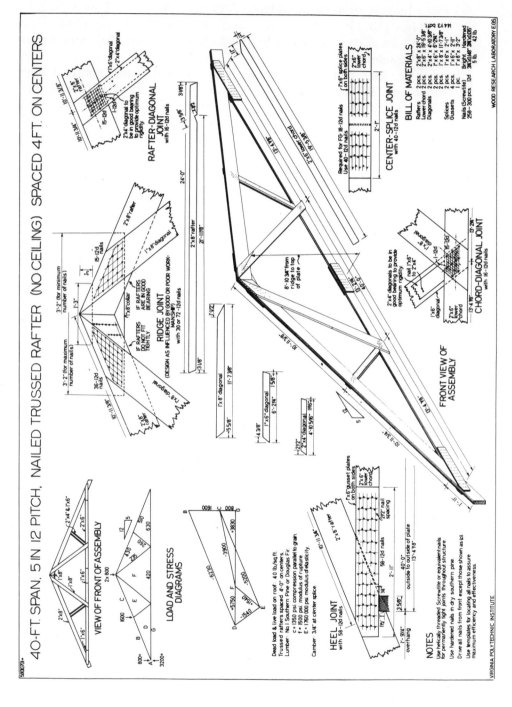

Figure 13-7. Nailed truss design. (*Courtesy Wood Research and Wood Construction Lab., Virginia Polytechnic Institute and State University*)

Truss Stress Analysis

Chapter 11 provides information on stress analysis and the use of free-body diagrams. With these procedures applied to successive joints, the stress in each member may be determined (Walker, 1974). A one-third pitch, "W" type truss shown in Figure 13-8, will be used to illustrate the procedure.

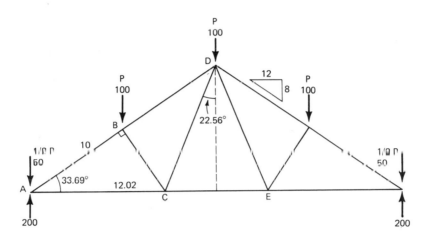

Figure 13-8.   Example of truss analysis.

Trigonometric values used in the example:

$$\begin{aligned}
&\text{Angle A} = 33.69° = \tfrac{1}{3} \text{ pitch} \\
&\text{Tangent } 33.69° \quad = 0.6667 \\
&\text{Sine} \qquad\qquad\;\; = 0.5547 \\
&\text{Cosine} \qquad\qquad = 0.8321 \\
&\text{Angle D} = 22.56° \\
&\text{Sine } 22.56° \qquad\; = 0.3837 \\
&\text{Cosine} \qquad\qquad = 0.9235 \\
&\text{T} = \text{tension, C} = \text{compression}
\end{aligned}$$

1. $\Sigma F_y = 0$

$$200 - 50 - (0.5547 AB) = 0$$
$$AB = 150/0.5547$$
$$AB = 270.4 \text{ C}$$

2.

$\Sigma F_x = 0$

100

B

A   C

$AC - 0.8321AB = 0$

$AC = 0.8321 \times 270.4$

$AC = 225 \; T$

$\Sigma M_A = 0$

$(100 \times 8.321) - (10 \; BC) = 0$

$BC = 100 \times 8.321/10$

3.   100

B   D

A   C

$BC = 83.2 \; C$

$\Sigma F_x = 0$

$(0.8321 \; BD) - (0.8321 \; AB) - (0.5547 \; BC) = 0$

$BD = ((0.8321 \times 270.4) - (0.5547 \times 83.2))/0.8321$

$BD = 215$

4.   B   D

A   E

C

$\Sigma F_y = 0$

$(0.8321 \; BC) - (0.9235 \; CD) = 0$

$CD = 0.8321 \times 83.2/0.9235$

$CD = 75 \; T$

$\Sigma F_x = 0$

$AC - CE - (0.3837 \; CD) - (0.5547 \; BC) = 0$

$CE = 2250 - (0.3837 \times 75) - (0.5547 \times 83.2)$

$CE = 150 \; T$

Since the truss is symmetrical, the stress values for the remaining similar members correspond to those already determined. By dividing the stress value for each member by P (100 in this case) a coefficient is obtained that may be used to find the stresses for any value of P, as long as the loading is uniform and symmetrical. Table 13-1 provides the stress coefficients for four pitches of the truss shown in Figure 13-9. Similar tables for a variety of situations may be found in handbooks (National Lumber Manufacturers' Association, 1962).

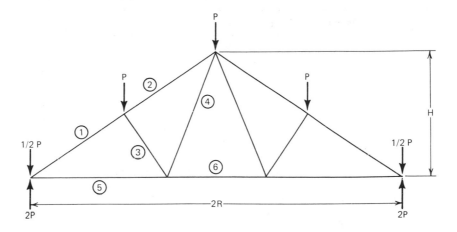

Figure 13-9. Truss member identification.

Truss Design

Tables 13-1 and 13-2 will provide stress coefficients and length-of-member data for use in the design of a simple "W" truss with two members in each top chord, two feet (600 mm) or less overhang at the eaves, and no ceiling load. The stresses in each of the members and joints may be calculated with the use of the tables. Once the stresses are known, an appropriate grade and size of lumber may be selected for a suitable truss spacing.

Since the truss design shown in Figure 13-9 is symmetrical, the procedure involves the loads and stresses for one side only. The *load* is the total uniform load to be supported by the trusses on both sides of the roof. For convenience, the load may be considered to be concentrated at the panel points (P). For Figure 13-9, P = Load/4 and H = Pitch × 2R.

The length (L) of members is determined from the length coefficients in Table 13-2.

The stress (G) in each truss member is determined by G = P × coefficient; the coefficient being chosen for the appropriate pitch in Table 13-1.

Table 13-1   Member Stress as a Coefficient of P

Member	Pitch	½	⅓	¼	1/6
1		−2.12	−2.70	−3.35	−4.74
2		−1.14	−2.15	−2.91	−4.43
3		−0.71	−0.83	−0.89	−0.95
4		0.50	0.75	1.00	1.50
5		1.50	2.25	3.00	4.50
6		1.00	1.50	2.00	3.00

A negative value indicates a stress in compression.

Table 13-2   Member Length as a Coefficient of H

Member	Pitch	½	⅓	¼	1/6
1,2		0.707	0.901	1.118	1.581
3		0.707	0.60	0.559	0.52
4,5		1.00	1.08	1.25	1.667
6		0.00	0.82	1.50	2.67

Safe Design Strength

Members in the top chord of the truss must be designed for strength in both bending and compression. Members in compression only, must be designed as columns. Lower chord members must be designed for safe strength in tension and also in bending if there is a ceiling load.

To determine the strength of a truss member as a *beam,* use the equation $WL/12 = f_bS$ for a *nailed* truss or $WL/8 = f_bS$ for a *bolted* truss.

Where:

$W =$ the uniform load perpendicular to the member in lb/ft (N/m)

$L =$ the length of the member in *inches* (m)

$f_b =$ the safe fiber stress in bending lb/sq in. (kPa)

$S =$ the section modulus. $S = 1/6\ bd^2$ in in.^{3} (m^3)

$b =$ the breadth of the member in in. (m)

$d =$ the depth of the member in in. (m)

Using a selected spacing and estimated load, the minimum satisfactory section modulus (S) is found for the member being designed. After solving for S, a member size may be selected for the wood to be used.

To check the strength of this member as a *column,* use the equation

$$C = F_cA \qquad \text{Where:}$$

$C =$ total safe axial load for a column in lb

$A =$ cross section area of member in sq in.

$F_c =$ the adjusted safe fiber stress in lb/sq in.

The value for F_c may be determined with the appropriate equation from the three given in the section on columns in Chapter 11.

For the slenderness ratio (l/d), l may be assumed to be the distance between purlins, and d the thickness of the member. In the case of a solid roof deck or purlins spaced less than 2 feet (600 mm) apart, l may be considered to be 65 percent of the total member length and d the depth of the member.

The safe design load of the member (C) may then be compared to (G), the load value determined by the product of P and the coefficient from Table 13-1.

After determining a member size suitable for both bending and compression stresses, the effect of the combined loading may be checked with the interaction equation using actual expected forces.

$$\frac{G/A}{f_c} = \frac{BM/S}{f_b} \leq 1.0$$

If the sum of the two ratios is over 1.0, it will be necessary to reduce the truss spacing or to increase the size of the members.

Tension members should be checked to ensure that the imposed tensile load does not exceed the safe fiber stress in tension f_t.

$$f_t = T/A \qquad \text{Where:}$$

$T =$ tensile force on the member

$A =$ cross section area of the member

When members are subjected to both bending and tensile stresses, the design must be checked for each. It has been common practice to use the interaction equation:

$$\frac{T/A}{f_t} + \frac{BM/S}{f_b} \leq 1.0$$

However, as it has been shown that the bending load at failure is nearly independent of applied tensile load, it seems conservative to substitute 1.5 for 1.0 in the above equation (Senft, 1973).

Ordinarily the lower end of the top chord of a truss should rest on the plate. If the bottom chord is the member resting on the plate, the fastener between the top and bottom chord must be designed accordingly.

Truss Design Example

Given a building 32 feet wide with a ¼ pitch roof to be covered with aluminum roofing on purlins 2 feet on center. Using No. 2 dressed southern pine with 1,200 pounds per square inch safe fiber stress in bending (f_b), design the number one and five members of nailed trusses to be spaced 2 feet on center. The total uniform dead and live load is 38 pounds per square foot of roof surface. The modulus of elasticity (E) is 1,500,000 pounds per square inch, safe fiber stress in compression parallel with the grain (f_c) is 1,000 pounds per square inch and the safe fiber stress in tension (f_t) is 625 pounds per square inch.

Member number one.

$\text{H} = \text{pitch} \times 2 \times \text{run} = ¼ \times 32 = 8 \,\text{ft}$

$\text{L} = \text{coef.} \times \text{H} = 1.118 \times 8 = 8.94 \,\text{ft or } 107 \,\text{in.}$

$\text{P} = \text{L} \times \text{load} = 8.94 \times 38 \times 2 = 680 \,\text{lb of vertical load}$

$\text{G} = \text{coef.} \times \text{P} = -3.35 \times 680 = 2280 \,\text{lb in compression}$

$\text{W} = \text{vertical load} \times \% \text{ normal} = 680 \times 0.89 = 606 \,\text{lb normal}$
    to roof

Determine a safe size in bending.

$\text{BM} = \text{WL}/12 \text{ for a nailed truss}$

$\text{BM} = f_b\text{S}, \text{WL}/12 = f_b\text{S}$

$\text{S} = \text{WL}/12 \, f_b = 606 \times 107/(12 \times 1,200) = 4.5 \,\text{in.}^3$

$\text{d} = \sqrt{6\,\text{S}/\text{b}} = \sqrt{6 \times 4.5/1.5} = 4.24 \,\text{in. (value for b of}$
    1.5 in. was assumed)

A 2 by 4 in. is too small, choose a 2 by 6 in.
Check the 2 by 6 in. member in compression, S = 7.56 in.^{3}

With the truss rafter 1½ in. wide and the purlins 2 ft o.c.,

$l/\text{d} = 24/1½ = 16$

Check K. $\text{K} = 0.671 \sqrt{\text{E}/f_c} = 0.67 \sqrt{1.5 \times 10^6/1.0 \times 10^3} = 21.2$

$11 < l/\text{d} < \text{K}$ is found to be the situation; use the equation:

$\text{F}_c = f_c[1 - ⅓((l/\text{d})/\text{K})^4]$

$\text{F}_c = 1,000[1 - ⅓(16/21.2)^4] = 890 \,\text{lb/sq in.}$

$\text{C} = \text{F}_c\text{A} = 890 \times 8.25 = 7342 \,\text{lb}$

Checking C/G, 7,342/2,280 = 3.22, which is well over the requirement.

Check the combined effect with the interaction equation using the actual stress predicted with the 2 ft spacing.

$$\frac{G/A}{f_c} + \frac{BM/S}{f_b} \le 1.0$$

$$\frac{2280/8.25}{1,000} + \frac{(606 \times 107/12)/7.56}{1,200} = 0.276 + 0.596 = 0.872$$

A 2 by 6 in. member is safe for the 2 ft o.c. spacing.
Member number five.

Determine a safe size for the load imposed.

$T = P \times \text{coef.} \times \text{truss spacing}$

$T = 340 \times 3.0 \times 2 = 2040 \text{ lb}$

$A = T/f_t = 2040/625 = 3.26 \text{ sq in. sectional area}$

Assume a 2 in. nominal thickness (1½ in. actual) for b

$d = A/b = 3.26/1.5 = 2.17 \text{ in., choose a 2 by 3 in. bottom chord}$

It is unnecessary to use the interaction equation as there is no bending load imposed on the member.

Selecting a Truss

The width of a building, expected snow load, and the type of roofing material will all influence the selection of a truss. For spans of up to 36 feet (11 m), a single "W" truss with only two compression members is quite satisfactory. However, for spans of more than 36 feet (11 m), the use of additional members will reduce the required chord size. A king post (vertical member at the center) is desirable when a ceiling is to be installed. The pitch of a roof significantly affects the stresses in the truss members. The 5:12 ratio provides about the best balance and is recommended for long spans or heavy snow loads. A 4:12 ratio is suitable for most farm buildings in many areas, but a 3:12 should be selected only for short to medium spans in low snow-load areas.

Wide truss spacings, (e.g., 8 feet [2.44]) provide the greatest economy in labor and materials. However, a 4-foot (1.22-m) spacing allows the use of smaller size purlins and makes the installation of insulation easier when that is a requirement. Purlin spacing is largely determined by the maximum span of the roofing material that will be installed. Two feet (600 mm) is common. A 2-foot (600-mm) truss spacing is commonly chosen when a solid roof deck is being used.

Two feet (600 mm) is the maximum overhang for a truss without employing a design specifically for a long overhang.

Truss Installation

Trusses should be handled carefully during erection. Large trusses are very fragile and easily damaged by mishandling during transport or erection. They should be anchored to the supporting wall and cross braced as soon as they are placed. Trusses should not be erected during a heavy wind. While a complete, well designed roof system will withstand high winds, one or a few trusses can easily be blown over causing damage or personal injury.

Cross bracing should be installed on the first 16 feet (4.8 m) of each end and at intermediate points not more than 32 feet (9.8 m) apart. Stiffeners should be installed between the bottom chords. Figure 13-10 illustrates how the bracing and stiffeners may be installed.

While trusses are well braced and rigid themselves, it is necessary to anchor and brace them to the supporting walls in order to obtain a rigid building. Commercial anchors, plumber's tape, or wooden anchors should be used at each truss. Two or more will be needed for trusses installed on 8-foot (2.4-m) spacing over long spans. Knee braces should be installed between studs or poles and the truss every 8 to 12 feet (2.4 to 3.6 m) along a wall unless a diaphragm design or partitions make them unnecessary. Diaphragm construction is discussed in the previous chapter under pole building framing.

Figure 13-10.   Bracing for trusses.

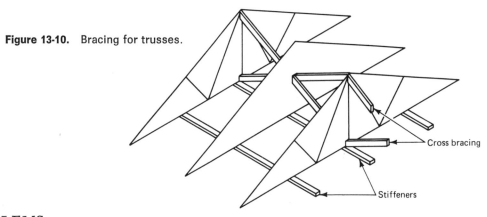

Cross bracing

Stiffeners

PROBLEMS

13.1   A 20-foot (6.1-m) wide building has a 5:12 pitch gable roof. Find the length of the rafter to the nearest eighth of an inch (5 mm). Determine the seat and ridge cut angles to the nearest tenth of a degree.

13.2 A gable roof building has a one-quarter pitch and is 24 feet (7.3 m) wide. The rafters are spaced 18 inches (450 mm) o.c. and are subject to the following vertical loads.

Snow and wind 28 lb/sq ft (137 kg/m²)
Roofing 200 lb/square (9.8 kg/m²)
Roof deck 2 lb/sq ft (9.8 kg/m²)

Use 0.89 of the total to obtain a load normal to the rafter.

a. Find the length of the rafter to the nearest eighth of an inch (5 mm).
b. Assume the rafter and tail are to be cut from the next even-numbered length. Choose a grade and size that will be adequate to support the load.

13.3 Assuming the same 24-foot (7.3-m) wide one-quarter pitch gable roof building and the same load conditions, find a safe truss spacing using 2- by 6-inch (38- by 140-mm) lumber with the following specifications:

Safe fiber stress in bending (f_b) = 1,500 lb/sq in. (10,335 kPa)
Safe fiber stress in compression (f_c) — 1,000 lb/sq in. (6890 kPa)
Modulus of Elasticity (E) = 1,500,000 lb/sq in. (10.3 × 10⁶ kPa)

Using Figure 13-9, find the forces involved in members one and five. Assume that P acts vertically and that the uniform *normal* load causing a bending force in member one is 0.89 of the vertical load.

REFERENCES

Midwest Plan Service. *Structures and Environment Handbook*. Ames, Iowa: Midwest Plan Service, 1977.

Midwest Plan Service. *Structures and Environment Handbook Supplement*. Ames, Iowa: Midwest Plan Service, 1974.

National Lumber Manufacturers' Association. *Wood Structural Design Data*. Vol. 1, 3rd ed. Washington, D.C.: National Lumber Manufacturers' Association, 1962.

Senft, John F. "Further Studies in Combined Bending and Tension Strength of Structural 2 by 4 Lumber." *Forest Products Journal*, October 1973, p. 36.

Walker, Keith M. *Applied Mechanics for Engineering Technology*. Reston, Va.: Reston Publishing Company, 1974.

Chapter Fourteen

Heat Transfer
and Solar Energy

The quality of the environment in agricultural buildings has become increasingly important as its influence on animal production, labor efficiency, and the value of products in storage has become economically more significant. The control of temperature, moisture, light, dust, and odors within buildings is essential for high production, maintenance of quality of stored produce, disease control, worker comfort, building and equipment longevity, and safety from explosion.

A knowledge of the basic factors involved in heat transfer and temperature control is necessary before a system can be designed and equipment chosen to control the environment in an agricultural building.

HEAT TRANSFER

Heat Terminology

Following is a list of definitions for terms used in dealing with heat.

Heat Heat is a form of energy. It is generally accepted that the molecules of a body are in constant motion and possess kinetic energy referred to as heat. Increased heat is indicated by more motion and energy. Heat is a measure of *total* kinetic energy of all the molecules of a body.

Temperature Temperature is the degree or intensity of heat. It is a measure of the *average* kinetic energy of the molecules of a body. Heat moves from an area of one temperature to an area of lower temperature. The difference in temperature between the two areas influences the rate of heat transfer.

Ambient temperature This is the temperature of the medium surrounding a body, for example, the room air temperature.

Btu or British Thermal Unit This is the unit of measure of quantity of heat in the customary system and is the heat required to raise the temperature of one pound of water one degree Fahrenheit.

Joule Joule is the unit of measure of quantity of heat in the SI system. One calorie of heat will raise the temperature of one gram of water one degree Celsius. This is equal to 4.186 joules (j). One kilojoule equals 0.948 Btu or 0.239 kilcalories.

Sensible heat Sensible heat is the heat which results in a *temperature change only* when a transfer takes place. It is sensible heat that is produced by a heating system, is lost through a building wall, or is removed by a refrigeration system.

Latent heat Latent heat is that heat which causes a *change in state* but no change in temperature. It is *latent heat of fusion* that is absorbed by ice as it melts at one temperature. It is *latent heat of fusion* that is removed as food is frozen for storage. In an evaporative cooler, which is a fibrous pad wet with water through which air is blown, it is *latent heat of vaporization* that is absorbed by the water as it changes to a vapor. Latent heat is given up to a dehumidifier as the vapor condenses back to a liquid. The amount of latent heat required for vaporization of water decreases with an increase in temperature. This is shown in Table 14-1 which lists the latent heat of vaporization for water at several temperatures.

Table 14-1 Latent Heat of Vaporization for Water

Degree F	Btu/lb	Degree C	kJ/kg
0	1,220	−17.8	2 838
20	1,219	−6.7	2 835
32	1,075	0.0	2 500
40	1,071	4.4	2 491
80	1,048	26.7	2 438
87	1,044	30.6	2 428
120	1,025	48.9	2 384
160	1,002	71.1	2 331
200	978	93.3	2 275
212	970	100.0	2 256

Thermal capacity   This is the amount of heat required to raise the temperature of a unit of mass of a material one degree. In customary units, one Btu will raise the temperature of one pound of water 1 degree Fahrenheit, while in metric units, one calorie will raise the temperature of one gram of water 1 degree Kelvin. However, the metric unit calorie is being abandoned in favor of the SI unit joule, and the thermal capacity of water is 4.187 joules to raise the temperature of one gram 1 degree Kelvin.

Specific heat   This is the ratio of the thermal capacity of a material to that of water. Being a ratio, specific heat has no dimensions. In customary units, the specific heat is equal to the thermal capacity numerically and may be treated as though it has the dimension Btu. However, in SI units the 4.187 joule thermal capacity of water must be used with the specific heat ratio.

Specific heat is used in determining the quantity of heat involved in heating or cooling a material. For example, specific heat would be used in determining the amount of refrigeration required to cool apples from harvest temperature down to storage temperature.

Total heat content   The total heat content of a body is greatly affected by its mass. A body with a large mass may have a considerably greater total heat than a body of lesser mass at a higher temperature. For example, the water under the ice in a lake will have more than enough heat to supply a heat pump to heat a home for an entire winter. A match, on the other hand, will burn one's finger, but the heat lasts only a few seconds. In the first case, the water, even at near freezing temperature, has tremendous heat content, while the match has very little even though the temperature is much higher. The mass makes the difference.

Heat Transfer

Heat energy moves from one place to another in one or more of the following modes—conduction, convection, or radiation.

Conduction   Heat movement by conduction involves the transfer of kinetic energy from molecule to molecule. Higher temperatures result in increased molecular activity and faster heat flow.

Conduction is the mode of heat transfer through opaque solids and across fluids in laminar flow. Although conduction also occurs in transparent solids and turbulent fluids, it is difficult to isolate that portion of the heat transfer attributable to conduction. Substances which transmit heat readily are termed thermal conductors; those that resist the flow of heat are thermal insulators.

An expression for heat flow by conduction is:

$$q = k_c \, A \, TD/t \qquad \text{Where:}$$

		Customary	*SI*
q =	rate of heat transfer by conduction	Btu/hr	(W)
k_c =	conductive heat transfer coefficient	$\dfrac{\text{Btu/(hr sq ft °F)}}{\text{in. thickness}}$	$\dfrac{\text{W/(m·°K)}}{\text{m thickness}}$
A =	surface area	sq ft	(m²)
TD =	temperature difference	°F	(°K)
t =	thickness	in.	(m)

The wide range of thermal conductivity found in various materials is illustrated by the k_c of 0.0684 (0.0098) for refrigerant 12 and 2,640 (380) for copper.

Specific equations for thermal conductance through various shapes may be found in the ASHRAE Handbook of Fundamentals (American Society of Heating, Refrigerating and Air-Conditioning Engineers, 1977). Heat transfer through nonhomogenous or composite materials will be discussed later in the chapter.

As an example of heat flow by conduction, assume a concrete tank with a wall thickness of 10 inches and a surface area of 65 square feet. If the water on the inside is 50°F and the air on the outside is 77°F, the total heat conduction through the tank wall in 10 hours, if the $k_c = 10$, will be:

$$q = k_c \, A \, TD/t$$

$$q = 10 \times 65 \times 27/10$$

$$q = 1,755 \text{ Btu/hr or } 17,550 \text{ Btu in 10 hr}$$

Convection The transfer of heat by the mass movement of a fluid is called convection. The movement may be caused by natural currents due to the variation in density for different temperatures of the material, or it can take place by the forced movement of the fluid with a fan, pump, or blower. When a measurable amount of fluid is moved from one location to another, such as transferring air in a ventilating system, the rate of heat transfer is given by the expression:

$$q = W\,S\,TD \qquad \text{Where:}$$

		Customary	SI
q =	heat transfer by convection	Btu/hr	(W)
W =	rate of fluid flow	lb/hr	(kg/s)
S =	specific heat of the fluid		
TD =	temperature difference between the fluid entering and the fluid being discharged	°F	(°K)

As an example of the rate of convected heat transfer by mass movement, assume the following: 100 pounds per hour air movement, specific heat of 0.24, and a temperature difference of 36°F. The rate of heat transfer is found by:

$$q = W\,S\,TD$$

$$q = 100 \times 0.24 \times 36$$

$$q = 864\ \text{Btu/hr}$$

In many cases however, convection involves heat transfer from a fluid through a wall into another fluid. In these cases the process becomes much more complex. Assuming that a wall surface is warmer than the surrounding air, heat travels through a thin laminar layer of air by conduction, then by conduction and convection through a buffer zone, and finally mostly by convection in a turbulent zone of air. The most important factor in the heat exchange is usually the conduction through the laminar layer of air. The following expression is used for heat transfer away from a surface by convection:

$$q = h_c\,A\,(t_s - t_f)$$

		Customary	SI
q =	heat transfer by convection	Btu/hr	(W)
h_c =	surface coefficient	Btu/(hr sq ft °F)	W/(m²·°K)
A =	surface area	sq ft	(m²)
t_f =	fluid film temperature	°F	(°C)
t_s =	surface temperature	°F	(°C)

The value for h_c is influenced by the fluid involved, the shape and surface condition of the body, the rate of fluid movement, and the temperature difference as well as other minor factors. Some idea of the order of magnitude of h_c for several situations may be obtained from the following:

Air, free convection	1 to 5	(6 to 30)
Air, forced convection	5 to 50	(30 to 300)
Water, forced convection	50 to 1,000	(300 to 6 000)
Water, boiling	500 to 10,000	(3 000 to 60 000)
Steam, condensing	1,000 to 20,000	(6 000 to 120 000)

The method for finding the value of h_c for several conditions may be found in the ASHRAE Handbook of Fundamentals (American Society of Heating, Refrigerating and Air-Conditioning Engineers, 1977).

Radiation   The transmission of energy by electromagnetic waves through space is called radiation. The emission of radiant energy occurs from the surface of bodies. The colder of two bodies will always absorb radiation until both bodies are the same temperature. The rate of exchange depends on the temperature difference and the nature of the surfaces.

When radiation strikes a surface, one or more of three things can happen. The radiation may be reflected, absorbed, or transmitted through the surface. Often it will be a combination of the three. Water, for example, reflects some of the sun's energy, absorbs some, and transmits some through to another surface. On the other hand, a dull, black surface will absorb most of the radiation from the sun, while a shiny, aluminum surface will reflect a high percentage of the radiation.

A body that has a surface capable of absorbing *all* radiation that falls on it is referred to as a black body. While there is no perfect black body, a dull, black surface very closely approximates the condition. A black body is not only the perfect absorber of radiant heat, but it is also the best emitter of radiant energy. The rate at which a black body emits energy is expressed by the equation:

$$q_b = A\,S\,T^4 \qquad \text{Where:}$$

	Customary	*SI*
q_b = rate of radiation	Btu/hr	(W)
A = surface area	sq ft	(m²)
S = black body constant	0.1713×10^{-8} Btu/(hr sq ft T)	(5.67×10^{-8} W m² T)
T = absolute temperature	°R	(°K)

Table 14-2   Temperature Scales Compared

| | Customary | | SI | |
	Fahrenheit	Rankine	Celsius	Kelvin
Boiling point of water	212	671	100	373
Freezing point of water	32	491	0	273
Absolute zero	−459	0	−273	0

Rankine = °F + 459; Kelvin = °C + 273

The closeness to which radiation approaches black body conditions depends on the nature of the surface at a given temperature. The radiation from any surface is expressed by the equation:

$$q = A E S T^4 \qquad \text{Where:}$$

$E =$ the ratio of emissivity of a surface to that of a black body

While the radiation from a single surface may be calculated with the above equation, ordinarily it is of greater interest to determine the net radiation exchange between two surfaces. When the higher temperature surface is much smaller than the other, the following simplified equation may be used:

$$q = A_1 E_1 S (T_1^4 - T_2^4) \qquad \text{Where:}$$

$A_1 E_1$ and T_1 apply to the higher temperature surface

For example, the surface of a small electric heater has one-half square foot of surface area that radiates toward the walls and ceiling of a room. The heater is 200°F and the walls are 65°F, while the emissivity ratio is 0.8. The net radiation is found as follows:

$$q = 0.5 \times 0.8 \times 0.1713 \times 10^{-8} (659^4 - 524^4)$$

$$q = 0.0685 \times 10^{-8} (1886 \times 10^8 - 754 \times 10^8)$$

$$q = 0.0685 \times 10^{-8} \times 1132 \times 10^8$$

$$q = 0.0685 \times 1132$$

$$q = 77.54 \text{ Btu/hr}$$

The value for E may vary with the temperature for some surfaces. However, on many surfaces the emissivity remains approximately constant. Such surfaces are called *gray*. Black paint is an example of a gray surface.

When radiation strikes a surface, the sum of the *absorptivity*, *transmissivity*, and *reflectivity* will equal one. In an opaque object the *trans-*

missivity will equal zero, and the *absorptivity* and *reflectivity* will equal one.

For some materials the emissivity and the absorptivity are nearly equal, while in others there is a considerable difference. Black paint is an example where they are nearly equal, the emissivity being 0.9–0.98 and the absorptivity 0.85–0.98. In contrast, aluminum varies considerably, the emissivity being 0.02–0.04 and the absorptivity 0.1–0.4. Both of these coefficients are also influenced by temperature as well as surface characteristics.

The so-called "greenhouse effect" is often discussed, although frequently with some errors in theory.

The sun has a surface temperature of approximately 100,000°F and emits about 90 percent of its radiation at wavelengths between 1 and 20×10^{-7} meters. Clear glass transmits 90 percent or more of the radiation in that range of wave lengths and most plastics do nearly as well.

When the radiation strikes an object within a greenhouse or other building, it changes to heat at a much lower temperature. Although radiation from those surfaces occurs it is at wavelengths much longer than the 4×10^{-6} meters above which glass and most plastics are opaque to heat radiation. The energy is effectively trapped within the glass or plastic enclosure. An exception is polyethylene which still passes considerable energy at this wavelength.

It should be remembered, however, that heat may be carried to the glass or plastic by radiation and convection and then be lost through them by conduction. As heat travels through these materials by conduction, small amounts of energy are radiated from their outer surface, although most is carried away by convection.

Combined Heat Transfer

While there are occasions when it is necessary to study heat transfer by a single mode, in the field of agricultural buildings it is the total heat transfer which is usually of interest. The transfer of heat from a warm air space through a solid medium to a cooler air space (as in the case of heat loss through a barn wall in winter) involves all methods of heat transfer including conduction, convection, and radiation. The wall may be constructed of several materials, each having a different resistance to heat flow. In addition, the surface layers of air on either side of the wall and the air space within the wall will resist the flow of heat.

With a knowledge of the heat-transfer resistance coefficients (R), the thickness of the materials from which a wall or ceiling is made, and the area of the surface, it is not difficult to find the heat transfer for each degree of temperature difference between the two surfaces.

In determining the heat transfer through either an homogenous or composite structure, the following terms are used.

		Customary	*SI*
R =	resistance to heat flow through a material	hr sq ft °F/Btu	(m²·°K/W)
R_t =	resistance to heat flow through a composite structure	hr sq ft °F/Btu	(m²·°K/W)
U =	thermal conductivity of a composite structure	Btu/(hr sq ft °F)	(W/(m²·°K))
U =	$1/R_t$, the reciprocal of total resistance		
k =	thermal conductivity per unit of thickness of a material	$\dfrac{\text{Btu/(hr sq ft °F)}}{\text{in. thickness}}$	$\left[\dfrac{W/(m^{2}·°K)}{\text{m thickness}}\right]$
C =	thermal conductivity of a single material in the thickness used	Btu/(hr sq ft °F)	(W/(m²·°K))
f =	conductivity of an air surface layer		
a =	conductivity of an air space		

To find the heat loss through a wall or ceiling section, it is first necessary to sum the R values for the layers of materials, including the air surface layer and any air spaces. The U value may then be found from $U = 1/R_t$. The R value for commercial insulation is often given on the package.

It should be noted that *only resistances* and not conductivities *may be added.*

The heat-transfer coefficients (R) of different materials vary according to the density and moisture content of the material. The R, or insulation values, for some of the more commonly used building and insulating materials are given in Table 14-3. U values for composite walls and ceilings may be calculated from these values using the procedure shown in Figure 14-1. However, for convenience, the U values for a number of wall and ceiling constructions are given in Table 14-4.

The heat transfer through a wall or ceiling may be determined with the following equation:

$$q = A\ U\ TD \qquad \text{Where:}$$

		Customary	SI
q =	rate of heat transfer	Btu/hr	(W)
A =	surface area	sq ft	(m²)
U =	conductivity	Btu/(hr sq ft °F)	W/(m²·°K)
TD =	temperature difference	°F	(°K)

The method for determining the conductivity (U) for a wall is illustrated with the example in Figure 14-1. The values for R are found in Table 14-3. The composite wall consists of the following layers. Outside air layer, one-half-inch plywood, an air space bounded by dull surfaces, 2 inches of polystyrene, one-half-inch gypsum board, and an inside air layer.

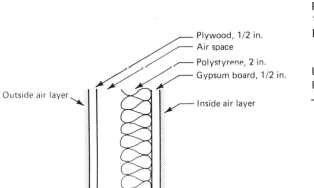

Layer	R
Outside air layer	0.17
½ in. plywood	0.62
Air space (dull surfaces)	0.94
Polystyrene (5 x 2 in.)	10.00
½ in. gypsum board	0.45
Inside air layer	0.61
Total (R_t)	12.79

$$U = 1/R_t = 1/12.79$$
$$U = 0.078 \text{ Btu/(hr sq ft °F)}$$

Plywood, 1/2 in.
Air space
Polystyrene, 2 in.
Gypsum board, 1/2 in.
Outside air layer
Inside air layer

Figure 14-1.   Heat transmission through a composite wall.

Table 14-3   Resistance to Heat Flow

Material	Thickness in inches	Customary Units		SI Units	
		per inch thickness	thickness as listed	per meter thickness	thickness as listed
		h·ft²·F/Btu·in.	h·ft²·F/Btu	(m·K)/W	(m²·K)/W
Air spaces					
Dull surfaces—					
wall	3/4		0.94		0.17
ceiling	3/4		0.77		0.14
One aluminum foil,					
2 spaces—wall	3/4		4.02		0.71
ceiling	3/4		2.7		0.48
Two aluminum foils,					
3 spaces—wall	3/4		6.79		1.2
ceiling	3/4		4.36		0.76

Note: Space dimensions, temperature difference, temperature levels, direction, dust, and position all influence the above values.

Material	Thickness in inches	per inch thickness	thickness as listed	per meter thickness	thickness as listed
Glass or rockwool	3-3½		11.0		1.94
Glass or rockwool	6-7		22.0		3.87
Expanded mica	1	2.27		15.73	
Shavings	1	2.22		15.39	
Polystyrene—					
molded beads	1	3.57		24.74	
extruded	1	5.00		34.65	
Polyurethane—					
extruded	1	6.25		43.82	
Urea formaldehyde—					
foamed	1	5.4		37.86	
Cellulose fiber	1	3.7		25.64	
Insulating board	½		1.32		0.31
Insulating board	25/32		2.06		0.36
Surfaces—					
Still air—inside			0.61		0.11
15 mph—outside			0.17		0.03
Fir or pine lumber	3/4		0.94		0.17
Fir or pine lumber	3½		4.35		0.75
Bevel siding	½		0.81		0.14
Plywood	¼		0.31		0.05
Plywood	½		0.62		0.11
Plywood	3/4		0.93		0.16
Hardboard, tempered	1	1.00		6.93	
Particleboard,					
medium density	1	1.06		7.35	
Gypsum board	½		0.45		0.08
Asbestos—					
cement board	⅛		0.03		0.005

Aluminum siding	—		0.61		0.11
Concrete and stone	1	0.08		0.55	
Concrete block	4		0.71		0.13
Concrete block	8		1.11		0.20
Conoroto block	12		1.28		0.23
Soil, sandy loam or clay, 10-20% moist.	1	0.1		0.69	

(From Handbook of Fundamentals, American Society of Heating, Refrigerating and Air-Conditioning Engineers, 1977)

Table 14-4   Heat Transmission and Resistance Coefficients for Some Building Components

	Customary Units		SI Units	
	U	R	U	R
Component	Btu/h ft² F	h ft² F/Btu	W/m²K	m²K/W
Glass, single pane (winter), vert.	1.10	0.91	6.25	0.16
Glass, single pane (winter), horiz.	1.23	0.81	6.98	0.14
double pane, 3/16 in. space	0.62	1.61	3.52	0.28
storm windows, 1/4 in. space	0.50	2.00	2.84	0.35
Plastic sheet, 0.125 in. thick (fiberglass)	1.06	0.94	6.02	0.17
double sheet, 1/2 in. space	0.81	1.23	4.6	0.22
Plastic film, .004 in. (polyethylene)	1.25	0.80	7.1	0.14
double film, 3/4 in. space	0.80	1.25	4.54	0.22
Glass block, 8x8x4 in.	0.56	1.79	3.18	0.32
Door, solid, 1 in. bare	0.64	1.56	3.63	0.27
panel, 1/2 in. bare	0.71	1.4	4.03	0.25
solid, 1 in. w/storm door	0.30	3.33	1.70	0.59
panel, 1/2 in. w/storm door	0.32	3.17	1.82	0.56
Concrete blocks, 8 in. not filled	0.53	1.89	3.01	0.33
12 in. not filled	0.49	2.04	2.78	0.36
8 in. filled	0.39	2.56	2.21	0.45
12 in. filled	0.34	2.94	1.93	0.52
Concrete wall, 6 in.	0.79	1.26	4.49	0.22
Concrete wall, 6 in., polyurethane 1" asbestos-cement board, 1/8"	0.13	7.54	0.75	1.33
Sheet metal wall	1.28	0.78	7.27	0.14
Plywood wall, 1/2 in. outside	0.71	1.40	4.03	0.25
Plywood, 1/2 in. outside & inside	0.34	2.96	1.93	0.52
Plywood, 1/2 in. outside, insulation, R=11, plywood, 1/2 in. inside	0.08	13.02	0.44	2.29
Sheet metal, insulation, R=11, plywood, 1/2 in.	0.08	12.40	0.45	2.18

Total Building Heat Loss

To find the total heat loss from a building, it is necessary to find the U value for each composite structure (wall, ceiling, window, door, and floor) and then multiply each by the area and the difference between the inside and outside temperatures. The heat loss for each of the parts may then be added to obtain the total.

The method for obtaining the total heat loss (q) from a building is illustrated with the following example. It is assumed that the U value for each part has been determined previously. The inside temperature is 60°F and the outside temperature is as listed. The floor and ceiling are isolated from outside temperatures.

Part	U	Area sq ft	Outside Temp	Temp Diff	q
Ceiling	0.05	1,000	5	55	0.05 × 1000 × 55 = 2,750
Wall	0.10	900	0	60	0.10 × 900 × 60 = 5,400
Windows	1.13	40	0	60	1.13 × 40 × 60 = 2,712
Door	1.00	100	0	60	1.00 × 100 × 60 = 6,000
Floor	0.50	1,000	50	10	0.50 × 1000 × 10 = 5,000
					Total 21,862

The total heat lost from the building is 21,862 Btu/hr.

To calculate with a high degree of accuracy the heat transfer through a wall framed with wood, it is necessary to determine the coefficient of conductivity (U) through the framing members as well as through the wall between the framing members. A weighted average may then be taken by multiplying each U value by the width through which it occurs, adding the two, and dividing by the total width of the section.

For example, assume that a wall has 2-inch studs spaced 16 inches on center. It is found that the U value is 0.5 through the studs and 0.1 between the studs. The average U will be $(0.5 \times 2 + 0.1 \times 14)/16 = 0.15$.

Walls, floors, or ceilings framed with metal of an irregular cross section present a special problem in determining heat transfer. A detailed method and example may be found in the ASHRAE Handbook of Fundamentals (American Society of Heating, Refrigerating and Air-Conditioning Engineers, 1977). In brief, the method involves adding the UA for various sections through which the heat flows in parallel, and adding 1/UA for sections through which the heat flows in series. "A" is equal to the surface area.

Constructing a Temperature Gradient

The construction of a temperature gradient on the cross-section diagram of a wall illustrates the heat movement through the wall and emphasizes the effect of insulating materials. The gradient diagram also serves as a starting point in checking for condensation on wall surfaces and within walls, a topic that will be discussed in Chapter 15.

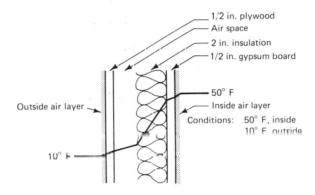

Layer (left side)	R	Deg/ Unit R_t	Temp. Diff.	Plane Temp. (left side)
Outer air layer	0.17	× 3.18 =	0.54	10.00
Plywood, ½ in.	0.63	× 3.18 =	2.00	10.54
Air space, dull surface	0.91	× 3.18 =	2.89	12.54
Polystyrene (5 x 2 in.)	10.00	× 3.18 =	31.77	15.43
Gypsum board, ½ in.	0.27	× 3.18 =	0.86	47.20
Inner air layer	0.61	× 3.18 =	1.94	48.06
Room air temp.	—		—	50.00
Totals	12.59		40.00	
40°/12.59 = 3.18 degrees per unit of R_t				

Figure 14-2. Temperature gradient across a wall.

The values t_1, t_2 . . . t_n, found with the following formulas, may be plotted on a cross-section diagram of the wall to show the temperature gradient. Figures 14-1 and 14-2 illustrate the procedure.

$$R_t = \Sigma R$$

$$Z = TD/R_t$$

$$t_1 = R_1 \times Z + t_0$$

$$t_2 = R_2 \times Z + t_1$$

$t_3 \ldots t_n$ similarly   Where:

$t_0 = $ the outside temperature

$t_1 = $ surface temperature of first layer

$t_2 \ldots t_n = $ succeeding temperatures

$R_t = $ sum of $R_1, R_2, \ldots R_n$

$Z = $ degrees per unit of R

$R = $ resistance to heat flow of a layer of wall material

Insulation

Buildings that are to be kept warm either by animal heat or supplementary heat will require that insulation be installed in the walls and ceilings to achieve efficient use of the heat. Insulating materials have a high thermal resistance that conserves heat in cold weather and reduces heat gain in hot weather. A dead air space up to three-quarters of an inch in thickness has a significant insulating value. Beyond that thickness, convection currents within the wall may actually increase the rate of heat transfer unless the currents are interrupted by the use of insulation.

How much insulation?   Because of the great difference in insulating values of the materials available, the amount of insulation installed should be expressed as R_t and not as inches or millimeters. The R_t level chosen for a building will depend on several factors:

1.   The climatic zone and the design temperature used. For example, the maximum heat loss from a 55°F (13°C) dairy stable in central Minnesota may be nearly twice as much as in Delaware. Consequently, nearly double the R value may be required in the Minnesota stable.

2.   The use of the building and the inside design temperature. A livestock shelter which must be ventilated to remove moisture but which depends on the animals as the only source of heat, will require an R value adequate to conserve the heat required for ventilation.

3. The cost of heating or cooling a building. When buildings are heated or refrigerated artificially, the fixed costs of insulation are charged off against savings in the cost of providing the heat or cooling for the building. High energy costs often justify installing the maximum amount of insulation that can be physically put into place. For example, wall cavities may be completely filled and ceilings filled to the maximum level that will still allow the necessary ventilation.

Choosing an insulation   Having determined how much insulating effect is required for a particular application, it is then necessary to choose an insulation that is suitable. Most insulating materials are bulky, lightweight, and porous, the numerous air pockets providing the insulating capabilities. Manufactured insulation is available in a variety of forms including reflective and fill types, batts, blankets, fiber and plastic panels, and foamed-in-place plastics. These insulating products are made from various materials including fiberglass, rockwool, mica, cellular glass, polystyrene, polyurethane, and urea formaldehyde. Some insulating materials are available in more than one form. No one material or form can possibly be best suited for all applications. A thorough knowledge of the characteristics of each material will allow an appropriate choice for each installation.

Some examples of the suitability of a type of insulation to an application are:

1.   Insulation for an existing wall may be limited to a fill type that can be poured or blown into the wall, a rigid type which can be cemented to a surface or a foamed-in-place plastic material.

2.   Blanket or batt material is often the least expensive to place within a new wall. It is easy to install and does not settle. Batts are designed to fit 16- or 24-inch (400- or 600-mm) stud spacings.

3.   Insulation placed between ceiling joists may be either batt or loose fill depending on cost.

4.   The insulating value of materials with shiny surfaces increases in effectiveness as the temperature rises. For example, aluminum roofing is much more effective in insulating against summer sun than against winter heat loss. To be effective, the shiny surfaces must not be in direct contact with any other material, but should abut an air space which cuts heat loss by conduction and convection.

5. Rigid insulation may have adequate structural strength to be installed under a concrete floor or a roof surface.

6. Some rigid insulating materials may be used as wall or ceiling surfaces. The saving in labor and cost of other surfacing material may make an otherwise expensive product the lowest cost when installed for the dual role.

7. Some materials are very porous and readily allow water-vapor transmission while others may be completely impervious. The latter may not need a vapor seal, while the former will need either an excellent vapor seal or good ventilation across its cold surface.

8. Although a number of insulation materials are classified as "self-extinguishing," "fire retardant," or "nonburning," serious flash fires can result under certain circumstances. For example, the asphalt-attached paper found on some batt or blanket material may burn rapidly even though the insulation itself does not. Also, some foam insulations, when exposed to high temperatures and restricted ventilation, may fail to live up to their billing of being "nonburning." It is advisable to check on local building codes and with an insurance company before making a final decision about the type of insulation.

Some of the more common insulating materials and their characteristics include:

1. Fiberglass and rockwool are of medium insulating value, very permeable and fireproof. They are available as loose fill, batts, and blankets, and fiberglass is available in low-density panels. The asphalt-attached vapor barrier found on some batts and blankets is flammable.

2. Cotton, cellulose, and shredded bark are of medium insulating value, permeable, and available as fill or blankets. They are usually treated to improve fire resistance and may have integral vapor barriers.

3. Shavings, sawdust, and straw are of rather low insulating value and have an affinity for moisture and vermin. It is usually poor economics to use them except for temporary purposes.

4. Expanded mica is of rather low insulating value, but it is inert and sometimes the only fill insulation that can be poured into a wall, particularly masonry-block walls.

5. Fiber insulating boards are of rather low insulating value but may be suitable for a wall or ceiling surface while at the same time offering some resistance to heat flow. In the thickness available for sheathing, they offer more insulation than plywood or lumber.

6. Cellular glass has a rather low insulating value but is impermeable and has sufficient structural strength for use under concrete floors that are to be heavily loaded.

7. Expanded polystyrene is available in extruded form or as molded beads. The extruded form has better-than-average insulating value and is relatively impermeable to water vapor. The molded bead form has a lower insulating value and is more permeable. Extruded polystyrene may be cemented to masonry walls, installed under concrete floors, and used for ceiling and wall surfaces in protected areas. However, the material is of varying flame resistance, and, if left exposed, care should be taken that code requirements are met.

8. Expanded polyurethane is available as extruded panels or it may be foamed in place. It has excellent insulating value and is non-permeable. It is often surfaced with paper, polyethylene, or aluminum. That which is not surfaced is prone to a decrease in insulating value. Its fire resistance is variable and it is usually recommended that the insulation be covered.

9. Urea formaldehyde is usually foamed in place. It has good insulating value and is reasonably flame resistant. However, it releases irritating fumes for several days after installation and has a tendency to shrink over a period of time.

In addition to the type of insulation for the application and the particular characteristics of the various insulating materials, the last and perhaps most important factor to consider is the cost per unit of R.

Specific and Latent Heat

Specific heat and latent heat values are usually used in relation to problems dealing with the heating or refrigeration of agricultural products. It is necessary to use the specific heat values for a product in finding the heating or cooling load imposed by processing or storage. If either the processing or storage involves a change of state, the latent heat values must also be considered. Specific heat may also be used in solving ventilation problems.

The following expressions would be used to find the total cooling load imposed on a refrigeration system in cooling a product from above freezing temperature to a below freezing temperature:

$$q_1 = W \times c_i \times (t_1 - t_f)$$

$$q_2 = W \times L$$

$$q_3 = W \times c_j \times (t_f - t_2)$$

$$q_t = q_1 + q_2 + q_3 \qquad \text{Where:}$$

		Customary	SI
q_t =	total heat removed	Btu	(kJ)
W =	weight of product	lb	(kg)
c_i =	specific heat above freezing		
c_j =	specific heat below freezing		
L =	latent heat of fusion	Btu/lb	(kJ/kg)
t_1, t_f, & t_2 =	initial, freezing, and final temperatures	°F	(°C)

Detailed values for specific and latent heats for many materials may be found in the ASHRAE Handbook of Fundamentals (American Society of Heating, Refrigerating and Air-Conditioning Engineers, 1977). A few representative values are given in Table 14-5.

Table 14-5   Specific and Latent Heats

Material	Boiling Temp		Specific Heat		Latent Heat of Vaporization	
	Degree F	Degree C	Above-Below Boiling		Btu/lb	kJ/kg
Water	212	100	0.49	1.0	970	2256
Air	−317	−194	0.24			
Refrig 12	−21.6	−29.4	0.14	0.25	75	177

Material	Freezing Temp		Specific Heat		Latent Heat of Fusion	
	Degree F	Degree C	Above-Below Freezing		Btu/lb	kJ/kg
Water	32	0.0	1.0	0.49	144	335
Milk	31	−0.6	0.93	0.49	124	288
Fruit	28	−2.2	0.86	0.45	122	284
Eggs	27	−2.8	0.76	0.40	100	233
Potatoes	29	−1.7	0.82	0.43	111	258
Beef	29	−1.7	0.74	0.40	100	233
Poultry	27	−2.8	0.79	0.37	106	247

| Cheese | 17 | −8.3 | 0.64 | 0.36 | 79 | 184 |
| Peas | 30 | −1.1 | 0.79 | 0.42 | 106 | 247 |

Material	Specific Heat
Concrete	0.16
Pine	0.67
Steel	0.12
Glass	0.20
Corn	0.25

The specific heat ratio is based on water. One Btu is the heat required to raise the temperature of 1 pound of water 1°F. In SI, 4.186 kilojoules is the heat required to raise the temperature of 1 kg of water 1°K.

As an example of the total heat to be removed from a product in reducing the temperature from field level to storage level, it is assumed that 1,000 pounds of peas with a field temperature of 65°F are to be frozen and reduced to a storage temperature of −15°F. Using the values in Table 14-5, the amount of heat to be removed is determined as follows:

$$q_1 = 1,000 \times 0.79 \times (65 - 30) = 27,650$$
$$q_2 = 1,000 \times 106 = 106,000$$
$$q_3 = 1,000 \times 0.42 \times (30 - (-15)) = 18,900$$
$$q_t = q_1 + q_2 + q_3 = 152,550 \text{ Btu}$$

SOLAR ENERGY

Background

The use of solar energy dates back to well before the beginning of recorded history. Archimedes is reported to have burned the Roman fleet in 212 BC by setting up a barrage of mirrors along the harbor walls to direct the beams of sunlight to a common point on the fleet (Williams, 1974). Whether this actually happened or not is academic. Of more significance is the fact that from the very beginning of the practice of agriculture, farmers have made use of solar energy in the greatest collectors of all, their crops. The sun has also been used for centuries to dry meat, fish, and fruit and even today examples of sun-dried products can be found throughout the world.

Investigation into the uses of solar energy between the 16th and 20th centuries was directed primarily at concentrating the sun's flux for high-temperature applications. Experimental solar furnaces for melting metals and solar-power steam engines captured the imagination of scientists. New interest in the utilization of solar energy was stimulated after World War II and solar heating became technologically feasible but remained economically prohibitive.

The real thrust into all phases of solar energy development came in the mid-1970s when the fossil fuel shortage and the accompanying rise in price, together with the increasing public concern over the safety of nuclear reactors, made it apparent that an alternative energy source was essential. Along with a multitude of ideas for harnessing and using the sun's clean energy were many related to its use in agriculture.

The purpose here is to look at the nature of solar energy and describe briefly some of the applications to agriculture that show promise. This discussion will by necessity be limited, as a comprehensive treatment would be voluminous. There has in fact, been more published about solar energy in the last decade than on any other subject covered in this book.

Solar Flux

Solar flux refers to the energy of the sun reaching the earth. While solar energy has high thermodynamic potential and is available in enormous quantities, it is at the same time both dilute and undependable. Its abundance is indicated by the total flux of 6469 megajoules that strike each square meter of the United States each year. The total is truly astronomical when multiplied by the area of the country. Indeed it is estimated that the sunlight falling on the earth could theoretically provide 100,000 times the total energy output of all existing power stations.

The fact that solar flux is dilute is illustrated by the same value of 6469 MJ. Divided by the 8,760 hours in a year, the average flux is only 0.738 MJ/m²h. That amount of flux would take 37 hours to produce the energy equal to that generated by 1 liter of fuel oil.

The dependability of solar energy is influenced to a great extent by geographic area. A portion of the northeastern United States receives less than 2,200 hours of sunlight per year. In contrast, practically all of the Southwest receives in excess of 3,400 hours of sunlight per year. Average solar energy over large areas is a misleading figure, however, due to seasonal and geographic variations. It is the day-to-day fluctuations in weather conditions, particularly periods of cloudiness, that make the sun's energy an undependable source of heat.

Solar Constant

The solar flux reaching a point normal (perpendicular) to the outer surface of the earth's atmosphere is given as 434.8 Btu/(sq ft hr) (4.587 MJ/ m²h). Due to the effect of the earth's atmosphere, the energy that reaches the earth's surface is given as 318 Btu/(sq ft hr) (3.61 MJ/m²h). In essence, the most energy available is approximately 300 Btu/(sq ft hr) (3.4 MJ/m²h) and that will occur only at a location where the sun's rays are perpendicular to the earth's surface.

The amount of energy that is actually available for collection is affected by a number of factors.

1.   *Latitude and season:* Because the earth is tilted 23.5 degrees on its axis in relation to the sun, there is a continuous change in the angle with which the sun's rays strike the earth. In the latitudes between 23.5 degrees North and 23.5 degrees South there will be two days each year in which the solar flux is perpendicular, while at latitudes farther north and farther south, the flux is never perpendicular.

2.   *Weather:* The frequency of cloudy weather has a strong influence on the actual radiation reaching the earth's surface. The bands marked by 20 degrees to 30 degrees North and South are relatively dry and receive approximately 90 percent of the incident radiation. The great deserts of the world fall within these bands. Both nearer the equator and nearer the poles there is much more cloudiness and considerably lower average solar energy actually striking the earth.

Within general climatic zones, there are local variations of frequency and density of cloud cover due to topography, bodies of water, and prevailing winds. Consequently, it is only by measurements and records that the solar radiation for a particular location may be predicted.

Collection

The type of device used to collect solar energy depends primarily on the application. Flat-plate collectors produce temperatures up to approximately 200°F (93°C) and are used mainly for heating water and buildings. Focusing collectors are used to obtain high temperatures by aiming a parabolic reflector at the sun and focusing the sun's reflected rays on a small surface where the energy is concentrated to produce a very high temperature. Another type of focusing collector is the parabolic cylinder which reflects the energy to a pipe parallel to its axis,

Table 14-6   Average Daily Solar Radiation on a Horizontal Surface
(megajoules/square meter)

Location	Lat.	Jan.	Feb.	Mar.	April	May	June	July	Aug.	Sept.	Oct.	Nov.	Dec.
Boston, MA	42°22'	5.7	8.4	12.1	15.4	20.1	21.1	21.1	17.8	14.4	10.2	7.2	5.0
Ithaca, N.Y.	42°27'	4.9	8.5	12.2	15.0	20.2	23.0	23.0	19.7	15.0	10.4	5.3	4.2
Ottawa, ON	45°20'	6.1	9.7	14.2	18.2	21.1	23.6	23.2	19.9	15.0	9.4	5.2	4.6
Columbus, OH	40°00'	5.5	8.5	12.6	16.8	20.9	(24.0)	23.1	17.8	13.5	10.4	5.4	4.9
Madison, WI	43°08'	6.4	9.2	14.0	16.5	19.8	(23.0)	23.2	19.7	16.4	11.3	6.3	5.6
Lincoln, NE	40°51'	8.1	10.8	14.7	18.0	21.0	23.1	22.8	21.6	17.5	13.8	8.8	7.3
Winnipeg, MB	49°54'	5.5	9.5	15.4	18.6	21.6	22.2	24.1	20.0	13.5	8.7	5.0	3.9
Great Falls, MT	47°29'	5.9	9.9	15.5	18.4	22.4	24.7	27.0	22.5	17.4	11.2	6.5	4.8
Seattle, WA	47°36'	2.9	5.4	10.4	15.6	18.9	19.6	20.5	18.3	12.8	7.2	3.7	2.5
Davis, CA	38°33'	6.8	10.7	17.1	22.2	26.9	29.7	29.1	25.9	21.1	14.6	9.0	6.2
Tucson, AZ	32°07'	13.3	16.5	—	27.6	—	29.5	26.0	24.7	24.1	18.6	15.0	12.8
Fort Worth, TX	32°50'	10.6	13.6	18.1	20.7	23.9	27.6	26.0	25.1	21.3	16.7	13.0	10.4
Columbia, MO	38°58'	7.4	10.7	14.9	18.5	13.6	24.1	24.4	21.1	19.2	13.6	9.5	6.7
Apalachicola, FL	29°45'	12.6	15.6	18.8	23.1	25.7	24.9	22.4	21.7	19.3	17.5	14.1	11.1
Greensboro, NC	36°05'	8.4	11.7	15.0	19.9	22.5	23.9	23.1	20.5	17.2	13.6	10.3	7.8

Extracted from Liu, B.Y.H. and Jordan, R.C.: Predicting Long-Term Average Performance of Flat Plate Solar Collectors, Solar Energy, Vol. 7, p. 53, 1963.

producing temperatures higher than those obtained from a flat plate but lower than those from a parabolic concentrator. The focusing collectors require costly, sophisticated equipment to track the sun in order to obtain the maximum solar flux at all times. A third type of collector, the photovoltaic cell, which converts sunlight directly into electricity, is still in the experimental stage.

While the flat-plate type is the simplest, it is the most important solar collector because of the broad range of potential applications. Basically most flat-plate collectors (Figure 14-3) consist of a wood or metal frame enclosing a black surface to absorb the heat with a circulating fluid, usually air or water, to carry the heat away. To prevent heat loss and improve effiicency, one or more transparent covers is usually placed over the collector surface and heavy insulation installed behind the plate and around the edges.

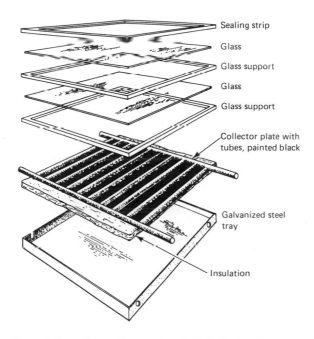

Sealing strip

Glass

Glass support

Glass

Glass support

Collector plate with tubes, painted black

Galvanized steel tray

Insulation

Figure 14-3. Typical-flat plate collector (exploded view). (*Courtesy* Cooperative Extension Service, Cornell University)

Regardless of the type of collector used, the amount of energy collected at a given time and place is directly related to the surface area of the collector. Although energy may be concentrated and temperatures raised, the total energy cannot be greater than that which strikes the collector surface. On the other hand, the design of the collector influences how effective it is in turning solar radiation into useful energy.

Collector Efficiency

The two types of parabolic collectors mentioned may reach 50 to 75 percent efficiency. Although flat-plate collectors can do as well theoretically, few of them reach these levels in actual use. Operating efficiencies range from below 25 percent to more than 50 percent depending on design and method of operation.

The efficiency of a collector is expressed as the percentage of energy reaching the surface of the collector that is retained and carried off by the circulating fluid. The efficiency of a flat-plate collector is affected by its orientation, the covering, the absorbing surface, the temperature at which it operates, and the insulation of the case.

To receive the maximum radiation, a collector should be set at an angle perpendicular to the sun's rays. Of the total amount striking the collector, some will be reflected from the transparent cover surface, some will be reflected from the absorbing surface back through the cover, some will be lost by convection through the cover, and some by conduction through the back of the case. The balance is carried away by the heat transfer medium to the place of use or to a storage.

Collector designs have been developed that minimize these losses. Antireflective coatings allow greater transmission through the cover to the absorbing surface. Certain spectral coatings for collector plates have been developed that have very high absorbtivity at wavelengths in the solar part of the spectrum but very low emissivity in the longer wavelength infrared portion of the spectrum. While these add to the cost of the collector, they are justified where relatively high operating temperatures are necessary. Double or triple covers reduce convection losses and a high R value reduces conduction losses through the insulated back.

To illustrate the effect of temperature on the efficiency of a flat-plate collector, let us assume that due to heavy cloud cover the collector is at ambient temperature; there will be no heat transfer either to or away from the collector. When the sun comes out, the collector temperature will rise and continue to rise until it reaches the balanced temperature situation of losing as much heat as it gains. The efficiency at this point will be zero. However, if water is circulated through the plate coils, the collector will be cooled and less heat will be lost. Some will be carried away for use. If the temperature of the plate could be reduced to ambient level, only a small radiant loss would remain and the efficiency would be very high. The temperature of the heat transfer medium (water or air) is often determined by the requirements of the storage or the use

Table 14-7   Ratio of Solar Energy Received at Fixed Position Flat-Plate Collectors to that of a Horizontal Surface

Latitude	45°	30°	45°	30°	45°	30°	45°	30°	45°	30°
Collector angle	0°	0°	45°	30°	60°	15°	90°	90°	*	*
Summer	1	1	1	0.84	0.76	0.66	0.34	0.15	1.48	1.35
Equinox	1	1	1.34	1.14	1.39	1.17	0.97	0.64	1.41	1.43
Winter	1	1	2.37	1.59	2.46	1.63	2.49	1.45	1.70	1.54

* North-south oriented horizontal collector that tracks the sun from east to west.

to which the heat will be put. For example, operating a collector at 50°F (10°C) is ineffective if the purpose is to warm 50°F (10°C) well water. For this situation a higher operating temperature would be required and the loss in efficiency would be unavoidable.

A combined solar collector-heat pump system makes the use of much lower collector temperatures possible. Although higher efficiencies result, the high initial cost discourages the use of such a dual system.

Absorber Plates and Transfer Mediums

Either air or water may be used as a transfer medium. The choice is often based on the type of storage or the use to which the energy will be put. For example, if the solar collector is designed to supplement the existing water-heating system, water would be the appropriate medium. On the other hand, if warmed air is desired for a drying process, it would be logical to use air as the medium.

Absorber plates that are painted black absorb about 95 percent of the radiation. Several methods of removing that heat are used. Collectors using water as a medium may be designed so that a thin layer of water sweeps down the open surface picking up the heat as it moves. Or they may be designed so that the water flows through tubes bonded to a metal plate. Either metal or plastic can be used satisfactorily for an open collector surface. When the water is carried in tubes, metal plates are desirable because of their high conductivity. Copper has the highest conductivity and the tubes are easily bonded to the plate. Aluminum also has good conductivity, but it is difficult to bond the tubes. Steel is the least expensive and has the lowest conductivity.

Air-medium collectors range from black-surfaced ducts through which the air is moved, to various finned-metal surfaces under a single or double transparent cover.

Glass, fiberglass reinforced plastic, or plastic films may be used for covers. Glass transmits over 90 percent of the energy and has a long life. Fiberglass reinforced plastic transmits about 80 percent of the energy and if Tedlar-coated will last more than 10 years. (Tedlar is manufactured by the E.I. DuPont de Nemours Company.) Ultraviolet-inhibited polyethylene and copolymer plastics transmit in excess of 90 percent of the energy, but they also lose an appreciable amount through reradiation. In addition they cannot be expected to last more than one to two years. Collector cases are usually made of wood, plastic, or metal, but regardless of the material from which they are constructed, provision must be made for expansion and contraction of glass covers. Plastic covers are not as critical in this respect.

Plastic-Duct Collector

When using solar energy for a drying operation, a plastic duct can serve as a variation of a flat-plate collector. A single layer black polyethylene duct, usually 3 feet (1 m) or more in diameter is kept expanded by the air which is blown through it. If a temperature rise of only 5 to 11°F (3 to 6°C) is adequate for the air being moved, the single-layer duct provides a simple and inexpensive collector. If, however, a greater temperature rise is required, the use of a clear plastic, air-inflated cover over the black duct will give both the higher temperature rise to the air and an improved efficiency (Figure 14-4).

Figure 14-4. Solar heated grain dryer using a duct collector.

Orientation of Flat-Plate Collectors

To explain how the most desirable orientation for a collector is determined, it is first necessary to understand how the sun's position is indicated. The two angles that indicate the position of the sun in respect to the earth are the azimuth and the altitude. The *azimuth* is the horizontal angle of the sun in relation to the true north meridian. In the morning it will be measured in an easterly direction and in the afternoon in a westerly direction. The *altitude* is the vertical angle the sun makes with the horizontal plane at the earth's surface.

Both the azimuth and the altitude of the sun are affected by the latitude of a location, the date, and the hour of the day. At the greater latitudes, the azimuth angles have a much greater daily range, while the altitude angles will be lower throughout the year. Table 14-8 gives winter and summer azimuth and altitude angles for latitudes of thirty to fifty degrees north.

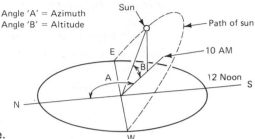

Angle 'A' = Azimuth
Angle 'B' = Altitude

Figure 14-5.   Azimuth and altitude.

Table 14-8   Azimuth and Altitude Angles

	30°N		35°N		40°N		45°N		50°N	
Winter	Azi	Alt	Azi	Alt	Azi	Alt	Azi	Alt	Azi	Alt
Noon	180°	36½°	180°	31½°	180°	26½°	180°	21½°	180°	16½°
10:A&2:P	148½	29	149¼	25	150½	20½	151½	16	152	12
8:A&4:P	126	11½	126	8½	127	5½	127½	2½	128½	0
Summer										
Noon	180	83½	180	78½	180	73½	180	68½	180	63½
10:A&2:P	83½	62½	105½	61½	114	60	121½	57½	127½	54½
8:A&4:P	81½	36½	85½	37	89	37½	93	37½	97	37

The location of the sun's rays at any latitude and moment of time is described by the combination of the azimuth and altitude angles. Ideally a flat plate collector should always be normal to the sun's radiation, that is, it should be perpendicular to the azimuth and the altitude angles. This can be accomplished by inclining and turning the plate to match the azimuth and altitude throughout the day. Since this would require expensive equipment, most collectors are installed to face within 5 degrees of true South and are often inclined to be normal to the average position of the sun during the period of the year when the solar energy is most needed. For winter use only, the most efficient collector angle is equal to the latitude plus 15 to 20 degrees. For year-round use, the latitude angle alone is satisfactory. For summer use only, the latitude minus 10 degrees is reasonable and for fall use, the latitude minus 5 degrees is a reasonable average. For example, if a collector is installed at 40 degrees N and is to be used only for summertime water heating, the rule of thumb would indicate 30 degrees (40 minus 10) as the best average angle for the collector. Looking at Table 14-8, one finds that at midmorning and midafternoon in the summer (10 a.m. and 2 p.m.) the altitude is 60 degrees.

Thus, installing the collector at 30 degrees would place it perpendicular to the sun's rays at those times. To be perpendicular, the sum of the sun's angle and the collector angle must equal 90 degrees. At noon, the collector would not be quite flat enough and at 8 a.m. and 4 p.m. it would be a little too flat. However, the 30 degrees is a good compromise for a complete day in midsummer.

Quite aside from solar collectors, another use for altitude angles is in designing the appropriate roof overhangs to give shading protection from the summer sun. For example, if it is desired to completely shade 6-foot-high, south-facing windows at noon in a house at 35 degrees N latitude, an overhang must be installed. The width of an overhang placed immediately above the windows can be determined as follows: From Table 14-8, the altitude at noon in midsummer is found to be 78½ degrees. The angle of the sun's rays with the window is then 11½ degrees (90 minus 78½) and the width of the overhang may be found with the expression:

$$\tan 11\tfrac{1}{2}° = \text{overhang/height}$$

$$\text{overhang} = \tan 11\tfrac{1}{2}° \times \text{height}$$

$$= 0.2 \times 6 \text{ ft}$$

$$= 1.2 \text{ ft}$$

If the overhang were to be installed at a higher location, the distance from the bottom of the window to the overhang would have to be used.

Storage

During periods in which solar radiation exceeds the heating requirements, energy from solar collectors may be stored in the form of sensible heat in water or in solids such as stone or concrete. At night, or during cloudy periods, the heat to warm the building or to heat the water is removed from storage. A more efficient but expensive storage makes use of the heat of fusion of Glauber's salt or sodium sulphate decahydrate ($Na_2SO_4 \cdot 10H_2O$). It melts at 90°F (32°C) and has a heat of fusion of 251 kJ/kg (108 Btu/lb). The principal advantage is the high heat storage capacity per unit of volume. However, Glauber's salt is expensive and has a tendency to deteriorate, necessitating replacement. Ordinarily water or stone storages can be designed to operate with about a 50°F (28°C) temperature rise. To be used for storage, stones should be uniform in size, either 1, 2 or 3 inches (25, 50 or 75 mm) in diameter. Under these conditions the specific gravity of the stones will be about 1.7. Stone has a specific heat of 0.2, and with the specific gravity of 1.7, will require nearly three times as much volume as water for equal storage capacity.

Potential for Solar Energy

The increased use of solar energy is largely dependent on the cost of other sources of energy. Although standardized procedures and equipment are not yet common, the technology to use solar energy is available. As the price of fuel increases and as collectors become more efficient and less expensive, solar energy will become more attractive. Two factors that appear to increase the practicality of solar energy for agricultural use are (1) year-round applications such as supplemental water heating, and (2) systems that are designed with low cost rather than high efficiency as the prime objectives as in the case of plastic-duct collectors for crop drying.

Energy from the sun is free, but solar energy delivery systems are not. But they can be economically feasible when they are used to provide supplemental heat to reduce the energy consumption of existing systems. An expenditure of an amount equal to 10 times the estimated average annual savings in fuel seems like a maximum feasible investment, since that would require something in excess of 10 years for payback unless fuel prices were to rise appreciably.

The use of solar energy in itself is not a solution to the problems of high fuel consumption. As with any heating system, the amount of insulation used has a significant impact on the total energy consumption. The fixed costs associated with solar energy systems are high enough to warrant extensive insulation in practically all applications. Adequate insulation is less expensive than a larger solar collector. Put another way, it is a waste of money to collect solar energy and then lose it because of inadequate insulation.

While a number of applications for the use of solar energy in agriculture have already proven their value, it is certain that many more will follow. A continued rise in the cost of fuel will surely hasten new developments, and with today's technology, the potential is enormous.

The farmer has for many years been harvesting some of the energy that flows freely from the sun. The following list of applications of solar energy to agriculture begins with some of those long-time practices and suggests new and more complex systems for today and the future.

1. Open-front livestock building facing south: this gives a drying effect on the bedding and alley floors.

2. Open-front building facing south with curtains or doors: closing up at night maintains a somewhat higher inside temperature.

3. Windows facing south: shutters or heavy curtains are essential to insure a net gain in heat.

4. Grain drying in the bin with warm air forced through a plastic-film duct collector: a disadvantage of this low temperature system for large grain handling operations would be the slower drying and reduced capacity relative to conventional drying operations.

5. Drying hay in stack-wagon units with air heated in an air-inflated triple-layer plastic duct that also serves as a roof over the stacks.

6. Grain or hay drying in a building roofed and sided with fiber-glass reinforced plastic to collect the necessary heat.

7. Attic collectors with or without storages, for heating farrowing and nursery sections of hog houses, hog finishing barns, poultry houses, and calf barns.

8. Air heaters for dehydration of fruits and vegetables either by direct radiation or by the circulation of preheated air.

9. Solar collectors for heating water for milkroom and home use.

10. Solar collectors to warm water which is stored in the porous concrete floor of a greenhouse and then used for nighttime heating.

11. Solar collectors to supplement the farm home heating and cooling system.

The potential value of solar energy as a means of meeting future energy demands is at last being recognized. Research and development in solar energy applications in agriculture are being supported on a significant scale for the first time and the U.S. Department of Energy predicts that solar energy could supply 25 percent of the total agricultural energy demand by the year 2000.

Planning a solar energy system for drying grain may be illustrated with the following example.

It has been estimated that to dry corn in the storage would require air that is 5°C over ambient temperature to be moved at the rate of 1 L/sec for each 9 kg of corn in the storage.

It is assumed that the storage, holding 9000 kg, is located near Madison, Wisconsin and will be operating effectively for about 10 hours per day in early October. The collector will be a single-thickness polyethylene duct, 1 m in diameter, oriented north and south. As the sun's rays strike an area 1 m in diameter throughout the day, it may be assumed that the duct has the characteristics of a north-south horizontal collector tracking east to west.

1. From Table 14-6, it is learned that in October Madison receives a daily flux on a horizontal surface of 11.3 MJ/m².

2. From Table 14-7, in the equinox season, a horizontal N-S oriented collector tracking east to west has a factor of 1.43.

3. As there is no cover on the collector it is assumed to be only 25 percent efficient even with the low temperature rise.

4. Heat/m² in 10 hours — 11.3 MJ/m² $\times$ 1.43 $\times$ .25 = 4 040 kJ/m² 10 h.

5. Air moved in 10 hours = 1 L/s $\times$ 9 000/9 = 1 000 L/s = 1 m³/s 1 m³/s = 3 600 m³/h $\times$ 10 hours of operation = 36 000 m³/10 h.

6. Heat required in 10 hours = 36 000 $\times$ 0.28 S.H. $\times$ 4.186 $\times$ 5°C = 210 974 kJ.

7. Duct area required = 210 974/4 040 = 52.2 m².

8. Duct length = 52.2 m²/1 m diameter = 52 m long.

PROBLEMS

14.1   Determine the total heat transmission (U) for a wall which has the following construction: ½ inch (12 mm) of plywood, aluminum foil centered in a 3½ inch air space, and ½ inch of plywood. Include the inside and outside air layer effects.

14.2   A building is 30 feet (9 m) wide and 60 feet (18 m) long. The walls are 10 feet (3 m) high and include 200 square feet (19 m²) of window and door area. The U values are: ceiling, 0.02 (0.114); walls, 0.05 (0.284); windows and doors 0.9 (5.11). Find the rate of heat loss from the building when the temperature difference is 56°F (31°C). Ignore any heat transfer through the floor.

14.3   Construct a temperature gradient for the wall described in problem 14.1 Keep the information for a later problem. Assume a temperature of 70°F (21°C) inside and 0°F (−18°C) outside.

14.4   Make a list of common insulating materials. Obtain price information and determine the cost per unit of R. Suggest an application for each material on the list.

14.5   Find the total heat required to thaw 660 pounds (300 kg) of frozen eggs removed from storage at 0°F (−17.8°C).

14.6   Find the total area of flat-plate collector surface required to collect an average of 300 megajoules per day in January. The collector, which averages 35 percent efficiency, is to be installed at an optimum angle for its location in Apalachicola, Florida. A storage is to be installed for a total of 600 megajoules with a 25°C temperature differential. What mass of water will be required?

REFERENCES

American Society of Heating, Refrigerating and Air-Conditioning Engineers. *Handbook of Fundamentals.* New York: American Society of Heating, Refrigerating and Air-Conditioning Engineers, 1977.

Baumeister, Theodore, ed. *Marks' Standard Handbook for Mechanical Engineers.* New York: McGraw-Hill, 1967.

Illuminating Engineering Society. *Lighting Handbook.* New York: Illuminating Engineering Society, 1966.

Henderson, S.M. and Perry, R.L. *Agricultural Process Engineering.* New York: Wiley, 1955.

Meinel, Aden B., and Meinel, Marjorie P. *Applied Solar Energy.* Reading, Massachusetts: Addison-Wesley Publishing Company, 1976.

Walpole, E.W., and Roan, T.M. *Potentials and Limitations of Solar Heating for Farm Buildings.* NA 74-106. St. Joseph, Mich.: American Society of Agricultural Engineers, 1974.

Weeks, S.A., and Wilson, G.E. *Solar Energy Systems.* Agricultural Engineering Extension Bulletin 421. Cornell University, Ithaca, N.Y.

Williams, J. Richard. *Solar Energy, Technology and Application.* Ann Arbor, Mich.: Ann Arbor Science Publishers, Inc., 1974.

Chapter Fifteen

Air, Moisture, and Temperature Relationships

The atmosphere in and around our homes and agricultural buildings contains primarily air and water vapor. Under most conditions the moisture cannot be seen, although if the temperature drops quickly, it forms a mist or fog in the air. The unseen moisture in the air also becomes visible when it condenses on a cool surface. High moisture levels, particularly when combined with high temperatures, seriously affect the comfort of both men and animals and the production of livestock as well.

Controlling the moisture level in the atmosphere is one of the more important aspects of maintaining a desirable environment in farm buildings. Examples in which moisture levels are significant include apple storages, in which a high humidity maintains the quality of the fruit; livestock buildings, in which it is desirable to keep humidity low enough to prevent condensation on walls; and heated buildings, such as the farm home, where moisture is often added in the winter to maintain comfortable conditions.

A number of terms used in dealing with air, moisture, and temperature relationships must be defined before a clear understanding of the physical and thermodynamic properties is possible.

Humidity ratio or absolute humidity This is the ratio of the mass of water vapor in the air to the mass of the dry air. Humidity ratio is not affected by a temperature change unless it drops below the saturation temperature. Humidity ratio is useful in calculating the amount of moisture involved in a process, such as the amount removed by ventilating a stable or the amount added by an evaporative cooler used in a greenhouse.

Relative humidity Relative humidity is the ratio of the density of water vapor in the air to the density of saturated water vapor at a given air temperature. A close approximation in ordinary terms is the ratio of vapor present in the air to the maximum amount of vapor that the air can hold at a given temperature. Relative humidity is expressed as a percentage.

Dry-bulb temperature Dry-bulb temperature is the air temperature as determined with a common dry thermometer or other dry temperature sensor. It is a measure of the temperature of the sensible heat in the air.

Wet-bulb temperature This is the steady-state temperature obtained by the evaporation of moisture from the wet wick on a thermometer. The temperature is taken after the thermometer has been exposed to a rapidly moving air stream. Wet-bulb and the associated dry-bulb temperatures are read from a psychrometer, an instrument consisting of a pair of thermometers indicating both temperatures in the same location. Many air, moisture, and temperature conditions in a room can be determined by using the wet- and dry-bulb temperatures and a psychrometric chart.

Wet-bulb depression Wet-bulb depression is the difference between a dry-bulb and wet-bulb temperature reading and is often required for use with psychrometric tables. It is also a useful factor in planning grain drying.

Vapor pressure Vapor pressure is the independent pressure exerted by the water vapor in the air. The vapor pressure is proportional to the humidity ratio. The natural tendency for pressures to equalize causes moisture to migrate through the wall of a building unless restricted by a vapor barrier.

Dew point The dew point is the saturation temperature corresponding to the actual vapor pressure of the moisture in the air. It is the temperature at which condensation just starts to occur on a polished metal surface. The probability of condensation on or within a wall is determined by comparing the actual temperature at a surface with the dew-point temperature at the same place.

Saturation temperature This is the same as the dew-point temperature. The relative humidity will be 100 percent and the wet and dry bulb temperatures will be equal.

Specific volume This is the volume of *dry air* per mass of dry air at a given temperature. Specific volume is read from the psychrometric chart at zero relative humidity, that is along the base-line of the chart.

Humid volume   This is the volume of *moist air* per mass of dry air at a given temperature and relative humidity. It is this value, found on a psychrometric chart, which is most useful in solving ventilation problems. Humid volume is used in converting the rate of air movement from volume to mass or vice versa.

Enthalpy   Enthalpy is the total heat content of an air-moisture mixture, referred to an arbitrary temperature base. Differences in enthalpy are useful in determining the heat transfer involved in the change from one temperature-humidity condition to another. The absolute value of enthalpy is of little significance.

Psychrometric charts   The psychrometric charts in Figure 15-1 A and B include all of the physical and thermal properties of moist air just defined.

The intersection of any two property lines establishes a point to which all other properties may be related. The chart is most useful in tracing the changes that take place in the various properties during ventilation, cooling, heating, and humidifying processes. The psychrometric charts in Figure 15-1 are based on standard sea level atmospheric pressure. They are simple and have a rather coarse scale but are adequate for most agricultural building environmental problems. For more exact information, a set of three or more larger charts with much finer scales and corrected to other atmospheric pressures may be used.

AIR-WATER VAPOR PROCESSES

The processes that go on in ventilating, cooling, heating, or controlling the humidity in a building can be most easily described with the use of a psychrometric chart. Several examples of these processes are shown in Figures 15-2, 15-3, 15-4, and 15-5 to help explain the use of the chart.

Moisture Transmission

Water vapor in the atmosphere exerts a pressure that is proportional to the amount of moisture present. This pressure, as stated in Dalton's Law, is independent from the air pressure. Inasmuch as warm air is capable of holding much more water vapor than cool air, a condition of considerably differing vapor pressures on opposite sides of a building wall is likely to exist. This pressure difference tends to equalize by the permeation of moisture from the high pressure to the low pressure side. Because warm air can hold more moisture than cool air, moisture almost always moves from a warm area to a cooler area.

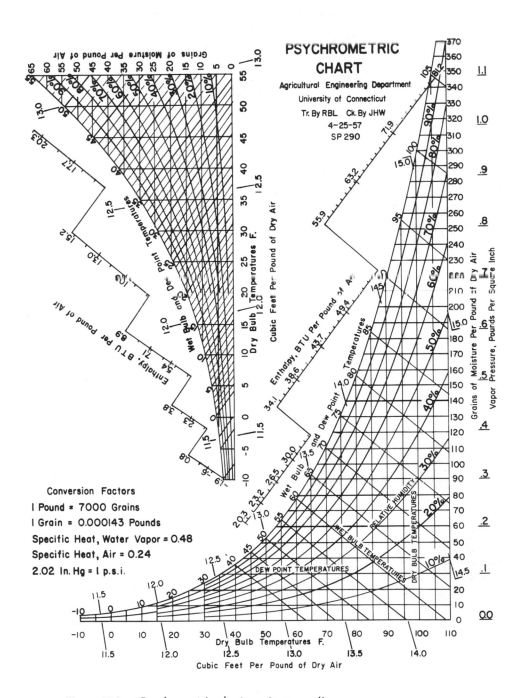

Figure 15-1a. Psychrometric chart, customary units.

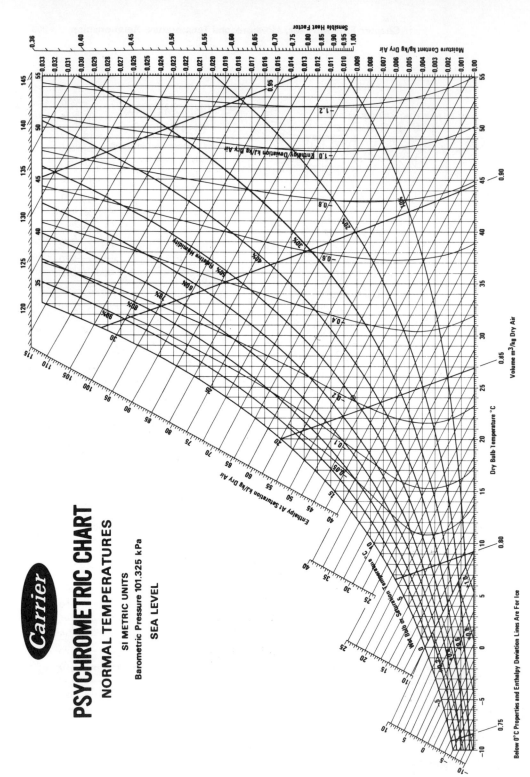

Figure 15-1b. Psychrometric chart, SI Metric units. (Reproduced by permission of Carrier Corporation, © Copyright 1978, Carrier Corporation)

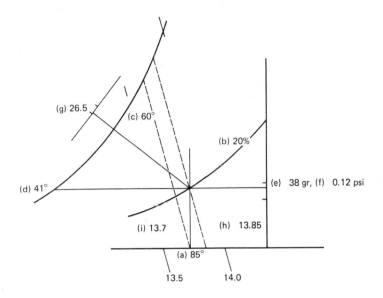

Figure 15-2. Reading the Psychrometric Chart (customary units).

A—85° dry bulb temperature

B—20% relative humidity

C—60° wet bulb temperature

D—41° dewpoint temperature

E—30 grains absolute humidity (also specific humidity or humid ratio)

F—0.12 psi vapor pressure

G—26.5 Btu/lb of air enthalpy

H—13.85 cu ft/lb humid volume

I—13.7 cu ft/lb specific volume

The SI chart is read in a similar manner.

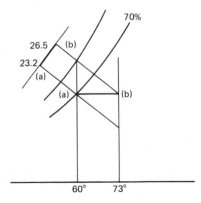

The process shown in Figure 15-3 illustrates what happens when a home is heated by a conventional heating system. Heat from the kitchen range would be similar except that moisture would more than likely be added at the same time. The heat required to raise the temperature of air from 60°F and 70% R.H. to 73°F when no more moisture is added or removed is 26.5 — 23.2 = 3.3 Btu/lb of air.

Figure 15-3. Sensible Heat Process (customary units).

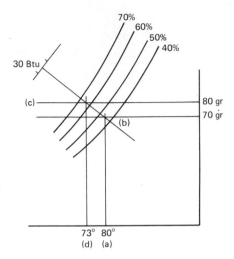

The process shown in Figure 15-4 illustrates what happens when an evaporative cooler is used to lower the temperature in a greenhouse. With no heat added or removed, 10 grains of moisture are evaporated per pound of air. Starting with 80°F and 44% R.H., the air is cooled to 73°F and 64% R.H. The relative humidity rises because of a drop in temperature as well as an increase in the absolute humidity.

Figure 15-4.   Evaporative cooling (customary units).

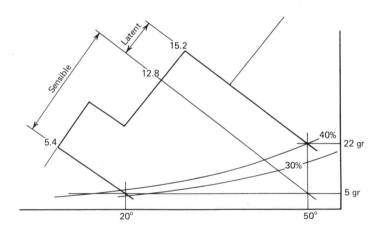

Figure 15-5.   Heating and humidifying (customary units).

The process shown here is typical for an animal shelter. Air enters, is warmed, picks up moisture and is then exhausted. In this case, air enters at 20°F and 30% R.H. and is warmed to 50°F. In rising to 40% R.H., 17 grains (22-5) per pound of dry air is evaporated and will be exhausted with the air. 9.8 Btu (15.2-5.4) of heat is required, of which 7.4 Btu (12.8-5.4) is sensible heat required to warm the air and 2.4 Btu (15.2-12.8) is latent heat required to evaporate the 17 grains of moisture. An example of a similar process is shown in the chapter on ventilation.

If, during the movement of vapor through a wall, the dew point temperature is reached, condensation will occur. The resulting free moisture can reduce the effectiveness of the insulation and cause paint failure and even structural failure due to rotting. Thus, all warm livestock and high humidity product storage buildings are designed with vapor barriers to prevent damaging condensation within the walls.

In order to understand air-moisture movement and to make the necessary calculations in a vapor transmission problem, it is necessary to understand the following terminology:

Vapor pressure Several units are used to indicate vapor pressure. They relate as follows:

$$1 \text{ in. Hg} = 0.49 \text{ lb/sq in.} = 13.6 \text{ in. water} = 25.4 \text{ mm Hg}$$

$$1 \text{ mm Hg} = 133.3 \text{ Pa} = 13.6 \text{ mm water} = 0.039 \text{ in. Hg}$$

Grain This is a unit of mass frequently used in the customary system. One grain equals 1/7000 of a pound or 0.065 grams.

Permeability Permeability is the property of a material that allows the transfer of water vapor. It is measured for a *standard thickness*:

Customary—grains/(sq ft hr in. Hg) for 1 in. of thickness (perm-inch)
SI—(grams)/(24 hr·m²·mm Hg) for 1 m of thickness

Permeance This is the property of a material that allows the transfer of water vapor for a *thickness as used*:

Customary—grains/(sq ft hr in. Hg) (perm)
SI — g/(24 hr·m²·mm Hg)

Permeability may be tested by either the dry-cup or the wet-cup method. The permeability of a thin material is measured by sealing a sample of the material to a standard test cup containing either water or a desiccant. In the dry-cup method, a desiccant provides near zero percent relative humidity inside the cup, while in the wet-cup method, water provides near 100 percent relative humidity. In either case, the cup is placed in a test location in which the relative humidity is approximately 50 percent. Weighing the cup each 24 hours over a period of several days establishes the rate of moisture movement through the layer of material being tested. The wet cup method usually gives a higher permeability value.

Moisture transmission through walls may be determined using the equation:

$$W = M\,A\,T\,DP$$

Where:

		Customary	SI
W =	total moisture	grains	(grams)
A =	area	sq ft	(m²)
T =	time	hr	(24 hr)
DP =	difference in pressure	in. Hg	(mm Hg)
M =	permeance	grains/(hr sq ft in. Hg)	g/(24 hr·m²·mm Hg)

If the wall section is not homogenous, the total M may be found as follows:

$$M_t = \frac{1}{\dfrac{1}{M_1} + \dfrac{1}{M_2} + \ldots \dfrac{1}{M_n}}$$

Table 15-1   Water Vapor Permeability of Building Materials

Material	Perm-inches*	Perms**	Method of Evaluation
Air	120		Special
Gypsum board		50	——
Interior plywood ¼ in.		1.9	——
Exterior plywood ¼ in.		0.7	——
Pine wood	0.4-5.4		——
Concrete	3.2		——
Roll roofing		0.05	dry cup
Aluminum paint		.3-.5	dry cup
Latex paint		5.5	dry cup
Mineral wool	116		wet cup
Blanket insulation and asphalt paper		0.04	dry cup
Expanded polystyrene			
Extruded	1.2		dry cup
Bead	2.0-5.8		dry cup
Polyurethane	0.4-1.6		dry cup
Polyethelyene (4 mil)		0.08	dry cup
Polyethelyene (8 mil)		0.04	dry cup
Aluminum foil (1 mil)		0.0	dry cup

* To obtain (grams–m)/(24 hr · m² · mm Hg) multiply by 0.017.
** To obtain grams/(24 hr · m² · mm Hg) multiply by 0.66.
(From American Society of Heating, Refrigerating and Air-Conditioning Engineers, 1977)

Vapor Barriers

A vapor barrier with a very low moisture permeability should be installed on the *warm side* of a wall or ceiling to prevent the penetration of any appreciable amount of water vapor into the insulation. The cold side of the wall or ceiling should be as permeable as possible. For dwellings it is recommended that a vapor barrier with a maximum rating of 1 perm (1.5 SI units) be installed except on cathedral ceilings where ½ perm (0.75 SI units) is desirable. Warm livestock and poultry buildings require a vapor barrier rating of at least ½ perm (0.75 SI units). The following levels are recommended for refrigerated storage walls.

30°F (—1°C) and higher	0.2 perms or less	(0.13 SI units)
0 to 29°F (—18 to —2°C)	0.1 perm or less	(0.07 SI units)
—1 to —40°F (—18 to —40°C)	0.01 perms or less	(0.007 SI units)

Care should always be taken to keep the vapor barrier as continuous as possible. Large sheets should be used, holes repaired, and joints well lapped and sealed. The vapor barrier should always be installed on the *predominantly warm side of the wall*. The justification for this recommendation can be verified by referring to the psychrometric chart.

Assume, for example, that it is 30°F and 100 percent relative humidity outside and 70°F and 30 percent relative humidity inside. Note that the vapor pressure is higher on the inside even though the relative humidity is much lower.

Only occasionally, and then for short periods of time, does one find a reverse situation. Moisture that penetrates a wall during such a period will soon be forced out again, usually in a matter of hours.

The attics of both agricultural buildings and homes benefit from year-round ventilation. In the warm months excess heat is removed, while during the winter, moisture that may have penetrated through the ceiling and insulation is removed, reducing the possibility of condensation. It is recommended that 1 square foot (1 m²) of net louver area be installed for each 300 square feet (300 m²) of ceiling area. The ceiling area is measured at the level of the eaves and the louver area is divided between the gable ends in a gable building or between the eaves and the ridge in a hip-roof design. To compensate for screening and rain deflectors, the gross area of louvers should be 2.25 times the net requirement.

Ceiling vapor barriers are strongly recommended in areas where the winter design temperature is 0°F (—18°C) or lower and is desirable for design temperatures up to 20°F (—7°C). Between 20 and 30°F (—7 and —1°C) no vapor seal is required if ventilation is adequate. When the design temperature is above 35°F (2°C) moisture may be moving in either direction due to alternate heating and cooling and a nonpermeable insulation is most suitable.

Condensation on Surfaces

When the humidity in a building is high, and the temperature-drop across the inside layer of air is substantial, the surface temperature of the wall is likely to fall below the dew-point temperature. Condensation will then occur *on the wall surface*. For example, if it is 55°F (12.7°C) and 80 percent relative humidity in a building, condensation will occur on any wall or window surface that is 50°F (10°C) or lower.

The remedies for this condition are (1) reduce the humidity, therefore reducing the dewpoint temperature, (2) insulate the walls more heavily, and (3) circulate air within the building. The latter two methods tend to raise the wall temperature.

Condensation Within a Wall

If a dew-point temperature is reached *within* a wall, condensation is likely to result. However, it is difficult to predict where the condensation will take place. Experience has shown that condensation rarely occurs within a very permeable material such as fiberglass or mineral wool even though temperatures are reached that might be expected to be below the dew-point temperature. Apparently vapor moves away from the plane as rapidly as it approaches the plane and saturation is never reached. However, where a sizeable change in permeability occurs, more moisture arrives at the plane than can leave and condensation takes place if the surface is below the dew-point temperature. A typical example is the inside surface of the sheathing of a wall insulated with mineral wool. If the vapor barrier is missing or defective, then condensation is likely to occur on this surface during cold weather.

The remedies for condensation within a wall are (1) use a less permeable vapor barrier, (2) increase the permeability of the outer wall surface, (3) reduce the humidity on the warm side of the wall, and (4) design the wall or ceiling section so that there is no reduction in permeability after the insulation so that the moisture can be readily removed by ventilation, for example, by having no floor above the ceiling level.

Predicting Condensation

In designing the insulation, vapor barrier, and ventilation for a building, it is important to determine that condensation is not likely to occur on the inner wall surface or within the wall structure itself. Methods of illustrating the probability of condensation are shown by the temperature gradients in Figures 15-6, 15-7, and 15-8.

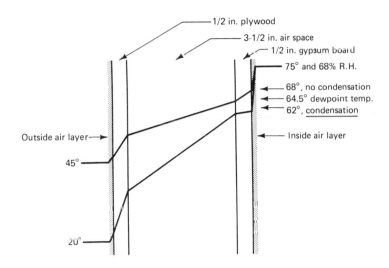

Layer (left side)	"R"	Degrees / unit of R 30° TD	55° TD	Temp at Plane 30°	55°
Outside air layer	0.17 × 11.6 =	2.0, × 21.2 =	3.6	45°	20°
Plywood	0.63	= 7.3,	= 13.4	47	23.6
Air space	0.91	= 10.6,	= 19.3	54.3	37
Gypsum board	0.27	= 3.1,	= 5.7	64.9	56.3
Inside air layer	0.61	= 7.0,	= 13.0	68	62
Total R	2.59		Room Temp.	75	75

30° / 2.59 = 11.6° / unit of R
55° / 2.59 = 21.2° / unit of R

Figure 15-6.   Condensation on a wall surface.

Referring back to Figure 14-2, the method for diagraming a temperature gradient was shown. Using the same procedure in figure 15-6, the inside surface temperature of the wall may be compared with the dew-point temperature to determine the probability of condensation. A 45°F (7.2°C) outside temperature causes a 68°F (20°C) inside wall temperature. As that is above the dew-point temperature of 64.5°F (18°C), no condensation will occur. However, if the outside temperature is 20°F (16.7°C) the surface temperature is below the dew-point and condensation will result.

The same general procedure used for the temperature gradient may be followed in determining dew-point temperatures to be plotted on the same scale. Having plotted both gradients, a theoretical plane of condensation is predicted if the gradient lines cross. In Figure 15-7, 63.5°F (16.9°C) is the temperature of such a plane.

This theoretical plane of condensation occurs within the insulation. However, as has been mentioned previously, condensation rarely occurs in a homogenous permeable material. Instead it occurs at the next sur-

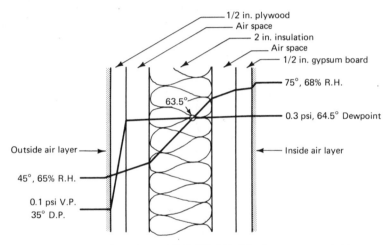

Conditions: 75° F, 68% R.H., 0.3 psi vapor pressure, inside
45° F, 65% R.H., 0.1 psi vapor pressure, outside

Layer (left side)	"R"	Temp. Diff.	"1/p"	V.P. Diff.	Plane Temp.	Vapor Press.	Dewpoint Temp.
Outer air layer	0.17	0.5	—	—	45.0	0.1000	35.0
Plywood	0.63	1.7	1.390	0.1930	45.5	0.1000	35.0
Air	0.91	2.5	0.008	0.0010	47.2	0.2930	63.0
Insulation	7.40	20.4	0.017	0.0023	49.7	0.2940	63.2
Air	0.91	2.5	0.008	0.0010	70.1	0.2963	63.9
Gypsum board	0.27	0.7	0.020	0.0027	72.6	0.2973	64.1
Inner air layer	0.61	1.7	—	—	73.3	0.3000	64.5
Inside air	—	—	—	—	75.0	0.3000	64.5
Totals	10.90	30.0	1.443	0.2000			

30°/10.90 = 2.75 degrees per unit of R
0.2 psi/1.443 = 0.139 psi per unit of "1/p"

Figure 15-7. Condensation within a wall.

face that is lower in permeability, which in this case is the inner surface of the plywood.

A vapor barrier (Figure 15-8) should have been placed just under the gypsum board. The large vapor-pressure drop across such a barrier would keep the dew-point temperature gradient under the actual temperature gradient throughout the wall and eliminate the danger of condensation within the wall.

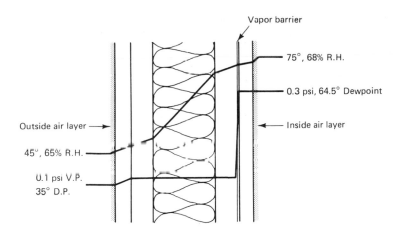

Figure 15-8. A vapor barrier prevents condensation within a wall.

PROBLEMS

15.1 A wet-bulb temperature of 50°F (10°C) and a dry-bulb temperature of 66° F (19°C) are read from a psychrometer. For these temperatures, read the following factors from a psychrometric chart:

> Relative humidity
> Absolute humidity
> Dewpoint temperature
> Humid volume
> Specific volume
> Enthalpy

15.2 Air enters a swine barn at 20°F (−6.7°C) and 50 percent relative humidity. It is exhausted at 65°F (18.3°C) and 50 percent relative humidity. How much heat and moisture are exhausted each hour when the air is moved at a rate of 500 cubic feet per minute (233 L/s)?

15.3   Using the information from Problems 14-1 and 14-3, determine whether condensation is likely to occur on the inside wall surface when it is 0°F (−18°C) outside and 70°F (21°C) and 50 percent relative humidity inside.

15.4   A building wall is constructed with an inside surface of gypsum board, 3½ inches (89 mm) of fiberglass and wood boards on the outside. When the outside conditions are 0°F (−18°C) and 80 percent relative humidity and the inside conditions are 70°F (21°C) and 30 percent relative humidity, would condensation be likely to occur *within* the wall? Superimposed temperature and dew-point temperature gradients will help to determine the answer. What is the effect of a polyethylene vapor barrier under the gypsum board?

REFERENCES

American Society of Agricultural Engineers. *Agricultural Engineers Yearbook.* St. Joseph, Mich.: American Society of Agricultural Engineers, 1977.

American Society of Heating, Refrigerating and Air-Conditioning Engineers. *Handbook of Fundamentals.* New York: American Society of Heating, Refrigerating and Air-Conditioning Engineers, 1977.

Midwest Plan Service. *Structures and Environment Handbook.* Ames, Iowa: Midwest Plan Service, 1977.

Chapter Sixteen

Ventilation

One of the important considerations in designing housing for farm livestock is the provision for a comfortable and healthy environment in which it is possible to attain maximum production. Likewise, buildings for storing agricultural products are designed to maintain maximum quality and to minimize losses.

To achieve these objectives, the control of heat and moisture, as discussed in previous chapters, as well as dust and odors, assumes a major role. By employing sophisticated equipment such as supplemental heaters, air filters, humidifiers, and machinery for the continuous removal of manure, it would be possible to maintain an ideal environment. However, such methods are not economically feasible for commercial farms unless production or quality are improved markedly.

Ventilation alone, which involves moving air through a building either by natural convection currents or with fans, will provide adequate conditions at reasonable cost for many agricultural enterprises. In other cases, however, supplemental heat, refrigeration, or atmosphere modification are required to maintain an optimum environment.

The following examples briefly illustrate the range of systems, from the very simple to the complex, as they are used to control the environment in farm buildings.

1. In a free-stall dairy barn, temperature is of little consideration, and a very simple system using natural convection removes sufficient moisture to prevent condensation under ordinary circumstances.

2.   In a cage poultry house, wall and ceiling insulation conserves enough animal heat to maintain a warm temperature while ventilation removes excess moisture and odors.

3.   In a farrowing house, low animal density and the need for a warm room temperature make the use of supplemental heat necessary. Ventilation controls moisture and odors.

4.   Potatoes that are to be stored are harvested late enough in the season so that cool nighttime air moved through the bins is adequate to obtain storage level temperatures. No refrigeration is necessary.

5.   Apples destined for storage are harvested earlier in the season during relatively warmer weather. To provide the required storage temperatures, mechanical refrigeration systems are essential. In addition, atmosphere modification is used to achieve maximum storage periods.

PHYSIOLOGICAL CONSIDERATIONS

Before designing a system for environmental control, it is important to understand the physiological characteristics for the enterprise to be housed. This includes both the heat and moisture needed as well as that produced by the animals or product.

Poultry and other farm animals are spoken of as being homeothermic; that is, they maintain relatively constant body temperatures, usually within a 2 to 3°F (1 to 2°C) range. Normal temperatures for the more common farm animals and humans are given in Table 16-1.

Table 16-1   Normal Temperatures of Farm Animals and Humans

| Animal | Rectal Temperatures | |
	°F	°C
Chicken	107.1	41.7
Dairy cow	101.5	38.6
Beef cow	101.0	38.3
Pig	102.5	39.2
Sheep	102.3	39.1
Horse	100.2	37.9
Humans	98.6	37.0

The hypothalamus gland is the body temperature regulator and stimulates mechanisms to counteract either high or low ambient temperatures. For example, increased metabolic activity and greater conversion of feed-to-heat energy are used to counteract low ambient temperatures. In contrast, increased respiration and blood circulation in the skin counteract high ambient temperatures. Of the animals listed in Table 16-1, only horses and humans have the physiological means to perspire to any great extent. Other animals depend on rapid respiration for most of their cooling under high temperature conditions and are much more likely to suffer seriously during periods of higher-than-normal temperatures. Extended periods in which the ambient temperature is above body temperature may very well prove lethal. This is particularly true if the humidity is also high, because the cooling effect from respiration is then seriously reduced. Table 16-2 lists typical heat and moisture production values for animals.

Table 16-2 Typical Moisture and Heat Production by Animals
(Total heat equals sensible heat plus latent heat)

Livestock	Ambient temperature		Moisture per hour		Total heat per hour	
	°F	°C	grains/lb	grams/kg	Btu/lb	kJ/kg
Dairy Cow	20	7	4.7	0.67	3.9	9.1
	50	10	7.4	1.06	3.4	7.9
	80	27	12.7	1.82	2.9	6.7
Dairy calves						
5 weeks	—	—	7	1.0	4.5	10.5
12 weeks	—	—	16	2.29	6.5	15.1
6 months	—	—	—	—	4.0	9.3
Swine						
50 lb (23 kg)	60	16	20	2.86	7.2	16.7
	70	21	25	3.58	6.8	15.8
Swine						
100 lb (45 kg)	60	16	13	1.86	4.7	10.9
	70	21	15	2.15	4.3	10.0
Swine						
200 lb (90 kg)	50	10	7.4	1.06	3.7	8.6
	60	16	7.9	1.13	3.3	7.7
Layers	55	13	20	2.86	9	20.9
	90	32	34	4.86	6	14.0
Broilers						
2 weeks	85	29	—	—	24	55.8
7 weeks	75	24	75	10.73	12	27.9
Sheep	50	10	—	—	5	11.6

Dairy cattle Cows produce well in a temperature range of 40 to 75°F (4 to 24°C) and a relative humidity that does not cause condensation on building surfaces. In fact, production is not significantly affected by temperatures down to 10°F (−12°C) as long as the fluctuations are not too rapid or frequent. However, production will start to drop at 75°F (24°C) and may get as low as 50 percent at 90°F (32°C) or higher.

Calves   Calves appear to be more sensitive to drafts and poor ventilation than to temperature level. In fact, one of the most successful housing methods isolates each calf in a small, well bedded shed which provides the only protection against weather extremes.

Beef cattle   Beef cattle gain well at temperatures below 75°F (24°C). Low temperatures and exposure tend to decrease feed conversion efficiency slightly but may actually increase the daily rate of gain. Some protection from snow and severe wind is desirable.

Swine   Swine make their best gains at about 68°F (20°C), although a range of 50 to 75°F (10 to 24°C) does not show a marked effect. Supplemental heat is usually needed to provide a temperature of 85 to 90°F (30 to 32°C) for newborn pigs. This can be gradually reduced to 70°F (21°C) during the first three weeks. The best gains will be made if this temperature is continued until market age. Brood sows will do well at 60°F (16°C) but suffer badly at temperatures of 80°F (27°C) and above. Feeder pigs show reduced gains above 70°F (21°C) and actually lose weight at 100°F (38°C).

Sheep   Sheep need protection from wind, rain, and snow, but tolerate a wide range of temperatures without significant effect. At temperatures below 45°F (7°C) at breeding time ewes have shown improved reproductive efficiency. Heat lamps for newborn lambs are desirable for the first few days when lambing occurs in cold weather.

Horses   Horses should be protected from wind, rain, and snow, but tolerate a wide range of temperatures without discomfort. If they are to be kept in an enclosed, insulated building, supplemental heat will be required to maintain a 45 to 50°F (7 to 10°C) temperature level because of the low animal density.

Poultry   Environmental requirements for poultry vary greatly with age. Chicks, started at 95°F (35°C) may have the temperature gradually reduced to 75°F (24°C) over the first few weeks. Meat birds, both broilers and young turkeys, make most efficient gains at 70 to 75°F (21 to 24°C). Laying birds produce the greatest number and largest sized eggs at 55 to 75°F (13 to 24°C). The best feed conversion efficiency is achieved between 70 to 75°F (21 to 24°C). Temperatures below 45°F (7°C) increase feed consumption significantly while temperatures over 75°F (24°C) result in a drop in egg production. A continued rise in temperature to 100°F (38°C) or more may well prove lethal. A relative humidity of 60 to 70 percent should help to control dust while still allowing adequate body cooling through respiration. High humidities at high temperatures create more lethal conditions because of a breakdown in this mode of cooling.

Inasmuch as working and living conditions are related to the success of an agricultural operation, it seems fitting to include physiological information for human beings along with that for the farm enterprises.

Most *humans,* when dressed in light clothing, seated and at rest, find 77°F (25°C) comfortable in winter and 78°F (26°C) in summer (Koch, Jennings, and Humphreys, 1960). At 72°F (22°C) most people feel slightly cool regardless of humidity, while at temperatures above 77°F (25°C) they feel warm, and an increase in humidity above 45 percent intensifies the feeling of warmth. At the most comfortable temperature, only humidities of more than 70 percent produce any change in comfort.

The metabolic heat produced by adult humans varies with weight and activity from as low as 250 Btu per hour (264 kJ/h) while sleeping to around 750 Btu per hour (791 kJ/h) at moderate work and up to 2,500 Btu per hour (2638 kJ/h) at sustained heavy work.

As shown in Table 16-3, agricultural products, when held in storage, have individual temperature and humidity requirements. Like animals, they also give off heat energy.

Table 16-3 Environmental Requirements for Product Storages

Product Area	Temperature °F	°C	Humidity	Remarks
Milkroom	50-90	10-30	90% max	Prevent freezing and condensation
Eggs	55	13	60-80%	
Apples	28-34	−2- +1	85-90%	Controlled atmosphere desirable
Potatoes	50-60	10-16	85-90%	First 7-10 days
	39-40	4	85-90%	Fresh and seed use
	45-55	7-12	85-90%	As required by processing use
Grain	—	—	Under 14% moisture	
Hay	—	—	Under 20% moisture	

Potatoes produce 1,100 to 1,700 Btu per ton (1275 to 1975 kJ/tonne) each 24 hours when held at storage temperature and about 50 percent more at 60°F (16°C). They also produce enough moisture to maintain humidity and to require periodic ventilation. Apples produce 600 to 800 Btu per ton (700 to 925 kJ/tonne) each 24 hours at 32°F (0°C). The amount is twice that at 40°F (4°C) and eight times as great at 60°F (16°C).

Greenhouse temperature requirements vary considerably with individual crops. Ventilation is largely related to the control of maximum temperature, although humidity control to prevent excessive condensation is also a factor. Added humidity or carbon dioxide may be required for some crops.

VENTILATION OF INSULATED BUILDINGS

A large proportion of automatically controlled ventilating fans are installed in well insulated buildings where the control of temperature and moisture are primary concerns. The proper selection and installation of ventilation equipment will provide the air volume required for uniform air mixing, moisture control, and necessary temperature levels.

Fans and Blowers

Fans used to move ventilation air through buildings are classified as *axial flow fans* or *centrifugal blowers*. With the axial flow (propeller) type, the air is moved parallel with the fan shaft by two or more radially mounted blades. Centrifugal blowers discharge air at right angles to the "squirrel cage" shaft-and-blade assembly. The choice of a fan or blower depends to a large extent on the static pressure conditions under which it must operate.

Static pressure   When a fan either exhausts air from or blows air into a reasonably tight building, a difference in pressure between the inside and outside will develop. The pressure difference is small and is most easily measured with a manometer calibrated in inches (millimeters) of water. A simple manometer (Figure 16-1A) may be constructed from plastic tubing. A more easily read commercial manometer is shown in Figure 16-1C. A draft gauge, also shown, is readily portable and does not have to be mounted with as much precision as a manometer.

Fan ratings   The ability of a fan to move air is inversely proportional to the static pressure against which it must discharge. A fan performance curve illustrating this is shown in Figure 16-2.

The performance for fans in cubic feet per minute (m^3/s or L/s) is plotted versus static pressure, ranging from zero, or free-air delivery, up to the maximum level against which the fan is expected to operate. Fans for farm ventilation are most often chosen on the basis of their capacity at ⅛-inch (3.2-mm) static pressure. The pressure drop across air inlets is usually less than one-half of this amount. However, many fans are equipped with automatic louvers which are opened by air pressure and if they become dusty they can cause much of the eighth-inch (3.2-mm) pressure drop.

The Air Moving and Conditioning Association (AMCA) has estab-

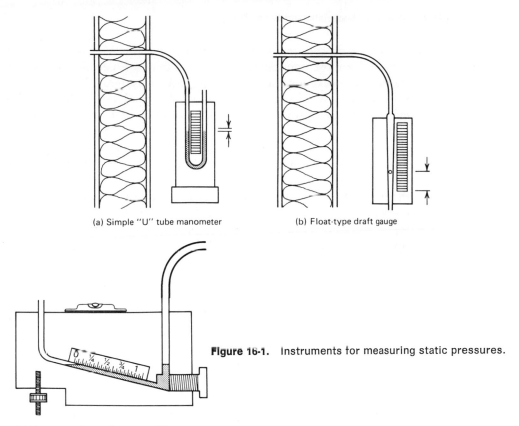

(a) Simple "U" tube manometer

(b) Float-type draft gauge

Figure 16-1. Instruments for measuring static pressures.

(c) Manometer for small pressure differences

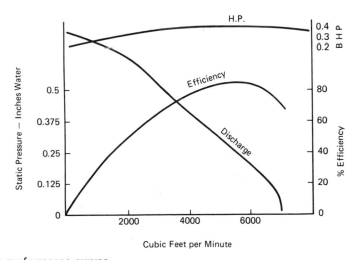

Figure 16-2. Fan performance curves.

lished test procedures for fans. Fans bearing the AMCA label should be chosen for most ventilation systems as they are certified to deliver the stated volumes of air at the specified static pressures. A few manufacturers provide an air-volume per watt rating. This combines both fan and motor efficiencies and provides a useful indication of comparative operating costs.

Choosing a fan   Propeller fans are the most commonly used type for the ventilation of agricultural buildings. They are the least expensive, exhibit high efficiency at low static pressure, and are easy to install and maintain. A two-blade propeller fan is suitable for static pressures under one-fourth of an inch (6 mm). Four-bladed fans are suitable for pressures up to three-eights of an inch (10 mm) and some six-blade designs for up to 1 inch (25 mm) or more. Multiblade fans tend to be less noisy.

Centrifugal blowers, although they are comparatively more expensive, will operate well against the pressures expected from long ducts. The blades on blowers may be forward-curved, radial, or backward-curved. The latter type offers the best combination of efficiency and quiet operation for agricultural applications.

In selecting a fan model from performance tables in a catalogue, the volume for a wall-mounted fan may usually be taken at ⅛-inch (3.2-mm) static pressure, while for use with a duct of less than 10 feet (3 m), capacity at one-fourth of an inch (6 mm) should be chosen. For longer ducts, fans rated at a higher pressure, or perhaps a blower, will be needed.

Many fans are belt-driven and may therefore be subject to changes in speed of operation. A knowledge of the effects brought about by changes in speed is desirable and may prevent some unfortunate results. Briefly stated, they are as follows.

- Fan capacity is proportional to speed.
- Static pressure is proportional to the square of the speed.
- Horsepower required is proportional to the cube of the speed.

Note that if the speed is *doubled,* as it might be by substituting a 3,450 RPM motor for a 1,725 RPM model, the power requirements increase *eightfold.*

Motors should be either a split-phase or a capacitor-start type with built-in thermal overload protection and bearings lubricated for long periods of operation. Fully enclosed frames are also advisable for dust and moisture protection.

A *shroud* or ring that fits fairly closely around the fan (Figure 16-3A), and in effect becomes a bell-shaped nozzle through which air flows, will improve efficiency substantially as compared to a plain circular opening. Fans with no ring are suitable only for free-air circulation within a room.

(a) A close fitting shroud improves fan efficiency. The metal guard is essential for
safety. (*Courtesy* Aerovent Fan and Equipment Inc.)

(b) The protective hood is made of corrosion
proof fiberglass reinforced plastic (*Courtesy* Aerovent Fan and Equipment Inc.)

Figure 16-3.   Ventilating fans.

Shutters should be designed to operate very easily to keep static pressure losses at a low level. Motor-operated shutters are expensive but offer the least resistance to air flow. Shutters need to be cleaned on a regular basis to prevent excessive pressure drop. A *hood* for weather protection is desirable. Welded wire guards should be installed over the fan to prevent accidental contact with the operating blades.

Fan Location

The location of fans will vary in different buildings, but generally midpoint on the lee side of a building up to 100 feet (30 m) long is satisfactory for exhaust fans. If the building is longer, the fans may be grouped at various points. Fans may be installed to exhaust directly from a high level on the wall or from a short distance above the floor. Although it appears that less heat would be removed at the lower level because of the lower temperature, in fact there is no particular advantage because the moisture level (humidity ratio) is also lower. As a result, the removal of an equal quantity of moisture requires a longer period of operation and approximately the same total amount of heat as compared to fans exhausting directly from a high level. In any case, high-level exhaust is desirable in warm weather. While mid-ceiling location is ideal, it usually requires an outlet duct.

If there is a particularly odorous area in a building, such as a manure pit, locating exhaust fans adjacent to that area should help to prevent the spread of odors.

Outlet ducts should be designed to provide 1½ square feet (0.15 m²) of inside cross section area per 1,000 cubic feet per minute (472 L/s) of fan capacity. The duct should be insulated to an R of 3 (0.5) or more to prevent condensation.

Air Inlets

Inlet location, shape, and size to a large extent influence the distribution of air throughout a ventilated building. Although fans determine the rate of air exchange, they have little effect on distribution within a radius of 50 feet (15 m). Experience has shown that a continuous "slot" inlet around the perimeter of the ceiling of a building provides uniform air distribution. However, the inlet opening should be interrupted at any place where it is within 10 feet (3 m) of an exhaust fan. An adjustable baffle (Figure 16-4) should be installed along the slot so that air is directed down along the wall surface, or alternatively, out along the ceiling. This not only distributes the air uniformly but also provides a wiping action that helps to keep the wall or ceiling free of condensation. Another inlet design, suitable for high animal densities, consists of one or more baffled slots running the length of the ceiling and spaced so that each slot provides ventilation for an equal area.

The total opening of any type of inlet should cause an air velocity of between 700 and 1,000 feet per minute (3.5 and 5 m/s). This will occur if the static pressure difference across the opening is 0.04 to 0.08 inches (1.0 to 2.0 mm) of water. Although one might calculate velocity by dividing the fan volume by the inlet area, the velocity in a tight building is likely to be somewhat higher due to the *vena contracta* of the air stream in the inlet opening. The vena contracta effect, occurring in any nonstreamlined opening, is one of narrowing the air stream to 0.6 to 0.8 of the sectional area. The actual value is difficult to determine due to the variety of inlet shapes. A small draft gauge, similar to that shown in Figure 16-1B, with the tubing connected to the bottom, provides a simple means of checking velocity when the end of the hose fitting is held in the inlet opening.

The inlet openings should be adjustable so that the desired range of inlet air velocity is maintained throughout the year. This often means a winter opening of less than half of that needed in the summer. The open-

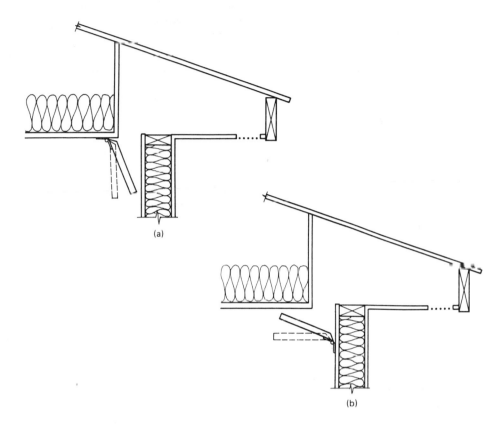

(a)

(b)

Figure 16-4. Alternative methods of baffling slot inlets.

ings may be adjusted about four times during the year to give at least 600 feet per minute (3 m/s) velocity with the minimum fan capacity expected for that season. Then as additional fan capacity is automatically cycled on and off with changing temperatures, the velocity will be in the desired range. However, care must be taken to ensure that the maximum desired velocity will not be exceeded with the maximum expected fan capacity during the period. If more precise control is desired, a pressure sensor and actuator can maintain a uniform static pressure and velocity regardless of the fan capacity that may be in operation at any particular time. Typical design parameters for inlets are shown in Table 16-4. If a damp spot develops in a localized area of a building, increased inlet opening adjacent to the area often remedies the problem. Additional fan capacity in the area is *not* likely to help.

While supply air for a slot inlet may be brought in from the attic

Table 16-4   Ventilation Inlet Parameters
(vena contracta = 0.8)

Static pressure water column		Velocity		Area of inlet	
inches	mm	ft/min	m/s	sq inches/ 100 cfm	sq meters/ m³/s
0.020	0.5	570	2.9	31.58	0.437
0.040	1.0	806	4.1	22.34	0.309
0.060	1.5	986	5.0	18.24	0.252
0.080	2.0	1140	5.8	15.79	0.218
0.100	2.5	1274	6.5	14.14	0.195
0.125	3.2	1424	7.3	12.65	0.175

in the winter and from the outside through the soffit in the summer, this design entails extra construction costs and management problems. It is quite satisfactory to use outside air the year around if the inlet supply opening is at the outer edge of the soffit. This location reduces the problem of drafts during cold, windy weather. The opening should be covered with three-quarter-inch (19-mm) hardware cloth to prevent the entry of birds. Screening should not be used as it will plug up with dust.

Inlets cannot be installed and forgotten; they must be managed. Since it is difficult to predict crack area in a building, there is no substitute for actual measurement of air velocity or pressure difference at the inlet openings. A direct-reading draft gauge may be used to adjust inlet openings to give 700 to 1,000 feet per minute (3.5 to 5 m/s) or a manometer may be used instead with corresponding readings of 0.04 to 0.08 inches (1 to 2 mm) of static pressure.

Fan Controls

Most livestock buildings are sufficiently large to require several fans, thus allowing some flexibility in the type of controls that will provide the required conditions. The least complicated controller is an on-off thermostat with a set temperature. One or more fans may be operated continuously to provide the minimum ventilation for severe temperature conditions. An optional thermostat may be set to serve as a safety device to prevent freeze-ups in severe weather. Additional fans may be controlled by thermostats set at near the minimum inside design temperature for the building, for example, 50°F (10°C). The balance of the fans may then be controlled with thermostats set at the maximum desired temperature, perhaps 70°F (21°C). The result will be some continuous operation and some cycling operation during moderate weather, while the balance of the fans will operate only in warm weather. It should be noted that the continuous ventilation at a minimum level is a requirement in any system employing ceiling-level inlets. Stopping all fans will cause a natural reversal of air flow with attendant condensation problems unless the inlets close automatically.

Temperature-sensitive, electronic controllers designed to be used with specific motors can provide continuously varying fan speeds. Although their original cost is somewhat higher and motor efficiency slightly lower, they should insure more uniform environmental conditions. The range of modulation makes them suitable for up to one-half of the total fan capacity required. Thermostatic control is best for the balance of the fan capacity needed for summer heat removal. For small buildings with only one fan, a two-speed motor, controlled by a thermostat with two set temperatures, may be used.

For most animal housing, thermostats are located about 6 feet (2 m) high near the center of the building. They will not operate satisfactorily if they are mounted too low. Either filled-type or bimetallic-type thermostats are adequately resistant to dust and moisture. From time to time, humidistats and program timers are proposed for ventilation controllers. However, thermostats seem to be the most dependable and satisfactory.

Exhaust vs Pressure Systems

The discussion of ventilation to this point has been based on the use of *exhaust* fans (that is, air is exhausted from a building creating a negative pressure that causes fresh air to enter through the inlets as well as any cracks that are present). With a *pressure* system, fresh air is charged into a building through one or more distribution ducts, while stale air is forced out through outlet openings and cracks.

Although exhaust systems are more common and generally simpler, there are circumstances where the pressure system is desirable. For example, if air in a building is very dusty or corrosive, a pressure system allows the fan to move fresh air, thereby avoiding the problems of dust accumulation and corrosion at the fan. A pressure system may also work better in a building where excessive crack area makes it difficult to design a satisfactory inlet system. Many old buildings fit into this category. A pressure system is often used for continuous recirculation of air within a building.

Distribution Ducts

Polyethylene tubes punched with holes along their length provide inexpensive distribution ducts. Ordinarily they are sized to give an air velocity through the duct of 800 to 1,200 feet per minute (4 to 6 m/s). Usually two rows of holes are spaced uniformly at 24- to 30-inch (600- to 750-mm) intervals along the tube. The total hole area should equal approximately 1.5 times the cross-section area of the duct. Polyducts are not only used with pressure systems but may be used as inlets with exhaust systems as well. They would be sized in the same manner.

CLIMATIC DATA

The successful design of environmental control systems requires accurate climatic information such as the design temperatures shown in Figures 16-5 and 16-6. As with snow loads, discussed in an earlier chapter, a comparison of the national and regional maps will illustrate the desirability of obtaining data for local areas whenever it is available. Figure 16-7 provides average temperature data that may be used for estimating heating or ventilating costs.

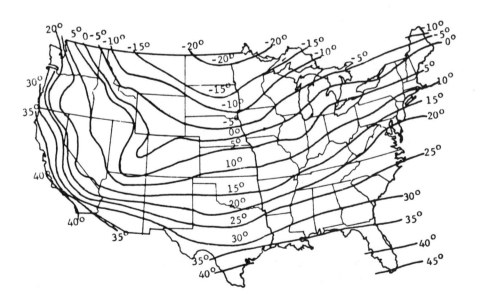

Figure 16-5. Winter design isotherms. Actual temperatures are expected to be higher than these values 97½ percent of the time in December, January, and February. (American Society of Agricultural Engineers)

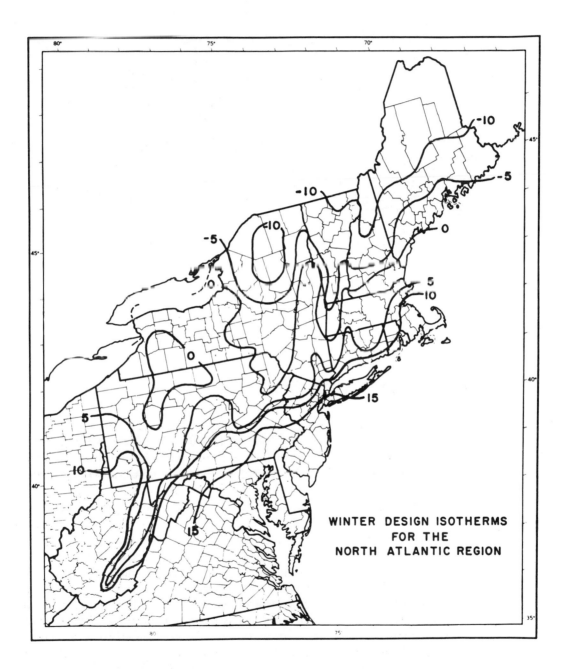

Figure 16-6. Winter isotherms for the North Atlantic region. (*Courtesy* College of Agriculture Extension Service, The Pennsylvania State University)

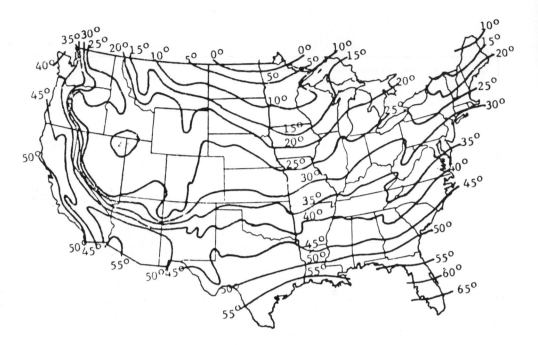

Figure 16-7. Average daily temperatures for January in the United States. (American Society of Agricultural Engineers)

Heat and Moisture Balance

In order to maintain a desired temperature and a reasonable level of moisture within an enclosed livestock building during the winter months, it is necessary to maintain a heat and moisture balance. In many cases this is possible with ventilation alone if the building is well insulated and is housing the number of animals for which it was designed.

Heat is supplied primarily by the animals. However, lights, equipment, and such sources as solar energy, supplemental artificial heat, and even a manure pack may also contribute to the total amount.

The heat produced by animals may be categorized as sensible and latent. The body heat given off by convection and radiation is sensible heat. The latent heat of vaporization is released during condensation of the moisture that has been respired by the animals in vapor form. Consequently, when using the *total* heat value given in Table 16-2, all moisture removed in the ventilation air must be considered to be vaporized before being exhausted and the heat required to accomplish the vaporization must be included in the total heat required for ventilation.

Moisture is contributed from four sources: incoming air, animal wastes, animal respiration, and feed and water. Moisture is removed by ventilation and in the waste material removed from the building. In rare cases ventilation can theoretically remove all moisture entering the building. In practice, enough should be removed to prevent condensation and uncomfortably humid conditions for animals and workers.

Although heat- and moisture-balance calculations may be completed with the use of specific heat and latent heat values, it is more convenient to use a psychrometric chart (Figure 15-1, A or B). An example of a heat and moisture balance will be completed to illustrate the use of the psychrometric chart and several other procedures previously discussed. The following situation is assumed:

A central New York State farm has sixty 1,500 pound cows housed in a 36- by 140- by 8-foot stable with 200 square feet of window and door area. R values are: window and door, 2; ceiling, 15; and wall, 12. The relative humidity outside is 80 percent and inside, 60 percent.

From Figure 16-6, the outside design temperature may be taken as 0°F; from Table 16-2, the heat and moisture produced by dairy cows are interpolated to be 3.5 Btu/(hr lb) and 7.4 grains per pound; from Figure 15-1, 0°F and 80 percent relative humidity equal 0.8 Btu enthalpy and 5 grains absolute humidity, 45°F and 60 percent relative humidity equal 15.0 Btu enthalpy and 26 grains absolute humidity; from Figure 15-1 the humid volume at 45°F and 60 percent equals 13 cubic feet per pound.

Heat input	60 × 1,500 × 3.5 =	315,000 Btu/hr
Moisture input	60 × 1,500 × 7.4 =	666,000 gr/hr
Heat loss from building		
Ceiling	36 × 140 × (1/15) × 45 =	15,120 Btu/hr
Wall	(2 × 8(36 + 140) − 200) × (1/12) × 45 =	9,810 Btu/hr
Windows & door	200 × (1/2) × 45 =	4,500 Btu/hr
Total heat loss		29,430 Btu/hr
Heat available for ventilation	315,000 − 29,430 =	285,570 Btu/hr
Lb of air moved	285,570/(15 − 0.8) =	20,111 lb/hr
Moisture removed	20,111 × (26 −5) =	422,331 gr/hr
Total fan capacity	13 × 20,111/60 =	4,357 cu ft/min
Fan capacity per 1,000 lb animal	4,357/(60 × 1.5 =	48.4 cu ft/min
Moisture to be removed from stable in waste	(666,000 − 422,331)/7,000 =	34.8 lb/hr

The 48.4 cubic feet per minute fan capacity per 1,000-pound animal unit is close to the recommended capacity for continuous operation given in Chapter 18. This is logical since the conditions chosen for the example are near the coldest to be expected in the area. A similar analysis made at a warmer temperature (e.g. 75°F (24°C)) might well show the need

for an additional 200 cubic feet per minute (5.6 m³/min) of fan capacity for each 1,000-pound (454-kg) animal unit. In between these two rates, fan capacity controlled by thermostats set at 55 to 60°F (13 to 16°C) would cycle on and off somewhat in relation to outside temperature.

Note on the psychrometric chart that of the 14.2 Btu required to change from inlet-air to exhaust-air condition, 10.3 Btu warmed the air from 0 to 45°F and the remaining 3.9 Btu vaporized and warmed the moisture.

About two-thirds of the moisture produced by the animals was removed by ventilation while the balance would be removed with the manure.

A similar analysis for a smaller number of animal units or a poorly insulated building might indicate the need for one or more of the following:

- A lower ventilation rate
- A lower inside design temperature
- The need for supplemental heat

Exposure Factor

A comparison of the heat loss per animal unit for two or more buildings, may easily be made with the aid of their *exposure factors* determined from the equation:

$$EF = \Sigma(A_iU_i)/N \qquad \text{Where:}$$

		Customary	*SI*
EF =	exposure factor	Btu/(hr °F)	(W/°C)
A_i =	surface areas of various parts of the building	sq ft	(m²)
U_i =	coefficient of heat transfer for the areas	Btu/(hr sq ft °F)	(W/(m²·°C))
N =	animal units: for cattle	1,000 lb	(454 kg)
	other animals	1 animal	1 animal

The American Society of Agricultural Engineers has published a series of design graphs (Figure 16-8) in which the exposure factor and outside temperature are used to determine desirable ventilation rates. While Figure 16-8 applies to dairy cattle, graphs for beef, swine, and poultry may be found in the Annual Agricultural Engineers Yearbook (American Society of Agricultural Engineers, 1977).

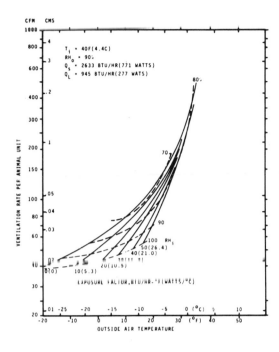

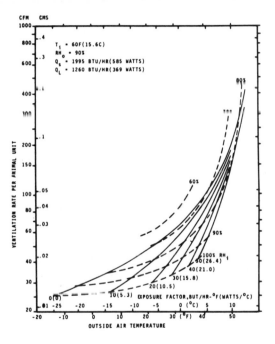

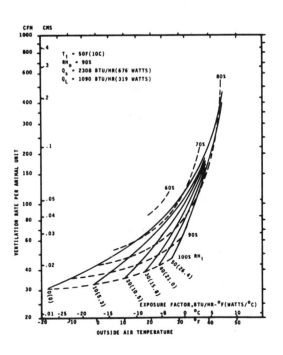

Figure 16-8. Design graphs for predicting ventilation performance for dairy cattle. (From *Agricultural Engineers Yearbook*, 1977, American Society of Agricultural Engineers)

VENTILATION OF UNINSULATED COLD BUILDINGS

Cold buildings used to house livestock require attention to proper ventilation design if a desirable environment is to be maintained. Just as in a warm building, animal heat is a factor that helps remove moisture. However, orientation of the building and construction details that promote free air movement are more essential.

Location and orientation   Location and orientation of the barn on high land with one side (the back side of an open-front building) facing the prevailing wind will help provide the air movement and pressure differences required for successful operation. Wind blowing perpendicular to the ridge of a building tends to cause a positive pressure on the windy side and a negative pressure on the lee side, thus promoting air movement within the building.

Roof pitch   A roof pitch of no less than 4:12 is desirable. Air movement appears to be sluggish under very low pitches while very steep slopes seem to carry inlet air off without adequate circulation within the animal zone. Also, the steeper pitches are more expensive and more difficult to work on during construction.

Sidewall height   Sidewall height that provides adequate clearance for animals and equipment is usually satisfactory. Ten feet (3 m) over alleys or 12 feet (3.5 m) in bedded manure-pack areas are minimum desirable heights.

Eave and ridge openings   These are necessary throughout the year. In addition, provision must be made to open the sidewalls during mild weather. It is recommended that the eaves have a continuous opening equivalent to 1 inch (25 mm) for each 10 feet (3 m) of barn width. This opening can usually be provided by leaving the space between the plate and the underside of the roof open. Unless blowing snow proves to be a problem, the space should be left open all year. If a hinged baffle seems necessary, it should not close off more than one-half of the required opening.

To be compatible, the ridge opening should be 2 inches (50 mm) for each 10 feet (3 m) of building width. Ordinarily, no ridge cap is necessary. While a cap keeps out rain, it often causes an increased snow problem. If a cap is installed, it should never be wider than twice the width of the opening and it must be high enough to allow a vertical distance between the top of the roofing and the bottom of the cap equal to one half of the ridge opening. As an example, a 60-foot (18-m) barn should have 6-inch (150-mm) openings at the eaves, a 12-inch (300-mm) opening at the ridge, and a ridge cap should be no more than 24 inches (600 mm) wide with a minimum vertical clearance of 6 inches (150 mm). When a ridge cap is not used, the exposed rafters should be flashed down to the first purlins in order to prevent decay due to moisture accumulation between the rafter and purlins.

Sidewall openings   These may be provided by hinged panels that will allow a continuous 2-foot (0.6-m) opening for the length of the building. If panels are mounted on a track to allow horizontal adjustment, they must be 4 foot (1.2 m) high to provide an equivalent area of opening.

Condensation   Condensation will occasionally appear on the underside of the roof in the best of systems. However, this can be kept to a minimum by following the suggestions for roof slope and ventilation, as well as other controlling factors such as animal density, purlin design, roof material, insulation, and the location of other buildings.

Housing the number of animals for which the building was planned provides the maximum heat to support air circulation. A truss spacing that allows 2- by 4-inch (38 by 89 mm) purlins to be laid flat will provide the best air movement. Six- and 8-inch (140- and 184-mm) deep purlins should be avoided as they tend to create dead air pockets. A solid roof deck or insulation under the roofing will help to prevent condensation. However, either one adds to the construction cost and, in the case of the insulation, moisture which can collect between it and the roofing may cause a serious corrosion problem with a metal roof. The use of corrugated asphalt roofing in place of metal may provide that slight increase in surface temperature that could prevent condensation. However, the asphalt roofing should have a white, mineral surface to prevent excessive absorption of summer heat.

VENTILATION COOLING SYSTEMS

For some enterprises, ventilation systems are designed to provide cooling. For example, in enclosed livestock buildings, surplus fan capacity above that required for winter ventilation is used for summer cooling. Potato and nursery storages use cool, nighttime air to lower the temperature to storage level. Greenhouse systems require large fan capacity which is used primarily for cooling.

However, when the outside air temperature is excessive, air movement alone is not effective and evaporative cooling becomes an alternative. Water dripping over shredded wood or cellulose pads creates a large wet area. Air drawn through the wet pads is cooled by the evaporation of the water. The range of pad area to air volume is approximately 0.5 to 0.7 square feet (0.05 to 0.07 m²) per 100 cubic feet per minute (47 L/s) of air flow, although the manufacturer's recommendations should be followed for specific installations. Efficient evaporative coolers are capable of reducing air temperature to within 5°F (3°C) of the initial wet-bulb temperature of the air being drawn through the pads. The cooled air will have a relative humidity of 85 to 90 percent.

The value of an evaporative cooling system depends on its application and on the typical wet-bulb temperatures for the region. In the eastern half of the United States wet-bulb temperatures at midday are commonly 12 to 17°F (7 to 9°C) below dry-bulb temperatures. Thus, lowering the temperature 7 to 12°F (4 to 7°C) with an evaporative cooler is feasible. However, in the event of an unusually hot spell, air passing through the cooling pads may still be above 80°F (27°C) and be very high in humidity. This is a condition that might be fine in a greenhouse but is unacceptable for broilers and other animals that depend on respiration for body cooling at high temperatures.

In contrast, in the western half of the United States, excluding western Oregon and Washington, wet-bulb temperatures are commonly 25 to 30°F (14 to 17°C) below dry-bulb temperatures. Under these conditions cooling the air 15 to 20°F (8 to 11°C) is possible without raising the relative humidity above 60 to 70 percent. The air is not only cooled appreciably, but humidity is still low enough to have little effect on animal comfort. Evaporative cooling is obviously much more practical in the drier regions of the country and should be considered on the basis of economic feasibility.

SPECIFIC ENTERPRISES

Ventilation requirements for specific enterprises will be discussed in the chapter devoted to housing for each of those enterprises.

PROBLEMS

16.1   In areas where summer temperatures may be extreme, spray systems are recommended for cooling hogs. Why should the spray fall directly on the hogs instead of evaporating in the air near the pens?

16.2   Figure 16-2 shows hypothetical performance curves for a fan. At what static pressure and discharge rate is the fan most efficient?

16.3   A poultry house in central Pennsylvania houses 10,000 layers averaging 4 pounds (1.8 kg) each. The inside temperature is maintained at 60°F (15.6°C) and the relative humidity averages 70 percent. Ninety percent of the animal heat is available for ventilation. Choose an outside design temperature for the area. What is the maximum possible ventilation rate at that design temperature? How much moisture is being removed?

16.4 For the poultry house and flock in problem 16.3, what ventilation rate will be required to remove 95 percent of the animal heat when it is 90°F (32°C) and 70 percent relative humidity outside and 95°F (35°C) and 70 percent relative humidity inside?

16.5 How much inlet area would be needed to match the ventilation rate determined in questions 16.3 and 16.4?

16.6 A dairy barn in central Wisconsin has an exposure factor of 5 (2.7). Using Figure 16-8 determine the correct ventilation rate per 1,000-pound (455 kg) animal unit to maintain the inside temperature at 50°F (10°C) while the outside temperature is at design level for the region.

REFERENCES

American Society of Agricultural Engineers. *Agricultural Engineers Yearbook.* St. Joseph, Mich.: American Society of Agricultural Engineers, 1977.

American Society of Heating, Refrigerating and Air Conditioning Engineers. *Handbook of Fundamentals.* New York: American Society of Heating, Refrigerating and Air Conditioning Engineers, 1977.

Bodman, Gerald R. *Non-Mechanical Ventilation of Animal Housing Facilities.* Pennsylvania State Agricultural Engineering Monograph No. 706. University Park, Pa.: Penn State University, 1976.

Koch, Walter, Jennings, B.H., and Humphreys, C.M. *Environmental Study II—Sensation Responses to Temperature and Humidity Under Still Air Conditions in the Comfort Range.* American Society of Heating, Refrigerating and Air Conditioning Engineers Transactions, Vol. 66, 1969, p. 264.

McCurdy, Joseph A., Irish, W.W., and Light, Robert G. *Ventilating Insulated Dairy Buildings.* Pennsylvania State University College of Agriculture Extension Service Special Circular 83, University Park, Pa., 1967.

Midwest Plan Service. *Structures and Environment Handbook.* Ames, Iowa: Midwest Plan Service, 1977.

Chapter Seventeen

Construction Cost Estimation

The subject of construction cost estimating will be discussed from the standpoint of the builder or his estimator. However, an understanding of the process of estimating by a buyer can be a helpful aid in choosing which of several contracts to accept. A farmer also can determine what a building constructed with farm labor is likely to cost.

In order to estimate the cost of construction, an estimator must be well acquainted with all building terms, be able to identify all parts of a building, and have a good knowledge of the various materials available to be used in construction (Figure 17-1). It is the estimator's responsibility to read a set of plans and specifications, estimate what materials and labor will be necessary, determine what parts of the job may be subcontracted and what they will cost, estimate an allowance where a definite cost figure is difficult, and determine a contract price including profit and overhead. It is also useful for the estimator to be conversant with code rules pertaining to such things as foundation depths, ceiling heights, window size, and service entrance size, and thus be able to point out any noncomplying specifications.

The estimated cost of such items as land, permits, clearing, excavation, water supply, sewage disposal, and landscaping may also be included as contract items or allowances.

Regardless of the size of the project, it is more important that the estimate be complete than precise. For example, it is not necessary to know exactly how every last stud will be used so that an exact number may be obtained; but it would be very costly indeed to forget to include the studs as a whole.

Many rules of thumb or conventions have been developed that are surprisingly accurate and reduce considerably the time and effort required to make an estimate. These rules take into account such factors as cutting waste, the difference between nominal and actual size, pattern matching, and breakage.

COST vs ALLOWANCE

An estimator will include, as a cost, all items in which the specified materials are relatively standard and the builder will be supplying the labor as well as items on which a subcontractor will give a definite bid price. There is relatively little chance that the cost of these two types of items will change appreciably during construction.

On the other hand, there are many items on which the estimator simply does not have adequate information to calculate a definite cost. Therefore, an estimated allowance is included and the buyer either pays any extra cost or receives a discount if the estimated allowance proves to be too high.

Examples of allowances range all the way from the cost of an excavation where ledge may be encountered, to light fixtures or floor coverings which come in a wide range of qualities and prices and are likely to be chosen by the customer well after construction has been started.

ESTIMATE SHEETS

A worksheet for each type of job should show all of the items, quantities, units, unit prices, and costs or allowances that are needed. Obviously a worksheet for site clearing and excavation might look quite different from one for the electrical work.

Once the worksheets have been completed, a summary sheet should be compiled that might have the following format:

Estimate Summary

Job _____ Location _____ Date _____

Work Sheet Title	Item	Subcontractor, Remarks	Cost	Allowance

These sheets allow the estimator or builder to have immediate access to items when discussing them with the buyer.

MAKING THE ESTIMATE

It is desirable to develop the estimate in the sequence in which work will be completed and the order in which materials will be needed on the job.

It is helpful to keep a separate sheet on which to list all surface

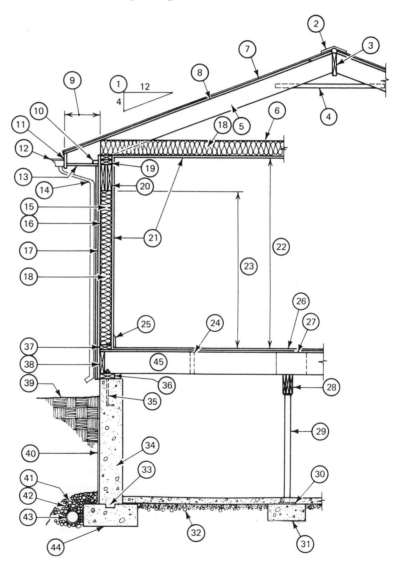

areas and wall lengths as they are calculated. Many of these values will be used several times over but need be calculated only once. For example, the square foot of floor area may be used for estimating concrete for the basement slab, subflooring for the main deck, various materials for the finish floor, and even the labor cost for closing in the building.

The following examples of rules and procedures can aid in the process of cost estimating.

1. A medium-size bulldozer can clear approximately 1,200 square feet (110 m²) of land per hour or excavate approximately 40 cubic yards (30 m³) per hour.

2. In estimating concrete, use full dimensions with no allowance for corners. Round up the results to compensate for form inaccuracy and waste. The delivered cost of a small quantity of concrete to make up for any shortage is very expensive.

3. Concrete blocks may be estimated on the basis of 1.2 blocks per square foot (0.09/m²) of gross wall surface. This will allow for a limited amount of breakage.

4. Floor and ceiling joist numbers may be determined by dividing the length of the area to be covered by the joist spacing and then adding 1. Estimates must take into account usable lengths and any openings that will need to be framed with headers or double joists.

5. The subflooring should be determined on the basis of the gross floor area for plywood, while with lumber, an additional amount must be included to account for the waste in cutting and the loss of width due to the tongue and groove.

6. In determining the number of studs required, allow one per

Figure 17-1. Parts identification for typical section of a house.

1. Pitch triangle
2. Ridge cap
3. Ridge board
4. Collar tie
5. Rafter
6. Ceiling joist
7. Roofing
8. Sheathing
9. Overhang or tail
10. Nailer
11. Facia
12. Gutter
13. Soffit
14. Leader or downspout
15. Stud
16. Sheathing

17. Siding
18. Insulation
19. Plate
20. Header
21. Gypsum board or plaster
22. Finish height
23. Window & door height
24. Bridging
25. Baseboard
26. Finish floor
27. Subfloor
28. Carrying beam or girder
29. Column
30. Concrete floor

31. Column footing
32. Gravel
33. Footing key
34. Foundation wall
35. Anchor bolt
36. Sill
37. Shoe or sole
38. Header
39. Grade
40. Waterproofing
41. Building paper
42. Crushed stone
43. Footing drain
44. Footing
45. Floor joist

foot (1/300 mm) of gross wall length. This will provide for cripple studs, jack studs, and nonweight-bearing headers.

7.   Choose the size for all weight-bearing headers on the basis of the size required for the largest opening. This is done to simplify construction procedures.

8.   Shoes and plates may be determined from gross wall lengths.

9.   Sheathing quantity, when using plywood, as with subflooring, is based on gross area. An extra amount must be included for tongue and groove lumber and diagonal installation.

10.   Rafter numbers may be determined the same as joists with proper allowance for overhangs at the gable ends and the rafter tails at the eaves.

11.   The estimated roof deck area should also take into account any overhang at the gable ends and eaves.

12.   The quantity of nails to close a building in, including framing, floor deck, roof deck, and sheathing, may be assumed at 100 pounds for each 1,000 square feet ($50 \text{ kg}/100 \text{ m}^2$) of floor area.

13.   Labor for the framing is often estimated on the basis of finished floor area.

14.   Siding and roofing are usually sold by the square (100 sq ft) and should be based on gross areas. One or two extra squares of roofing will allow for a starter course as well as valleys and ridges.

15.   The electrical system estimate is usually based on a cost per opening (switch, outlet, or fixture) plus the cost of the service entrance. Fixtures should be listed as an allowance, with the customer's choice either raising or lowering the actual cost. Outside outlets must be protected with ground-fault interrupters at extra cost.

16.   The plumbing estimate is often based on the number of major fixtures located in the kitchen, laundry, and bath. In addition, a cost for connecting equipment such as a dishwasher and disposal unit will be included.

17.   A hot-water heating system is likely to be based on floor area for radiation plus the cost of the boiler and burner. Zoned systems will add further to the cost. Hot air systems are likely to be based on a cost for each feed and return opening, plus the cost of the furnace and blower.

18.   Insulation needs are estimated on the basis of gross wall, ceiling, and floor areas.

19.   Inside wall and ceiling coverings such as gypsum board or paneling are based on gross areas.

20.   In estimating finished floor coverings, an allowance for matching must be included as follows: sheet vinyl and carpeting—10 percent; various tiles—0 to 5 percent, unless there is a special pattern consideration; hardwood flooring—30 percent, to take care of cutting waste and difference between nominal and actual size.

21.   Labor for all interior trim work is often estimated on the basis of finished floor area.

22.   Cost estimates for inside painting are usually based on medium sized rooms. Large rooms are counted as two. Two coats of paint per room with no more than two colors in the house is typical. An extra charge is assessed for more than two colors.

23.   Outside painting is usually based on the area to be painted, plus a charge for each window and each lineal foot of trim.

24.   An estimated charge should be included for cleaning during construction and at the completion of construction. This is a cost that is frequently overlooked.

While there are many details omitted from the foregoing list, it does cover the major parts of a home. The pertinent parts of the list may be selected for use in estimating the cost for other buildings.

The experienced estimator will not overlook the many little items that can add up to a substantial amount. Good specifications and a working list will help to prevent the omission of such items as joist hangers, bridging, screen for soffit vents, door stops, and others.

The following list of items is often given an *allowance* estimate.

- Site clearing and excavation
- Electrical fixtures and floor coverings
- Kitchen cabinets and appliances
- Bathroom vanities, cabinets
- Inside painting and wall papering
- Landscaping but not seeding
- Septic tank and drainage field
- Well and water pump

Overhead and Profit

Whether a builder works out of a tool box in his pickup truck or has a headquarters building and a large staff, he has overhead—nonproductive costs that must be considered. If he does not include these costs in his bid prices, he is only hastening the day when he will be out of business. Following is a list of typical overhead items.

- Secretarial services
- Office supplies
- Insurance and bonding
- Taxes and license fees
- Advertising
- Tools and depreciation
- Travel and entertainment
- Accounting and legal fees

- Utilities
- Office rent and equipment
- Education and subscriptions
- Interest and commissions

The overhead costs may be estimated as a percentage of the construction cost. Depending somewhat on the number of jobs completed during the year, it typically runs 6 to 10 percent. However, the most satisfactory method is to estimate the total overhead cost on the basis of previous years' records and then prorate that cost over the number of jobs expected during the year.

Profit is determined by a number of factors, not the least of which is the economic situation and building market at the time the estimate is made. Five to 10 percent of construction cost is probably a reasonable range. The amount of subcontracting used on a job can also influence the profit margin for the principal contractor.

The Buyer's Viewpoint

Let the buyer beware of the lowest and highest of several bids. The chances are that neither is a very good indication of actual cost. The buyer should go over the "allowance list" with each bidder and find out what items are so listed and how much has been estimated in each case. The chances are good that when differences in allowances are reconciled, the various bid prices may be much closer than they originally appeared.

"Bargain" jobs seldom turn out to be real bargains. Changes that are made during construction are likely to be expensive and allowances that have been given low estimates seem to have a way of growing larger.

PROBLEMS

17.1   Identify all of the numbered parts in Figure 17-1 without referring to the key.

17.2   Starting with information developed in problems 4.2 and 7.2, complete an estimate for materials, labor, and overhead.

REFERENCES

Boyd, James S. *Practical Farm Buildings.* Danville, Ill.: The Interstate Printers and Publishers, Inc., 1973.

Lytle, R.J. *Farm Builder's Handbook.* Farmington, Mich.: Structures Publishing Company, 1973.

Part Two

Housing for Specific Enterprises

Part II deals with housing for specific enterprises. Unlike the enduring principles discussed in Part I, the design of housing for livestock and farm products tends to evolve continuously. What is common practice today is likely to be improved upon or even changed radically tomorrow. New ideas are continually being tested for achieving maximum efficiency in handling materials and utilizing labor efficiently, for controlling the environment more precisely, and for obtaining maximum production or maintaining superior product quality. For this reason, the discussions in Part II will often be more general, limited in some cases to such basic requirements as space and environmental needs, yet providing a base from which new ideas may be developed.

AN EXAMPLE OF CHANGE: THE MANUFACTURED BUILDING

An example of the change in buildings for agriculture is the increased use of manufactured buildings delivered to the farm ready to use. Early manufactured buildings were not popular, but as quality has improved and complete environmental control systems have been included, sales have increased at a rapid rate. There are advantages that were not at first considered. For example, in many states these buildings are not considered real estate; thus, there may be tax advantages. The

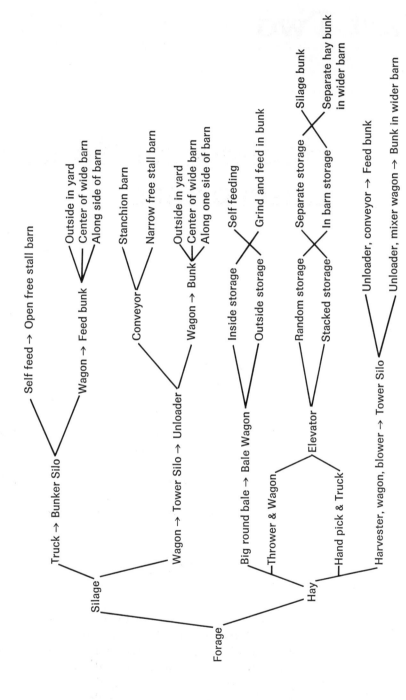

Figure II-1.   Example of multiple material handling system.

buildings may be readily sold and moved, a definite advantage to the tenant farmer. Portability also allows a change in the management system or even a complete change in enterprise without suffering the expense of renovating or abandoning a permanent building.

A SYSTEMS APPROACH

It is a rare case in which several alternatives for the mechanization of an agricultural enterprise do not exist. Furthermore, these alternatives may occur at several steps along the production path. Figure II-1 illustrates a number of possibilities in the choice of equipment and handling of forage from field to dairy cow. Similar diagrams can be drawn for grain, milk, manure, and even the herd itself.

In a systems approach all of the possible methods of managing and handling the necessary items for an enterprise are considered both separately and in combination. Once the overall combined system has been decided upon, it is possible to choose a structure to house that system. The materials-handling system will influence the size and type of building, type of frame, floor material, strength of members, and amount of insulation. The system chosen will affect such things as the type of silage and hay storage and the amount of land area required. The interaction between the system and the building also affects labor efficiency and investment. A systems approach to planning the buildings for an enterprise is essential if the most efficient, comfortable, and economical combination is to be obtained.

Chapter Eighteen

Housing for Dairy Cattle

Dairy cattle housing systems are among the more complex of agricultural structures. When undertaking new or modified construction, there are several basic requirements that planners should attempt to meet. For the cows they include:

1. Adequate shelter from wind, rain, snow, and temperature extremes.

2. Layout and equipment that does not subject the animals to undue stress or chance of injury.

For the operator they include:

1. A design and construction that meets all federal, state, and local requirements relating to building, sanitary, safety, and environmental regulations.

2. A system that is efficient in the handling of the cows, feed, milk, and waste products.

3. A system that uses capital efficiently for an economically sound enterprise.

4. A system that is integrated into the total farm operation in terms of its location in relation to other buildings (including neighbors), feed storage, roads, utilities, and manure disposal.

The manner in which these requirements are met will differ according to climate, farm organization, land values, and markets. For example, farmers in the upper Midwest and southern Ontario may integrate dairying with other farm enterprises, including the production of most of the feed. With a herd size of 30 to 60 cows, a traditional stanchion or tie-stall barn seems to best meet their needs. Where severe winters make a warm barn desirable, satisfactory environmental conditions are more easily maintained in a stable barn than in a free-stall barn. Investment per cow for the small to medium sized herds is usually less and while this system requires considerable attention to individual animals it allows for maximum production.

In extreme contrast, the typical dairy operation in the Southwest consists of several hundred cows divided into strings confined to unpaved yards that require scraping only twice a year. Shelter consists of approximately 20 square feet (2 m²) of sunshade per animal. Feeding is in fenceline bunks and milking is done in large milking parlors. Although some cropland may be contiguous with the dairy operation, in many cases all feed is purchased and only enough acreage is included for the yards, buildings, and such pastureland as is necessary for waste-water disposal.

In warm, humid regions, open-side free-stall barns with paved alleys, often flush-cleaned, are more suitable. Forage may be grown on the adjoining farmland or purchased. Flush cleaning is feasible in areas where the water source is adequate to supply up to 100 gallons (380 L) per day for each cow and where that much waste water can be easily disposed of on the land. The volume of fresh water may be reduced somewhat by recycling waste water.

In colder areas of the country, as herds have increased in size to 80 cows or more, free-stall barns and milking parlors have become common. The degree of confinement often increases as the climate becomes colder and snowfall greater. Although there are proponents of warm systems for very cold climates, there is little evidence to indicate that warm barns influence milk production or cow comfort. The only benefit is related to worker comfort. However, the ventilation problems associated with warm systems in cold regions appear to outweigh that advantage.

HOUSING SYSTEMS

Stable Barns

Popular for herds of 30 to 60 cows, stable barns provide the facilities for feeding, resting, and milking in one location. The herdsman moves from cow to cow for milking and must stoop each time to have access to the cow's udder. The high degree of individual animal attention that is required for good herd health and maximum production is easily provided. A warm, well-ventilated stable is a pleasant place to work during the winter and provides an attractive display of breeding stock. For small sized herds the construction cost is often less than for a free-stall and parlor system. Two rows of cows, facing out, will consolidate all cleaning and milking operations in one alley and help to keep barn walls clean. Either stanchions or tie stalls may be used to restrain the cows. In spite of extra labor required to tie cows, the greater freedom of movement that the tie stalls allow for the animals makes them the choice in most new or modified systems. Of the several styles of tie stalls available, the simple New York stall consisting of a single horizontal pipe 8 inches (200 mm) ahead of the curb and approximately 3 feet (1 m) above the stall floor appears to have the most advantages, particularly in terms of cost. The pipe can double as a water or vacuum line or it may be separate and designed to revolve so that all animals may be unhooked by the herdsman at one time.

Stalls of adequate width and length reduce injuries and keep cows clean. However, when the stall is too long, a cow drops more manure on the platform. Placement of the gutter at an angle to the stall platforms at the time of construction provides stalls of varying lengths suitable for all the animals in the herd. German farmers often use 3-foot (1 m) wide gutters combined with gutter grates that can be positioned to adjust the length of each stall.

Table 18-1   Dairy Stable Dimensions

	Customary Units	SI Units
Tie stalls—width	4½–5 ft	1.3–1.5 m
length	5¾–6½ ft	1.7–2 m
Platform slope	1:50–1:25	1:50–1:25
Feed alley—width	6–6½ ft	1.8–2 m
Service alley—width	6–6½ ft	1.8–2 m
Cross alley—width	4½ft	1.4 m
Gutter width	16–18 in.	400–450 mm

Various alley and manger designs are used, but the most popular is a simple flat feed-alley without a raised manger. Stall platforms may be bedded with straw, shavings, or sawdust. Rubber mats may be used to minimize the amount of bedding required.

To be competitive with other systems in terms of labor, stable barns must have mechanized handling of materials. Milking is most efficient with a clean-in-place pipeline. However, a dumping station that pumps milk to the cooler from a portable receiver is nearly as efficient and considerably less expensive. Feeding can be done with a conveyor system or

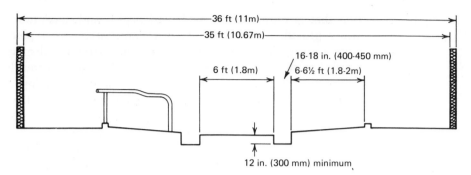

Figure 18-1. Critical dimensions for a dairy stable. Apportion remaining dimensions as space permits.

with a self-propelled cart. Of the two, the conveyor is more labor efficient, but the cart requires less investment and permits individual feed control.

To meet the high standards of cleanliness required in a dairy stable, the wall and ceiling surfaces should be smooth, easily cleaned, and moisture resistant. A choice of several materials varying in cost and quality is available. Fiberglass panels are waterproof, durable, and expensive. MDO plywood offers a satisfactory surface at medium to high cost, and painted exterior-type plywood is the least expensive.

Free Stalls and a Milking Parlor

Free-stall systems which are compatible with several methods for feeding, milking, and removing manure, show improved labor efficiency when compared to a stanchion system. With a herd size of 80 cows or more, the initial investment can be less than for a stall barn. While it is not as easy to give individual attention or to observe the cows closely, milking in an elevated parlor does allow eye-level observation of the cow's udder, and the freedom of animal movement can improve heat detection.

There are at least five variations in the degree of shelter provided by free stall systems:

1. *Enclosed warm* systems with heavy insulation and mechanical ventilation eliminate extreme fluctuations in temperature and problems with frozen manure. However, the cost of operating the fans is significant, particularly during mild weather, and even with thermostatic control there are likely to be periods in which condensation will occur in some parts of the barn. This happens because of the large areas of wet alley surface and because the cows tend to group together in some places

while leaving other areas unoccupied, resulting in heat deficiency in those areas. As temperature declines and moisture level remains constant, the relative humidity will increase until condensation occurs, either in the air as fog or on inside surfaces of the building. The effect may be minimized by heavy insulation, maintaining maximum animal density, and using a layout designed for uniform animal distribution and heat production during feeding and resting.

2. *Enclosed cold* systems have little or no insulation and depend on natural air currents for ventilation. Openings along the eaves and at the ridge provide for ventilation in the cold months, while large openings along the sidewalls allow free air movement in mild weather. With the enclosed cold system, most snow problems are eliminated and, with the animals completely confined, there is no runoff from a yard to increase disposal problems.

3. *Covered cold* systems, while not providing quite as much protection from snow and wind, do allow sunshine into the building through the open south side.

4. *Partially open* systems have reduced barn area per cow but compensate for this with a paved yard. Provision for yard cleaning and yard runoff are necessary.

5. *Open* systems with covered free stalls but open feeding and exercise areas are practical in mild climates and are the least expensive. The free-stall barn may be sided or not, depending on local conditions. Water flushing of the alleys may be practical where temperatures, water supply, and disposal areas are suitable. Although initial costs will be increased by the flush system, savings in labor will result.

Free-Stall Barns

Materials In order to install the required insulation in a warm system barn, frame construction on a concrete foundation is preferred. However, pole construction is ideal for all cold system, free-stall buildings. An open roof deck with metal roofing, together with siding of vertical boards, plywood, or metal provides economical construction. A roof pitch of at least 4:12 is desirable for adequate air movement. While rigid-frame, metal buildings may be used, roof pitches are often rather low and purlins quite deep, restricting free air movement from eave to ridge. This situation results in ventilation problems and premature corrosion of frame and roof covering.

Stall dividers made of 2-inch (38-mm) wood or metal are satisfactory. Wood that comes in contact with the ground should be pressure-preservative treated. Stall curbing may be made of either concrete or wood. Wood curbing is designed with two pieces, one pressure-preservative treated and fastened securely to the stall posts for permanence, and an untreated member on the alley side that can be easily replaced when it becomes worn.

Concrete is the most durable material for alleys and yards. Because it tends to become slippery, concrete should be given an antiskid, broomed finish when it is placed. In addition, it is common practice to cut half-inch (13-mm) grooves into the surface in a pattern that runs at an angle to the direction of scraping to avoid catching the scraper blade. Coarse, aluminum oxide grit worked into the surface as it sets is another method of reducing both slipping and floor wear. This surface also wears away the cow's hooves enough to reduce the frequency of regular trimming.

Barn layout   In direct contrast to the stable barn where a cow feeds, rests, and is milked in one place, the free-stall housing system allows the cow to move to a different area for each of these activities with free access to feed and water.

The objective in planning the layout for a free-stall system is to meet the requirements of the cow in a minimum suitable area, to allow effective movement of the herd and permit efficient handling of feed and manure. If the layout provides a separate area specifically designed for each function, efficiency will be maximized.

A cow requires a clean, dry place to rest without being bothered by other cows. When she gets up after resting she normally defecates. To keep her resting area clean, a neck rail forces her to back into the alley as she gets up where the manure collects and is mechanically removed by one of several methods. The alley must be wide enough so she has no trouble getting into or out of her stall. Feeding is done in a separate area so that the stall will remain clean. Filling the feed bunk is accomplished with a conveyor or a mixer wagon. At milking time the herd is gathered together in one or more groups in a holding area. A mechanical crowd gate may be used to minimize delays. After milking, the cows return to the feed and rest areas.

Although many different floor plans have been used over the years, there has been an evolution to straight rows of stalls and considerably reduced area per cow. However, there are still a number of different designs being used, the choice of which depends on herd size, feeding program, climate, site characteristics, and owner preference.

All of the specifications in the following list do not necessarily apply to every barn, but where they do apply, they will contribute to cow comfort and labor efficiency with a minimum of investment. These specifications are for large milk cows. If a barn is being planned for a small breed, some dimensions, i.e. stall size, should be reduced.

1.   Free-stall alleys, a minimum of 7½ to 8 feet (2.2 to 2.4 m) wide.

2.   Free-stall to silage-bunk alley, a minimum of 12 feet (3.7 m) wide.

3.   Silage bunk to blank wall, a minimum of 10 feet (3 m) wide.

4.   Hay rack to silage bunk on opposite side of the alley, a minimum of 13 feet (4 m) wide.

5.   Individual free stalls, 3½ to 4 feet (1.1 to 1.2 m) wide with length dependent on the average animal size of the herd and stall arrangement. Single row of stalls: stalls 6½ to 7 feet (2 to 2.1 m) long including curb.

Two facing rows: stalls 6 feet (1.8 m) long if stall fronts are left open
        except for top rail at 4-foot (1.2-m) level.
Other dimensions: Side rails, 4 feet (1.2 m)
        Bottom rails, 15 inches (380 mm)
        Slope from stall front to curb, 5 inches (125 mm)
        Curb height, 10 to 12 inches (250 to 300 mm) depending on length
        of alley and method of removing manure.

6.   Adequate cross alleys, 8 feet (2.4 m) wide and no dead-end alleys, providing ease of animal movement. Cross alleys should be raised to the stall curb level to keep manure in the main alleys during scraping.

7.   Approximately 15 square feet (1.4 m²) of holding area per cow, with a slope up to the milking parlor entrance; a slope aids in cleaning and induces the cows to face the parlor entrance.

8.   Provision to divide the herd into groups. Grouping allows feeding in accordance with the level of production. Groups should not exceed 100 cows.

9.   No turns in the entrance to the milking parlor. Single pass alleys, such as parlor return alleys, should be only 32 to 36 inches (0.8 to 0.9 m) wide to prevent cows from turning.

10.   Breeding, hospital, and calving areas adjacent to the milking parlor and arranged so that cows may be easily diverted to them.

11.   Access for vehicles into alleys, even in barns with mechanical scrapers and conveyor feeders.

Figure 18-2 shows the plan for a barn to be used with a relatively small free-stall housing system. If used as an open shed with cows having access to a paved strip at least 10 feet (3 m) wide along the bunk, the area per cow and length of bunk is quite generous. If, however, the plan is used for a closed barn, the floor area and bunk length per cow are probably near the minimum.

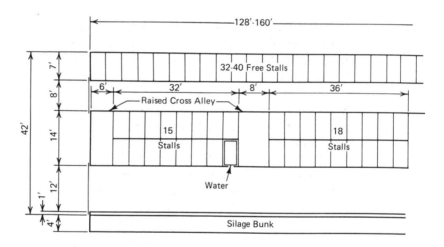

Figure 18-2.   Open side barn, 80-104 free stalls. *Variations:* eight to ten 16 ft. increments of length. (a) 42 ft. wide, open side, feed on one side of bunk, 67 sq. ft./cow, 1.6 bunk/cow; (b) 40 ft. wide, open side, center stalls reduced to 6 ft.; (c) gateway in bunk, feed both sides, 83 sq. ft./cow, 3 ft. bunk/cow; (d) 46 ft. wide, closed barn, 74 sq. ft./cow, 1.6 ft. bunk/cow; (e) 44 ft. wide closed barn, center stalls reduced to 6 ft.

Figures 18-3 and 18-4 show plans for barns to house larger herds either with medium or high animal density. If a warm, free-stall system is desired, the high density plan shown in Figure 18-4 has the better chance of successful ventilation as there would be only about two-thirds as much wet alley surface per cow (Figure 18-3). Figure 18-5 shows an elevation through the stalls for the high-density plan with a drive-through feed alley similar to the plan given in Figure 18-4.

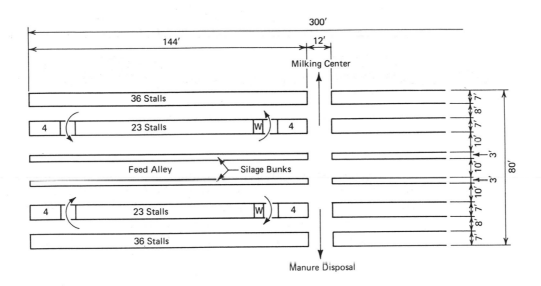

Figure 18-3. Closed barn, 268 free stalls. *Variations:* (a) 80 ft. wide, 10 ft. wide drive-through feed alley, 89.5 sq. ft./cow, 2.1 ft. bunk/cow; (b) 69 ft. wide, 5 ft. bunk with conveyor, 77 sq. ft./cow, 2.1 ft. bunk/cow.

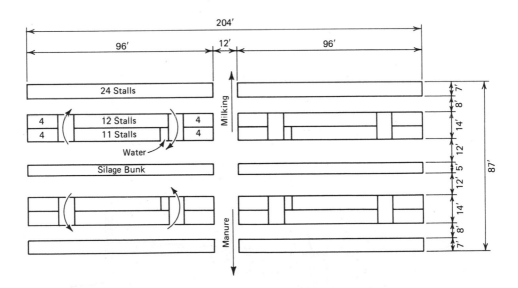

Figure 18-4. High density closed barn, 252 free stalls. *Variations:* (a) 87 ft. wide, 5 ft. bunk with conveyor, 70.4 sq. ft./cow, 1.5 ft. bunk/cow; (b) 98 ft. wide, 2-3 ft. bunks with 10 ft. feed alley, 78 sq. ft./cow, 1.5 ft. bunk/cow; (c) 83 ft. wide, double stalls reduced to 6 ft., 5 ft. bunk with conveyor, 67 sq. ft./cow, 1.5 ft. bunk/cow.

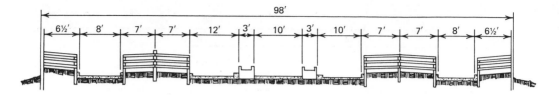

Figure 18-5.   Elevation of a high density free-stall barn.

Designs for free stalls   Stalls built on the site using wood, and commercial stalls made of steel are shown in Figures 18-6 and 18-7. Most have a sloping rear post set in the concrete curb or just inside the curb. Stalls should be bolted together for easy dismantling in the event that a cow "gets down." Cantilevered partitions, as shown in Figure 18-8, which are somewhat shorter than the others, allow cleaning or leveling the stall platform with a tractor-mounted blade. However, they need a sturdy support and bracing with a neck rail.

Free stalls should have a well-drained gravel base, but they must have a thick surface of clay or silt to reduce the formation of holes. Sand or gravel does not work well for a surface. Although more expensive, a concrete stall floor with mats requires less maintenance.

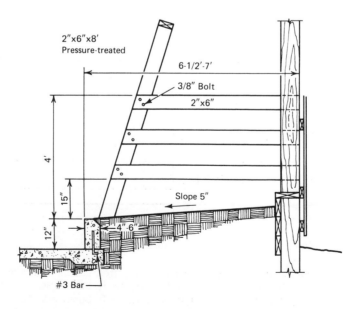

Figure 18-6.   Wood free-stall with overhead stiffener.

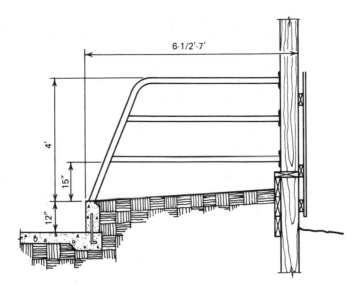

Figuro 18-7. Mctal frco stall partition.

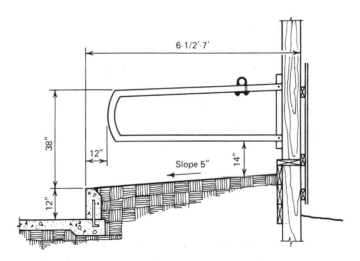

Figure 18-8. Steel cantilever free-stall partition.

Yard or Corral Systems

Open systems of this type are best suited to mild, dry climate zones. Variations include unpaved yards with 500 square feet (45 m²) per cow which are dry-scraped twice a year, semipaved yards with 350 square feet (33 m²) per cow and weekly scraping, or complete paving with 125 square feet (12 m²) or less per cow and daily scraping. The choice will depend on rainfall and availability of land both for yards and waste disposal.

Even the earthen yard should have paved areas at the feed bunks and water tanks, along at least one fence and around gates leading to the milking area. The semipaved yards should have approximately 50 square feet (5 m²) of paved area per cow.

Corral arrangement should provide for efficient feeding, good drainage, easy access for cleaning, and, above all, efficient, continuous movement of animals for milking. This can be achieved with either rectangular or pie-shaped layouts.

Rectangular corrals for herds of up to 400 cows have at least four basic arrangements (Figure 18-9).

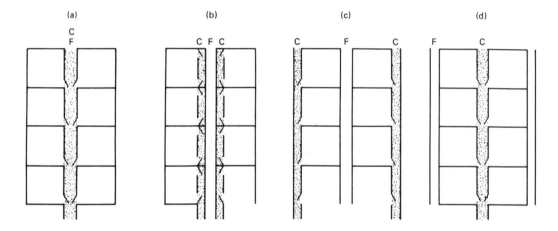

Figure 18-9. Four rectangular corral designs.

- Type A uses the center lane for feeding and moving cows.
- Type B uses the center lane for feeding and adjacent lanes for moving cows.
- Type C uses the center lane for feeding and outside lanes for moving cows.
- Type D uses the center lane for cows and the outside lanes for feeding.

Each of these types has advantages and disadvantages that must be weighed and a decision made as to the relative importance for a particular farm. The factors to consider include:

1. Types B and C with their double cow-lanes permit continuous flow of cows for milking. Types A and D would require a staggered shift to move the cows most effectively.

2. Type D has the most convenient feeding arrangement. Hay can be stacked close to where it will be fed and there are no gates to open or close when feeding silage.

3. Types C and D use the cow lanes as drains. Types A and B need perimeter drains.

4. Type B permits cows to be locked away from feed before milking. The other types require stanchions.

Combinations of rectangular yards with cross alleys are used for herds of 1,000 to 2,000 cows or more.

Pie-shaped corrals (Figure 18-10) are suitable for herds of 250 to 500 cows divided into groups of 40 to 60 cows. Thirty-degree divisions keep the area, yard length, and feed bunk length in good proportion. The most significant advantage of the pie-shaped arrangement is that all the corrals are closer to the milking parlor than in a rectangular layout. This permits strings of cows from very large herds to be moved to the milking facilities in a shorter time. A double pie-shaped system, with service facilities between, can handle up to 800 or 1,000 cows. However, expansion beyond that number is difficult.

In either yard system, 20 to 25 square feet (2 to 2.3 m²) of shade area should be provided for each animal. A sun shade with an eave height of 12 to 14 feet (4 m) and double that in width, when oriented north and south, will allow sunshine to strike all parts of the area under the shade at sometime during the day. This helps keep the surface dry and sanitary. If shades are built in the fence line, they must be located on both sides of the yard to insure shade for all animals throughout the day.

Hospital and Maternity Area

A treatment pen located near the milking center is an essential part of any dairy housing system. One 12 by 14-foot (3.7 by 4.3 m) pen for each 100 milking cows should be adequate. Two or three stanchions in the pen fence allow cows to be restrained for artificial insemination or treatment. Lift equipment, supported on an extra truss or beam, can be useful for elevating animals that get down and can't get up.

One maternity pen of approximately 13 by 13 feet (4 by 4 m) for each 25 cows in the herd is desirable. Designing and locating the pens so

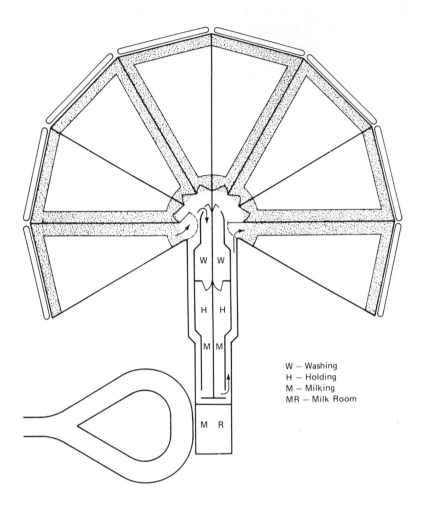

Figure 18-10.   Pie-shaped dairy corral for herds of 250 cows or more.

W — Washing
H — Holding
M — Milking
MR — Milk Room

they may be cleaned with a tractor scraper will reduce labor. A chute for receiving or shipping cows should be placed adjacent to one of the pens.

Milking Center

More than 50 percent of the total labor involved in a dairy enterprise is required for the milking operation and labor costs often exceed 75 percent of the total cost of milking. These factors combine to make the milking center of prime importance in the overall plan.

Milking parlor   While a number of parlor designs have been used, the two most common are the side opening (Figure 18-11) and the herringbone (Figure 18-12). Side opening units allow each animal to be milked at her own pace and to be closely observed. Cows may be easily cut out for treatment. The herringbone parlors are ordinarily less expensive, and because they hold the cows closer together, reduce walking distance to little more than half of that in the side opening system. Although the rate of milking varies more between operators than between systems, generally for similarly equipped systems and herds of equal production, the throughput of a double two side opening parlor will be 30 to 33 per hour, while that of a double-four herringbone parlor will be 34 to 37 per hour. Automated gates will improve the throughput of the side opening unit appreciably. Additional equipment such as crowd gates, stimulating sprays in the floor, and detaching units will increase the capacity of both types but appear to be more beneficial with the herringbone design.

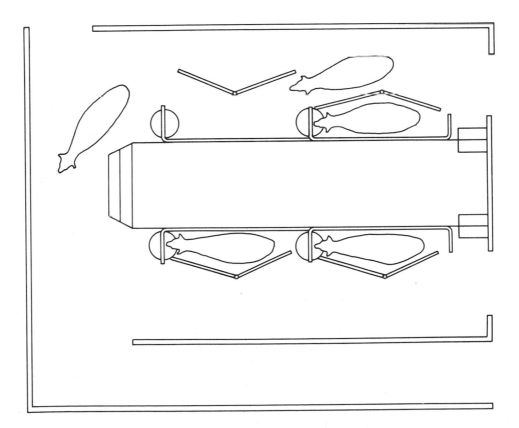

Figure 18-11.   Double-two side-opening parlor.

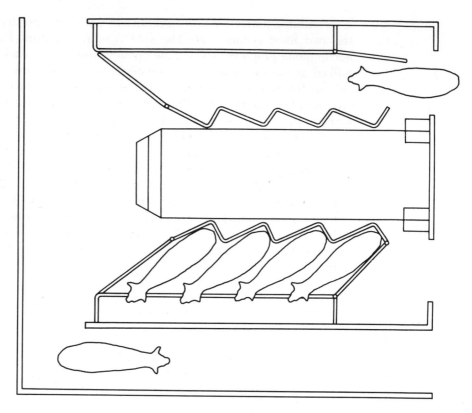

Figure 18-12.   Double-four herringbone parlor.

When relatively little mechanization is available, double-four herringbone parlors for one person or double-eight or -ten for two persons are most efficient. Double-three and double-six parlors seem less productive. Where considerable mechanization is installed, including a crowd gate, stimulators, and detachers, one person can work very effectively in a double-eight or double-ten parlor. Smaller sizes hardly justify the initial investment in mechanization.

For large herds of 400 cows or more, other parlor designs may be considered. The polygon herringbone design (Figure 18-13) is one of the most efficient, particularly when it is fully mechanized. With automatic milk unit detachers, a throughput of more than 100 cows per hour by one person is possible in a 24-stall unit.

While early milking parlors were equipped for feeding grain, many parlors are now being constructed with a saving in cost by omitting grain feeding facilities. This follows the recent trend to feeding a complete ration in the silage bunk.

Regardless of the type or size of parlor used in a system, there are

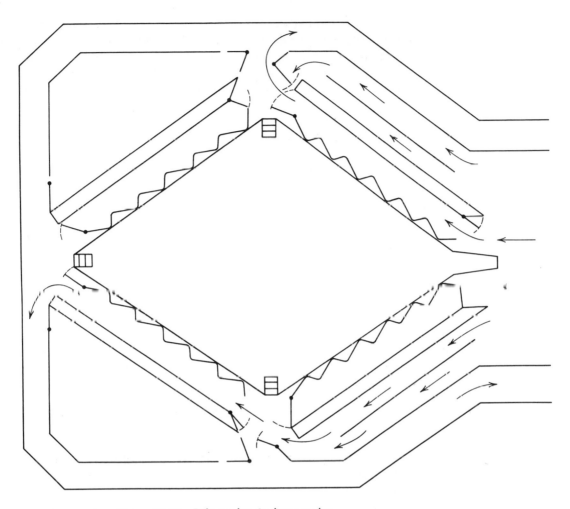

Figure 18-13. Polygon herringbone parlor.

a number of details common to all that contribute to efficient, safe, and comfortable operation.

1. A crowd gate to move the cows toward the parlor. Although a separate holding area and crowd gate are investments that can be eliminated by using a part of the feeding area for holding, the efficiency of the milking operation is enhanced by including them in the design.

2. A combined holding area and milking parlor, or a holding area and parlor separated by an overhead garage door that remains open during milking, can increase the efficiency with which cows move through the parlor. However, the walls and ceiling in the holding area must meet

the same sanitary standards as the parlor walls. In contrast, some herds-men prefer a split entrance door, hinged at either side, that opens toward the holding area. Closing the doors lightly against an entering cow hur-ries her along and at the same time positively stops the following cow. This system relaxes the requirements for sanitary construction in the holding area.

3.   A straight entrance into the parlor for the cows.

4.   Minimum steps or ramps for entering or exiting. However, a gradual slope upward toward the parlor induces cows to face the entrance.

5.   A floor-level 3 to 4 inches (75 to 100 mm) above the holding area.

6.   An insulated concrete foundation.

7.   Grates installed in the milking parlor floor behind the cows reduce manure splash. However, when they are used, a larger amount of manure enters the milking center waste system. This may be a prob-lem if milking center waste must be handled separately from the rest of the manure.

8.   Washable walls with at least 6 inches (150 mm) of concrete at the base.

9.   A minimum of 20 footcandles (200 lux) of general lighting and 50 footcandles (500 lux) at the cows' udders.

10.   Insulation and ventilation sufficient to prevent condensation on walls and ceiling.

11.   For maximum energy efficiency, heat removed from the milk may be collected at the refrigeration condenser and distributed as needed. Heat for the milking pit can be supplied by a duct from the compressor room, routed either under the floor with a discharge at the side of the pit, or above the ceiling with a discharge over the pit.

12.   Provision to separate exiting cows for special attention without having to leave the parlor pit.

13.   Exiting should be into an uncrowded dispersal area that may be cleaned with a tractor scraper. Exiting alleys in the parlor should

be only 32 inches (800 mm) wide to prevent turning and bunching of the cows.

Milk room Details of milk room construction are dictated by state and federal sanitary codes. Some general characteristics commonly required are:

1. A room with twice the actual area needed for equipment.

2. Floors sloped 1:48 to one or more drains.

3. A self-closing door and high threshold between the parlor and milk room.

4. A separate utility room.

5. An adjoining lavatory and toilet.

Materials for parlor and milk room Sanitation is of paramount importance in milk rooms and milking parlors, requiring construction materials that will withstand moisture and chemicals. Floors should be made of high quality concrete, and if the building is of frame construction, a concrete curb up to 12 inches (300 mm) high and smoothly coved to the floor facilitates cleaning.

Ceilings and walls should have a smooth, light-colored, water-resistant surface that permits thorough and easy cleaning and improves illumination. In addition, the walls and ceilings need to be progressively better insulated at lower design temperatures. In temperature zones above 20°F (−6°C), smooth masonry walls, finished with a waterproof surface, are both durable and easily cleaned. Filled core masonry walls are marginally satisfactory in the 10°F (−12°C) temperature zone. In both cases the ceiling should be insulated. In colder areas, frame walls that can be well insulated are the most practical.

Of the several surface materials from which to choose, fiberglass reinforced plastic paneling in sizes large enough to cover a wall without any seams has excellent resistance to moisture and wear and is easily cleaned. Although expensive originally, this is offset by the superior moisture protection and long life. MDO plywood has good overall characteristics at a medium cost. Exterior plywood, asbestos cement board, and tempered hardboard rate a little lower but are also lower in cost. All of these materials, with the exception of the fiberglass paneling, need painting with a glossy oil- or latex-base enamel. Epoxy may be used if recommended by the manufacturer specifically for these materials. Asbestos board should be painted to reduce the risk of fibers being released into the air. Fiberglass, asbestos cement board and hardboard need to be backed up with plywood in those areas of the milking parlor with which the cows come in contact. A polyethylene vapor barrier should be installed under all surface material.

Prefinished metal sheets, either steel or aluminum, rate well for installation as a ceiling. They are easily cleaned and reasonable in cost.

Ventilation Requirements

Details relating to ventilation of both cold and warm buildings are discussed in Chapter 16.

Open free-stall sheds   These should have a continuous ridge opening of 2 inches (50 mm) for each 10 feet (3 m) of barn width, while the back eaves should have 1 inch (25 mm) of opening for each 10 feet (3 m) of width. The south side of the building may be left completely open. If problems with blowing snow make it necessary to partially close the open side for a period of time, it is then desirable that the remaining opening be continuous rather than in two or three small openings. This will help prevent drafts. Summer ventilation is augmented by drop panels that provide a minimum 2-foot (600-mm) opening below the eaves for the length of the building.

Closed cold sheds   These may be ventilated similarly to the open design, except the eave openings and the drop panels should be on both sides.

Yard or corral systems   Even in these systems dairy cattle respond to modification of the environment. Although it is well known that production losses in the warm climatic zones are substantial during the summer months, in most cases sunshades represent the only effort to modify environmental conditions. Studies have indicated (Hahn, 1976) however, that high-producing herds show an 8 to 10 percent increase in milk production and a marked improvement in conception rate when they have the benefit of an evaporative cooler such as shown in Figure 18-14. A 4-foot (1.25-m) wide horizontal mat installed above an eave-level plenum is continually sprayed with water. Small fans installed along the back side of the plenum draw air through the wet mats and discharge the cooled air at an angle across the shade area. Shown to be a definite benefit in hot, dry areas, it is estimated to be economically feasible in some hot, humid areas as well.

Warm stable and free–stall barns   These require insulation and controlled air movement if temperature and moisture are to be maintained at satisfactory levels. Table 18-2 suggests insulation and ventilation values for both stable and free-stall barns.

All continuously operating fans should be controlled by low-limit

Figure 18-14. Evaporatively-cooled sun shade.

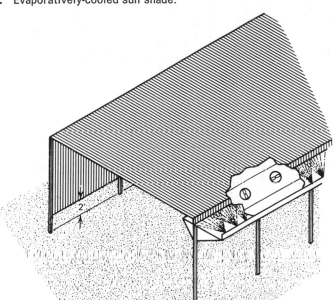

thermostats to insure against freeze-ups during periods of very low outside temperatures. Even with the amount of insulation indicated, some condensation may occur on surfaces when the temperature is extremely low. R values in excess of those shown reduce the chances for surface condensation in severe weather.

Locate all fans in one place except in a very long barn. While the middle of the protected side is ordinarily the recommended location, the fans can be located near an area such as a silo or manure pit to prevent the spread of odors. In mild weather, the fans should exhaust air from near the ceiling. In the winter there is little difference whether it is drawn from near the floor or the ceiling.

Slot inlets require a range of adjustment sufficient to maintain an inlet velocity of 700 to 1,000 feet per minute (3.5 to 5 m/s) at all ventilating rates. Twenty square inches of inlet area per 100 cubic feet per minute of fan capacity will usually produce a velocity within the desired range. (In SI units, 275 mm² of inlet area per 1 L/s of fan capacity will produce a similar relationship.)

Locate corrosion-resistant thermostats near the center of the barn and about 1 foot (300 mm) from the ceiling. The operating temperature may need to be reduced in midwinter.

Milking center   The milk room and milking parlor should be well

Table 18-2 Insulation and Ventilation Values for Dairy Barns

Design Temperature*		Minimum R Values				Ventilation per 1000 lb (450 kg) Animal Weight							
		Ceiling		Walls		Stable Barn				Free Stall Barn			
						Min.		Max.		Min.		Max.	
°F	°C	R_1	R_2	R_1	R_2	cfm	L/s	cfm	L/s	cfm	L/s	cfm	L/s
15	− 9.4	6.3	1.1	4.2	0.8	60	28.5	200	95	70	33.0	200	95
10	−12.2	7.6	1.3	5.1	0.9	55	26.0	200	95	60	28.5	200	95
5	−15.0	9.4	1.7	6.3	1.1	52	24.5	200	95	55	26.0	200	95
0	−17.8	15.2	2.7	10.1	1.8	50	23.5	200	95	50	23.5	200	95
− 5	−20.5	17.1	3.0	11.4	2.0	45	21.0	150	71	45	21.0	150	71
−10	−23.3	18.9	3.3	12.6	2.2	40	19.0	150	71	40	19.0	150	71

* See figure 16-5
R_1 = sq ft hr °F/Btu
R_2 = m²·K/W
(From McCurdy, Irish, and Light, 1967.)

insulated to conserve heat and prevent surface condensation. Suggested R values are given in Table 18-3.

Table 18-3   R Values for Milking Center Walls and Ceilings

| Design Temperature | | R Values | | | |
| | | Ceiling | | Wall | |
°F	°C	R_1	R_2	R_1	R_2
10	−12.2	11.4	2.0	8.0	1.4
0	−17.8	13.6	2.4	10.2	1.8
−10	−23.3	15.9	2.8	13.0	2.3

$R_1 = $ sq ft hr °F/Btu
$R_2 = $ m² · K/W
(Extracted from McCurdy, Irish, and Light, 1967.)

Ventilation for the milk room and milking parlor should control moisture and odors while preventing freeze ups or excessively high temperatures. A manually controlled exhaust fan may be located in the milking parlor to draw its inlet air through the milk room. Automatic louvers should be installed at both the inlet and outlet of the milk room. The fan capacity should be the equivalent of 6 to 12 air changes of the milk room each hour. Much of the heat needed to maintain comfortable conditions in the milk room can be collected from the milk cooling operation. During the two-hour milking period, 1,000 pounds (450 kg) of milk plus the electricity to operate the compressor will produce around 80,000 Btu (84 400 kJ). There will also be some loss from the lights and the water heater. In addition to these sources of heat, it is desirable to have 3 kilowatts of electrical heating capacity in the milk room and up to 15 kilowatts in the parlor. Figure 18-15 shows how one hinged panel in the

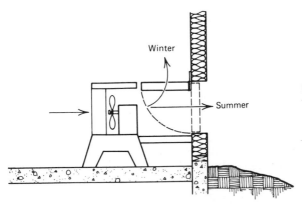

Figure 18-15. Hinged panel directs heat flow for summer and winter.

utility room wall can direct waste heat outside in the summer or conserve it for heating the milk room in the winter.

FEED MANAGEMENT

Feed storage and handling for a dairy enterprise should be set up as an integral part of the overall system.

Hay may be stored above a dairy stable for convenient feeding. However, ground level storages are usually easier to fill and offer some fire protection when they are located an adequate distance from the stable.

Hay for free-stall systems is almost always stored in a separate building, although for convenience several days' supply may be placed above the feed racks. Low-cost pole buildings are very satisfactory for hay storage.

Silage storage is discussed in detail in Chapter 23. As mentioned there, tower silos with mechanical unloaders are generally compatible with conveyor handling and feeding. A single conveyor may collect a complete ration including haylage from a silo, concentrate metered from the storage bin, high-moisture corn crushed as it is discharged from an airtight silo, and finally, corn silage from a silo. The complete ration is then conveyed and distributed along the feed bunk.

Conveyor feed systems can be highly automated and require very little attention during operation. Their cost is closely related to the length of the system. The longer the conveyor, the more it costs.

An alternative to the conveyor system is the use of a mixer wagon. The various ingredients to be mixed and fed may be picked up at several locations, including a horizontal silo. The feed ration is then mechanically mixed and distributed along the feed bunks. A mixer wagon has a fixed cost so that the more animals it serves, the more economical it becomes. However, depending on the layout, a barn may need to be built 10 to 12 feet (3 to 3.7 m) wider if a mixer wagon is used.

The horizontal silo, which can be used effectively with a mixer wagon but which is somewhat less efficient to unload, requires considerably less investment than a tower silo.

WASTE MANAGEMENT

The disposal of manure, wash water, and milk room waste is a major problem that must be dealt with in the overall dairy housing plan. Before planning begins, local and state authorities should be consulted on related health and environmental regulations. Once the waste management system has been designed, the proposed plans should be approved by the appropriate authorities before starting construction.

Moving Waste Out of the Stable Barn

If bedding is used, the manure can be easily handled with a gutter cleaner and elevator to move it to either a storage or a manure spreader. If bedding is not used, an alternative is a large-piston, manure-transfer pump that forces the manure from a pit in the barn to a liquid-manure storage. Another method, suitable when no bedding is used, is to let the manure drop through grates into a storage below. A system used effectively in Germany employs 3-foot (1-m) deep channels below the gutter grates in which the manure flows on a continuous basis to a sump at the end of the barn where it is periodically pumped into a storage. The channel has three essential characteristics: (1) it must be level, (2) it must have a 6-inch (150-mm) dam at the outlet end, and (3) it should not be more than 60 feet (20 m) long. In longer barns, the channels are arranged in steps with manure flowing from the uppermost level into the next and so on to the sump or cross channel.

Moving Waste Out of the Free-Stall Barn

Alleys in a free-stall barn may be scraped with a tractor-mounted blade or a skid loader with the manure being pushed off a loading ramp into a spreader or storage. Alternatively, it may push the manure into a pit from where the manure is moved to the storage with a gutter cleaner and elevator or with a large-piston, manure-transfer pump which can move the manure up to 300 feet (90 m) away from the barn. Mechanical scrapers discharging into manure elevators or piston-pump pits are suitable for rectangular barns with uniform width alleys.

If little or no bedding is used, a slotted floor with manure storage under the building is possible. If a slotted floor system with storage outside the barn is preferred, the manure can be moved in a continuous-flow channel similar to the German system described for stable barns, or with a scraper installed to work under the slots.

In mild climates, a hydraulic flushing system may be employed to clean free-stall alleys and adjacent areas. The amount of water required for flushing alleys can increase the manure storage requirements by 10 to 100 times unless the liquid is recycled. The system is most practical in areas where large quantities of water are used for irrigation and the water can be "borrowed" for flushing and then returned to the irrigation system after removal of the coarse solids.

Experience has shown that a slope of two to three percent and a minimum water velocity of 2 to 3 feet per second (0.6 to 0.9 m/s) is necessary to remove and transport wet manure. Successful cleaning action requires a uniform flow over the entire surface area of the alley. Tipping buckets or trapdoor tanks provide the rapid discharge required for flushing. The frequency of flushing is related not only to the amount of manure to be removed but also to the weather. In hot, dry weather, flushing must be done more frequently to prevent the manure from drying and becoming difficult to remove.

Moving Waste from the Milking Center

The term milking center applies to the milk room in a stable system and to the parlor and milk room in a free-stall system. The waste from a milking center includes milk and milk solids, chemicals, dilute manure, and clean water. The volume of these wastes varies greatly depending on management practices and equipment.

The practice of designing milk room and parlor floors to slope one-fourth to one-half inch per foot (20 to 40 mm/m) and locating the drains in one corner or in a gutter helps direct the flow of wash water and simplifies floor construction. A high threshold is required between the parlor and the milk room and is desirable between the milk room and utility room and lavatory as well. All drains should be of an approved material and equipped with traps and vents to prevent the discharge of odors into the center. Piping the milk room floor waste through a corner of the milking pit provides the operator with a visual check of any malfunction of equipment in the milk room. This would allow a shutdown before a major loss occurred.

If a liquid manure system is used, the milking center wastes may be included with the manure and serve as part of the diluting water. If a solid manure system is used, then the milking center wastes must be disposed of separately, as discussed later in the chapter.

Manure Storage

Climate permitting, manure may be spread daily as it is produced. However, more of the fertilizer value of the manure may be conserved and the spreading operation integrated with crop production if a means of storage is provided. In addition, environmental considerations may restrict spreading on snow or frozen ground, thus making storage facilities mandatory. Both the length of the winter season in northern areas and the length of the growing season in all areas indicate the desirability of at least 180 days of storage capacity.

Storing solid manure   If a considerable amount of bedding is used, manure may be stacked on a paved area sloped to a point from which the leachate may be drained away for approved disposal. The paved surface will reduce nutrient losses and help eliminate both pollution and fly problems.

If little or no bedding is used, the manure will need to be confined by walls constructed of concrete or pressure-preservative treated wood, or by building earthen dikes. An allowance of 2.5 cubic feet per 1,000 pounds of animal weight (0.07 m³/450 kg) per day of storage period is adequate.

One of the more successful means of draining precipitation from a solid or "as-produced" manure storage consists of picket dams (Figure 18-16). They are located at points along the storage wall where the manure level is expected to be lowest. One of the low points will be along the edge of the ramp used to enter the storage for loading out. Another will be at the point farthest from the spot where the manure is loaded into the storage. Vertical 2 inch (50-mm) planks mounted on heavy horizontal stringers are positioned to give three-quarter-inch vertical slots for the face of the dams. The recommended size and spacing for posts and stringers is given in Table 18-4.

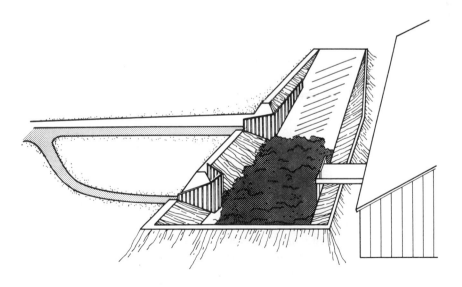

Figure 18-16.   Picket dam drain for solid manure.

Table 18-4   Member Sizes for Picket Dams

POSTS					
Length above ground		Size		Spacing	
ft	m	inches	mm	ft	m
0–4	0–1.2	4x6	89x140	5	1.5
5	1.5	6x6	140x140	4	1.2
6	1.8	6x8	140x184	4	1.2
7	2.1	8x8	184x184	3	1.0

HORIZONTAL SUPPORTS (Stringers)					
Below maximum manure level		Size		Spacing	
ft	m	inches	mm	ft	m
0–4	0–1.2	4x4	89x89	3.0	1.0
4–6	1.2–1.8	4x4	89x89	2.5	0.75
6–8	1.8–2.4	4x4	89x89	2.0	0.6

(From Louden, 1978.)

The posts are set 4 to 5 feet (1.2 to 1.5 m) into the ground and the concrete floor poured around them. In addition, a U-shaped reinforcing bar should be placed in the concrete around the post and extended at least 15 inches (380 mm) into the concrete floor. Bending the ends of the bar will form a secure anchor in the floor. The bottom stringer is placed at least 10 inches (250 mm) above the floor to allow unrestricted drainage. It is essential that all wooden members be pressure-preservative treated dimension or rough-cut lumber.

Constructing the ramp 40 feet (12 m) wide allows room for the spreader to be backed to the edge of the manure for loading. The ramp, with a slope of no more than 1:10 (rise:run) and preferably less, becomes a large collecting surface for precipitation. Grooves formed in the ramp's surface at the time of casting should be angled to drain this water toward the dam.

The leachate that drains from the manure is a strong pollutant to be disposed of in a safe manner. It may be combined with milking center wastes to be held in a lagoon, or it may be spread on a grass filter bed. In estimating the necessary capacity for a lagoon or grass filter bed, provision should be made for a leachate volume equivalent to a 24-hour storm over the storage area plus the volume of the milking center wastes. No milking center waste should be discharged into the picket-dam storage and under no circumstances should the leachate from the storage be allow to drain into a watercourse.

Storing liquid manure   Dairy manure without bedding is too high in moisture to handle easily as a solid but too thick to pump well. However, the addition of some water, including milking center wastes and precipitation over open storages, will dilute the manure sufficiently to allow handling it as a liquid.

The least expensive liquid manure storage consists of an earthen basin with banks sloped 1:2 to 1:3 (rise:run) inside and about 1:3 to 1:4 on the outside. Provision for agitating and pumping the manure may be made in one of three ways (Figure 18-17):

1.   By constructing a long, vertical concrete wall along one side and an 8- to 10-foot (2.4- to 3-m) wide paved strip at the bottom of the wall. Agitating and pumping may then be done from any place along the wall.

2.   By constructing a platform extending out into the storage from which the agitating and pumping may be done. A 10 to 20-foot (3- to 6-m) square concrete pad is needed under the platform.

3.   By constructing a roughened concrete ramp of 1:8 to 1:10 slope down into the bottom of the basin. In this case, a manure pump that extends 10 to 16 feet (3 to 5 m) behind the tractor and pumps up over the tractor to the spreader must be used. The tractor is backed to the edge of the manure for agitating and then loading.

Selecting the site for an earthen manure storage, whether close to the barn or 100 to 300 feet (30 to 90 m) away from the barn, should be given careful consideration. The soil must be heavy enough so that it will seal well. Any fresh-water pond, well, or natural waterway must be far enough from the proposed storage so that there is no danger of pollution. Although odors from such a storage are likely to be serious only when the manure is being agitated and removed, proximity to neighbors and the farm home must be taken into account.

The location of the storage will also be influenced by the availability of space and the method of loading. If manure is handled with a tractor scraper or a mechanical alley scraper and barn-cleaner extension, the storage must be located very close to the barn. However, the use of a large-piston transfer pump allows the storage to be 150 to 300 feet (45 to 90 m) away from the barn. A capacity of 2½ to 3 cubic feet (0.07 to 0.08 m³) per 1,000 pounds (450 kg) of animal weight per day of storage is adequate, although some excess bank height should be allowed to prevent any possibility of overflow. In most regions a six-month storage period is recommended and a one-year period should be considered.

The soil type will influence the angle of the bank slopes. Neverthe-

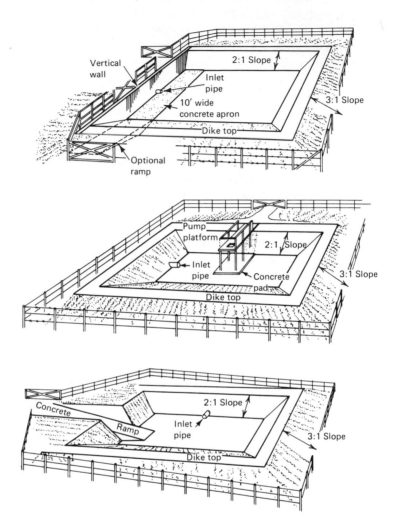

Figure 18-17. Three designs for agitation and pumping of liquid manure. (*Courtesy* Cooperative Extension Service, University of Wisconsin)

less, the inside should be as steep as possible while the outside of the banks should be seeded, and if they are kept to less than 1:3 (rise:run) they can be mowed more easily. Providing the ground water level allows it, the basin may be 10 to 12 feet (3 to 3½ m) deep or for the ramp design shown in Figure 18-17, even deeper. Care should be taken that no surface water drains into the basin. Agitation from one location up to distances of 60 to 80 feet (18 to 25 m) is satisfactory in most storages.

However, if the basin is larger than that, additional agitation points should be provided.

Above-grade storage   Above-grade storage should be considered in areas of high water table, shallow soils, or where insufficient area is available for an earthen basin. Generally they are not such an attractive nuisance to children and are considered safer. They may be made of wood or concrete staves, poured concrete, or corrosion-protected steel. Each of these materials is satisfactory, but in each case care must be taken to provide a good foundation and adequate strength for the large forces present. These tanks may extend into the ground a few feet (1 m) if that does not interfere with emptying.

Filling can be accomplished with a large-piston transfer pump through the bottom or, alternatively, with a standard manure pump from a sump, or from a gutter cleaner into an elevator and over the side.

Agitation and removal of the manure from an above-ground tank may be done in either of two ways. The manure may be drained into a sump and then pumped back into the tank, recirculating until the agitation is complete. Finally it is pumped into the spreader for disposal. The second method is similar except that the pump is connected directly to the outlet of the storage tank.

Because above-grade storages have straight sides, they collect less precipitation. Consequently, the smaller volume of 2 to 2½ cubic feet (0.06 to 0.07 m^3) per 1,000 pounds (450 kg) of animal weight per day may be used to calculate the storage volume required.

Below-ground storage   Storage below slotted floors requires good management to be successful. It is desirable for the continuously operating ventilation fans to exhaust air from the pit area. However, even then, as there is no assurance that all of the toxic gases will be removed during periods of agitation and pumping, the animals should be removed and the building left open while the manure is being pumped out.

The four principal gases released during agitation are carbon dioxide, methane, ammonia, and hydrogen sulphide. The first two are asphyxiants when they replace air, the ammonia is a powerful irritant, and the hydrogen sulphide is poisonous and easily lethal in the concentrations produced by the manure. The importance of caution and care in working with an underfloor system cannot be overemphasized.

Although the animal density may be increased and labor efficiency improved by the use of a slotted floor and a below-floor storage, the management of a liquid manure system using storages outside the building is generally less expensive and ventilation problems are less likely to develop. Slat material and design are discussed in Chapter 10.

Disposing of milking center wastes   Milk solids, cleaners, and sanitizers do not degrade easily, so provision for the safe disposal of milking center wastes is essential. If a liquid manure system is used, the milking center wastes may be diverted into the manure storage where it will contribute to the necessary dilution. However, if the manure is handled as a solid, the milking center wastes must be disposed of separately. There are several methods from which to choose, but each requires careful management.

1. A grass filtration bed is simple and free of trouble if it is designed correctly. There should be no low areas or concentrated point of discharge that will cause pooling and killing of the vegetation. Furthermore, there should be no erosion or anaerobic conditions from overloading. But most important, there must be no drainage to a water course.

The recommended design criteria include the following:

(a) Five to 10 square feet of area per gallon of daily discharge. (12 to 25 m²/ 100 l)
Fifty to 100 square feet (4.5 to 9 m²) per cow should be adequate for most herds.

(b) The land must slope, but not more than 5 percent. Contoured furrows may be used for steeper areas.

(c) Reed canary grass or tall fescue is recommended for planting on the filter bed as they are resistant to wet conditions.

(d) The effluent should be distributed either through a manifold with holes spaced along its length, or over the edge of a shallow settling basin. The distribution edge of the settling basin should extend deeply enough into the ground to avoid any displacement due to frost action.

(e) A settling tank with a capacity of 20 gallons (75 L) per cow in the line between the milking center and the filter bed will prevent the accumulation of solids on the filter area.

(f) Animals should be fenced out of the area and the grass harvested periodically.

2. A lagoon large enough to avoid overflow is another proven method for disposing of milking center wastes. The effluent from the lagoon is distributed on cropland when soil conditions are suitable. Although the quantity of waste water is a variable factor, generally a 4- to 5-foot (1.2- to 1.5-m) deep lagoon with 100 square feet (9 m²) of surface area per cow will be adequate for mild temperature zones. Increasing the surface area to 130 square feet (12 m²) is desirable for colder regions.

3. An automatic spray irrigation system that discharges on to a suitable grass-covered area can avoid some of the distribution problems that may occur with a grass filtration bed. On the other hand, more equipment and attention to operation is required. The system includes a pit which collects the waste material from the milking center, a float-switch-

controlled pump, lines, and a number of sprinkler heads. The pit should be sized to hold 3 to 4 days waste discharge. This limits sprinkling to approximately twice a week. The number and capacity of the sprinkler heads should limit the rate of application to three-eighths of an inch (9.5 mm) per hour. It is imperative that the pump match the sprinkler capacity while maintaining a minimum of 40 pounds per square inch (275 kPa) of pressure at the sprinkler. The effect of gravity and friction head must also be considered in the selection of lines and pump.

Septic tank and drainage field systems have been installed to handle milking center wastes on many farms. However, the waste is so resistant to degradation that the system usually proves to be little more than a holding tank that must be pumped out at frequent intervals.

Regardless of the system selected, care should be taken to avoid point discharge of untreated water.

Toilet waste must *not* be included with the manure or milking center waste. It should be disposed of through a separate septic tank and drainage field system or be piped into a city sewer.

Disposing of waste from open lots Unpaved lots are usually scraped and cleaned periodically and the manure spread on cropland. Paved yards need to be scraped more often and a storage may be required that is suitable for the consistency of the manure.

Runoff from either unpaved or paved yards must be handled in a way that prevents pollution. The subject is discussed in detail in Chapter 19.

HOUSING FOR CALVES

Newborn calves are particularly susceptible to respiratory and digestive disorders. While the complete management program influences the survival and healthy growth of the young calf, housing is a major factor. The most important characteristics of calf housing are that it be clean, dry, free from drafts, and separated from older animals. Temperature is not an important factor. Even in the northern states and Canada, the most compelling reasons for warm housing are worker comfort and ease of handling the liquid supplement fed to the calves during the first six weeks.

Calves may be successfully housed in a variety of shelters including:

- A cold hutch or individual calf shelter.
- A cold barn in which the temperature fluctuates with the weather.
- A warm barn maintained at 50 to 60°F (10 to 15°C) throughout the winter.

Hutches   Calves housed in individual hutches with plenty of bedding do as well or better than those in a warm barn. Hutches should be a minimum of 4 by 4 feet (1.2 by 1.2 m) with a 4- by 8-foot (1.2- by 2.4-m) outdoor run. Each hutch must be thoroughly cleaned and moved to a new location each time a new calf is housed. Deep bedding should be maintained at all times. Hinging the roof at the front edge allows the roof to be lifted so that feed buckets may be placed in racks at the back of the hutch.

Cold barns   The most important consideration in a cold barn is good natural ventilation obtained by a roof slope of at least 4:12, a ridge opening of 2 inches (50 mm) per 10 feet (3 m) of barn width and an eave opening of 1 inch (25 mm) per 10 feet (3 m) of barn width. If the barn is open on the south side, the rear eave opening is still required. The use of old dairy stables for housing calves is not satisfactory because it is difficult to provide adequate natural ventilation. In the winter they tend to be too damp and in the summer they may be too hot.

Warm barns   A warm barn provides comfortable working conditions and greater labor efficiency but is more costly to build and operate. It must be well insulated and ventilated and have a source of supplemental heat. Old dairy stables may be satisfactory, but only if they are completely renovated and equipped for adequate environmental control. Conditions in the building should be maintained at near 50°F (10°C) with less than 80 percent relative humidity.

Using the moisture balance techniques discussed in Chapter 16, it may be shown that for fully occupied housing, approximately 11 cubic feet per minute (18 m³/h) of ventilation for each 100 pounds (45 kg) of animal weight will be required to keep the relative humidity at 80 percent or less. The balance equations will indicate a rate of nearly four air changes per hour. That is, the fans should move air at a rate equivalent to four times the volume of the room each hour. This much air movement will supply the necessary fresh air and will keep the relative humidity below 80 percent. When this much air is introduced, warmed and exhausted on a 0°F (−10°C) day, it is readily shown that the calves produce only about half the heat required for a heat and moisture balance. It is difficult to determine an exact balance as the heat and moisture produced by calves varies considerably during the first six months after birth. Nevertheless, the animal heat must be supplemented with artificial heat.

Table 18-5 suggests supplementary heat requirements for two levels of insulation and three outside design temperatures. The supplemental heat may be supplied by unit heaters suspended from the ceiling or by electrical heaters installed in metal, fresh-air distribution ducts extending the length of the room. The minimum ventilation should be operated on a continuous basis while the room temperature is maintained at the desired level by the thermostat-controlled heaters.

Heat balances calculated for the moderate temperatures of spring and fall will indicate the need for additional ventilation of up to eight air changes per hour during these seasons. Fans providing this amount of ventilation should be controlled by a thermostat set a few degrees above the heater thermostat to prevent the heaters from operating during periods of increased ventilation. For summer heat removal, total fan capacity should provide an air change every one to two minutes.

Table 18-5   Estimated Supplemental Heat Required in a Warm Calf Barn*

| | | | | Watts/100 lb (45 kg) of animal weight | | |
| | R Value | | Outside | | | |
	Cust.	SI	Design Temp	−10°F −23°C	0°F −18°C	10°F −12°C
Wall	12	1.1				
Ceiling	20	3.5		160	115	70
Wall	6	1.1		195	140	90
Ceiling	15	2.6				

* Based on a 1,250 sq ft (116 m²) building housing forty 150 lb (68 kg) animals at 50°F (10°C).
Customary R = sq ft hr °F/Btu
SI   R = m² · K/W

If inlet distribution ducts are used, they should be adjusted manually each season to produce an inlet velocity of 700 to 1,000 feet per minute (3.6 to 5 m/s). If unit heaters are used in combination with slot inlets, it is advisable to divide the adjusting baffles into lengths of approximately 6 feet (2 m) so that alternate baffles may be closed tightly in the winter. Even then the remaining baffles will be opened only one-fourth of an inch (6 mm). Although the complete environmental system just described should maintain good overall conditions within a warm calf barn, zone heating with infrared heat lamps should be provided for young and sick calves.

Stalls and pens   Calves should be kept in individual stalls or pens, or in a hutch for the first six to eight weeks. This allows for individual attention to feeding and helps to prevent the spread of disease. The stalls or pens may be constructed of wood, plywood, welded wire, or sheet metal. To prevent the spread of disease, it is best to design the stall or pen dividers so that the calves cannot lick each other. Stalls should be 2 by 4 feet (0.6 by 1.2 m) while pens should be 4 feet (1.2 m) wide and from 4 to 8 feet (1.2 to 2.4 m) long. In each case a rack to hold two buckets for milk and grain should be installed along a feed alley.

A wide variety of pen and stall designs are used in both the cold and warm barns. Pens are usually bedded with straw, ground corn cobs, shavings, or sawdust. Stalls in cold barns are perhaps best located at floor level and bedded. Stalls in warm barns are frequently raised several inches above a rear gutter so that manure may be flushed away. These raised stalls may be completely slotted or the front may be tight and bedded. If elevated stalls are used in a cold barn, the front half should be bedded. Many operators feel that when the raised, slotted-floor stalls are used in a warm system, the temperature should be a few degrees warmer than is needed with partially or completely bedded stalls.

A 100-cow milking herd would typically require housing for 20 calves under two months of age. Assuming stalls are used, a barn width of 20 to 24 feet (6 to 7.2 m) is adequate for two rows, while 36 to 44 feet (11 to 13 m) are needed for four rows. Walls and ceilings constructed of smooth, easily cleaned materials facilitate the maintenance of the sanitary conditions that are essential for successful housing of dairy calves. A feed storage and preparation area should be located near the calf pens. Hot water is important for washing equipment and mixing feed.

HOUSING FOR HEIFERS

Convenience and reasonable cost are prime objectives in planning housing for heifers. Buildings abandoned for other purposes are frequently used for young stock housing. While they may meet the reasonable cost objective, they seldom are very convenient. For this reason, new housing at a higher initial investment is often justified.

At weaning, calves should be grouped together with others of their age. Seven- to 10-animal groups are ideal, but with careful management larger groups are satisfactory. Typical groups might include animals aged two to seven months, 7 to 12, 12 to 18 and 18 to 24 months. Timid animals may be moved to a lower age group while aggressive animals may be moved up.

A number of successful housing systems are used. They include:

- Loose housing
- Free stalls
- Sloped floor facility
- Warm, slotted-floor system
- Dry lot or pasture

Loose housing A bedded-pack, loose-housing system is most satisfactory when plenty of home grown bedding is available and the area is well drained.

Free stalls The free-stall system with scraped alleys is a popular choice and works well if the free stalls are sized correctly for the animals in the group. The following sizes of free stalls are suitable:

2 - 7 months	2.5 x 4.5 ft	(0.76 x 1.4 m)
7 - 12 months	2.8 x 5.0 ft	(0.85 x 1.5 m)
12 - 18 months	3.2 x 6.0 ft	(1.0 x 1.8 m)
18 - 24 months	3.5 x 6.8 ft	(1.1 x 2.0 m)

The stalls may be constructed so that the length is adjustable. In that way the operator can make adjustments to improve on the cleanliness of the stalls.

Figure 18-18 illustrates how a series of gates may be used to separate the animals into age groups and control their movement for feeding, cleaning the alleys, and handling individual groups.

Sloped floor facility An open barn with a paved resting area 18 feet (5.5 m) wide, sloped toward the front 1:12 is suitable for milder climates. The action of the animals' hooves moves most of the manure to a litter alley. The balance dries, aided by midwinter sunshine that reaches to the back of the floor area through the open side of the shed roof building. Feeding is done at a covered bunk across the litter alley from the rest area. A 5-foot (1.5-m) wide platform in front of the feed bunk designed with the same slope of 1:12 is also self-cleaning. Only the litter alley must be scraped. Including the 6½- to 9-foot (2- to 2.75-m) litter alley, a total area of 20 to 30 square feet (2 to 2.8 m²) per heifer is available. (Figure 18-19).

The resting area is divided into 12-foot (3.7-m) sections to divide the various age groups. Gates extending across the litter alley from the resting-area partitions to the feed bunk complete the pen. Swinging the gates confines the animals to the resting area to allow cleaning the litter alley or handling individual groups.

Warm slotted-floor housing system Slotted-floor housing with no free stalls allows high animal density and improves labor efficiency. A warm, insulated building with mechanical ventilation insures the effective movement of the manure between the slats. The floor remains dry and clean enough to rear clean animals. Manure may be handled in shallow pits with mechanical scrapers or by storing the manure in deep pits for periodic removal.

Dry lot or pasture In mild climates, heifers may be grown successfully in dry lots or on pasture with an open building that gives protection from storms and offers shade in hot weather.

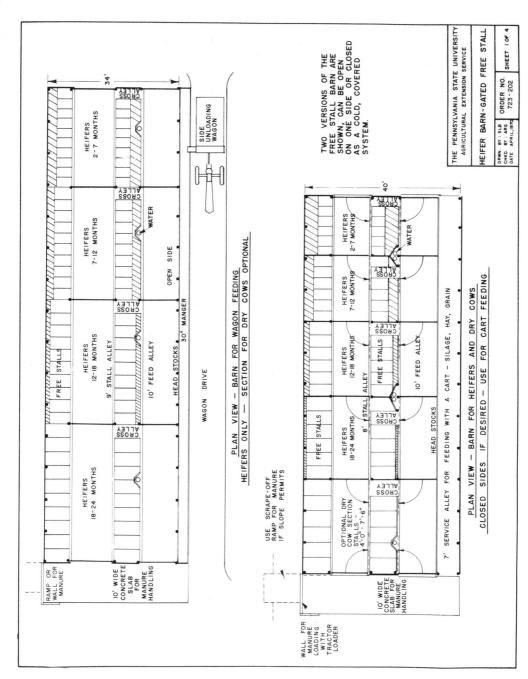

Figure 18-18. Young stock barn, free-stall system. *(Courtesy Agricultural Extension Service, The Pennsylvania State University)*

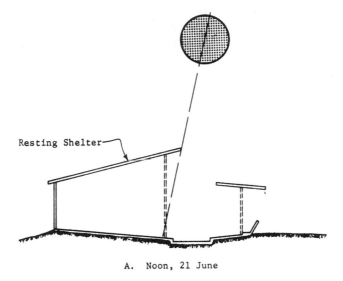

A. Noon, 21 June

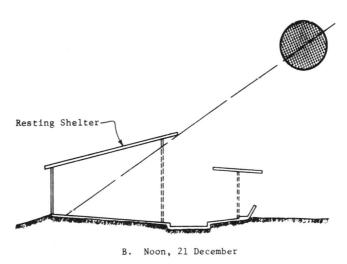

B. Noon, 21 December

Figure 18-19. Young stock barn, sloped–floor facility. (Collins and Murley, 1975)

HOUSING FOR VEAL CALVES

In order to produce a market carcass with light pink muscle tissue and white fat, veal calves are fed an iron-free diet. The result is an animal that is anemic, weak, and susceptible to disease, making environmental conditions particularly critical. Although research has yet to produce definitive values for temperature and humidity, 60 to 65°F (16 to 18°C) and 80 percent relative humidity are typical recommendations.

Fresh air circulation throughout the shelter, adequate to maintain uniform conditions, may reduce the humidity to below the desired level. A system designed with a proportioning damper that circulates a mixture of fresh air and room air, allows both adequate air movement and maintenance of the desired humidity. The damper is controlled by a proportioning thermostat which allows more fresh air to enter the system as outside temperatures rise. Air is distributed through plastic or metal ducts running the length of the barn. The number and size of holes in the ducts are based on an air velocity of 800 to 1,000 feet per minute (4 to 5 m/s). Figure 18-20 shows a cross section of the proportioning system.

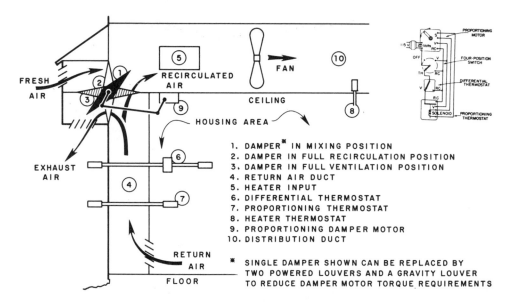

Figure 18-20. Schematic cross section of positive pressure, constant air flow ventilation system. (*Courtesy* Cooperative Extension Service, University of Massachusetts)

Elevated stalls with slotted floors and either gutters behind the stalls or a flush system under the stalls may be used (Figure 18-21). Plywood or wood, rather than metal, is used for stalls and all bedding is avoided to insure that no iron is available to the calves. Ordinarily a building width of 44 feet (13.4 m) is required for four rows of stalls including two feed alleys and three litter alleys (Figure 18-22). However, it is possible to reduce the barn width to 36 feet (11 m), including three feed alleys, if water flushing under the stalls is used for manure

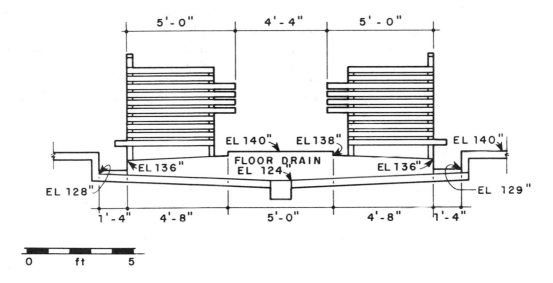

Figure 18-21. Typical standard double stall row for veal calves. (*Courtesy* Cooperative Extension Service, University of Massachusetts)

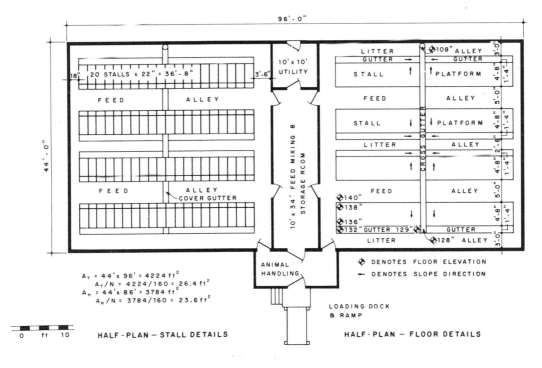

Figure 18-22. 160-stall standard veal calf barn (two 80 stall groups). (*Courtesy* Cooperative Extension Service, University of Massachusetts)

removal. The barn width may be further reduced to 28 feet (8.5 m) if calves are fed from the back of the stalls. The four rows of stalls would have only two combined feed and litter alleys. Although cost per animal is reduced with the narrower design, it increases the demands for good management. A wash and feed preparation area adjacent to the animal stalls should provide dry feed storage and adequate hot water for washing equipment and preparing the milk supplement.

PROBLEMS

18.1   Draw a scale floor plan for a stable barn equipped with tie stalls for 60 cows. Include space for maternity and hospital pens but not calf pens. In addition make a cross section drawing showing the alley and stall dimensions and the contour of the floor.

18.2   Draw a scale floor plan for a high density free-stall barn for 160 milking cows. Include a means for dividing the herd into two approximately equal groups. Show a holding area to be used in conjunction with the milking parlor. Although it may be assumed that they will be located elsewhere, indicate the requirements for maternity and hospital pens.

18.3   Draw a scale floor plan for a building to house replacement animals for the herd in either problem 18.1 or 18-2. Plan on housing animals from 2 months to 24 months of age.

18.4   Give your recommendations for the housing of calves from birth to 2 months of age for the herd in either problem 18.1 or 18.2.

18.5   Assume that the 60 cows in problem 18.1 average 1,500 lb (680 kg) in weight. Suggest ventilation system capacity for each season of the year for an outside design temperature of 10°F (−12°C). Include recommendations for inlet design.

REFERENCES

Bickert, William G., and Armstrong, Dennis V. *Herringbone and Side-Opening Milking Parlors.* Michigan State University Cooperative Extension Service Bulletin E1034. East Lansing, Mich., 1976.

Bickert, William G., and Armstrong, Dennis V. *Polygon Milking Parlors.* Michigan State University Cooperative Extension Service Bulletin E1035. East Lansing, Mich., 1976.

Bodman, G.R., and Bodman, M.E. *Environmental Control Systems for Calf Nurseries*. Paper No. 73-4552. St. Joseph, Mich.: American Society of Agricultural Engineers, 1973.

Bodman, Gerald R. *Non-Mechanical Ventilation of Animal Housing Facilities*. Pennsylvania State University Cooperative Extension Service Agricultural Engineering Extension Monograph No. 706. University Park, Pa., 1976.

Brevik, T.J., and Bringe, A.N. *Controlled Environment Housing for Dairy Calves*. Fact Sheet A2578. University of Wisconsin Cooperative Extension Programs. Madison, Wis., 1974.

Brevik, T.J., and Bringe, A.N. *Uninsulated Housing for Dairy Calves*. Fact Sheet A2576. University of Wisconsin Cooperative Extension Programs. Madison, Wis., 1974.

California Agricultural Extension Service. *Dairy Design*. Davis, Calif.: University of California, 1968.

Collins, W.H., and Murley, W. Ray. *Replacement and Dry Cow Facilities*. Paper No. 75-4561. St. Joseph, Mich.: American Society of Agricultural Engineers, 1975.

Eichhorn, H., Boxberger, J., and Senfert, H. *Flüssigmist*. Beton-Verlag, GmbH, Düsseldorf, 1972.

Gaunt, Stanley N., and Harrington, Roger M., ed. *Raising Veal Calves*. University of Massachusetts Cooperative Extension Service. Amherst, Mass., 1975.

Graves, R.E. *Earth Storage Basins for Liquid Manure*. University of Wisconsin Cooperative Extension Program No. A2795. Madison, Wis., 1976.

Hahn, Leroy. *Cows' Response to Cooling*. Confinement. Vol. 1, No. 3. Champaign, Ill., 1976.

Larsen, H.J., Cramer, C.O., and Tenpas, G.H. *Dairy Calf Health Birth to Weaning in Four Different Environments*. Paper No. 76-4547. St. Joseph, Mich.: American Society of Agricultural Engineers, 1976.

Louden, T.L., "Picket Dams Provide Drainage for Semi-solid Stack." *Dairy Herd Management*, Vol. 15, No. 5. Minneapolis, Minn., 1978.

McCurdy, J.A., Irish, W.W., and Light, Robert G. *Ventilating Insulated Dairy Buildings.* Pennsylvania State University College of Agriculture Extension Service Special Circular 83. University Park, Pa., 1967.

Midwest Plan Service. *Livestock Waste Facilities Handbook.* Ames, Iowa: Midwest Plan Service, 1976.

Midwest Plan Service. *Dairy Housing and Equipment Handbook,* 3rd ed. Ames, Iowa: Midwest Plan Service, 1976.

Chapter Nineteen

Housing for Livestock

BEEF CATTLE

Beef cattle require only minimal shelter, the principal need being for protection from wind and storm and during calving time in winter. Experience has shown that beef animals convert a sufficient amount of food to heat to maintain body temperature. Consequently they do not suffer from the cold as long as they are dry. On the other hand, they do require protection from the hot summer sun. In some regions of the country, cow-calf herds are left on range or pastureland much of the year with little more than natural or artificial shade for shelter. Facilities for feeder cattle vary from mammoth feedlots where only space for feeding, drinking, and resting is provided, to total confinement buildings with mechanical feeding systems and slotted floors for manure removal.

Beef production is ordinarily considered to be a low-margin enterprise and even small savings in investment or improvements in labor or feed efficiency can spell the difference between profit and loss. Successful beef operations vary from a few animals on a general farm to thousands of animals in a feedlot. The small operator can be successful when he has a completely integrated system of feed production, feed use, manure management, and labor distribution—crops in the summer, cattle in the winter. The large feedlot is profitable because of the economy of scale even though all feed is purchased and manure becomes a nuisance instead of a resource.

Since it has been shown that the rate of gain by beef animals is influenced only minimally by weather conditions or the shelter provided, the type and amount of housing provided is often determined by climatic and management factors rather than the requirements of the animals. For example, in the Southwest, the mild, dry climate may indicate an open lot as the most practical. However, in the northern humid areas, high snowfall, wind, and difficulty in draining a yard without causing pollution may justify a complete confinement system.

Types of Housing

Although beef housing systems vary greatly, they may be classified as:

- Open lot system
- Barn and lot system
- Total confinement system

Each of these systems has characteristics making it suitable under certain conditions or circumstances.

Open lot system   In areas where adequate space, good drainage, and moderate annual precipitation prevail, open yards with limited shelter for feeding and resting are sufficient, reasonable in cost, and may be designed for high labor efficiency. Figure 19-1 illustrates a typical open lot.

Typically feeding is done in fenceline bunks supplied from mixer wagons or trucks driven along the alleys between the yards. The width of the alleys is influenced not only by the equipment used but by the need to accommodate snow accumulation in the winter. Where snow accumulates, the alley may need to be two to three times as wide.

A paved strip along the feed and watering areas keeps the animals out of the mud at least part of the time during periods when the ground is saturated. Sloping the concrete slab 1:12 away from the bunk helps to keep it clean. As the animals move around, the manure tends to work to the lower edge. A low step in front of the feedbunk effectively keeps manure out of the bunk because cattle will not back up onto a raised level.

Good yard drainage is essential. Ideally yards should be located on a southern slope to allow the maximum drying effect from sunshine. A slope of four to five percent will allow runoff from rain or melting snow to drain from the yard to a settling basin and then on into a holding pond or lagoon.

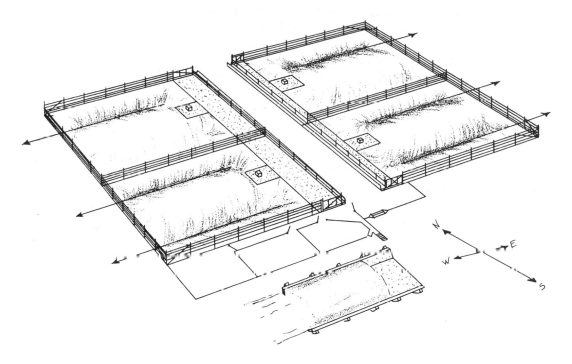

Figure 19-1. Open feedlot with fenceline feed bunks. (*Courtesy* Cooperative Extension Service, University of Missouri)

Under most conditions dry resting areas can best be provided with earthen mounds (Figure 19-1). They are constructed by pushing earth from the sides of the yard toward the center line, thus lowering the grade for controlled drainage along the edges and raising the grade in the center for an improved resting area. With this arrangement, about one-third of the yard width will ordinarily remain firm enough for resting even during heavy rains. The length of the mound may be determined from the estimated useful width and the resting area needed per animal.

The mound will need to be stabilized. This may be done by working chopped straw, bedded manure, or agricultural lime into the surface. If lime is used, 10 pounds per square yard (5 kg/m²) should be disked into the top 4 inches.

Depending on seasonal weather conditions and natural landscape features, a windbreak fence and/or a sunshade may be the only protection provided.

If space for yards is limited or drainage is questionable, a yard may be completely paved. The area required per animal will be only 10 to

20 percent of that needed for unpaved yards. However, facilities for handling runoff will be just as essential and it will be necessary to scrape manure from the yards more often.

Individual circumstances allowing, feed storage and processing structures should be located north of the yards to avoid continuous shadows on the lot and allow the full benefit of the sun to be available for thawing and drying.

Barn and lot system   In cold, humid climates barns that provide shelter from wind, rain, and snow, and a bedded resting area may increase animal comfort enough so that improvement in feeding efficiency will at least partially offset the investment in the building. Barns for this purpose are usually built with one side open to the east or south to afford protection from the prevailing wind.

As shown in Figure 19-2, a paved area extending a short distance in front of and into the building will help improve conditions during rain or snow and spring thaw. To insure good drainage, the floor of the barn should be slightly raised and sloped toward the open side.

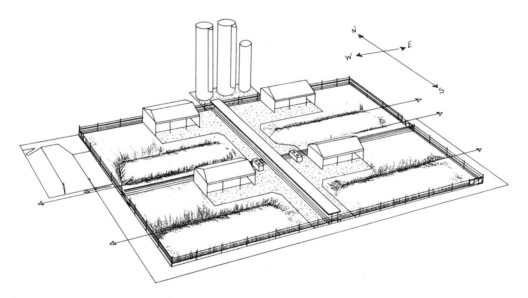

Figure 19-2. A barn and lot system. (*Courtesy* Cooperative Extension Service, University of Missouri)

The yards may be partially or completely paved depending on drainage and space available. As in open lots, complete paving allows a reduction in the area required. In unpaved yards, earthen mounds similar to those described under the open-lot system will encourage the animals to rest outside, thus reducing the bedding needed and the amount of manure to be removed from the barn.

The considerably smaller yards required when resting space is provided within the barn make mechanical bunk feeders practical. Most mechanical feeding systems are limited in length to approximately 150 feet (46 m). This length limits the number of cattle and lots that can be developed around one mechanical feeder system and the storage facilities related to it. Approximately 300 head is the maximum number of cattle that can be fed by one feeder system. The feedbunks may be either centered in a yard or built into a fence between two yards. Yards for small herds are usually laid out in a rectangular arrangement. For larger enterprises, however, fan-shaped layouts with the feed center at the apex allow multiple mechanical feeders to be serviced from one storage facility. This type of layout (Figure 19-3) will accommodate 500 head of cattle.

Sloping the feedbunk aprons 1:12 will help to keep them clean. Bunks that are oriented approximately north and south allow sunshine to strike the apron on each side for part of the day. Locating the feed center at the north end of the lot also prevents shading the bunks.

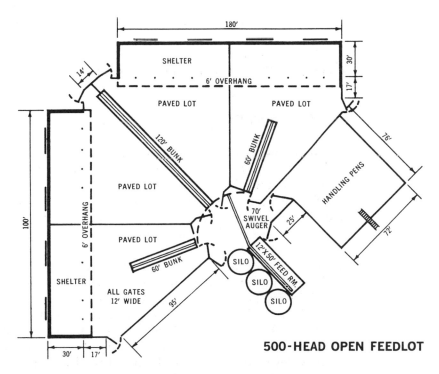

Figure 19-3. Fan shaped lot design saves on feeding equipment. (*Courtesy* Granite City Steel Division of National Steel Corporation)

In areas of high wind and heavy snowfall, special consideration should be given to structure location and orientation, windbreaks, snow fences and swirl areas. These factors are discussed in Chapter 3.

Total confinement system   Total confinement barns offer more complete protection and more comfortable working conditions in regions where heavy snow, severe winds, and poor drainage make open systems difficult to manage.

A bedded barn can be satisfactorily used for a small herd when bedding is available at low cost. However, labor requirements for handling the bedding and removing the manure tend to be high.

A slotted floor system eliminates the cost and labor associated with bedding, and at the same time animal densities can be increased considerably. Slats may be used over the entire floor area or they may be used in the center 40 percent of the floor with the solid floor area on either side sloped 1:10 to facilitate the movement of manure toward the slotted area.

If the entire floor is slotted, it is common practice to construct the pit deep enough to store manure for up to six months. If only part of the floor is slotted, it is usually combined with a shallow pit and a mechanical manure scraper which removes the manure daily. Where these systems have been used in cold barns in northern regions, freezing has been a problem with the shallow pit but not with the deep pit.

Water flushing of sloped, solid floors is suitable only in mild climates where it is difficult to justify any type of confinement housing.

Cow-Calf Facilities

Beef cows that are bred to calve in the spring may be wintered outdoors. Protection from wind should be available from natural landscape features, plant windbreaks, or fences.

Confining the cows to a pasture near the farmstead a short time before calving, allows the cows to be observed and helped if necessary. The pasture area should be large enough to allow animals clean surroundings and freedom from interference from other cows and calves. The failure of a newborn calf to get the colostrum milk from its mother because another calf nurses the cow, considerably reduces its chances for survival.

If calves are born early in the spring, an open-sided shed with several 8- by 12-foot (3.4 by 3.6 m) bedded pens in which the cow and calf may be kept for two to three days is beneficial. A water supply and electrical service are essential. A heat lamp over a protected corner of the pen provides warmth for a newborn calf until it is dry and has nursed. After two or three days calves are able to tolerate normal weather conditions without difficulty.

Site Selection and Building Design

Any beef cattle housing system should be located on a site that provides good drainage and sufficient space for the facilities as well as easy access for large trucks. It should also be located far enough from the farm home and from neighbors so that odors will not become a problem.

Buildings and equipment should be economical but rugged enough to stand the rigors of housing large animals. Pole barns with trussed roofs to give a clear span are suitable for bedded housing. Corrugated roofing permits the economy of an open roof deck. Sides may be of metal, wood, or plywood. However, metal siding, particularly aluminum, is not rugged enough to withstand the activity of heavy beef animals. For this reason metal siding should be protected where animals are apt to damage it. This can be accomplished with a board wall 4 feet (1.2 m) high along the interior perimeter of the building and fencing around the outside. All wood that will come in contact with either the ground or the manure pack should be pressure-preservative treated.

Buildings constructed with a full slotted floor will have a concrete foundation permitting either a frame sidewall and truss construction or a rigid frame design.

Environmental Control

Sufficient air movement is required in both the open barn and the cold confinement systems to remove moisture in winter, heat in summer, and odors from manure throughout the year. Either type of barn may be ventilated without the aid of fans if the following factors are observed:

1.   The building should be oriented at right angles to the prevailing wind and on relatively high ground. The winds will then increase air movement through the building.

2.   A roof pitched 4:12 or 5:12 and constructed without deep purlins allows free air movement along the underside of the roofing.

3.   Openings at the eaves equivalent to 1 inch (25 mm) for each 10 feet (3 m) of building width and an opening at the ridge equal to 2 inches (50 mm) for each 10 feet (3 m) of width are essential for free air movement. No ridge covering is required, but if one is desired, the free distance above the opening should equal half the width of the opening. Animal heat plus the effects of wind will provide enough air movement through these openings to control moisture during the winter months.

4. For summer ventilation, provision should be made for opening at least 25 percent of the wall area to allow air to circulate freely at animal level.

More information about ventilation may be found in Chapter 16.

Feed Storage and Management

Feeding programs are so varied that it is difficult to establish general storage requirements. Silage storage and grain handling and storage will be discussed in later chapters.

Hay storage in humid areas may be in low-cost, pole-type structures. Adjacent feeding facilities will keep labor requirements at a minimum. In dry regions, stacks or large bales may be stored in the open on high, well drained land. A movable fence allowing the animals access to one stack or bale at a time reduces wastage. However, portable feed racks or the use of equipment that processes the hay for bunk feeding offer alternative methods that will further reduce waste.

Manure Management

In managing the manure from a beef cattle enterprise one should strive for:

1. The prevention of pollution of streams, lakes, and groundwater.

2. The conservation of nutrients to provide maximum value to crops.

3. High labor efficiency in handling the wastes.

4. A feasible level of investment in storage facilities and handling equipment.

The methods used to obtain these objectives will be influenced by the type of housing system, the climate of the region, and the ultimate disposal of the manure.

Management methods for each of the three housing systems (open lot, barn and lot, and total confinement) will be discussed.

Open-lot systems, and barn-and-lot systems   At the time of construction, diversion drainage should be installed to intercept surface water so it will not drain onto the feedlot and increase the amount of runoff. In addition, eave troughs and drains should be installed on barns to direct rainwater away from the lot and keep it out of the waste handling system.

The solid waste can be scraped from an unpaved yard periodically and spread on cropland. This is usually done when the moisture level of the manure is low. Paved yards will need much more frequent scraping and storage facilities may be required. A paved storage with a picket dam as described in Chapter 18 and shown in Figure 18-16, is designed for holding solid manure. Approximately ¾ cubic foot (0.02 m³) per animal will be needed for each day of the storage period.

All open yards will have liquid runoff from heavy rains or melting snow which contains high levels of pollutants and must be prevented from entering any natural waterway. Therefore, if the runoff is not immediately dispersed over adjacent grassland in an acceptable manner, a holding pond is required to store the runoff until conditions are suitable for disposal on crop or pasture land. The effluent will usually be distributed through an irrigation system. The amount of runoff is estimated on the basis of rainfall records. Local rainfall data is the most satisfactory for design purposes. In addition to the runoff, the size of a holding pond will be influenced by the length of the holding period, the accumulation of solids, and the net effect of rainfall and evaporation.

In the eastern part of the United States and Canada the rainfall and evaporation are roughly equal and have little effect on the storage capacity of a holding pond. In much of the western part of the United States and Canada evaporation exceeds rainfall significantly. This increases the effective storage capacity of a holding pond used for periods of several months. Evaporation is of little significance, however, if the holding pond is emptied frequently.

During an intense storm of short duration, a large volume flow picks up solids and carries them along in the runoff. A *settling basin,* installed between the lot and the holding pond, greatly reduces the accumulation of these solids. With a detention period of 20 minutes or more, up to 85 percent of the solids can be removed from the runoff before it enters the pond. Detention period is defined as the time required for the flow volume to equal the design volume of the basin. In other words, a 20-minute detention period is assumed if the drained basin is large enough to hold the expected runoff for the 20-minute period. Additional capacity will be required to hold the settled solids. The amount of accumulated solids will be influenced by the area of the lot and the frequency with which the settling basin is cleaned.

A porous dam or a vertical, perforated pipe outlet may be used to restrict the flow to give the required detention time and to drain the basin at the end of the storm. Such dams can be constructed of planks with either horizontal or vertical spacing. A ½-inch (13 mm) expanded metal screen, installed so that it tips away from the top of the dam approximately 30 degrees, will help to keep the dam from plugging. The reverse slope produces a self-cleaning action. In addition, periodic scraping of the surface of the dam is necessary for proper operation.

Table 19-1   Flow Values for Perforated Pipe or Porous Dam
Based on a pipe with 12 square inches (7,740 mm²) of opening per foot (300 mm) of length or 1 inch (25 mm) of spacing between vertical pickets per foot of height. An orifice constant of 0.6 is assumed.

| Depth | | Flow | | Depth | | Flow | |
ft	m	cu ft/hr	m³/hr	ft	m	cu ft/hr	m³/hr
0.5	0.15	348	9.7	3.5	1.07	6,480	181
1.0	0.31	990	27.7	4.0	1.22	7,943	222
1.5	0.46	1,818	50.9	4.5	1.37	9,450	265
2.0	0.61	2,808	78.6	5.0	1.53	11,040	309
2.5	0.76	3,900	109.0	5.5	1.68	12,780	358
3.0	0.92	5,148	144.0	6.0	1.83	14,550	407

Settling basin design   A settling basin (Figure 19-4) is designed on the basis of the maximum expected runoff flow for a relatively short period of time. The one-hour rainfall expected one year in 10 is commonly used. It may be assumed that the first half inch (13 mm) of heavy rain will be retained on an unpaved yard, while one-fourth of an inch (6 mm) will be retained by a paved yard that is scraped frequently.

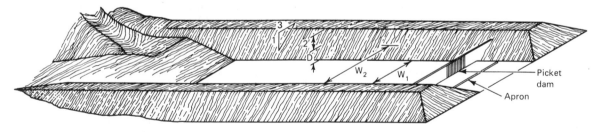

Figure 19-4.   Settling basin with a picket dam.

The following steps are used in designing a settling basin:

1.   Determine the *peak runoff rate* per hour based on local rainfall records and lot area. Subtract the first half inch (13 mm) for an unpaved yard or quarter inch (6 mm) for a paved yard.

2.   Find the *basin surface area* by dividing the rate per hour in cubic feet by 4 feet (m³ by 1.2 m).

3. Find the design *depth of the liquid* by multiplying the detention period in hours by 4 feet (1.2 m).

4. Determine the additional *basin depth for solids* accumulation with the formula:

$$D_b = (A_y \times D_y)/(A_b \times TC) \qquad \text{Where:}$$

D_b = depth of solids in basin

A_y = area of yard

D_y = depth of solids lost from yard annually

A_b = surface area of basin

TC = times cleaned annually

The *design depth* is equal to the depth of the liquid plus the depth of the solids.

5. Find the *total area of openings* in a perforated pipe or porous dam that will match the maximum expected runoff flow rate. This is done by dividing the runoff rate by the appropriate flow value for the design depth. Table 19-1 gives the flow rate for a single 1-inch (25-mm) vertical opening or 12 square inches per foot (25 mm²/mm) of length for perforated pipe. As the flow through an orifice is proportional to area, larger pipes or multiple dam openings may be used to obtain the required capacity.

6. Select an arbitrary width (W_1) for the bottom of the basin. Using a 1:3 slope (rise:run), determine the *width* (W_2) *at the design depth* (Step 4). Use the formula: $W_2 = W_1 + (2 \times \text{depth} \times \text{slope ratio})$.

7. Find the *length of the basin* with the formula:

$$\text{Length} = 2 \times A_b/(W_1 + W_2) \qquad \text{Where:}$$

A_b = surface area of basin

W_1 = width at bottom

W_2 = width at surface

8. Determine the dike and dam height with the following criteria:
The *dike height* should be 2 feet (0.6 m) higher than the design depth. The porous dam or perforated pipe may be 1 foot (0.3 m) above the design depth.

9.   Design the *slope of the bottom* of the basin to be no more than 0.5 percent and as uniform as possible to prevent ponding.

10.   Ancillary features that are highly recommended include:
   (a) A ramp over the dike that will allow solids to be removed with a tractor loader.
   (b) An apron installed under the dam and extending downstream several feet.
   (c) A reverse-sloped, expanded metal screen in front of the dam.
   (d) A dike width sufficient to allow mowing and easy maintenance.
   (e) A presettling basin constructed in the lower corner of a paved yard using a protected perforated pipe or a dam. The solids accumulated are then removed in the course of regular yard cleaning.

An example for the design of a settling basin has the following information given: Yard size, 200 by 400 feet, unpaved; 6-inch solids runoff annually; and the basin will be cleaned eight times a year. Design a basin for a 25-year, one-hour storm of 2.5 inches using a picket dam and a 30-minute detention time.

1.   2.5 in $-$ 0.5 in. $=$ 2 in./hr $\times$ 200 $\times$ 400/12 in. $=$ 13,333 cu ft/hr

2.   13,333/4 $=$ 3,333 sq ft surface area

3.   4 $\times$ 0.5 hr $=$ 2 ft liquid depth

4. D_b $=$ 80,000 $\times$ 0.5 ft/3,333 $\times$ 8 $=$ 1.5 ft solids depth
   2 ft $+$ 1.5 ft $=$ 3.5 ft design depth

5.   13,333 cu ft/hr/6,480 $=$ 2.06 times the area of 1 picket, therefore use 2 picket openings

6. W_1 $=$ 12 ft, chosen arbitrarily
   W_2 $=$ 12 $+$ 2 $\times$ 3.5 $\times$ 3
   W_2 $=$ 33 ft

7.   The length $=$ 2 $\times$ 3,333/12 $+$ 33 $=$ 148 ft long

8.   The dike height should be 3.5 $+$ 2 $=$ 5.5 ft

9. The slope of the basin bottom $= 0.005 \times 148 = 0.74$ ft $= 8$ in.

10. Include ancillary features listed.

The holding pond below the settling basin should have adequate capacity to hold the runoff from a 25-year frequency, 24-hour storm, and to hold effluent for the required storage period. In mild climates the storage period may be less than a month, while in colder climates a six-month storage is likely to be necessary to allow disposal at suitable times in relation to soil conditions and the cropping season.

In some areas feedlot runoff may be disposed of by infiltration on an adjacent grassland area. The distribution channel, after a settling basin, must be designed with a very low slope in order to obtain uniform distribution.

Confinement housing If manure is to be stored under a slotted floor, 10 foot (3m) of storage depth below the floor will allow up to 180 days of storage time. If a scraper system is used, the storage area is based on 1 cubic foot (0.03 m³) per 1,000 pounds (450 kg) of animal weight for each day of storage required. Liquid manure storage facilities are discussed in Chapter 18.

It is imperative that a building with manure storage below the floor have all ventilation openings wide open before manure is agitated and removed. The noxious gases released when the manure is disturbed can be dangerous, even fatal, to both animals and workers.

Equipment

Every beef farm, regardless of size or type, must have facilities for sorting, treating, weighing, loading, and unloading animals. Designing these facilities for efficiency pays bigger dividends. A well planned corral saves time and labor and helps to prevent human injuries as well as bruising and more serious injuries to animals. Veterinarians will be more willing to provide their services where conditions are safe and convenient. Basic facilities needed are:

1. A crowding pen where animals are forced into a working chute.

2. A working chute where animals can be treated individually or sorted and directed to a desired location.

3. A squeeze chute where an animal can be immobilized for special treatment.

4. A loading chute for loading or unloading stock trucks and trailers.

For the small herd, a crowd gate in the corner of the yard with an alley leading to a head gate for treating and a chute for loading and unloading is adequate (Figure 19-5).

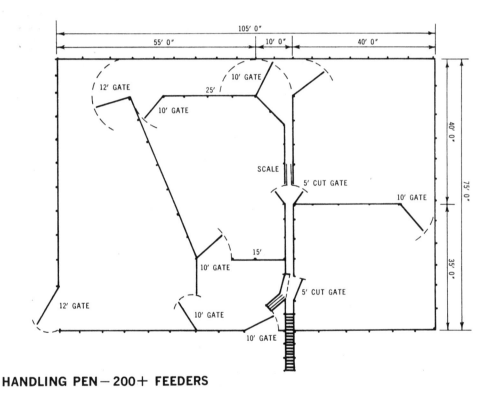

HANDLING PEN — 200+ FEEDERS

Figure 19-5. Handling pen for a small herd. (*Courtesy* of Granite City Steel Division of National Steel Corporation)

For larger herds, however, the handling facilities are more complex. A funnel-shaped crowding pen facilitates movement of cattle from a large area to a smaller area. The use of large, curved alleys to direct the flow of cattle recognizes that cattle tend to move more easily if they cannot see where the animals ahead are going. Sorting gates that are well designed and properly located within the alleys provide for easy sorting and cutting toward a loading chute, scales, or a squeeze. Roofing over the handling and treatment areas provides more comfortable working conditions during inclement weather (Figure 19-6). In this plan the weighing of animals could be done with portable scales located adjacent to the headgate.

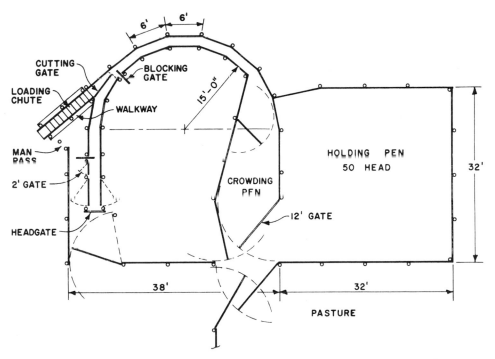

Figure 19-6. Corral for a medium sized herd. (*Courtesy* Cooperative Extension Service, University of Wisconsin)

The fences in a corral should be strong, smooth, and high enough so that wild or crowded animals will not be hurt or damage the fence. Yard fences are commonly built with 2- by 6-inch (38 by 140 mm) lumber although metal is also suitable for fence construction. In the crowding area and working chute, the fence should be 6 feet (2 m) high and have solid walls to prevent balking. However, a single 4-inch (100-mm) slot at the 4-foot (1.2-m) level is thought to keep cattle from jumping. If range animals are being handled, because of their wilder nature, a restraining board running along the top center of the working chute may be necessary to prevent jumping. Jumping is dangerous as an animal is likely to fall, often on its back, and be injured seriously. It is also difficult to get even an uninjured animal on its feet again.

Table 19-2 Specifications for Housing Facilities for Beef Cattle

Space requirements per animal:	Customary	SI
Open lot		
unpaved—no buildings	160–540 sq ft	15–50 m²
paved—no buildings	50–80 sq ft	5–7.5 m²
sunshade	20–25 sq ft	2–2.5 m²
mounds in yard	25–30 sq ft	2.5–2.8 m²
Barn and lot		
rest area in barn	20–30 sq ft	2–3 m²
unpaved lot	100–300 sq ft	9–28 m²
paved lot	25–35 sq ft	2.5–3.2 m²
mounds in yard	25–30 sq ft	2.5–2.8 m²
Total confinement		
bedded floor	25–40 sq ft	2.5–3.5 m²
slotted floor	18–20 sq ft	1.7–1.9 m²
calving pen 1/12 cows	100 sq ft	9 m²
isolation pen 1/20–40 head	50 sq ft	4.5 m²
Feed space per animal		
Once- or twice-a-day feeding		
cows	24–30 in.	600–760 mm
feeders	22–28 in.	560–710 mm
calves	18–22 in.	460–560 mm
Continuous feed		
roughage	6–8 in.	150–200 mm
grain	4–6 in.	100–150 mm
Number water fountains 50–75 head	1	1
Corrals		
Holding and crowding pens	15–20 sq ft	1.4–2 m²
working chute width		
under 600 lb	18 in.	460 mm
600–1,200 lb	22 in.	560 mm
over 1,200 lb	26 in.	660 mm
Working chute width		
sloped sides, top and bottom		
under 600 lb	15 & 20 in.	380 & 500 mm
600–1,200 lb	15 & 24 in.	380 & 600 mm
over 1,200 lb	16 & 26 in.	400 & 660 mm
Chute and fence height	5 ft	1.5 m
Post spacing		
chute	6 ft	1.8 m
yard	8 ft	2.4 m
Circular chute radius	16.5 ft	5.0
Feed alley (feedlot)	13–33 ft	4–10 m

If cattle are to be prevented from turning around, the width of the chute is critical and should be constructed to fit the animals most commonly handled. Where both cows and calves will be handled, the sides should be sloped being wide enough at the top to accommodate the cows and narrow enough at the bottom to keep the calves from turning around.

Planning the Beef Cattle System

As with any farm enterprise, it is important to carefully prepare a complete plan for the entire system. The plan should include a topographic layout of the site, the facilities for sheltering and handling the cattle, storage and equipment for feed, and the facilities for storing and handling waste. It is much easier to change a plan than alter a completed structure.

SWINE

Cash receipts from swine sales in the United States are surpassed only by those for beef and dairy cattle. Although the most efficient of the large animals in converting feed into meat products, swine do not tolerate temperature extremes well and controlled environment is essential for the most successful enterprise. Confinement housing contributes to labor efficiency, faster gains, and greater animal density. Specialization and growth in size of operations, typical of agriculture as a whole, has occurred, and along with increased size and concentration have come the problems of waste management and odor control.

Production Programs

Swine production occurs in three stages: (1) farrowing and nursing baby pigs up to three to eight weeks of age, (2) growing the pigs to 14 to 16 weeks of age, and (3) finishing to 22 to 24 weeks when the pigs will be ready for market. Some farms are organized to handle all three stages in a farrow-to-finish operation. Other swine enterprises may be limited to feeder pig production or growing and finishing for market.

The choice of a production alternative is a management decision based on several factors including the availability of capital, skilled labor, feed supply, and markets. For example, top-quality labor and skilled management are required for the farrowing and starting operation. Feed costs are not critical. For a finishing operation, however, the most important requirements are an adequate source of feed grains, a reliable source of feeder pigs, and a ready market. To carry through the whole operation from farrow to finish requires top management, considerable investment, and a good source of feed.

The production program and the management system together will determine the facilities required for a particular farm.

Management Systems

Management systems include: (1) pasture and portable houses, (2) concrete lot confinement, and (3) total confinement.

Pasture system   The pasture system is suitable only in mild climate areas and even there the winter season may produce temperatures that will cause a slower rate of gain and reduced feed conversion efficiency. Labor demands are likely to be high and sufficient land for rotating the pasture on a three-year basis is required. The principal advantage is low investment in buildings.

Concrete feedlot system   With open front buildings for shelter, this system reduces the land and labor required and allows greater automation of the feeding system. Although rate of gain and feed conversion efficiency will improve, they will still not be as high as in the total confinement system. The considerably greater animal density introduces a manure disposal problem.

Total confinement system   This system provides the ideal conditions that allow for multiple farrowing practices and continuous operation throughout the year under a wide range of climatic conditions. Ventilation will keep moisture and odor under control while supplementary heat and cooling systems can maintain near optimum temperatures. The high density housing allows for maximum automation and labor efficiency. The principal disadvantage is high investment. However, with skilled management, increased production volume, and efficiency in feed and labor utilization, the annual cost per animal marketed is likely to be less than for an animal raised in either the pasture or open-lot systems.

Building Requirements

In the mild climate regions where a pasture management system is practiced, small houses with one or two farrowing pens are commonly used. Built on skids, the houses are easily drawn to a clean location as required. Sunshades, also on skids, may be necessary if natural shade is not available. Pasture housing requires enough land to permit a three-

Table 19-3 Space Requirements for Swine Breeding Stock

	Per Sow		Per Boar	
	Customary	SI	Customary	SI
TOTAL CONFINEMENT				
Concrete floor	30–35 sq ft	2.3–3.3 m²	35–40 sq ft	3.3–3.7 m²
Partial slotted floor	20 sq ft	1.9 m²	25 sq ft	2.3 m²
Full slotted floor	15 sq ft	1.4 m²	20 sq ft	1.9 m²
Tie stalls	2 ft x 6 ft	0.6 x 1.8 m		
OPEN LOT				
Shelter resting area	25–30 sq ft	2.3–2.8 m²	30–35 sq ft	2.8–3.3 m²
Concrete lot	20 sq ft	1.9 m²	30 sq ft	2.8 m²
Dirt lot	100–200 sq ft	9.5–19 m²	150–250 sq ft	14–23 m²
PASTURE				
Pasture lot per acre (hectare)	10–12 sows	25–30 sows	5–10 boars	12–15 boars
Shelter	20–25 sq ft	1.9–2.3 m²	15–20 sq ft	1.4–1.9 m²
FEEDING AND WATER SPACE				
Self feeder (grain or complete feed)	2–3 sows per hole		2 linear ft	0.6 m
Supplement feeder	3–5 sows per hole		1 linear ft	0.3 m
Water space	1 waterer per 12 sows		1 waterer per 3 boars	

(From Granite City Steel Division of National Steel Corporation, 1977) year rotation schedule; that is, a farrowing house can return to the original area every third year.

In partial or total confinement systems, separate buildings or sections within a building are often provided for each stage of hog production: (1) gestating gilts and sows, along with the necessary number of boars, (2) farrowing sows and the baby pigs through weaning, (3) growing pigs up to approximately 100 pounds (45 kg), and (4) finishing hogs up to market weight. A large herd may even have an intermediate area (a weanling unit) for use between weaning and growing, while smaller operations often combine growing and finishing. The smallest farms complete the farrow-to-finish cycle in one location. Size and intensity of operation largely determine how many separate sections are required.

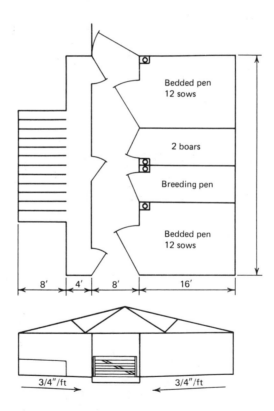

Figure 19-7. Open–front gestation house. Layout may be repeated as necessary.

Breeding–Gestating Buildings

Complete confinement buildings for gestating sows are increasing in popularity for several reasons, including easier control over feeding and reduced incidence of parasites. They also release good land for crop production. There are, however, reasons why this is not suitable on all farms. The large investment required for a total confinement building cannot be justified if capital is limited, ample marginal land is available, the farmer is operating on rented land, or if there are limited rather than continuous farrowings during the year.

A partial confinement barn with pens for groups of 5 to 20 sows is shown in Figure 19-7. With five to six animals in a pen, individual feeding stalls are necessary to limit each sow to her own allotment of feed. Restricted feeding space is provided for one-third of the animals in the barn and they are moved in groups to the feeding pens.

Total confinement gestation buildings may be designed with pens and partially slotted floors or with individual tie stalls (Figure 19-8). While the tie stalls require somewhat more floor area, they simplify the restrictive feeding program and prevent fighting. Mechanical feeding can reduce the width of the barn by eliminating one or more feeding alleys.

Farrowing Buildings

If gilts are farrowed only once a year, building investment must be kept to a minimum. Farrowing on pasture may be the answer. When sows are farrowed twice a year, a greater investment is justified. With careful scheduling, buildings can be kept simple and provided with a minimum of environmental control equipment. When sows are grouped so that farrowing is continuous throughout the year, investment in a slotted-floor system with supplemental heating and considerable automated equipment becomes economically feasible.

Farrowing usually takes place in either a stall (Figure 19-9), or an individual pen (Figure 19-10), with sloped floors to prevent any accumulation of liquid. The variation in details of design is almost unlimited. However, both stalls and pens will have guard rails to prevent the sow from lying on the young pigs and there will be a creep area at the side or in front of the sow, provided with extra heat from a warmed floor panel or from a radiant heater above the creep. Sometimes both sources are used for the first few days when a temperature of 90°F (32°C) is desirable. Since the temperature is decreased 2°F (1°C) daily until 70°F (21°C) is reached, both sources are not likely to be needed past the first few days.

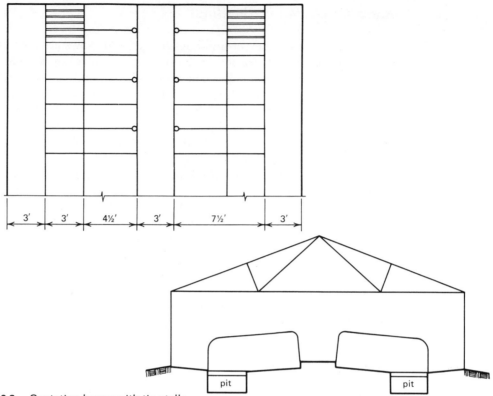

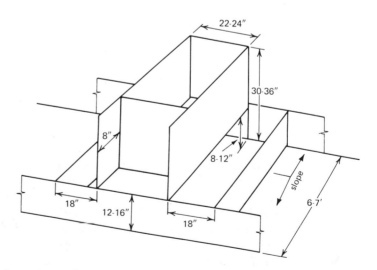

Figure 19-8.   Gestation house with tie stalls.

Figure 19-9.   Dimensions for a farrowing stall.

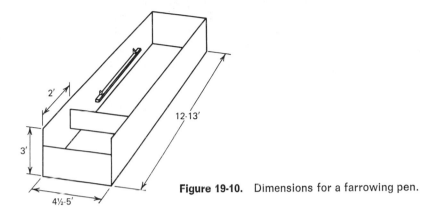

2'

3'

12-13'

4½-5'

Figure 19-10.   Dimensions for a farrowing pen.

A creep feeder and water cup should be provided to encourage the young pigs to feed and drink before they are weaned.

The choice between stalls (crates) or pens in a farrowing building is often determined by whether the building is used for farrowing only or for farrowing and growing. The stalls are advantageous for the single-use system, while pens are more convenient in the multipurpose building where partitions can be easily removed to enlarge the pens for the growing operation.

Feeding in a stall rather than turning the sows out to a common feeding floor is more efficient and avoids the odor problems and cleaning associated with feeding floors. Although stalls may face in or out, the face-in arrangement permits easier feeding from a single alley, and the sows tend to be calmer when they can see another animal. Slotted floors allow the manure to fall into pits where it accumulates for a period of time. A face-out arrangement is preferable when a solid floor is used, with the stalls sloping down to a center alley that is cleaned daily.

In pig production, disease and parasite control are critical during the first few weeks after birth. Sanitation therefore becomes one of the most important factors in a farrowing operation. The thoroughness with which cleaning can be done is affected by the scheduling of the farrowing pens. If sows are brought into a single-room farrowing building in rotation, it means that individual stalls or pens must be cleaned and dried as each sow and litter are removed. One-room farrowing barns obviously can never be completely sanitized. An alternative to this is to arrange the breeding schedule in such a way that the building is filled in about one week and used for six weeks. At the end of this period all animals are removed and one week is used for complete cleaning and drying. This eight-week cycle is continued throughout the year. However, the necessary interruption of the breeding schedule in order to have the sows farrow on an 8-week cycle decreases the reproduction rate of the herd.

The delay of rebreeding may be avoided by having multiroom buildings that are used on a cycle that allows one week for complete cleaning and drying. The two-room house shown in figure 19-11 would work on an eight-week, continuous-breeding cycle but has little advantage over

FARROWING BUILDINGS WITH STALLS

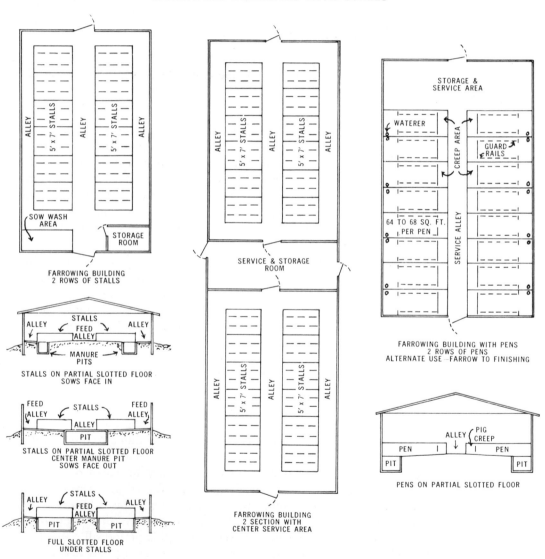

Figure 19-11. Farrowing buildings with stalls. (*Courtesy* Granite City Steel Division of National Steel Corporation)

Table 19-4 Space Requirements for a Farrowing House

	Stall		Conventional Pen		Long Narrow Pen	
	Customary	SI	Customary	SI	Customary	SI
Gilt	22 in. x 6 ft (11 sq ft)	0.56 x 1.8 m (1 m²)	6 ft x 8 ft (48 sq ft)	1.8 x 2.4 m (4.5 m²)	5 ft x 14 ft (70 sq ft)	1.5 x 4.3 m (6.5 m²)
Sow	24 in. x 7 ft (14 sq ft)	0.6 x 2.1 m (1.3 m²)	8 ft x 8 ft (64 sq ft)	2.4 x 2.4 m (6.0 m²)	5 ft x 14 ft (70 sq ft)	1.5 x 4.3 m (6.5 m²)
Pigs	18 in. each side	0.46 m	Creep in corner*		Creep in end of pen	

* Both conventional pen and long narrow pen have a guard rail 8 inches (200 mm) high and 8 inches (200 mm) from pen side in addition to creep.

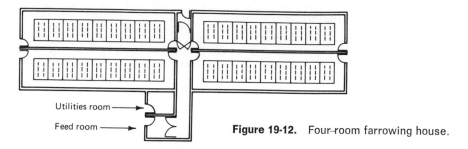

Utilities room ⟶

Feed room ⟶

Figure 19-12.   Four-room farrowing house.

the single-room system. However, in a house with four rooms (Figure 19-12), each isolated from the other and from outside contamination as well, groups of sows with their litters can be taken through the farrowing-nursing stages on a rotation without interruption of the breeding schedule. Each room is emptied, cleaned, sterilized, and dried for one week at the end of each cycle. This system provides a superior sanitation program and allows greater uniformity in the age of the young pigs removed from the house. Multiroom farrowing houses are suited to large herds of 100 or more where management becomes most critical. Typical cycles are shown in Figure 19-13.

Figure 19-13.   Typical Cycles for One, Two, and Four Room Farrowing Houses.

N = Nursing	F = Filling	C = Cleaning	W = Weaning

Single Room:
5 week cycle
F N N N C, F N N N C, F N
8 week cycle (early weaning)
F N N N W W W C, F N N N
8 week cycle (late weaning)
F N N N N N N C, F N N N
Breeding on a 5 or 8 week cycle is required.

Double Room:
8 week cycle (early weaning)
1st room   F F F F N N N C, F F F F N
2nd room   F F F F N N N C, F F F F N
Continuous breeding cycle.

Four Rooms:
8 week cycle (early weaning)
1st room   F F N N N W W C, F F N N
2nd room   F F N N N W W C, F F N N
3rd room   F F N N N W W C, F F N N
4th room   F F N N N W W C, F F N N
8 week cycle (late weaning)
1st room   F F N N N N N C, F F N N
2nd room   F F N N N N N C, F F N N
3rd room   F F N N N N N C, F F N N
4th room   F F N N N N N C, F F N N
Continuous breeding cycle.

Growing Pens

Each stage in a pig's life requires specific housing, feeding, and environmental conditions. During the growing stage, from weaning to about 100 pounds (45 kg) of weight, the maximum rate of gain and the highest feed conversion efficiency takes place in an environment where the temperature is between 60 and 68°F (16 and 20°C) and the humidity is moderate. Separate facilities for the growing stage can provide these optimum conditions.

Design recommendations include 20 to 25 pigs per pen with a water fountain and continuous feeding in each pen. A larger number per pen is likely to reduce the rate of gain. Full-slotted floors are desirable for growing pens as the young pigs are likely to be messy.

Some farmers who practice early weaning (three weeks old) are using 3- by 3½-foot (0.9- by 1-m) weaner cages. The cages, which are stacked two high and hold about 12 pigs up to 30 pounds (14 kg), have automatic feeding, watering, and manure-removal systems similar to poultry layer cages. At 30 pounds (14 kg) the pigs are divided into two cages of six each.

Finishing Pens

In mild climates an open-front building with a paved dry lot can be used for finishing each group of 20 to 25 pigs (Figure 19-14). About 6 square feet (0.6 m²) per animal, both inside and on the paved yard, will be needed. For confinement housing, pens may be arranged so that those on one side of a central alley are one and one-half times as wide as those on the other. This allows groups of younger animals to be started in the smaller pens and then simply moved across the alley when they have outgrown the pen. The principal reason for this arrangement is to promote a calm and secure social relationship among the pigs. Whenever possible, swine groups should be kept together from weaning to market to avoid fighting and stress that will reduce gain. Partially slotted floors are an efficient way to handle the waste. An alternative is the use of deep, narrow gutters at the rear of a row of pens with a sloping floor. One water fountain and feeder per pen is adequate. Figure 19-15 shows two pen layouts and four floor arrangements for growing and finishing operations.

Location and Type of Construction

After a production program and a management system have been decided upon, all of the buildings that are planned initially or for

Table 19-5   Space Requirements for Growing and Finishing Hogs

	Weaning to 75 lb (35 kg)		75–125 lb (35–55 kg)		125 lb (55 kg) and over	
	Customary	SI	Customary	SI	Customary	SI
TOTAL CONFINEMENT (10–20 head per pen)						
Slotted floor (full or partial)	4 sq ft	0.4 m²	6 sq ft	0.6 m²	8–10 sq ft	0.7–.9 m²
Solid concrete floor	4 sq ft	0.4 m²	6.7 sq ft	0.7 m²	9–10 sq ft	0.8–.9 m²
Additional building space (storage, isolation, etc.)	1 sq ft	0.1 m²	1 sq ft	0.1 m²	2 sq ft	0.2 m²
CONCRETE LOT (20–25 head per pen)						
Shelter floor area	6 sq ft	0.6 m²	7 sq ft	0.7 m²	8 sq ft	0.7 m²
Concrete floor	8 sq ft	0.7 m²	12 sq ft	1.1 m²	12–15 sq ft	1.1–1.4 m²
PASTURE						
Animals per acre (hectare)	20–30 head	50–75 head	15–20 head	35–50 head	10–15 head	25–35 head
Shade	5–6 sq ft	0.5 m²	6–8 sq ft	0.6–0.7 m²	8–12 sq ft	0.7–1.1 m²
FEEDING AND WATER SPACE						
Self feeder (grain or complete feed)	6–8 head per hole		4–6 head per hole		3–5 head per hole	
Supplement feeder	8–10 head per hole		8–10 head per hole		6–8 head per hole	
Waterer	20–25 head per cup		20–25 head per cup		10–15 head per cup	

(From Granite City Steel Division of National Steel Corporation, 1977)

OPEN FRONT FINISHING BUILDINGS

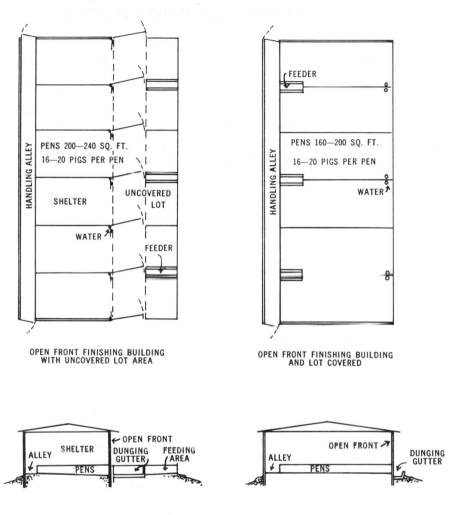

OPEN FRONT FINISHING BUILDING
WITH UNCOVERED LOT AREA

OPEN FRONT FINISHING BUILDING
AND LOT COVERED

Figure 19-14. Open–front finishing buildings. (*Courtesy* Granite City Steel Division of National Steel Corporation)

future expansion should be located on a plan. As discussed in Chapter 3, there are a number of factors that must be considered. A swine enterprise creates strong odors and large amounts of manure. Careful planning is necessary to minimize these problems. Therefore it is worthwhile to review some of the questions that pertain especially to livestock operations.

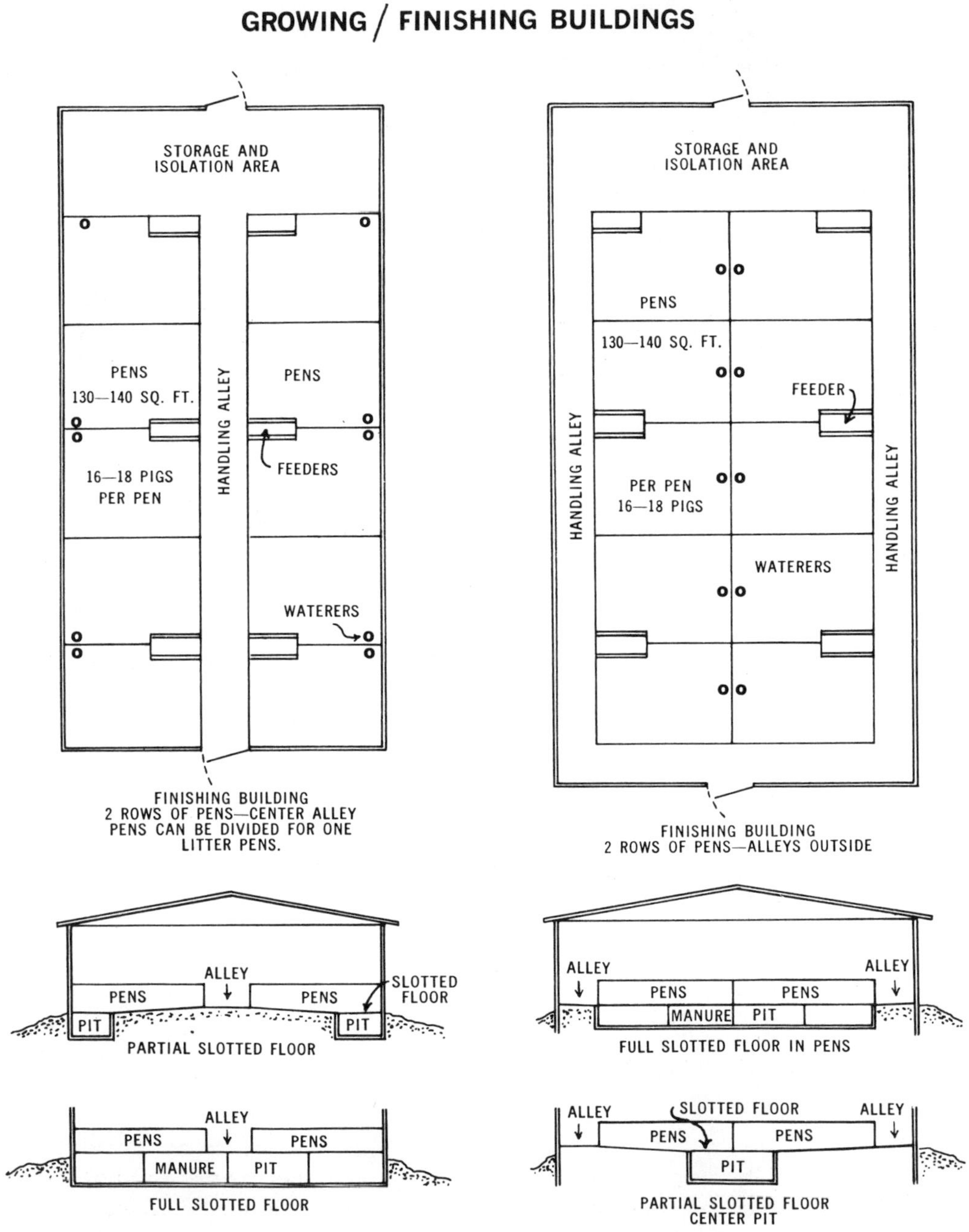

GROWING / FINISHING BUILDINGS

Figure 19-15. Growing and finishing buildings. (*Courtesy* Granite City Division of National Steel Corporation)

1.   Will all local and environmental regulations be met?

2.   Is the location well drained?

3.   Is there adequate space and suitable topography for manure storage?

4.   Are adequate utilities, such as water, available?

5.   Will prevailing winds and proposed building separation minimize odor problems?

6.   Will buildings be arranged for easy movement of animals from one unit to another without risk of spreading disease?

7.   Can feed, animals, and waste be moved efficiently?

Materials of Construction

Since most confinement buildings are single story and must be heavily insulated in both walls and ceiling, frame construction on a concrete foundation is the most practical. Placing 2 inches (50 mm) of rigid polystyrene on the inside of the outer concrete form will allow the insulation to bond securely to the wall. Asbestos cement board is later installed over the insulation for a neat, durable finish. The use of 2- by 6-inch (38 by 140 mm) studs will provide added strength and allow adequate space for the insulation. The ventilation inlets should be constructed at the time the walls and roof are being built.

Roof framing using clear-span, trussed construction eliminates any interference with pen location and facilitates any future modifications.

Either exterior-type plywood or sheet metal installed horizontally is suitable for the outer wall covering. After the insulation is in place, the studs should be covered with a vapor barrier before the inside wall surface is installed. Exterior plywood is a suitable material for both walls and ceiling, but the bottom 3 feet (1 m) of any wall exposed to the pigs should be covered with three-eighths-inch (9.5-mm), high density asbestos cement board to prevent damage from chewing.

Concrete is the universal choice as the material with which to pave yards and build solid floors in swine houses. It is hard, durable, and easy to clean. As slotted floors have become popular, concrete has been the common choice for slat construction, again because of its durability and reasonable cost. However, a number of other materials including wood, steel, aluminum, and plastic have been used. Concrete is heavy to install but is relatively nonskid. The edges of the slats should be slightly rounded. Wood is inexpensive and light in weight but does not wear well and often warps and becomes slippery. The expected life is only two to four years. Expanded metal has worked well for pigs under 50 pounds (23 kg) but has not held up well for larger hogs. Early steel slats produced a satisfactory floor but had a short life due to corrosion. Aluminum is considerably more expensive than steel but is much more corrosion resistant. Some aluminum slats lock together for greater stability and strength. They have perforated openings punched in a staggered pattern in either of two widths, three-eighths of an inch (9.5 mm) for the farrowing house or five-eighths of an inch (16 mm) for the growing and finishing house.

Early slotted floors were designed with narrow slats. Experience appears to have shown, however, that 8-inch (200-mm) slats with a 1-inch (24-mm) opening are best for all ages. The area under the sow should be covered with a piece of plywood or flat, expanded metal for two or three days at farrowing time to give the baby pigs a chance to become adjusted. It is generally recommended that a spacing of either three-eighths of an inch (9.5 mm) or 1 inch (25 mm), but not an intermediate value, may be used successfully for farrowing house floors. The baby pigs get their legs caught in the intermediate-sized spacing and the incidence of crushing by the sow increases. Casting the slats for the rear of the stall to a 1¼-inch (32-mm) spacing will improve the cleanliness of the farrowing stall.

A discussion of slat dimensions and strengths is presented in Chapter 10.

Environmental Control

Swine are more sensitive to temperature than other domestic animals due in part to their lack of a protective coat of wool, hair, or feathers. Because of this, growing pigs respond to the temperature of their housing to a greater degree than other livestock. Newborn pigs need a temperature of 90°F (32°C) just to survive. The temperature is then gradually lowered until 70°F (21°C) is reached at about three weeks of age.

Research has shown that 70°F (21°C) is the optimum temperature for growth up to 150 pounds (68 kg). From 150 pounds (68 kg) up to market weight, 70°F (21°C) remains the optimum level but temperatures down to 60°F (16°C) do not appreciably affect the rate of growth. At 90°F (32°C) and above, however, larger pigs suffer from excessive heat and actually lose weight.

Feed conversion is also dramatically affected by temperature level.

The highest rate of feed conversion in pigs up to 150 pounds (68 kg) occurs at 70°F (21°C) while the most efficient use of feed is obtained at 60°F (16°C) during the finishing stage.

Although prices of feed and fuel vary, and future prices are uncertain, in general it is safe to say that fuel is cheaper than feed and therefore it is economically feasible to provide some artificial heat during cold weather up to the age of 18 weeks and, under ecrtain circumstances, right on through to market age.

Insulation   Given the importance of relatively high inside temperatures under all climatic conditions, high levels of insulation are essential. Table 19-6 suggests minimum R values for mild, cold, and very cold zones. With these levels of insulation, a carefully installed 4-mil (0.1-mm) polyethylene vapor barrier is also important.

Table 19-6   Minimum R Values for Swine Buildings

Temperature		Wall		Ceiling	
°F	°C	R_1*	R_2**	R_1*	R_2**
10	−12	9	1.6	12	2.1
0	−18	13	2.3	18	3.2
−10	−23	17	3.0	24	4.2

* R_1 = sq ft hr °F/Btu   ** R_2 = m² · K/W

Ventilation   Good ventilation in a swine barn controls humidity, odors, and the spread of disease. Supplemental heat is usually necessary during the winter. Although minimum ventilation will add to the heat load, it is essential for the removal of moisture and odors and for drawing in fresh air to dilute the air-borne disease organisms. As outside temperatures moderate, fans are used to move more and more air through the building to maintain the inside temperature at the optimum level.

Fans, driven by enclosed capacitor or split-phase motors with built-in overload protection, should have a capacity rated by AMCA at one-eighth-inch (3-mm) static pressure. Auxiliary equipment, such as shutters, guards, and hoods, is essential.

Fans may be located high on the wall on the protected side of the building. They may be grouped together in buildings up to 100 feet (30 m) long, but in longer buildings they should be divided into pairs and located at intervals along the wall. Locating thermostats for all fans at one point near the center of the building at eye level permits easy adjustment.

The distribution and circulation within the room is determined largely by the design and location of the fresh air inlets. They can be located either at the junction of the ceiling and walls or near the center of the ceiling. In either case, air which is a few degrees warmer may be brought in from the attic in the winter while for summer ventilation the side slots are supplied by air coming in through the soffits under the eaves. In the summer, the center inlet must be supplied by an insulated duct extending to gable-end louvres. Regardless of the vent location, baffles should direct the incoming air along the ceiling for winter ventilation. There the cool air mixes with the warm air uniformly and drafts are avoided. Summer ventilation is most effective when the inlet baffles are positioned so that the air is directed down toward the floor, thus providing the greatest cooling effect on the animals.

Air should pass through the inlets at high velocity to insure good distribution and maximum mixing. An inlet opening of not over 20 square inches per 100 cubic feet per minute of fan capacity (275 mm² per L/s) will cause an air velocity of 700 to 1,000 feet per minute (3.6 to 5.0 m/s) and insure good ventilation. The velocity can be checked directly with a draft gauge or with the use of a manometer which will give the static

Table 19-7A   Customary Units
Ventilation Rates and Supplemental Heat Values for Swine Houses
(Wall R= 17, Ceiling R = 24)

	Ventilation Rates cu ft/min per animal				Supplemental Heat Btu/hour per animal				
	Rate 1*	Rate 2*	Rate 3*	°F	Outside temperature °F				
					−20	−10	0	10	20
Sow and litter	20	60	240	60	2,150	1,900	1,650	1,400	1,150
Growing—									
Finishing Pigs									
20–40 lb	3	12	36	70 ⎫	300	250	200	150	100
40–100 lb	5	20	48	60 ⎭					
100–150 lb	7	25	75	60 ⎫	500	400	300	200	100
150 lb up	10	35	100	60 ⎭					
Sows and Boars									
200–250 lb	10	35	120	50 ⎫					
250–300 lb	12	40	180	50 ⎬	125	75	25	0	0
300 lb up	15	45	250	50 ⎭					

R = sq ft hr °F/Btu
For Wall R = 13 and Ceiling R = 18 increase heat values 4%
    Wall R = 9 and Ceiling R = 12 increase heat values 8%
* Rate 1 is for continuous operation and is put on a 35°F thermostat for freeze protection only.
   Rate 2 is in addition and would be controlled to come on at 5°F above heater shutdown.
   Rate 3 is in addition and would be controlled to come on at about 72°F for high room temperature control.

pressure across the inlet opening (Figure 16-1). A static pressure of 0.03 to 0.06 inches (0.75 to 1.5 mm) indicates a satisfactory velocity. A discussion of the term "exposure factor" and its relation to air flow rates in a ventilation system is found in Chapter 16. A series of design graphs to be used with the exposure factor in planning swine building ventilation can be found in the annual Agricultural Engineers Yearbook (American Society of Agricultural Engineers, 1977).

Supplemental heat As explained in Chapter 16, a heat balance is calculated by estimating the heat loss through the building walls and ceiling as well as the amount of heat removed by ventilation. From this total the heat produced by the animals is subtracted, leaving a balance to be supplied by a heating system. Table 19-7 provides approximate supplemental heat values and ventilation rates for swine buildings.

Heating systems should be designed for safe, economical, and dependable operation.

Space heating For small buildings, gas or electric unit heaters, which can be suspended from the ceiling, help to circulate air as well as supply heat. For larger buildings a central, hot water heating system,

Table 19-7B SI Metric Units
Ventilation Rates and Supplemental Heat Values for Swine Houses
(Wall R = 3, Ceiling R = 4.2)

	Ventilation Rates L/s per animal				Supplemental Heat Watts per Animal				
					Outside temperature °C				
	Rate 1*	Rate 2*	Rate 3*	°C	−29	−23	−18	−12	−7
Sow and litter	9.3	28	112	16	630	557	483	410	337
Growing— finishing pigs									
9–18 kg	1.4	5.6	17	21 }	88	73	59	44	29
18–45 kg	2.3	9.3	22	16 }					
45–68 kg	3.3	11.7	35	16 }	147	117	88	59	29
68 kg up	4.7	16.3	47	16 }					
Sows and boars									
91–114 kg	4.7	16.3	56	10 }					
114–136 kg	5.6	19.0	84	10 }	37	22	7	0	0
136 kg up	7.0	21.0	117	10 }					

$R = m^2 \cdot K/W$
For Wall R = 2.3 and ceiling R = 3.2, increase heat values 4%.
    Wall R = 1.6 and ceiling R = 2.1, increase heat values 8%.
* Rate 1 is for continuous operation and is put on a 2°C thermostat for freeze protection only.
  Rate 2 is in addition and would be controlled to come on at 3°C above heater shutdown.
  Rate 3 is in addition and would be controlled to come on at about 22°C for high temperature control.

isolated in a fire-resistant room, will supply the necessary heat to maintain the room temperature. In addition, hot water can be used for heating floor slabs for creep and weaned pig areas.

The general heating can be supplied by black iron pipes mounted on the walls. Finned pipes or radiators should not be used because of dust. For the same reason, hot air systems are not satisfactory unless the normal filter area of the blower is doubled. It should be remembered that with continuous fan operation there will be a small negative pressure in the building. This could adversely affect the combustion and flue draft of unit heaters or central heating systems that are not isolated. The best heating installations overcome this by providing fresh air from outside the building to support combustion. All burners, regardless of type, should be vented to the outdoors.

Creep heating   Newborn pigs require a very warm environment starting at 90°F (32°C) at birth with a gradual decline to 70°F (21°C) by the end of two or three weeks. At the same time, the sow is most comfortable at 60°F (16°C). Either floor or radiant heat in the creep area can supply the localized requirements of the young pigs without overheating the room for the sow.

Floor heat may be supplied to the creep areas by hot water pipes or electric heating cables set in the concrete. A hot water system will be less expensive to operate and is particularly convenient to use if the boiler is also supplying heat for the room. Electrical heating permits individual control of the temperature at each creep in the building.

Fiberglass stall pads that cover slotted floors have electrically heated areas to provide for young pigs. Other slotted floor covers are designed to be used with quartz radiant heaters or heat lamps.

A relatively simple design for installing hot water pipes in a solid slab consists of preparing a smooth grade on which 2-inch (50-mm) thick pieces of polystyrene are placed in all locations where creep heat is desired. A pair of pipes, joined together at the far end of the house to form a loop, are laid across the polystyrene. Insulation is then placed around the pipes between the pieces of polystyrene insulation (Figure 19-16). A second pair of pipes is placed in the same manner leaving 12 inches (300 mm) between each of the four pipelines. Black iron, copper, or high temperature CPVC pipe may be used. Concrete is then poured over the entire area, 4 inches (100 mm) thick between the insulation and 2 inches (50 mm) over the insulation. Water heated to 140°F (60°C) and circulated through the lines will produce an 85 to 90°F (29 to 32°C) floor-surface temperature over the insulation when room temperature is 60°F (16°C). In calculating the size of a heater to supply a floor-piped system of this type, the loss of heat between the warmed areas will be about 10 Btu/(hr ft) (10 W/m) of pipe, while the loss within the heated areas will be about 35 Btu/(hr ft) (34 W/m) of pipe. The heat for a small system may be supplied by an electric, gas, or oil domestic water heater. For larger systems, a home heating system may be used.

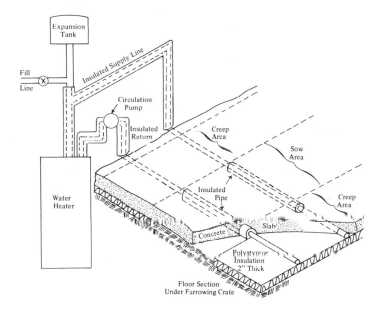

Figure 19-16. Hot water heating of creep-area floor. (*Courtesy* Cooperative Extension Service, University of Missouri)

To illustrate the method of calculating heating capacity, assume a 24 by 36 by 8-foot farrowing house with ten 5-foot stalls in two rows. In each stall, a 3-foot area is heated and a 2-foot area is unheated. The outside temperature is 0°F and the inside is 60°F. The average R is 20.

1. 10 stalls $\times$ 3 ft = 30 ft heated $\times$ 4 lines = 120 ft
    10 stalls $\times$ 2 ft = 20 ft unheated $\times$ 4 lines = 80 ft

2. 120 ft $\times$ 35 Btu/hr ft = 4,200
    80 ft $\times$ 10 Btu/hr ft = 800

3. The total heat per hour = 5,000 Btu

4. This is well within the supply capabilities of a water heater. However, total heat for the house should be calculated to determine the type of heater required.

5. A 24 x 36 x 8-ft house has 1,824 square feet of surface area.

6. $1,824 \times (1/20) \times (60 - 0) = 5,472$ Btu/hr wall and ceiling loss.

7. 20 cfm $\times 10 \times 60° \times 0.018 \times 60$ min. $= 12,960$ Btu/hr ventilation loss.

8. Total loss $= 18,432$ Btu/hr.

9. A 6,000 W electric water heater or a 30,000 Btu input gas heater would be adequate.

10. The 5,000 Btu for the creep floor heat does not add on to the total loss for the house; it is part of the radiation capacity of the system and at 44°F outside temperature would maintain a 60°F air temperature in the room without further radiation.

11. The total heating system should have two circulating pumps controlled by two thermostats. One thermostat would sense slab temperature and control water flow to the slab, while the other would sense air temperature and control water flow to wall-mounted pipes.

When electric cable is used to warm creep floors, it is imbedded in a slab of concrete. Proper installation is crucial to avoid failure from burning out. Two inches (50 mm) of polystyrene insulation is covered with a sheet of ⅛-inch (3-mm) asbestos cement board to which the cable is carefully wired using the recommended spacing. A careful check to see that the wires do not come in contact with the insulation and that they are not crossed should be made before a 1½-inch (38-mm) layer of concrete is poured. Either crossed wires or contact with the polystyrene will produce temperatures that melt the plastic insulation on the cable and cause it to burn out.

Cables are available with a number of different wattage ratings per unit length. Based on 30 to 40 watts per square foot (320 to 430 W/m²) the proper spacing can be calculated. The installation can be simplified by the use of units in which the cable has been prespaced on a metal mat. A thermostat with the sensing bulb inserted in a conduit imbedded in the slab should be installed for each three to four stalls and a fuse and switch installed for each pen.

Heat lamps or quartz radiant heaters above the creep area should be equipped with guards and suspended by adjustable chains. As a safety precaution it is wise to use ceiling-mounted outlets and cords that are just long enough to serve the lowest level at which the heater will be used. If for some reason the heater falls, the cord will be pulled out.

Cooling Feeder hogs subjected to high summer temperatures tend to gain more slowly or actually lose weight, while sows tend to be uncomfortable and lose their appetites at temperatures over 80°F (27°C). To avoid these problems, a number of cooling methods are employed.

For animals on pasture, shades and wallows are beneficial.

In the dry western half of the United States and Canada, evaporative coolers can reduce air temperatures by 10 to 20°F (6 to 11°C). However, they are not well suited to eastern areas where temperature reductions over 6 to 9°F (3 to 5°C) are seldom practical.

The use of spray nozzles is one of the most practical methods of providing cooling for feeder hogs. One to two minutes per hour will wet the animal's skin and allow cooling by evaporation. The system consists of a theromstat set at 75 to 80°F (24 to 27°C) which operates a solenoid valve in the waterline supplying the nozzles. The nozzles should be of the hollow cone type producing a coarse spray pattern at the rate of about 0.05 gal/min (0.2 L/min) per pig at line pressure. The coarse droplet size is important since the beneficial effect comes from wetting the pig and not evaporating water into the air. A time clock in series with the thermostat limits the spraying time.

Zone cooling has proved beneficial for sows confined in stalls. An insulated plywood duct extending the length of the room is located just above the front of the stalls. At each stall a small blower is installed in the duct with a short length of 2½-inch (6-mm) flexible tubing that carries the air toward the stall. In the summer the tubing is bent down so that the sow can stand in the cool airstream. In areas where outside air is too warm and humid to supply the necessary cooling, air conditioners have been installed in the duct to provide about 1,200 Btu per hour (350 W) of cooling for each sow. In the winter the tubing may be bent up to promote air circulation in the room and provide the minimum continuous ventilation. The small blowers should have a capacity of at least 50 cubic feet per minute (1.5 m³/min) at ½ inch (13 mm) of static pressure. Depending on blower capacity and outside temperature, the use of every third or fourth fan can provide the necessary minimum continuous ventilation. Outlet openings in the building wall may need to be provided, but overhead inlets used in conjunction with larger exhaust fans should be closed tightly to prevent exhausting moist air into the attic.

Feed Management

Corn is the basic ingredient in hog finishing rations and requires the greatest storage space. Dry corn is usually stored in steel bins. High-moisture corn is commonly stored in glass-lined steel or concrete oxygen-limiting silos in the whole kernel form and then mixed on the farm with purchased concentrate using grinder-blender-proportioners. Concentrates and purchased feeds are usually stored in 5- to 20-ton hopper-bottom steel or fiberglass bins.

Self-feeders on pasture are filled from self-unloading feed wagons. Yard feeders near the fence line can be filled from the same type of wagon. However auger feeders that run the length of the barn and fill each of the feeders have the advantage of requiring less labor and allowing the feeder to be located in the ideal location which is usually close to the rest area.

Feed is distributed by augers in totally confined growing and finishing operations. Where floor feeding is practiced, either feed carts or auger conveyors are used. The choice is often determined by the size of the enterprise and whether a time clock operation is desired.

For feeding in gestation barns equipped with stalls, automatic feeders that travel on rails above the sow stalls meter out a predetermined amount of feed as indicated by the tab position at each stall. This insures the correct individual ration of feed for each animal. Other automatic feeders accumulate a preset amount of feed and then drop it simultaneously into the feeders allowing all animals in a room to be fed within a few seconds. This prevents the emotional disturbances associated with sequential feeding along the row of stalls. Automatic feeders can eliminate the need for one or more feed alleys, resulting in a saving in building costs that would partially offset the cost of the feeder. On smaller farms where individual feeding is practiced, feed carts are used in both the farrowing and breeder-gestation barns.

Table 19-8   Estimated Feed Requirements for Swine

	Customary	SI
Annual Feed Requirements for Sows:		
Corn grain	1,820 lb	825 kg
Protein supplement	580 lb	260 kg
Feed Requirements per Pig:		
40–210 lb (18–95 kg)		
Pig starter	12 lb	5 kg
Pig grower	70 lb	32 kg
Corn grain	490 lb	225 kg
Protein supplement	75 lb	34 kg

(From Granite City Steel Division of National Steel Corporation, 1977)

Waste Management

A well planned, complete waste management system is absolutely essential in a swine production enterprise. A complete waste disposal system is needed to maintain healthy livestock in sanitary conditions, to avoid polluting air and water, and to comply with local, state, and federal environmental regulations.

The methods of waste disposal vary with the type of waste being handled.

Hogs that are raised on pasture naturally distribute the manure throughout the area and thus reduce handling to a minimum. Wastes from bedded solid-floor houses are handled as solids and spread with a conventional spreader, while drainage from manure stacks, runoff from lots, and manure from unbedded floors and slotted floors are handled as liquids, and spread with liquid manure spreaders or through irrigation systems.

Completely slotted floors reduce labor requirements at the barn to a minimum. However, because hogs always tend to dung in the same place, partially slotted floors are probably a better choice since they require only a minimal increase in labor while saving significantly on the original investment. Locating the water fountain over the slotted area and the feeders near the resting area encourages the pigs to dung over the slotted portion of the floor while keeping the solid area clean.

Although the full slotted floor is usually designed with pits that are capable of storing manure up to 180 days, many herdsmen prefer to store the manure outside the building because of odors and toxic gases. In that case, the smaller pits under partially slotted floors are completely adequate in size.

Table 19-9 Lot and Floor Slopes

	Customary	SI
Paved lots and Feeding floors	¼-1 in./ft	20-80 mm/m
Finishing pens	½-1 in./ft	40-80 mm/m
Farrowing pens (no bedding)	½-¾ in./ft	40-60 mm/m
(bedding)	¼-½ in./ft	20-40 mm/m
Slotted floors	level	level

(From Granite City Steel Division of National Steel Corporation, 1977 and Midwest Plan Service, 1972.)

Manure Storage

Manure storage facilities are essential for most farms to meet environmental regulations and to hold the manure until a convenient or advantageous time to spread it on the land.

Types of storage include:

Paved areas Paved areas are used to stack bedded manure. The floor should slope toward a picket dam that will drain off the seepage from snow and rain. Picket dams are discussed in Chapter 18 and a dam is shown in Figure 18-16.

Pit storages   These are located under slotted-floor buildings. The problem of odors and toxic gases at the time of agitation discourages many from using this method. Hydrogen sulphide and ammonia are strong irritants and can be lethal in sufficient concentrations. Carbon dioxide and methane are odorless but cause asphyxiation. Excellent ventilation and great care are imperative at the time of agitation and pumping.

Holding ponds or tanks   These are used to hold manure up to six months or longer. Some anaerobic decomposition may occur, but the primary purpose is simply storage. Holding ponds should be located so that there is no possibility of polluting streams or lakes. In areas of porous soil structure, sealing may be necessary.

Tanks may be either above ground, requiring the manure to be pumped from the barn, or below grade into which the manure flows by gravity. Both ponds and tanks present potential odor problems when they are agitated and pumped. A location well away from the farm home and from neighbors will minimize the likelihood of complaints.

Lagoons   Lagoons are designed to cause bacterial decomposition of the manure. Anaerobic lagoons have a deficiency of air and frequently cause some odor problems. Often they become simply holding ponds that need to be pumped periodically. Aerobic lagoons require sufficient surface area to enable the sun and air to bring about complete decomposition, leaving the water clear and without scum or odor. Both aerobic and anaerobic lagoons are most satisfactory in mild climates.

Settling basins   These are used as temporary detention ponds to allow settling of a high percentage of the solid material from yard runoff as it flows into a lagoon. The basin is cleaned periodically and dries out between storms. Settling-basin design is discussed in detail in the section on beef cattle.

Oxidation ditches   Oxidation ditches are equipped with large agitators that stir air into the manure. Considerable decomposition results and odors are reduced to a minimum. However, costs are high, management difficult, and much nutrient value is lost.

Moving manure from swine buildings   Gutters should be scraped and flushed down daily. Deep gutters, 6 inches (150 mm) wide by 30 inches (760 mm) deep, are allowed to accumulate material scraped and flushed into them for one to three days. They are essentially self-cleaning when allowed to drain. Pits under slotted floors are emptied either by pumping into above ground tanks or allowed to drain periodically into below grade storage. Three to four inches (100 mm) of water added to the pit immediately after draining facilitates cleaning the next time.

With proper design, German farmers successfully allow the channels under slotted floors to drain continuously. The design includes level channels up to 60 feet (20 m) in length with a 6-inch (150-mm) raised edge at the end of the channel. The channel is filled with water initially and thereafter the manure flows with a low angle of repose. If the building is more than 60 feet (20 m) long, multiple channels may be used with a 12-inch (300-mm) step down at the end of each succeeding level section.

Table 19-10 shows the approximate manure production from animals at various stages of development.

Table 19-10   Daily Manure Production from Swine

| Animal | Size | | Volume of Manure* | |
	lb	kg	cubic feet	liters (1/1000 m³)
Pigs	40	18	.04	1.1
	100	45	11	3.1
	130	68	.17	4.8
	210	95	.23	6.4
Sows and boars	300	136	.17	4.8
	500	227	.28	7.8
Sows and Litter			.54	15.1

* The values given are for manure and urine only.

If pens and alleys are flushed down with high pressure water, the storage volume required will nearly double. If manure is to be distributed through an irrigation system, from 20 to 60 percent of the storage may be needed for extra water.

Equipment

The equipment required for a swine enterprise will depend to a large extent on the production program and the management system being used. Feed-handling equipment and feeders will differ considerably from one farm to another. Farrowing stalls, for example, may be free standing or designed for anchoring to a wall at one end. They may be either commercial or home built. The same is true for many items used in swine production.

The wide range of equipment and the variety of designs from which to choose necessitate careful planning and complete integration of the entire system so that buildings and equipment are compatible throughout.

The Midwest Plan Service publications provide plans for many pieces of equipment needed for a swine operation. These plans include sorting chutes, loading chutes, breeding racks, pens and stalls, feeders, and fences.

Alarms   As with other complete confinement systems, the conditions in swine buildings can change rapidly in the event of either electrical or mechanical failure. Alarms that are both power- and temperature-sensitive are available and recommended for all completely enclosed buildings. An alarm may be wired directly to a location where it will always be noted, or it may be connected by leased telephone line. Prompt warning of even one failure can result in a saving of livestock worth many times the cost of the alarm.

SHEEP

Sheep make excellent use of pasture and forage crops and require relatively small amounts of concentrates. Capital investment for housing and equipment for sheep is low in comparison to that for other livestock. Labor needs are modest but unevenly distributed throughout the year, making the enterprise well suited to a diversified farm operation. Although sheep can be grown successfully over a wide geographic range, overall labor and production costs will be lowest where the grazing season is long and the winter forage requirements are the least.

Being well protected with a heavy fleece, sheep can withstand cold temperatures and need shelter only from rain, snow, and wind in the winter and from hot sun in the summer. Warmth is a factor only during lambing and in some instances, immediately after shearing. Open, naturally ventilated buildings, and well drained yards, securely fenced to keep out predators, satisfy most of the demands for shelter.

Management Systems

Many sheep farms maintain a breeding flock which is bred to lamb early in the year. After a two and one-half to three month period of nursing and creep feeding, the lambs are weaned and put on pasture to be finished for market while the ewes are pastured separately. One rather simple facility can satisfy the housing needs in this type of production program.

In some areas, pasture is not adequate to finish the lambs and they are sold at about 55 to 65 pounds (25 to 30 kg) as feeders to be fed grain and either hay or pasture until they reach market weight of 100 to 120 pounds (45 to 55 kg). Shelter for a feeder operation should emphasize labor efficiency and good care since the margin per animal is often quite small.

A somewhat greater investment may be justified for a third management system. The total flock of ewes is divided and managed so that the two groups lamb alternately on a four-month schedule. Each group of ewes lambs three times in 24 months and the facilities are used on a cycle of three times per year. With this more intensive use of facilities, a larger investment in buildings and equipment is feasible.

Site Selection

A well drained southerly slope is preferred for a sheep barn and yards. This orientation of the site offers protection from winter winds and exposure to maximum sunshine so that the yards will dry out faster and be easier to maintain. Sheep do not tolerate mud well; therefore grading and filling should be considered if the natural slope and drainage do not meet the necessary standards. As with all livestock enterprises, the topography should be such that there is no chance of pollution from yard runoff.

While easy access to the barns is important, locating the barns at least 150 feet (45 m) downwind from the farm home will minimize summer barnyard odors in the living area.

Building Design and Layout

Inasmuch as natural ventilation is recommended for most sheep barns, pole-frame buildings with truss roof construction are ideal. The clear span offers an opportunity to shift partitions and equipment without interference from posts and to bed and clean the barn with tractor-mounted equipment. Post-and-beam construction is less expensive but the numerous posts reduce flexibility and make manure removal more difficult. If the building is to house the flock only, an even-pitch, gable roof provides the best combination of natural ventilation, working height, and economy of construction. However, if hay and bedding are to be stored in the same building with the sheep, an offset gable roof shape, with the high side to the back, permits greater height in the area where the hay is stored. Facing the open side to the south or southeast provides wind protection and a maximum amount of sunshine.

Although a concrete floor is usually unnecessary, a concrete apron, sloped 1:25, extending from 4 feet (1.2 m) inside to 8 feet (2.4 m) outside will help maintain firm, clean conditions at the barn entrance. A hard-packed gravel floor with a slope of 1:50 toward the open front is recommended. An eavestrough along the open side that drains the water away from the building is essential. A paved area may be provided for shearing the small flock, while a shearing shed with crowd pens and a raised shearing floor will improve efficiency for large flocks.

Rough lumber, plywood, or metal siding are all suitable for exterior walls and either corrugated roofing on purlins or asphalt roofing on a solid roof deck provide ample protection.

Figure 19-17 shows a plan for a 42- by 60-foot (12.8- by 18.3-m) barn that will house a flock of 100 ewes and store the necessary hay and some bedding. By the time lambing starts, an area is available in the hay storage section sufficient to set up the portable lambing pens. Hay racks and panels are movable to allow flexibility in pen arrangement to suit the needs of the seasons. The south side is open to one or more yards. While this figure shows only one of an unlimited variety of layouts, the flexibility illustrated through the use of movable racks and panels should be a part of any plan.

Yards require a slope of 1:20 to 1:10 and should be of adequate size to remain in good condition; that is, animal density should not be so heavy as to work the yard into a quagmire with every rain storm. Enclosing the yard with a fence at least 4 feet (1.2 m) high is inexpensive insurance against the intrusion of dogs. In range areas where coyotes are a problem, yard fences need to be 6 feet (1.8 m) high and have a buried apron along the outside. The fence is constructed of two 4-foot (1.2-m) wide rolls of woven wire fence. The bottom strip is bent in the middle to a right angle and the 2-foot (0.6-m) apron buried lightly. The close-spaced, horizontal edges of the top and bottom fence strips are joined with wire clips between alternate vertical wires.

The efficiency of handling the flock will be improved with the installation of a permanent crowd gate and sorting chute. For a small flock, one leg of the chute should lead to a loading chute or portable dipping tank (Figure 19-17). In a large operation a permanent dipping tank or spray yard should be incorporated into the design.

Sheep are prone to infestation by internal parasites. Experience has shown that an effective way to reduce this problem is to confine the flock to slotted floor pens. This can be done on a small scale by mounting a slotted pen on a mobile home trailer frame. The entire pen can then be shifted to facilitate manure disposal. Large barns can also be constructed with slotted floors over a deep pit. The pit must have grade access for manure removal with a front-end loader. Slotted floors eliminate the need for bedding, require less labor, and allow for greater animal density, all of which help to offset the added cost of construction.

Environmental Control

Throughout most of the year an open-front building provides adequate shelter. To reduce the possibility of condensation under the roof, an open ridge and openings under the eaves at the rear of the building are recommended. One inch (25 mm) per 10 feet (3 m) of barn width will suffice at both locations, except that the ridge opening should be a mini-

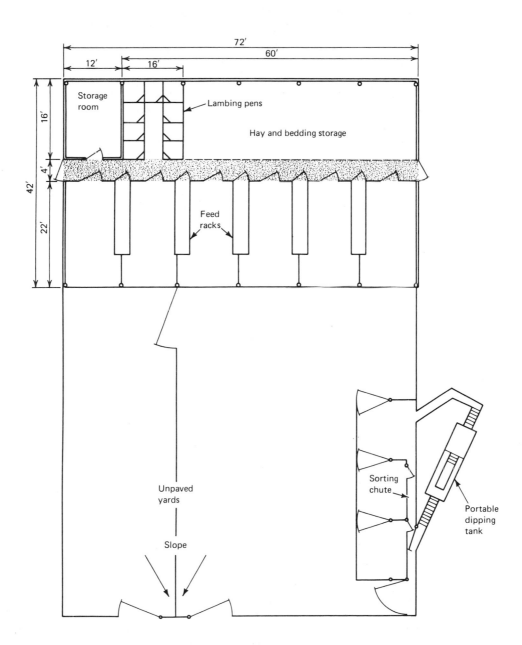

Figure 19-17. Facilities for 100 ewes.

mum of 4 inches (100 mm) to prevent freeze-ups. Summer ventilation is furnished by opening 4-foot (1.2-m) wide doors along the rear wall.

If a warm housing system is desired because of very early shearing or lambing the building should be of frame construction and insulated to an R of 4 (0.7) for the wall and an R of 8 (1.4) for the ceiling. A barn having both siding and interior wall covering along with hay storage above the flock would have an equivalent heat loss. The R values recommended are based on 0°F (−16°C) and a density of at least one ewe in 20 square feet (2 m²). If density is reduced by 50 percent, as it probably would be in a separate lambing room, the R values would need to be doubled.

In a draft-free, insulated building, very little natural ventilation takes place and moisture soon builds up. Failure to remove sufficient moisture results in damp conditions that are conducive to the development of pneumonia and scours. By ventilating with a fan at the minimum continuous rate of 6 cubic feet per minute (2.8 L/s) per ewe, the temperature should remain above freezing and the moisture balance at a reasonable level. Fan capacity should be at least doubled on mild days, or, alternatively, the building should be opened up for natural ventilation. In a reasonably tight building, an air inlet area of 20 square inches per 100 cubic feet per minute (275 mm² per L/s) of fan capacity will produce the recommended air velocity of 700 to 1,000 feet per minute (3.5 to 5 m/s).

Newborn lambs are able to withstand cold temperatures after they are dry and have nursed the ewe. A 250-watt heat lamp mounted in an approved frame, suspended with a chain over one corner of the lambing pen, will keep the lamb warm and hasten drying. The outlet into which the lamp is plugged should be above the lamp and the cord should be too short to reach the floor so if the lamp falls it will automatically pull the plug.

Feed Management

Hay should be stored as close to the flock as possible for greatest labor efficiency.

Grain may be processed and stored in an elevated bulk bin from which it is easily discharged into a feed cart or mixer wagon or augered to self feeders. Feeder lambs are supplied with grain on a continuous basis from self feeders. These may be filled with a conveyor system or from a mixer wagon if the location is suitable.

Young lambs should also be fed grain in a creep on a continuous basis to ensure maximum growth. A lamb creep is a fenced-off area containing a hay rack and a low grain trough. The fence is constructed to allow entrance of lambs while excluding ewes.

If silage is an important part of the ration, one of the following should be considered:

1. Self-feeding through a movable fence from a horizontal silo.

2. Feeding from a cart into bunks on either side of a covered alley.

3. Feeding with a mechanical bunk conveyor.

4. Feeding from a mixer wagon, perhaps as a complete ration.

A supply of clean water should be available at all times. Watering tanks may be float controlled and automatically protected from freezing.

Waste Management

Sheep manure has a moisture content of about 75 percent which is much lower than that of other livestock. With relatively little bedding, pens stay clean and dry and the manure is easily handled as a solid.

Runoff from yards, however, must be managed so that all environmental regulations are met and no pollution of natural waterways occurs. Surface runoff should be diverted away from the lots so that only the precipitation falling on the lots becomes polluted. In many cases the runoff from yards can be allowed to spread out on a grassed area. If the yards are large and rainfall substantial, it may be necessary to install a settling basin and a holding pond as described in the section on beef cattle. In any case, when planning the waste management system, the local authorities concerned with pollution control should be consulted to assure compliance with state and federal regulations.

Equipment

The equipment required for a sheep enterprise will vary according to size, feeding program, and climatic area, but it need not be elaborate or expensive. Each stage of production requires a somewhat different arrangement and different space needs. Lightweight but rugged portable equipment can help promote the needed flexibility.

Fenceline bunks contribute to efficiency with large flocks but may not be as useful as portable racks for smaller sized operations. Feeders of all types should be designed to reduce to a minimum the amount of chaff and other trash that works into the wool. Racks and troughs that can be tipped over for cleaning and shifted to form new pen locations are convenient.

Table 19-11   Specifications for Housing Facilities for Sheep

	Ewe and Lambs		Feeder Lambs	
	Customary	SI	Customary	SI
Pen space (open to lot)	12–16 sq ft	1.1–1.5 m²	6–8 sq ft	0.6–0.7 m²
Yard space	25–40 sq ft	2.3–3.7 m²	15–20 sq ft	1.4–1.9 m²
Solid floor confinement	15–20 sq ft	1.4–1.9 m²	8–10 sq ft	0.7–0.9 m²
Slotted floor confinement	10–12 sq ft	0.9–1.1 m²	4–5 sq ft	0.4–0.5 m²
Lambing pens	4 x 4 ft	1.2 x 1.2 m		
Creep space/lamb	2 sq ft	0.2 m²		
Feeder space				
Grain—group fed	12–18 in.	300–450 mm	8–12 in.	200–300 mm
Grain—self fed			3–4 in.	75–100 mm
Hay and silage—group fed	12–18 in.	300–450 mm	8–12 in.	200–300 mm
Hay and silage—self fed	6–8 in.	150–200 mm	3–4 in.	75–100 mm
Waterer	1/35	1/35	1/35	1/35
Water per day	2 gal	7.5 L	1½ gal	5.7 L
Feed requirements/day				
Hay	4–5 lb	1.8–2.3 kg	Varies with season	
Grain	¾–1½ lb	0.3–0.7 kg	2–3 lb	0.9–1.4 kg
Silage (only roughage) (2–3 tons silage = 1 ton hay)	12–15 lb	5.5–6.8 kg	4–6 lb	1.8–2.7 kg
Bedding requirements/day	1 lb	0.5 kg	½ lb	0.2 kg
Manure production/day	6 lb	2.7 kg	3–4 lb	1.4–1.8 kg

Pairs of hinged panels 4 feet (1.2 m) long and 2½ feet (0.75 m) high are useful for lambing pens and for isolating sick animals.

Ample lighting in the barn and yards is important, particularly during the lambing season. An electrical service adequate to supply lighting, water heaters, heat lamps, and other equipment is essential.

Well maintained, woven-wire fences not only keep sheep confined to pasture areas but discourage predators as well. Three-wire electric fences are satisfactory, but sheep must be trained to avoid them since their heavy coat of wool insulates them from shock. Training should be done soon after shearing by placing a little feed behind the wires so that the sheep must touch the wire to reach the feed. Electric fences are also effective in keeping dogs and other predators out of the sheep lots.

HORSES

The rising popularity of pleasure horse riding has increased the interest in and the need for both horse barns and riding facilities. Well designed stables contribute to the ease and pleasure of caring for horses, and an attractive, well constructed building adds to the pride of ownership. Because horses are large and spirited animals, and because individuals are generally more intimately involved with them than with other farm animals, prime consideration in planning a horse barn and related facilities must be given to the health and safety of both the animals and the people who will come in contact with them.

Horse Barns

The barn, whether it be large or small, should be well planned, durable and attractive. It must provide shelter from wind, rain, and snow, be adequately ventilated, and be located in a well drained area. A slope of 1:20 away from the entrance and soil that is naturally well drained help maintain firm surface conditions. This is particularly important if the horses are allowed to run in a paddock adjacent to the barn. If natural conditions are not adequate, gravel fill may be necessary. As with other livestock housing, it is desirable to locate a horse barn downwind from the home. A distance of 150 feet (45 m) is usually sufficient.

Barn layout Many pleasure horse barns house one to three horses and are designed to be aesthetically pleasing in appearance, using such features as gambrel roofs, cupolas, and window shutters. Vertical boards and battens, novelty siding, or texture 1-11 plywood are practical and attractive siding materials. Barns are often designed for outside service with a roof overhang for weather protection.

Figure 19-18a. Two-stall horse barn with Dutch doors. (USDA 5838)

Large barns with either box stalls or tie stalls may be designed with a central alley and inside service for maximum convenience and protection from the weather. The width of the barn is typically 36 feet (11 m) and the length in increments of 12 feet (3.6 m) as required. With tie stalls the barn can be somewhat narrower.

An alternative design places two rows of box stalls back to back with outside service on both sides of the barn. Eight-foot (2.4-m) roof overhangs provide protection. The overall width is typically 40 feet (12 m) with the length in increments of 12 feet (3.6 m). While this design does not offer as much convenience or protection, the outside doors somewhat improve fire safety.

Single-story gable roof designs employing either frame or pole construction, are suitable for either small or large barns and are adaptable to either inside or outside service plans.

Stalls and alleys   Horses may be confined in either tie stalls or box stalls. Although box stalls require approximately twice as much space, they are recommended because pleasure horses often fail to receive adequate and regular outdoor exercise, and a box stall permits limited exercise inside. On the other hand, tie stalls require less bedding and are easier to clean. They can often be constructed in buildings that are not suitable for box stalls. The width of a horse barn is determined by the size of the box stall or the length of a tie stall plus the width of the alley.

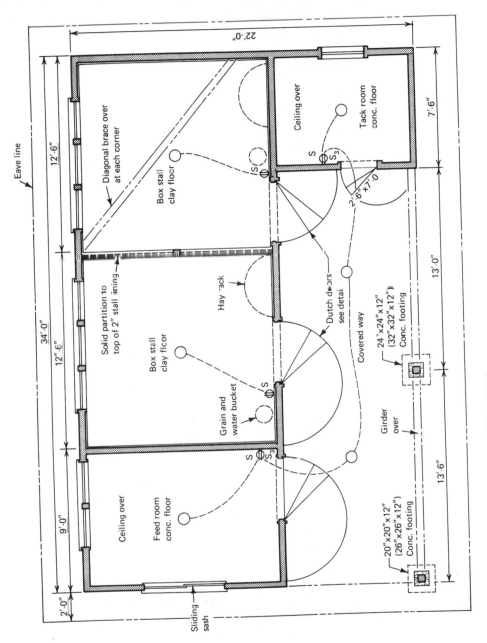

Figure 19-18b. Floor plan for two-stall barn. (USDA 5838)

Table 19-12 lists the recommended sizes for alleys, stalls, and stall equipment. It should be emphasized that young animals require generous sized stalls just as older horses do.

Table 19-12   Specifications for Housing Facilities for Horses

	Customary	SI
Box stall size		
Foals to 2 years	10x10 ft	3 x 3 m
Mature mares and geldings	12x12 ft	3.7 x 3.7 m
Stallions	14x14 ft	4.3 x 4.3 m
Tie stall size		
Foals to 2 years	5x9 ft	1.5 x 2.7 m
Mature animal	5x9-12 ft	1.5 x 2.7-3.7 m
Stallion	Not recommended	
Ceiling height		
Horse alone	8 ft	2.4 m
Horse and rider	12 ft	3.7 m
Doors		
Stalls	4x8 ft	1.2 x 2.4 m
Barn alley, horse and rider	12x12 ft	3.7 x 3.7 m
Alleys	8 ft minimum	2.4 m minimum
	12 ft is best	3.7 m is best
Hay mangers	L x W x D x H	L x W x D x H
Foals to 2 years	30x18x20x34 in.	760x450x500x860 mm
Mature animals	36x24x24x40 in.	900x600x600x1000 mm
Grain box		
Foals to 2 years	18x12x6x34 in.	450x300x150x860 mm
Mature animals	24x12x8x40 in.	600x300x200x1000 mm
Water requirements per day	8–12 gal	30–45 L

Alleys of adequate width for easy handling of the horses are not only more convenient but are also safer. A minimum door and alley height of 8 feet (2.4 m) is acceptable if a horse is *never* mounted inside. However, if animals will be mounted within the building, a minimum height of 12 feet (3.7 m) is essential.

Full-length, sliding doors, with a bottom guide to prevent them from being pushed out, are convenient for box stalls opening onto an inside alley. Swinging doors are sometimes used but they are not as satisfactory because of the space required to swing open. When box stalls open to the outside, Dutch doors, with 4-foot (1.2-m) high lower sections, allow for light and ventilation. Latches must be strong and easy to operate from both inside and outside the stall but not so simple that the horse can open the door. A 4- to 8-foot (1.2 to 2.4 m) roof overhang offers weather protection and shade for both horse and attendant.

Stall and alley construction Sturdy, rugged construction is imperative for all facilities. Stall walls should be constructed of 2-inch (38-mm) lumber, preferably tongue and groove, which is bolted together. Stall posts may be made of 6- by 6-inch (140 by 140-mm) wood or 5-inch (125 mm) steel with welded channels to hold the partitions. Box stalls should have 5-foot (1.5-m) high, solid walls topped with a 2-foot (0.6-m) open metal or wood stall guard to allow free air movement. The guard may be constructed of pipe, steel bars, expanded steel, welded steel, or wood. Whatever material is used, it must be spaced to keep the horses from reaching one another. A height of 6 feet (1.8 m) for the front half and 4 feet (1.2 m) for the rear half is adequate for tie stalls.

Suitable stall and alley floors may be constructed of any of the following materials:

1. Packed clay on a well drained, gravel base.

2. Treated planks mounted on 4 by 4 inch (89 by 89 mm) pressure-preservative treated "sleepers" set in concrete.

3. Artificial turf on concrete.

4. Wooden blocks laid in concrete.

5. Broomed concrete (although this is a last choice).

Sloping tie stall floors 1:50 toward a 2- by 14-inch (50 by 350 mm) concrete gutter makes them easier to keep clean and dry. Concrete feed alleys are easiest to sweep clean. Concrete floors are also preferable in the wash area and feed and tack rooms.

Tack room Although horses do not require or benefit from a warm environment, horse owners usually enjoy a warm tack room. A simple, dust-free storage for tack is adequate, but frequently tack rooms are equipped with a desk, chairs, water and toilet facilities, and thermostatically controlled heat. It's a matter of personal choice.

Feed and Bedding

The feed area should be kept as dust free as possible and the grain storage should be in vermin-proof bins. For small quantities, garbage cans or wooden bins with tight covers are satisfactory. For large enterprises, commercial- or home-built bins or hopper-bottom bins with mechanical unloading are used.

The hay and bedding storage is most convenient if located in the same building. This may be in a loft or in a room on the ground floor. In either case, an open front or wide doors provide convenient unloading from trucks and easy distribution to the mangers. However, danger from fire will be somewhat reduced by having a separate storage nearby.

The hay and bedding storage space required will depend on the number and size of animals and the length of the storage period. Each horse will consume about 10 cubic feet (0.3 m³) of hay per week and an equal amount of straw or other bedding is likely to be used. Grain consumption will range up to about 2 cubic feet (0.06 m³) per week.

An adequate supply of clean, fresh water is essential for a healthy horse. Inasmuch as up to 12 gallons (45 L) of water are required daily for each horse, a frost-free hydrant or a waterline and faucet protected with heating tape is convenient. An electrically heated water bowl can be located in a box stall partition to serve two horses, or, if installed outside in a lot, it will be adequate for 8 to 10 horses. Where several horses are released from tie stalls at the same time, a frost-free watering tank is desirable.

Manure Handling

Manure is easily handled as a solid and should be disposed of daily when possible. A concrete slab on which to store the manure will reduce the incidence of flies. A carefully chosen location for the manure storage will prevent pollution of water sources and allow the leachate to be drained away to a grassed area or a seepage field.

Ventilation and Lighting

Horses do not require warm surroundings, but they do not easily tolerate drafts, dampness, and high humidity. Like all animals, they produce heat and moisture. The moisture must be removed from the barn to prevent condensation and damp conditions and to reduce odors. The most effective method of moisture and odor control is through proper ventilation.

If the barn is always open, a 4-inch (100-mm) ridge ventilator or gable-end louvers should be adequate. If the doors are closed tightly at night, 4-inch (100-mm) eave openings are also necessary.

Completely enclosed stables will need to be well insulated and ventilated. Since the animal density is usually low in a horse barn, particularly one with box stalls, additional heat in the range of 4,100 to 5,100 Btu per hour (1200 to 1500 W) per stall will be needed to supplement animal heat. A minimum of 50 cubic feet per minute (25 L/s) per stall of continuous ventilation should be provided plus at least 100 cubic feet per minute (50 L/s) additional capacity which is thermostatically controlled. An allowance of approximately 20 square inches of inlet area is required for each 100 cubic feet per minute of fan capacity (275 mm² per L/s).

A small, adjustable window for each stall will provide both light and warm weather ventilation. Any windows within reach of horses must be protected with wire mesh.

Each stall should have a protected lamp; a 100- to 150-watt bulb is adequate in most cases. Two lamps with a total of 300 watts are desirable for foaling stalls. A duplex outlet should be provided for each two stalls and an alley light provided every 12 feet (3.6 m).

Riding Rings

The great increase in pleasure horse riding has led to more horse shows and competitions of all types. While outdoor rings are relatively inexpensive, there is a growing demand for all-weather riding that can be satisfied only with indoor rings.

The National Horse Show Association recommendation on dimensions for outdoor rings is 120 by 240 feet (36.6 by 73.2 m) and for indoor rings 110 by 220 feet (33.5 by 67 m). Perhaps the first factor to consider in planning an indoor facility is that the recommended size will cost well into six figures. Smaller sized rings may be satisfactory in many cases. Eighty to 100 feet (24 to 30 m) in width has been recommended as a minimum for horse shows, while equitation classes may be conducted in a ring as small as 50 by 100 feet (15 by 30 m).

The larger sized buildings will require either bowstring or metal trusses for the long spans. The 50-foot (15-m) width can be satisfactorily spanned with a wood gable truss. Sidewall construction and foundations require careful engineering because of the tremendous snow loads that the building must be able to withstand. For example, the roof of a 100- by 220-foot (33.5 by 67 m) ring might easily accumulate a 360-ton (330-tonne) snow load.

Regardless of the size, a 16- to 18-foot (5 to 5.5 m) ceiling height is recommended for safety in jumping events. The design of the lighting system must take into account the prevention of shadows as well as the level of lighting. Fluorescent lights cast fewer shadows and are less expensive to operate than incandescent lamps. Transparent panels in the roof provide some natural light during the day.

Sandy loam on a firm, well drained base makes an excellent floor. Gravel, sand, or dusty materials are not suitable.

A safety feature that is strongly recommended is a knee board installed around the inside perimeter of the ring. It consists of a solid 2-inch (38-mm) wall sloping from a point 18 inches (450 mm) from the base of the wall to a point 5 feet (1.5 m) up on the wall. This will help to prevent rider injuries.

An adequate spectator section can be provided with a lean-to addition along one or more sides of the ring. While stalls may be located around the perimeter of the ring at minimal cost, a stall barn perpendicular to the ring will be more efficient. When stalls are located around the ring, it is best to provide outside doors and a roof overhang so that horses may be moved while the ring is in use.

Fences

Wood fences have been traditional for horse paddocks and, when well maintained, are attractive enclosures on the rural landscape. However, they are expensive to construct and require considerable maintenance. Nevertheless, wood fences are the safest type of fencing for horses and are a necessity for small enclosures such as show rings, training rings, corrals, and stallion pens.

Woven-wire fence with a board top is less expensive and provides good visibility while at the same time preventing horses from "riding down" on the fence. Chain link, welded pipe and cable fences are also satisfactory for horses. Barbed wire should never be used and electric fences are questionable. Horses have to be trained to an electric fence and some never learn to respect its action. Two ways in which electric fences can be useful are as a top wire above a woven-wire fence to prevent riding down and as a divider fence for rotational grazing. Two wires are needed for the latter with the top wire 36 to 40 inches (1 m) high. Pressure-preservative treated posts, 5 inches (125 mm) in diameter, set on 8-foot (2.4 m) centers, 3 feet (1 m) into the ground will give adequate support for any type of fence.

If fences cut across bridal paths, consideration should be given to gates that can be opened without dismounting. Plans for gates and many other items of equipment used with horses are described in the Midwest Plan Service Horse Handbook (Midwest Plan Service, 1971).

PROBLEMS

19.1   Plan an open unpaved feed lot for 200 beef animals. Show the feeding and resting areas and the location of the feed storage facilities. Be sure to indicate the size of the yard.

19.2   Using the plan developed for problem 19.1, assume that the maximum one hour rain for a 10 year recurrence period is 1½ inches

(38 mm). Also assume that 4 inches (100 mm) of solids will drain off the yard each year and that a settling basin will be cleaned 8 times a year. Design a settling basin with a 20 minute detention time, to be installed in the drainage channel to a holding pond.

19.3 What size holding pond will be required to provide for a 6 month storage period? Assume a maximum of 24 inches (600 mm) of precipitation during the period and that evaporation equals precipitation on the pond surface.

19.4 Using a four-room design, plan a building to provide farrowing facilities for the 80 sows on a farm. Within the same building or one attached to it, provide facilities for growing the pigs from 8 weeks to 14 weeks of age.

19.5 Plan a separate building to provide space for finishing to market weight the pigs moved from the growing area in 19.4.

19.6 Make recommendations for the environmental control system for the farrowing house section of the building in problem 19.4. Indicate the level of insulation, supplemental heat, and ventilation. Assume a winter design temperature of −10°F (−23°C).

19.7 Design the facilities for feeding 500 lambs, including an open shed and yard with provision for self feeding of grain.

19.8 Plan a barn for eight horses, including a central alley, tack room, and feed room.

REFERENCES

American Society of Agricultural Engineers. *Agricultural Engineers' Yearbook*. St. Joseph, Mich.: American Society of Agricultural Engineers, 1977.

Brevik, T.J. *Housing Your Flocks*. University of Wisconsin Cooperative Extension Program A2830. Madison, Wis., 1977.

Clemson University Cooperative Extension Service. *Beef Cattle Plans for South Carolina*. Clemson, S.C.: Clemson University Cooperative Extension Service, 1977.

Clemson University Cooperative Extension Service. *Hog Shelters and Equipment for South Carolina*. Agricultural Engineering Handbook

No. 14. Clemson, S.C.: Clemson University Cooperative Extension Service, 1977.

George, R.M., and Ricketts, R. *Feeding Slaughter Cattle.* Columbia, Mo.: University of Missouri Extension Division, 1968.

Granite City Steel Division of National Steel Corporation. *Farmstead Planning Beef Manual.* Granite City, Ill.: Granite City Steel Division of National Steel Corporation, 1977.

Granite City Steel Division of National Steel Corporation, *Farmstead Planning Swine Manual.* Granite City, Ill.: Granite City Steel Division of National Steel Corporation, 1977.

Krenzberger, F.L., et al. *Sheep Handbook.* University Park, Pa.: Pennsylvania State University.

Maddex, Robert L. "Recommended Housing for Horses." *Electricity on the Farm.* Vol. 43, No. 1, 1970.

Midwest Plan Service. *Beef Housing and Equipment Handbook.* Midwest Plan Service MWPS-6. Ames, Iowa, 1975.

Midwest Plan Service. *Horse Handbook, Housing and Equipment.* Midwest Plan Service MWPS-15. Ames, Iowa, 1971.

Midwest Plan Service. *Livestock Waste Facilities Handbook.* Midwest Plan Service MWPS-18. Ames, Iowa, 1975.

Midwest Plan Service. *Sheep Handbook, Housing and Equipment.* Midwest Plan Service MWPS-3. Ames, Iowa, 1974.

Midwest Plan Service. *Swine Handbook.* Midwest Plan Service MWPS-8. Ames, Iowa, 1972.

Muehling, A.J. *Swine Housing and Waste Management.* University of Illinois Department of Agricultural Engineering. Urbana-Champaign, Ill., 1969.

Myer, D.J. *Cattle Handling Corral Design.* University of Wisconsin Cooperative Extension Programs. Madison, Wis., 1976.

Turnbull, J.E., and Bird, N.A. *Confinement Swine Housing.* Canada Department of Agriculture Publication 1451. Ottawa, Canada, 1971.

Chapter Twenty

Poultry Housing

CHICKENS

Changes in poultry housing in recent years have been rapid and dramatic. The transition from the old farm chicken coop with a few hundred birds to a modern, environmentally controlled cage house for thousands of birds represents one of the greatest advancements ever made in housing for an agricultural enterprise. Automated equipment for feeding, watering, egg pickup, ventilating, and manure removal has promoted egg production to one of the most efficient of farm operations. It is now recognized that good housing also contributes to the overall increase in production efficiencies.

Increased bird densities and improved insulation have transformed the poultry house from one of the most difficult buildings to ventilate into one where optimum conditions are readily obtainable. High summer temperature is much more likely to be a problem than is severe winter weather.

Poultry Housing Requirements

Poultry production, like other animal enterprises, is divided into several phases organized to serve specific egg and meat markets. Breeding flocks supply eggs to hatcheries which in turn produce day-old chicks for broiler and layer replacement needs. Commercial laying flocks produce eggs for the fresh market as well as the bakery and processed food industries. Broiler production is a very intensive operation consisting of starting and finishing birds for market in eight to nine weeks with four to five flocks being shipped per year.

Each of these phases, with housing requirements peculiar to its own needs, will be discussed separately.

Three housing systems are prevalent in various regions of the country:

1. *Open housing* with little more than a roof and roll-up curtains on the sides.

2. *Window houses* that depend on natural ventilation, particularly in mild weather.

3. *Windowless, environmentally controlled houses* which are well ventilated, warm throughout the year, and depend on automatic fan ventilation.

Further, the birds within the house may be *floor managed* or confined in a *cage system*. Each of these two systems has applications to the various phases of poultry production.

Housing for the Breeding Flock

Breeder flocks are floor managed in either window or environmentally controlled houses. Considerable supervision is required in feeding and disease control in order to produce high quality eggs for the hatcheries. Labor efficiency is improved with automatic feeders and waterers which are often located on a slotted floor area. The floor litter in the balance of the house consequently stays drier and the moisture to be removed by the ventilating system is reduced. Nests are banked in lines along the outside wall or on either side of a center alley for convenient egg collection.

Housing for Laying Hens

Open houses utilizing cage systems are popular throughout the South where a mild year-round climate makes insulation and mechanical ventilation unnecessary. The cage system is protected with only a light reflective roof and roll-up curtains on the sides. Emergency cooling systems and rooftop sprinklers may be installed for periods of unusual hot weather. Investment is low and environmental conditions are reasonably uniform.

In the rest of the country, many lightly insulated, floor-managed houses, often with open fronts, are still being used. Although they offer some protection from weather extremes, they do not provide either the environmental conditions or the labor-saving facilities for a modern and efficient laying enterprise.

Newly established commercial laying operations are predominantly controlled environment buildings using cage systems that permit high bird density. The buildings are well insulated, windowless structures up to several hundred feet in length. The width is determined by the type and arrangement of the cages but usually ranges between 38 and 52 feet (12 and 16 m). While the cages are installed on only one floor level, the house may be essentially two stories high to allow space for manure storage for a period of up to 12 months.

Cage systems   Due to the influence of the cage systems on investment, environment, and labor efficiency, it is important to understand the advantages and disadvantages of each type before proceeding with a building design.

A number of different cage and housing systems have been developed during the past two decades. Although there are variations in equipment and design, cage systems may be classified by the number of levels of cages. Most of the early systems were flat deck, that is, just one level of cages. The introduction of the two-tier, stair-step cages (Figure 20-1) greatly improved the accessibility to the birds. With the advent of controlled-environment housing, cage designs continued to be improved until 3- and 4-tier cage systems became popular and allowed significantly increased bird density within a house. The four-tier system introduces some problems relating to air movement, ease of observation, and light distribution for the birds. Although all of these systems are in use, the three-tier is most common, offering good management possibilities and a high-density housing that offers a reasonable return on a per-hen investment.

The most common cage size is 12 inches (300 mm) across the front and 18 inches (450 mm) deep and usually holds four leghorn type hens. Several other front widths are available for differing numbers of birds. A more recent development is the so-called "reverse" cage which is 12 inches (300 mm) deep and 18 inches (450 mm) across the front (Figure 20-2). This shape allows all four birds to eat at one time, reducing competition and stress. The advantages of this cage are increased production, fewer cracked eggs, and lower mortality. The disadvantages are the necessity for a greater length of egg belt, feed chain, and water trough for a given number of cages, as well as more floor space for an equal number of tiers.

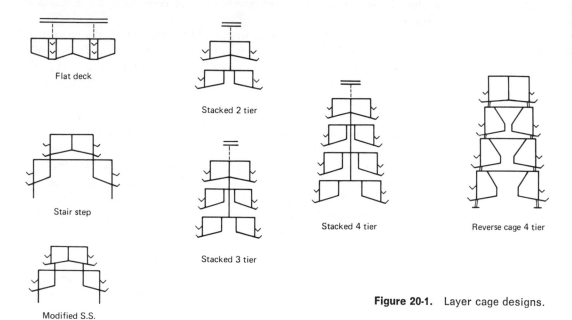

Flat deck

Stacked 2 tier

Stair step

Stacked 3 tier

Modified S.S.

Stacked 4 tier

Reverse cage 4 tier

Figure 20-1.   Layer cage designs.

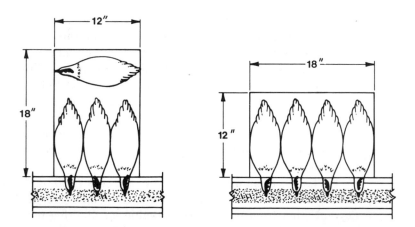

Figure 20-2.   Reverse cage design allows all birds to eat at one time. (*Courtesy* Northco Systems, A.R. Wood Manufacturing Co.)

The term *bird density* relates to two areas. The first is the area that each bird has in the cage. For example, each of the four birds in a 12- by 18-inch (300 by 450 mm) cage has 54 square inches (33 750 mm²) of space. The space that the birds have in the cage has an effect on egg production, livability, and feed consumed per dozen eggs produced (University of California Agricultural Extension Service, 1977). If the cost of the hen and the feed were the only considerations, one bird per cage would produce the most eggs on the least feed and with the best livability. However, when all costs, including those for the building, equipment, and labor are considered, either three or four birds per cage show the greatest return on investment. Three birds are best when egg prices are low, while four birds per cage show a greater return with high egg prices.

Bird density also refers to the building floor area per bird, and within the limits of good management, the more birds that can be housed in a building, the lower the cost of housing per bird. The type of cage and number of tiers will affect the bird density in the buildings as shown in Table 20-1.

Table 20-1 Cage Systems and Building Bird Densities

| | | | | House Width | | Area/bird | |
| | | | | ft | m | sq ft | m² |
Cage Type	Tiers	Cage Size	Rows				
Flat deck	1	12x18*	4	40	12.2	0.63	0.058
Modified S.S.	2	12x18*	4	40	12.2	0.63	0.058
Modified S.S.	3	12x18*	4	40	12.2	0.42	0.039
Stacked	3	12x18*	6	52	15.9	0.36	0.033
Stacked	4	12x18*	6	52	15.9	0.27	0.025
Reverse	4	18x12*	4	30	9.2	0.35	0.033
Reverse	4	18x12*	6	42	12.2	0.33	0.031
Stacked	4	19x19**	5	38	11.6	0.21	0.020

* 4 birds per cage and 54 sq in. (34 838 mm²) per bird
** 7 birds per cage and 51 sq in. (33 290 mm²) per bird

Feeders   Feed is stored in one or more metal feed bins outside the building from where it is automatically carried by conveyor to the feed hoppers at the end of each cage row. Several types of automatic feeders can be used effectively in the caged housing system:

1.   Chain or auger feed conveyors can be used in any of the systems discussed. The flat-deck system, however, is the only one in which four rows of cages are supplied simultaneously by one feeder loop designed to run between two rows of cages.

2.   Traveling hoppers riding a track along the cages while metering out feed into the trough are suitable for all but the flat-deck system.

3. A self-propelled and self-guided feed cart that travels along the walkway between the rows dispensing feed automatically requires an operator in attendance.

Layers should be encouraged to eat in order to maintain egg production, and the operation of the feeding system has a direct influence on the rate of feed consumption. Providing fresh feed, or merely stirring old feed stimulates eating (a ploy that can be used with a mechanical feeder controlled by a time clock to operate periodically). When feed is carried slowly along a long trough, chickens tend to "high grade;" that is, the first hens to have the feed pass by, pick out the coarse, high-energy bits of feed. The fines that are left for the birds at the end of the row contain most of the minerals and other additives. The result is that neither the birds at the beginning nor those at the end get a balanced ration. Uniformity of feed quantity and quality at all points along the cage row can be improved by various means. The traveling hopper and self-propelled feed carts put out the same feed for the length of the trough. Auger feeders are reported to continuously mix the feed. Some chain feeders operate at a high speed so that eating is discouraged until the chain stops moving.

Waterers   Water is critical to egg production and bird comfort. The water system in each house must be adequate, reliable, and free of contamination from feed, manure, or bacterial growth.

Three methods of supplying water to cages are in common use. Perhaps the simplest is a sloping trough that runs the length of the cage row with water flowing past each cage. To get the required slope and yet keep the water trough and feed trough parallel it is necessary to slope the entire building 4 inches per 100 feet (100 mm/30 m). To save water and reduce disposal problems, the troughs are usually supplied with water on a limited basis, for example, 30 minutes, six times a day. With proper maintenance, leaks that cause wet manure problems seldom occur. Some poultrymen feel that trough systems contribute to feed waste because of the amount that washes off the chickens' beaks and runs away down the drain at the end of each trough. While troughs can be readily checked to see that water is available at each cage, they are not suitable for medication because of wastage.

A second system is a water cup in which the flow is activated by the chicken. Any feed dropped in a cup is picked up again. It also lends itself to medicating birds through the watering system. The principal disadvantage is leaking and the resulting wet spots in the manure. The cup also has little reserve in the event of a supply shutoff and each cup must be checked individually to insure its functioning.

The third type is a nipple waterer. Mounted overhead, the bird has to push up on the valve to get water. Apparently some birds never learn to do this well enough to satisfy their needs.

Egg collection   Cages contribute to quality egg production by maintaining as closely as possible the characteristics of the egg as laid. The interior quality of the egg is maintained by rapid cooling. In a cage, the eggs immediately roll away from the body heat of the birds to a holding tray or collection belt. With properly designed cages there are fewer cracked eggs than in conventional nests and, with the absence of manure in the cages, the number of dirty eggs can be drastically reduced.

Eggs roll out the front of the cages either onto an egg tray for hand pickup or onto a collecting belt. Eggs collected by hand are placed on flats carried on a self-guided cart. In the case of four-tier systems, self-propelled elevator carts are used. Mechanical collectors employ belts to carry the eggs to the end of the cage rows where they are lowered to a single level and carried by cross conveyor to the egg packing or processing room.

A decision on whether or not to invest in an automated egg collection system should be made in terms of the initial cost versus potential savings in labor. While the hand collection of eggs represents a major portion of the total labor required in an egg production enterprise, the labor saved by the use of a mechanical egg collector is significant only if the eggs are carried directly to a fully automated processing machine.

Figure 20-3. Three-tier cage laying system. (*Courtesy* Big Dutchman)

Egg handling   Eggs are human food and must be treated accordingly. Periodic outbreaks of salmonella emphasize this point. State agencies are becoming more concerned and are establishing sanitary requirements. Some currently recommended facilities and conditions are:

1.   The building and surroundings shall be free of rubbish, waste, foul odors, insects, rodents, and other vermin.

2.   Open windows shall be screened. Doors shall be rodent proof and equipped with self-closing devices.

3.   There shall be adequate drains with approved traps and vents.

4.   The water shall be ample and potable.

5.   Floors, walls, ceilings, etc. shall be easy to clean.

6.   Lavatory and toilet facilities shall be available.

7.   Facilities for cleaning and sanitizing equipment shall be available.

Egg cooling room   Ten cubic feet of room volume per 1,000 layers for each day of required holding period should allow adequate space for storage needs. It is advisable to insulate to an R of 15 (2.6) and to use specially designed refrigeration equipment for cooling to 55°F (13°C) and 60 to 80 percent relative humidity. Approximate refrigeration capacity needed for storage rooms is as follows: 5,000 birds—6,800 Btu per hour (2000 W); 10,000 birds—11,700 Btu per hour (3400 W). Home air conditioners should not be used. They are inefficient at the required temperature and are designed to remove moisture rather than maintain it.

Manure handling systems   The flat deck, full stair-step, and reverse cages with a slant back all allow manure to drop to the floor or pit below. The modified stair-step cage is also available with a slant back. The stacked cage designs must all be equipped with dropping boards which need to be scraped every one to two days to remove the manure, or equipped with plastic belts that convey the manure to the end of the cage row. Several types of mechanical scrapers designed to be used with specific cages are used successfully.

The manure which drops from the cages may be handled in one of three ways:

1.   Manure collects on the floor beneath the cages and is scraped

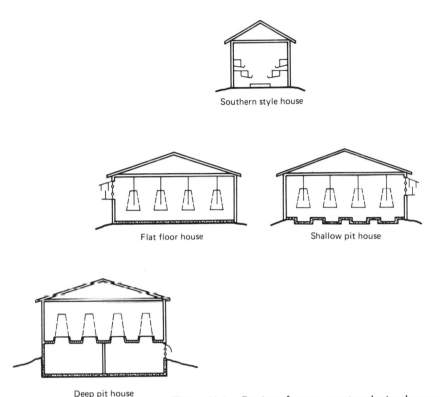

Southern style house

Flat floor house   Shallow pit house

Deep pit house   **Figure 20-4.** Designs for cage system laying houses.

on a two- to three-week cycle with scraper blades mounted on a small tractor.

2. Manure collects in shallow pits, 12 to 14 inches (300 to 350 mm) deep, which are then scraped with cable-pulled pit scrapers on a daily basis.

3. Manure collects in a deep pit 8 to 10 feet (2.5 to 3 m) below the cage floor. Cleaning is required not sooner than six months and may not be necessary for considerably more than a year if the ventilation system works well. Manure may be removed when it is most convenient and advantageous to spread on cropland.

The manure handling system dictates much of the building design. For example, if the flat-floor, tractor-scraping system is used, the cages must be suspended from the building trusses, adding a considerable weight that enters into the truss design and spacing. Obviously the deep-pit house requires a much different wall construction. Since the pit may be constructed below grade, the importance of good drainage cannot be over-emphasized. With dry floor conditions and proper ventilation, the manure will form into ridges and valleys and dry sufficiently for easy handling with mechanical equipment. Reducing the moisture from 80 percent to 60 percent will reduce the volume by one-half. Hen manure releases strong odors whenever it is disturbed, but the odor is somewhat less objectionable when the manure is dry. The well designed deep-pit system would also cut down, but not eliminate, odor problems by holding the manure undisturbed for a long period in a dry condition. High ground-water and wet manure on the other hand, make handling very difficult and increase odor levels considerably. The deep-pit storage allows manure to be removed at convenient times while the other two systems require some means of disposing of the manure at frequent intervals throughout the year.

Each of these systems can present problems such as ground water in the deep pits, cable corrosion and breaking with the pit scrapers, and wet spots and scraper breakdowns with the flat-floor system. On the other hand, with good management, any of them will work satisfactorily. A major factor in deciding which system is best for a specific case is the manner and timing of manure disposal once it is out of the house.

The least expensive method of handling the manure will be the flat-floor system, providing the self-propelled scraper can be used in several houses. The deep-pit system is the most expensive because of the additional cost of constructing a two-story house.

Housing for Pullet Rearing and Broiler Production

Raising broilers and replacement pullets involves brooding and growing the chicks to either market age or the ready-to-lay stage. Housing, equipment, and management procedures during the first few weeks are similar and will be discussed as one.

Since baby chicks are very susceptible to disease, it is important to thoroughly clean and sanitize the house and equipment before starting the brooding operation. A smooth, concrete floor and easily cleaned surfaces on the walls and ceiling will aid in the process.

Most chicks for layer replacement or broiler production are started on the floor with either portable or centrally heated brooders. A central, hot-water heating system with the boiler located in a separate room provides maximum safety from fire. The heating pipes are located along one wall with a hinged hover that is lowered to confine the heat.

More popular however, are gas-fired brooders suspended by chains from the ceiling. They are preferred by many because of the free air movement on all sides. The brooders are raised to the ceiling level when heat is no longer required.

As the chicks grow they are allowed to spread out to use a greater amount of floor area. Compared to the first week, two to three times as much space will be needed by the time they reach seven to eight weeks of age. Since heating and ventilating the entire building is inefficient at the start, "end-room" brooding is recommended. One end of the house is closed off and used for the first four to five weeks and then the growing birds are allowed to spread out over the whole floor area. Mechanical feeders and an automatic water system reduce labor requirements to a minimum. Placing the feed and water equipment on a slotted floor section helps to keep the litter in good condition and reduce ventilation requirements.

Once the chicks are past the brooding stage of four to five weeks, open housing may be used in mild climates. However, the practice of year-round production and the proven benefits of a uniform temperature of near 70°F (21°C) throughout the growing stage suggests that closed, environmentally controlled houses are feasible in nearly all geographic areas.

Cage brooding and growing of replacement pullets is increasing in popularity as new construction occurs. The benefits include higher bird density in the house, easier handling of the birds, no litter, less bruising, and fewer disease problems. Combination cages often have a cage partition that confines the chicks to the front half of the cage for the first two weeks making vaccination and debeaking easier.

Some cage brooding systems require a room temperature of 90°F (32°C) at the start, while others have a hot-water heating line running just above each pair of cages. The localized heat source allows lower room temperatures and gives the chicks the opportunity to choose their own comfort level.

Experience has shown that pullets grown on the floor can be put into either floor- or cage-managed laying houses. However pullets grown in cages do not adapt well to floor-managed operations.

Cage rearing of broilers has been plagued with problems of deformed legs and breast blisters, both of which reduce market quality. However, research is developing new cage floor materials which should alleviate the problems and, as building and labor costs rise, there will undoubtedly be an increased use of cages for brooding and rearing both broilers and replacement pullets.

Site Selection and Building Design

Since buildings for all phases of poultry production tend to produce considerable odor, the site should be well downwind from neighbors and the farm home. As with all farm buildings, a well drained site is desirable. This is particularly true for deep-pit laying houses as they may be partially below grade. Foundation drains are essential to protect against wet manure problems. While in mild climates some structures are built without foundations, generally a good foundation not only forms a sound base for the building, but it also allows a tight seal to the floor that prevents rodents and other vermin from entering the house.

Frame construction is popular because of the ease with which insulation can be installed and because rodents cannot penetrate the wall. The size and spacing of the studs are influenced by wall height and truss loads. For example, a house with suspended cages would require 2- by 6-inch (38 by 140 mm) studs, while a brooding and growing house might be adequately framed with 2- by 4-inch (38 by 89 mm) studs.

Trusses that will be supporting cages as well as the usual snow and wind loads must be designed specifically for the job. Bracing between trusses and between the wall and trusses is essential.

Although there are a number of materials suitable for use as exterior wall covering, sheet metal, which is reasonable in cost and requires little maintenance, is one of the best. Installing the panels with the pattern horizontal and nailing in the flat will contribute considerable bracing effect. Although many laying houses have been built with plastic foam panels serving as both insulation and interior wall surface, the practice is questionable inasmuch as some of the plastic materials are flammable. While foil covering offers some protection, it may not satisfy insurance underwriters' requirements. Plywood and metal are suitable for interior walls and ceiling but are somewhat expensive. Gypsum board is economical and fire resistant and, although it is subject to deterioration when exposed to high humidity, it should be possible to maintain satisfactory conditions within a high-density house so that this would not become a problem. With a suitable interior wall covering, the most economical insulation may then be selected for installation within the wall and ceiling. A vapor barrier installed between the wall covering and the insulation will prevent moisture from entering the wall.

The installation of reflective roofing will reduce summer attic temperatures and have a small but significant effect on the temperature inside the house.

Environmental Control

Temperature is the most important environmental factor in poultry housing. Young chicks need very warm surroundings just to survive. Older chickens, both layers and meat birds, exhibit their best feed conversion efficiencies at 70 to 75°F (21 to 24°C). However, production drops rapidly as temperatures rise above 80°F (27°C) and temperatures above 100°F (38°C) may be lethal.

Humidity is important in only two circumstances. Very low humidity tends to cause objectionably dusty conditions and high humidity combined with a very high temperature interferes with the bird's natural cooling mechanism and contributes to high mortality.

Brooder and Growing House Operation

Baby chicks are started with a temperature of 90 to 92°F (32 to 33°C) at the edge of the hover. After the first week the temperature is dropped 5°F (3°C) per week until 70°F (21°C) is reached. Seventy degrees F (21°C) room temperature is then maintained until broilers are marketed or replacement pullets reach eight weeks of age at which time a small decrease in temperature is acceptable. While birds of more than five weeks of age will gain well at temperatures below 70°F (21°C) feed conversion efficiency will drop significantly.

Table 20-2 suggests insulation and ventilation levels for windowless houses. Only the minimum ventilation rate is required until the heating system is shut off. The thermostatically controlled fan circuits are then activated allowing increasing rates of ventilation as temperatures rise due to animal heat and warm weather.

Table 20-2 Insulation and Ventilation Schedule for Brooding and Growing Houses

Design Temperature		Wall R		Ceiling R	
°F	°C	Customary	SI	Customary	SI
−10–0	−23–(−18)	12	2.1	16	2.8
0–10	−18–(−12)	8	1.4	12	2.1
10–20	−12–(−7)	4	0.7	8	1.4

Thermostat Set Point		Fan Capacity per Bird	
°F	°C	cu ft/min	L/s
90 (Heater)	32	0.2	0.09
75 (Fan)	24	0.6	0.28
78 (Fan)	26	0.8	0.38
85 (Fan)	29	1.25*	0.60
	Total	2.85	1.35

* For pullets over 8 weeks old, add 1.5 cfm (0.7 L/s)

Fan and motor characteristics are discussed in Chapter 16. Fans that are installed high on the wall and spaced along the protected side of the building perform well.

Inlet baffles should be adjusted to give a velocity of 700 to 1,000 feet per minute (3.6 to 5 m/s). A manometer reading of 0.04 to 0.08 inches (1.0 to 2.0 mm) will insure a velocity in this recommended range.

Broiler houses are given 24-hour lighting to encourage maximum feed consumption and rate of gain. In windowless houses, pullets are started on 14½ hours of light and decreased 15 minutes a week to nine hours at 22 weeks. This routine postpones the start of laying but produces larger eggs when production begins. When the pullets are moved to a windowless layer house, a 14-hour day length is used throughout the laying period. The light program for pullets to be housed in window laying houses requires special planning.

Laying House Operation

Suggested levels of insulation for three temperature zones are given in Table 20-3. Thermostat set points and ventilation rates per bird are also provided. These apply to both floor-managed and cage-managed houses. However, due to the much lower bird density in a floor-managed house, the temperature may remain below 60°F (16°C) during periods of low outside temperature. Although a 65 to 70°F (18 to 21°C) set point is listed in the table, if satisfactory air and moisture conditions can be maintained with minimum ventilation, a set temperature of 70 to 75°F (21 to 24°C) will reduce feed consumption. Egg production, egg size, rate of gain, and mortality rates are essentially equal at temperatures between 60° and 75°F (16 and 24°C), but feed consumption is significantly less at the high end of the range (University of Connecticut Cooperative Extension Service, 1978).

Exhaust fans for floor-managed houses and for shallow-pit or flat-floor cage houses are located high on the wall and installed singly or in groups spaced not more than 100 feet (30 m) apart. Since fans for cage houses are often placed in light-trap structures, grouping will simplify construction. The light traps allow free air movement, but prevent the entrance of light. This permits the control of "day length" within the house with a timed lighting system.

Exhaust fans for deep-pit houses are located in the wall of the pit area. A protective hood will ordinarily be adequate as a light trap. In all types of houses, those fans which will be operating continuously during cold weather should be spaced uniformly along the length of the building. Fan and motor characteristics are discussed more fully in Chapter 16.

Table 20-3 Insulation and Ventilation Schedule for Layer
and Breeder Houses
Based on 4-lb (1.8 kg) birds

Design Temperature		Wall R		Ceiling R	
°F	°C	Customary	SI	Customary	SI
−10–0	−23–(−18)	12	2.1	16	2.8
0–10	−18–(−12)	8	1.4	12	2.1
10–20	−12–(−7)	4	0.7	8	1.4

Thermostat Set Point		Fan Capacity per Bird	
°F	°C	cu ft/min	L/s
45	7	0.25	0.12
60	16	0.25	0.12
65–70	18–21	1.5	0.71
75	24	3.0	1.4
	Total	5.00	2.35

Inlets determine the distribution of air throughout the house. Slot inlets along the perimeter of the ceiling or along the length of the ceiling over the cages may be equipped with baffles that both direct the flow and control the velocity of the incoming air. The slot inlets at the perimeter of the ceiling allow summer air to be drawn through the soffits where it is usually slightly cooler than in the attic. A velocity of 700 to 1,000 feet per minute (3.6 to 5 m/s) insures uniform distribution. This velocity range is indicated by a manometer reading of 0.04 to 0.08 inches (1.0 to 2.0 mm). Since ventilation rates vary by a factor of 10 at different times of the year, it is essential that the baffles be easily adjustable. Commercial controls are available that automatically adjust the inlet opening in relation to static pressure differences, thus eliminating the need for manual adjustment. More complete mixing of the cool, inlet air with the warm air of the house takes place when the baffles direct the air along the ceiling (Figure 16-4B). Chapter 16 includes a discussion of the term "exposure factor" and how it is related to air-flow rates in a ventilation system. A series of design graphs to be used with the exposure factor in planning poultry house ventilation is found in the annual Agricultural Engineers Yearbook (American Society of Agricultural Engineers, 1977).

During heat waves, when outside dew-point temperatures of 70°F (21°C) or higher are accompanied by dry-bulb temperatures of 104°F (40°C) or higher, ventilation alone will not protect birds against heat prostration and some type of supplemental cooling will be needed.

Fog nozzles that periodically spray water directly on the chickens provide an emergency means of reducing mortality due to heat. Sprinkling the roof of the poultry house is another emergency measure that will lower the inside house temperature a few degrees. This will be most effective if the roof happens to be a dark color and if ventilation air is drawn from the attic area.

Evaporative coolers are capable of dropping air temperatures to within 5°F (3°C) of the existing wet-bulb temperature, but in doing so, the relative humidity is raised to about 85 percent. This high humidity largely offsets the advantage of evaporative cooling for poultry in the eastern United States or Canada. In the western half of the United States, wet-bulb temperatures are low enough so that considerable cooling is possible without reaching unacceptably high relative humidities. Permanent evaporative coolers may be considered feasible under these conditions.

The rather minimal light levels required in poultry houses are usually supplied with one 25-watt bulb per 100 square feet (9 m²). An exception to this is the bottom level of a four-tier cage system which may be so shaded by the upper tiers that additional lighting is required.

With thousands of birds depending on electricity for light and ventilation as well as feed and water, it is imperative to have an emergency standby generating plant. Capacity should be large enough to operate all of the fans plus part of the balance of the equipment. Feeders and other equipment may be operated in rotation, but if the weather is hot, all of the fans must operate continuously. The generating plant should be located in a dust-free room and be equipped with an automatic starter and alarm system.

TURKEYS

Although it has been customary to grow market turkeys on range, the risks of predators and adverse weather, together with the trend toward year-round production has brought about a shift to total confinement housing. As the growing and finishing stages have changed from a seasonal to a full-time operation, the demand for increased year-round egg production is forcing the move to total confinement housing facilities for the breeding flock as well. In mild temperature zones, an insulated ceiling and fan ventilation will provide adequate winter conditions while large sliding wall panels are opened for summer ventilation. In colder climates well insulated houses similar to those suggested for chickens are more practical for both breeding and growing flocks.

Mechanical feeders and waterers are required for labor efficiency in the floor-managed houses. Installing them on a partially slotted floor area helps keep the litter dry and simplifies ventilation.

Table 20-4 provides information on insulation and ventilation for turkey houses and Table 20-5 gives information on space requirements.

Table 20-4   Insulation and Ventilation Schedule for Turkey Houses

Design Temperature		Wall R		Ceiling R	
°F	°C	Customary	SI	Customary	SI
−10–0	−23–(−18)	12	2.1	16	2.8
0–10	−18–(−12)	8	1.4	12	2.1
10–20	−12–(−7)	4	0.7	8	1.4

	Thermostat Set Point		Fan Capacity per Bird	
	°F	°C	cu ft/min	L/s
Brooding	90 (Heater)	32	0.5	0.24
Growing	65–70	18–21	5.0	2.4
Growing	80	27	15.0	7.1
Breeders	45	7	0.75	0.35
Breeders	60	16	0.75	0.35
Breeders	65	14	5.0	2.4
Breeders	75	23	15.0	7.1

Table 20-5   Poultry Housing Space and Equipment Requirements

LAYING FLOCKS

	Light Breeds		Heavy Breeds	
	Customary	SI	Customary	SI
Floor space				
Floor	1¼–2½ sq ft	0.12–0.23 m²	1½–3 sq ft	0.14–0.28 m²
Cage	0.2–0.7 sq ft	0.02–0.07 m²	0.3–1.0 sq ft	0.03–0.09 m²
Feeders	3 in.	75 mm	4 in.	100 mm
Waterers	¾ in.	19 m	1 in.	25 mm
Nests	4–5/nest	4–5/nest	4–5/nest	4–5/nest

Table 20-5   continued

BROILER AND REPLACEMENT PULLETS

	0–4 weeks		4–10 weeks		10–20 weeks	
	Cust.	SI	Cust.	SI	Cust.	SI
Floor space						
Open house	0.5 sq ft	0.05 m²	0.9 sq ft	0.08 m²	2 sq ft	0.19 m²
Controlled Env.	0.5 sq ft	0.05 m²	0.8 sq ft	0.07 m²	1.3 sq ft	0.12 m²
Feeders	1 in.	25 mm	2 in.	50 mm	4 in.	100 mm
Waterers	0.2 in.	5 mm	0.4 in.	10 mm	1 in.	25 mm

TURKEYS

	Breeders		Growing	
	Customary	SI	Customary	SI
Floor space				
Open house	8–10 sq ft	0.7–0.9 m²	6 sq ft	0.6 m²
Controlled Env.	5–8 sq ft	0.5–0.7 m²	4 sq ft	0.4 m²
Roosting space	12–15 in.	300–375 mm	12–15 in.	300–375 mm
Nests	2' x 5'	0.6 x 1.5 m		
	(20–25 hens)	(20–25 hens)		
Feeders	4 in.	100 mm	4 in.	100 mm
Water troughs	1/100	1/100	1/100	1/100

(From Granite City Steel Division of National Steel Corporation, 1971)

PROBLEMS

20.1   A poultryman wishes to construct a deep pit house in which to install "reverse" cages 8 rows wide, 4 tiers high. Using this configuration, determine the width and length of the building necessary to house 30,000 layers.

20.2   Design a schedule showing the thermostat set point, number of fans, fan capacity, and fan location for each step in the ventilation capacity required for the 30,000 layers in problem 20.1. Suitable models of fans are available to the poultryman which deliver either 7500 cubic feet per minute or 12,000 cubic feet per minute at ⅛ in. S.P. (3540 and 5665 L/s).

20.3 What is the total inlet area required to match the maximum fan capacity operating at 70°F (21°C) or lower? What is the total inlet area required when all fans are operating?

20.4 Investigate the cost of insulating materials and materials suitable for interior walls and ceilings for cage laying houses. Taking into consideration economy, insulating value, ease of installation, fire safety, and durability, recommend a wall and ceiling construction for a cage house.

REFERENCES

American Society of Agricultural Engineers. *Agricultural Engineers Yearbook*. St. Joseph, Mich.: American Society of Agricultural Engineers, 1977.

Cooperative Extension Service for the Six New England States, *Poultry Management and Business Analysis Manual*. Cooperative Extension Service for the Six New England States Bulletin 566. Storrs, Conn., 1972.

Granite City Steel Division of National Steel Corporation. *Poultry Production Planning Manual*. Granite City, Ill.: Granite City Steel Division of National Steel Corporation, 1971.

University of California Agricultural Extension Service. *Poultry Scratch No. 5*. Riverside, Calif.: University of California Agricultural Extension Service, June 1977.

University of Connecticut Cooperative Extension Service. *Poultry News*. Storrs, Conn.: University of Connecticut Cooperative Extension Service, April 1978.

Chapter Twenty-One

Greenhouses

Greenhouses provide an ideal environment for propagating and growing horticultural crops. Often the crop yield is several times greater than is possible in the open field. Although the investment necessary to control temperature, humidity, air composition, and lighting can be considerable, the high monetary value of the crops grown justifies the investment.

Crop production in greenhouses is a rapidly growing industry. At the present time there are more than 3,500 acres under glass in the United States that are used primarily for growing flowers and potted plants. In addition there are more than 4,000 acres of plastic-covered greenhouses. An ever increasing number of these lower cost houses are being used for starting flower and vegetable plants (bedding plants), for growing vegetable crops, and for propagating and wintering nursery stock.

INVESTMENT

The investment in a house is justified by the value of the crop grown and the length of the period the house is used each year. For example, the investment in a house to be used year-round for producing cut flowers is amortized over a long period of time. Housing costs become less important while labor and other production costs increase in importance. Under these conditions a permanent type of house, perhaps glass covered, is easily justified.

In contrast, seasonal use of a house for the production of bedding plants or wintering nursery stock cannot justify a large investment and temporary, plastic-covered houses are generally used.

Hobby greenhouses have become increasingly popular. Frequently they are attached to the home or another building which can house the heating system and provide storage. Minimal equipment for environmental control is usually adequate even though conditions throughout the house may not be uniform. In fact, the variety of plants grown may make just such a situation useful.

TYPES OF GREENHOUSES

Commercial greenhouses may be classified in several different ways. One division is into free-standing and gutter-connected houses.

Free Standing Greenhouses

These houses are suitable for a single range (house) or for a large number of ranges. Some space will be required between houses for maintenance operations and, in northern climates, for snow accumulation. There are a number of suitable frame designs from which to choose.

The quonset house This house is one of the simplest styles. For spans up to 10 to 12 feet (3 to 3.5 m), a semicircular frame may be constructed with thin-wall conduit (EMT). For greater spans, galvanized pipe, aluminum extrusions, or arched trusses are employed. Either plastic film or fiberglass makes a suitable covering. An inflated, double layer of polyethylene film, fastened at the base of the sides and at the ends with specially designed anchors works well on the curved surface and can be put in place with minimal labor. Because they are often constructed without any foundation and are considered temporary structures, quonset houses may not be subject to local building codes. The low, arch shape with its nearly flat center area makes them prone to snow overloading and to problems with dripping from condensation. Also, because of the curved sides, they are primarily suited to growing or storing crops on the floor rather than on benches.

Gothic arch houses These are framed with metal or laminated wood rafters and have a pleasing appearance. Their steeper sides allow benches to be used and they are not as subject to dripping or snow overloading. Covering is done in the same manner as on the quonset house.

Gable greenhouses With an even pitch, gable houses may be

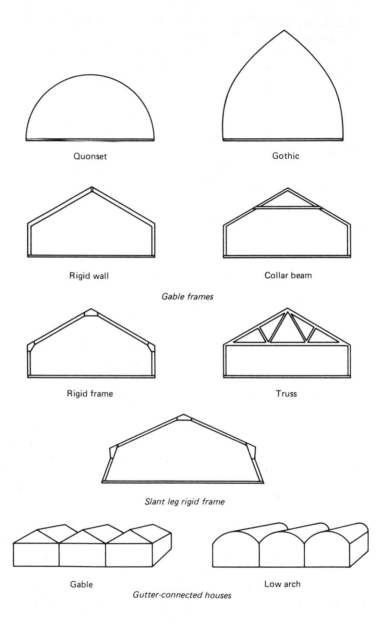

Figure 21-1. Types of greenhouse frames.

framed in a number of ways. Relatively narrow buildings with rigid side-walls may use rafters without bracing, thus allowing maximum light to reach the crop. Houses up to 24 feet (7.2 m) wide may be framed with rafters braced with collar beams, while rigid frame construction will tolerate widths up to 40 feet (12 m). The widest houses, up to 60 feet (18 m), are spanned with trusses, usually fabricated of metal to keep shading at a minimum. The slant-leg rigid frame is ideally shaped to use the inflated double-layer covering.

The gable shape will accept any type of covering and with a sufficiently steep pitch, (6:12 for glass, more for plastic), dripping from condensation is negligible. Either floor or bench crops are easily managed.

Gutter-Connected Greenhouses

Sometimes referred to as ridge and furrow houses, gutter-connected greenhouses are a series of gable or low-arch structures connected together at the gutter level. The individual bays vary from 10 to 25 feet (3 to 8 m) in width and usually have a minimum clearance of 8 feet (2.3 m) under the gutters.

The primary advantage of the gutter-connected house is the ability to cover a large ground area with a minimum of exposed wall area, thus reducing heat loss by as much as 25 percent. Also less time is needed to travel to various points within the enclosed area than between several free-standing houses of equal total space. Perhaps the biggest shortcoming is the difficulty in removing snow with any means except heat. Consequently this type of greenhouse is most suitable in regions of limited snowfall. Gutter houses require many supports which may interfere somewhat with operations. However, with additional investment, flat trusses may be used to obtain up to 36 feet (11 m) of clear span in which to work.

The arched frames are suitable for either plastic film or fiberglass covering while the gable frames are suited for standard glass, fiberglass panels, or "big pane" glass that extends from eave to ridge.

STRUCTURAL MATERIALS

Wood, galvanized steel, and aluminum are all commonly used for greenhouse frames.

Because of the characteristically lightweight construction of greenhouses, when using *wood*, only top grade lumber should be selected. The high moisture environment that exists in a greenhouse makes it essential that the most decay-resistant wood be used. Although a few species such as black locust, osage orange, red cedar, and redwood are naturally decay resistant, the use of preservative-treated lumber for all but temporary greenhouses is desirable. Only the water-borne type of preservatives, as described in Chapter 4, should be used. If plywood is used for gussets in rigid frame construction it must be exterior grade and preservative treated. The edges of the plywood should be painted to prevent moisture from causing delamination. Glue used in the fabrication of trusses or frames should be of the waterproof, resorcinol type. Casein glues should never be used for greenhouse construction.

Steel is commonly used for commercially manufactured greenhouses. Because of the high moisture conditions all steel should be protected from corrosion by paint or galvanizing. It is preferable to do the galvanizing after all cutting and welding of the frame members have been completed.

Aluminum extrusions are gaining favor for greenhouse construction because of the minimal amount of maintenance and the resistance to corrosion. Both steel and aluminum permit the use of slim structural members thereby reducing shading to a minimum.

COVERING MATERIALS

For many years glass was virtually the only covering used in greenhouses. But during the last two decades greenhouse coverings have undergone revolutionary changes. Today we have, in addition to glass, a multitude of plastic materials with a wide range of cost and quality. In addition they vary considerably with respect to ease of installation, light transmission, and durability.

Glass

Glass, the standard by which other materials are rated, transmits the most light (90 percent) and lasts the longest, but it is expensive. In the past, double-strength glass has been used. More recently, however, triple-strength, or tempered glass, has been introduced permitting the use of larger panes. This in turn allows framing members to be spaced farther apart, reducing both the cost and the shading effect of the frame. Glass requires special structural members and glazing techniques to insure airtight and watertight construction. Increased light diffusion and reduction of shadows can be achieved with the use of frosted glass.

While glass retains its inherent light transmittance over many years, light reduction does occur as dirt, algae, and surface etching build up. The caulking and sealing of the glass panes presents a maintenance problem.

Fiberglass Reinforced Plastic

Polyester panels reinforced with fiberglass are considerably more impact-resistant than ordinary glass and have a longer life than plastic films. However, the polyester in the panels will burn rapidly and fire insurance is not easily obtained. The light transmission, although highly diffused, is about 85 percent. Weathering will reduce light transmission considerably unless the surface is cleaned and resurfaced with acrylic sealer every four to five years. Fiberglass reinforced plastic, manufactured with 15 percent acrylic combined with the polyester, improves both the light transmission characteristics and the durability. However, the best resistance to weathering is provided by a thin film of Tedlar (registered by E. I. DuPont de Nemours and Company) (polyvinyl-fluoride) laminated to the surface of the panel, which should increase its life expectancy to as much as 20 years.

Fiberglass plastic is available in 4, 5, and 6 ounce per square foot (1.2, 1.5 and 1.8 kg/m²) corrugated panels and 4 ounce per square foot (1.2 kg/m²) flat materials in rolls. The corrugated panels, which are stronger, are installed on purlins while the flat material is usually used for end walls.

Fiberglass panels are installed with ring-shank nails or screws. A flexible sealing compound used in the one to one-and-one-half corrugation overlap, and sealing washers under the nail or screw heads insure against air and water leaks. Formed wood or foam rubber strips are used to seal the upper and lower ends of the panels. The manufacturer's recommendations should be followed in regard to purlin and fastener spacing.

Larger sized quonset houses with extruded aluminum frames may employ cables to hold the fiberglass panels in place. The cables, which are anchored at the base on either side of the house, run in the panel valleys over each frame member and hold the panels securely in the concave groove in the outside of the frame.

Polyethylene (PE)

Polyethylene film, with light transmitting characteristics similar to glass, is the least expensive covering available. PE is a less effective barrier to heat radiation than other coverings and houses tend to cool rapidly when the sunlight decreases in the afternoon. Condensation that may appear at about the same time, however, can reduce this radiant loss by up to 50 percent.

Regular polyethylene ordinarily lasts only one season because it is destroyed by ultraviolet radiation from the sun. Two improved film coverings, ultraviolet (UV) inhibited PE and copolymer material combining PE and vinyl, are now available and will last for two seasons. Only greenhouse grade films should be used, as there is a tendency for others to split along the folds occurring in the original package. Originally PE was used almost entirely for temporary or seasonal operations. However, the introduction of a number of metal and plastic devices for anchoring the edges of the plastic and the use of an air-inflated, double-layer covering has increased its use on many permanent greenhouses. Air inflation will be discussed in detail later.

Other Materials

There are several other plastics that have been used or considered for greenhouse covering but are not now common for one reason or another. *Acrylic* is particularly clear and, resisting breakage, lasts nearly as long as glass. It has the added advantage of being somewhat flexible. However, it costs appreciably more than glass and other materials. *Polyester* and *vinyl* both have good resistance to weathering but both are expensive and are available only in sheets too narrow to be practical for greenhouses. *Polyvinylfluoride* has excellent weatherability, but it also is too expensive to use as a covering. As mentioned previously, it is used as a thin laminate to increase the life of fiberglass panels. *Polyvinylchloride* panels tend to darken enough in two to four years to make them unsuitable for greenhouse use.

The multitude of coverings available makes the choice of the "best" one difficult. Individual circumstances will govern the final selection. Estimates have shown that when original cost, labor for installation, and maintenance costs are considered, the annual cost for all of the materials commonly used for greenhouse covering is remarkably similar.

Double-Layer Polyethylene Covers

It has long been recognized that two layers of plastic film significantly reduce heat loss from a greenhouse. However, the necessity of using wooden spacers and furring strips to secure the plastic film and create an airspace between the layers not only increased the labor required but reduced the amount of light entering the greenhouse due to the thickness of the framing members. The inflated double-layer system has overcome these problems and at the same time allows the installation of two layers of plastic with even less labor than a single sheet. The single sheet must be fastened along most of the framing members. In contrast, in the inflated double-layer system, the two layers are draped over the rafters and then anchored only at the base of each side and at the ends of the building. Typical anchors are illustrated in figure 21-2. Once secured around the edges, a small blower type fan, running continuously, pumps air between the layers keeping them separated and rigid. The air space becomes an effective barrier to heat loss and the rigidity prevents the plastic from flapping in the wind and tearing. Snow also slides off the smooth, curved surface more easily.

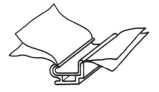 

Figure 21-2. Polyethylene anchors.

With this system there is less condensation on the underside of the plastic resulting in fewer dripping problems and longer periods between watering.

Installation of an Inflated Double-Layer Cover

1. On houses to be covered with inflated double-layer systems, the frame members may be safely spaced up to 4 feet (1.2 m) apart.

2. All corners should be smoothed and all rough places taped to prevent the plastic from being punctured or chafed.

3. On a calm day the double layer of PE may be draped over the greenhouse frame and secured at the edges along the base of each side and along the end frames (Figure 21-2).

4. A small squirrel cage blower that will deliver 100 to 150 cubic feet per minute (47 to 70 L/s) at 0.5 inches (13 mm) of water pressure will be needed for each 5,000 square feet (465 m²) of area to be inflated. A simple "U" tube manometer made from a piece of plastic tubing will also be needed to measure the pressure (Figure 10-1). The pressure is regulated with a sheet metal valve that can be adjusted to partially cover the fan inlet.

5. The blower should be mounted high enough on an end wall so that it draws in outside air without the possibility of being closed off with snow. The use of outside air prevents condensation from forming between the layers of plastic. A connection is made from the blower outlet to the inner layer of plastic with clothes-dryer vent tubing.

6. On houses with a ridge, it will be necessary to connect the two sides with a piece of vent tubing in order to equalize the pressures. If the greenhouse rafters are more than 18 feet (5.5 m) long, the plastic should be secured at the midpoint of the rafters from end to end on the house in order to prevent excessive stresses that might cause premature failure of the plastic. An air connection will be needed across the secured point.

7.   After the connections are completed, the pressure may be adjusted to 0.25 inches (6 mm) of water by changing the size of the blower opening.

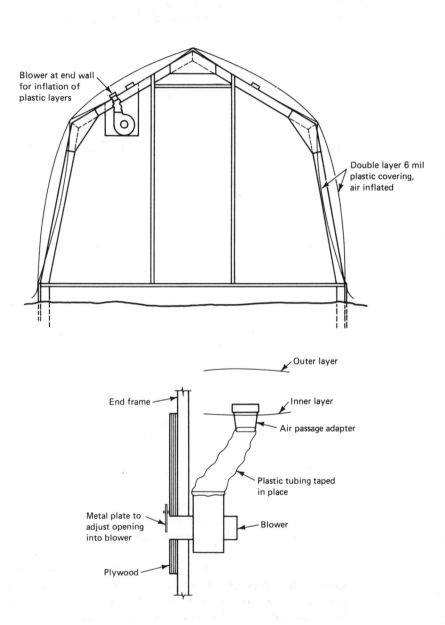

Figure 21-3. Installation of blower for inflating double layer of polyethylene covering.

GREENHOUSE SITE AND ORIENTATION

Greenhouses should be located away from buildings and trees that may cast shadows. The time of year, time of day, and latitude all influence the length of shadows cast. For example, at latitude 40°N (Philadelphia, Columbus, Denver), the angle of the sun's rays near noon in midwinter is only about 25° above the ground. Obviously this means that very long shadows are cast and that greenhouses should be located well away from trees or buildings that may reduce the amount of sunlight. As a general rule, objects on the east, south, or west sides of a greenhouse should be two and one-half to three times their height away from the house to avoid unwanted shadows. Windbreaks, as long as they meet this distance requirement, are desirable, as they can make a significant difference in the heat loss from the house.

A greenhouse site should be level and well drained. This may pose no problem for a small hobby house, but for a large commercial range, desirable sites may be difficult to find in rolling country. Except for houses used solely for holding over nursery stock, water and electricity are essential services.

In latitudes south of 40°N, a *north to south* orientation of the building ridge is desirable for the best lighting. Houses north of 40°N benefit from an *east to west* orientation, particularly in midwinter. However, the gutters in gutter-connected greenhouses tend to cast long lasting shadows that reduce production. Therefore this type of house should be on a *north to south* axis regardless of latitude. Also, houses that will be used primarily for spring production are best oriented north and south.

STRUCTURAL REQUIREMENTS

Regardless of the type of frame or the covering material, greenhouses should be strong enough to withstand expected wind and snow loads, and in some cases, loads imposed by equipment or crops. For example, tomatoes tied to the roof frame may impose a load of 4 pounds per square foot (0.19 kPa).

U.S. Weather Bureau wind velocities are reported for a 30-foot (9-m) height. Most greenhouses, being relatively low, would be subject to a wind pressure of about 75 percent of that caused by the 30-foot (9-m) velocity. The pressures caused by wind are discussed in Chapter 9 and wind velocities are shown in Figure 9-3. Inasmuch as greenhouses are lightweight structures and the maximum wind pressures, particularly on the low, semicircular roof shapes, tend to impose lifting forces, it is imperative that the supports be well anchored.

Snow loads vary greatly from one region to another and local conditions must be considered in designing a house. However, in the case of heated greenhouses, the likelihood of a heavy snow load is reduced because the snow tends to melt and slide off. Polyethylene-covered houses hasten the shedding process with the motion of the plastic.

Design loads of 10 to 12 pounds per square foot (0.48 to 0.58 kPa) have proven satisfactory even in the northeastern United States. The exception to this rule of experience is the gutter-connected house where there is no place for the snow to go except into the gutter to melt. A 20 pounds per square foot (0.96 kPa) design load and a generous sized heating system to hasten melting are both advisable.

Foundation requirements will vary with the type of house, but in general they are as important for anchoring a house as for supporting it. Piers or foundations of at least 18 inches (450 mm) in depth or below the frost level are necessary.

GREENHOUSE HEATING

The successful operation of a greenhouse requires near optimum temperatures for plant growth. Although sunlight and ventilation contribute greatly to maintenance of the required temperature, it remains the function of the heating system to provide the necessary heat at night and during periods of cloudy weather. Since the cost of heating represents a substantial part of the total cost of production, an efficient system, together with steps to keep heating requirements to a minimum, is essential.

Table 21-1   Heating Cost as a Percentage of Total Cost for
Various Greenhouse Crops

Cut flowers	15–20%
Potted plants	15–20%
Bedding plants	10–15%
Vegetables	35–45%
Nursery stock	5–10%

Heat loss   Heat is lost from a greenhouse in several ways. Of greatest significance is the loss of heat by *conduction* through the walls and roof. Temperature differences and fans used for air circulation provide the natural and forced *convection* currents that carry the warm air to the surfaces where the conduction takes place. On the outside, natural convection and wind carry the heat away.

Infiltration   The natural exchange of inside air with outside air through cracks and openings (infiltration), is the second most important means of heat loss. The amount varies considerably, as shown in Table 21-2.

Table 21-2 Typical Infiltration Losses

New Houses	Air Exchanges per hour
Double polyethylene cover	0.5 –1.0
Glass or fiberglass	0.75–1.5
Old Houses	
Glass—good maintenance	1–2
Glass—in poor condition	2–4

Ventilation Even in periods of relatively cold weather when artificial heat is necessary, some ventilation may be required for moisture control. Heat will be lost in the air that is exchanged. In the most severe weather, infiltration alone will provide adequate ventilation.

Radiation losses Radiation losses from glass and fiberglass houses are low. By comparison, polyethylene (PE) transmits as much as 80 percent of long wave-length (low temperature) radiation. This can be a significant source of heat loss when the greenhouse humidity is low and no condensation is occurring. If however, as is frequently the case, moisture does condense on the inner surface of the PE, the radiation loss is reduced to a level which is not much more than glass. Although the double-layer PE houses are not as likely to have condensation, the radiation loss is considerably less than in a single-layer house. The generally tighter construction of the PE-covered houses balances the high radiation losses so that the overall loss from glass- and PE-covered houses is similar.

Heat loss calculation To find the total expected heat loss and determine the size of an adequate heating system, it is necessary to obtain the following information:

1. The surface area of the glass- or plastic-covered portions of the greenhouse.

2. The surface area of walls, ends, or other parts of different construction.

3. The "U" value for each type of construction from Table 14-3 or by calculation.

4. The estimated infiltration rate from Table 21-2.

The heat loss by conduction through the surfaces may then be found with the equation:

$$q_c = A\ U\ TD \qquad \text{Where:}$$

		Customary	SI
q_c =	Conducted heat loss	BTU/hr	(W)
A =	Surface area	sq ft	(m²)
U =		BTU/(hr sq ft °F)	(W/(m²·K))
TD =	Temperature difference	°F	(K)

The heat loss by infiltration may be found with the following equation:

$$q_i = C\ V\ SH\ TD \qquad \text{Where:}$$

q_i =	infiltration heat loss	BTU/hr	(W)
C =	air changes per hours		
V =	volume of house	cu ft	(m³)
SH =	Specific heat of air by volume of house	0.018	(0.339)
TD =	temperature difference	°F	(K)

The total heat loss, q_t, is the sum of $q_c + q_i$.

Although some winter ventilation will be required, under the minimum temperature conditions used for design purposes, the infiltration should provide enough air exchange to maintain a satisfactory level of humidity. As an example of estimating the heat loss from a greenhouse assume the following conditions:

0°F outside
60°F inside
2 layers PE on top
Fiberglass ends and sides
House is located in a protected area
U values, from Table 14-3:
2 layers of PE = 0.80
Fiberglass = 1.06

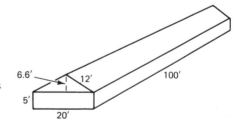

Conduction loss: $q_c = A\ U\ TD$

Roof   2,400 × .80 × 60° = 115,200
Ends   332 × 1.06 × 60° = 21,115
Sides 1,000 × 1.06 × 60° = 63,600

q_c total   = 199,915 Btu/hr

Infiltration loss: $q_i = C \, V \, SH \, TD$

House volume $= 10,000 + 6,600 = 16,600$ cu ft

$$1 \times 16,600 \times 0.018 \times 60° = 17,928 \text{ Btu/hr}$$

Total heat loss: $q_t = q_e + q_i$

$$199,915 + 17,928 = 217,843 \text{ Btu/hr}$$

If the greenhouse is located in a windy area it is good insurance to add 10 percent to the calculated heat loss before selecting a heating system. After having decided on the type of heating system, one that is large enough to supply the total estimated loss should be selected. Although considerable excess capacity will cost more initially and be somewhat less efficient to operate, up to 10 percent extra capacity will provide a desirable margin of safety for very severe weather conditions.

Heating Systems

The most beneficial growing conditions result when temperatures remain nearly constant and are uniform throughout the greenhouse. Heat can be distributed in the house by natural convection from pipes or radiators along the sidewalls, or by forced hot air from free-standing furnaces or suspended unit heaters. Although solar heating systems can reduce the total fuel requirements, they have little effect on the requisite size of a heating system.

Hot water systems Hot water, or in the case of older houses, steam, supplied to black iron or finned pipes along the walls of greenhouses has been the standard heating system for years. Due to the mass of heated metal and water, these systems tend to cycle slowly and maintain a uniform temperature. Steam boilers and some hot water boilers supply steam for soil sterilization which is a useful feature. However, they are expensive to install.

In gutter-connected houses, hot water radiation is frequently installed in a horizontal position at a level just below the bottom of the gutters. Although this location is not ideal for heat distribution, it does prevent the heating system from interfering with work operations. Modulating controllers that vary the temperature of the water in relation to outside conditions are able to maintain a more uniform greenhouse temperature.

Hot air systems Hot air heaters may be free-standing oil or gas burners with built-in blowers or they may be smaller unit heaters suspended from the roof supports. The unit heaters can be fired with gas or oil or they may be supplied with heat from a hot water heat exchanger.

All of the burners, regardless of type, must be vented to the outside of the house.

For houses up to 60 feet (18 m) long, the heating requirements may be divided between two units, one at each end oriented so that they discharge air along opposite sides of the house. This provides continuous air circulation and reasonably uniform temperature.

Unit heaters and polyethylene duct system   The unit heater and a PE duct distribution system provide an economical method of heating and circulating the air to maintain uniform conditions throughout the greenhouse. In periods of mild weather, fresh air may be introduced through the system.

For houses up to 30 feet (9 m) wide, a single duct down the center of the house (Figure 21-4) is connected to a fan and heater unit mounted on one end wall. Fresh air for heating and recirculation may be drawn in at the sides of the unit or through the louvres in the end wall. For houses more than 30 feet (9 m) wide, two or more parallel units will be needed.

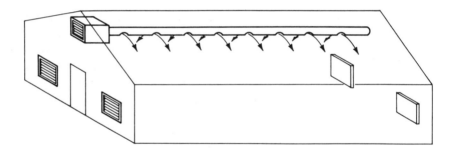

Figure 21-4.   Polyethylene duct system.

While individual ducts may be up to 150 feet (45 m) long, the most uniform conditions will be maintained if units are located at both ends with ducts extending toward the center for any house more than 120 feet (36 m) long.

In the case of gutter-connected houses with a horizontal overhead heating system, fans and PE ducts are beneficial just to recirculate the warm air for more uniform conditions.

Polyethylene duct design   Although PE ducts are supplied by manufacturers ready for installation, the consumer should check them for the following characteristics:

1.   A uniform hole spacing of approximately 2 feet (600 mm).

2.   The total hole area should be equal to one and one-half to two times the duct cross-section area.

3.   The holes should be about 30 degrees below the horizontal on each side.

4.   One duct is adequate for houses up to 30 feet (9 m) wide. Two or more are needed for wider houses.

5.   While ducts are available up to 150 feet (45 m) long, it is better to start them from both ends and limit their length to 100 to 120 feet (30 to 36 m).

6.   The system should be designed to recirculate the air, heat the recirculated air, or draw in fresh air as conditions require.

Temperature control Thermostats need to be of a type that will tolerate high humidity. They should be located at eye level near the center of the house and shielded from direct sunlight. Although they should not be in a stagnant air location, neither should they be in the airstream from a fan or distribution duct. Electronic temperature controllers with up to seven or eight set points are able to control a sequence of events over a range of temperatures. For example, the lowest point might control heat; the next step, air circulation; the next, minimum ventilation; the next two, additional ventilation, and finally, cooling.

Sources of Heat

It has been pointed out that heating systems may be fired with various fuels. The choice of fuel will depend on availability, cost, and convenience. Table 21-3 A and B provides a comparison of different heat sources.

Table 21-3A   Heat Output from Fuels—Customary

Fuel	Unit	Btu/Unit	Typical Efficiency	Fuel Units per 100,000 Btu heat output
#2 Oil	gal	140,000	70%	1.02 gal
Coal	lb	12,500	65%	12.3 lb
Natural gas	cu ft	1,000	80%	125 cu ft
LP gas	gal	92,000	80%	1.36 gal
Electricity	kwh	3,413	100%	29.3 kwh

Table 21-3B   Heat Outputs from Fuels—SI

Fuel	Unit	Kilojoules/unit	Typical Efficiency	Fuel Units per 100,000 kJ heat output
#2 Oil	liters	39 022	70%	3.66 L
Coal	kilograms	29 012	65%	5.30 kg
Natural gas	cu meters	37 252	80%	3.36 m³
LP gas	liters	25 643	80%	4.87 L
Electricity	kWh	3 600	100%	27.78 kWh

Multiply the cost of the fuel per unit times the units in the last column to obtain values for comparison.

Seasonal Heat Requirements

Heating degree-days is a useful index in determining fuel requirements. Although the index is designed for use as an aid in estimating annual heating costs for homes or for scheduling fuel oil deliveries, with proper adjustments it can be useful for estimating fuel requirements for greenhouse heating.

Heating degree-days are determined by subtracting the average of the maximum and minimum temperatures for a 24-hour period from 65 degrees F. Any negative value is taken as zero. For example, a minimum of 20 degrees F and a maximum of 30 degrees F for a day would result in 40 degree-days—(65 −[20 + 30]/2 = 40). An oil company might find from its records that a customer uses one gallon of oil for every five degree-days. With that knowledge and a record of accumulated degree-days since the last oil delivery, the date of the next delivery can be pinpointed.

The total heating needs for a home for any period (probably a heating season) may be estimated by the following equation:

$$F = \frac{q_f\,DD\,k}{Btu/f} \qquad \text{Where:}$$

F = Units of fuel

q_f = Total heat loss from the home per °F each hour

DD = degree-days for period

k = a constant

f = Unit in which fuel is measured

The degree-days must be for the local area and for the period required. Local weather stations have the information. The value for k is influenced by the sources of heat other than the heating system. These include occupants, lights, equipment, and solar energy.

To use this equation effectively for a greenhouse, it becomes necessary to consider the average hours of sunshine per day in determining a value for k (Figure 21-5).

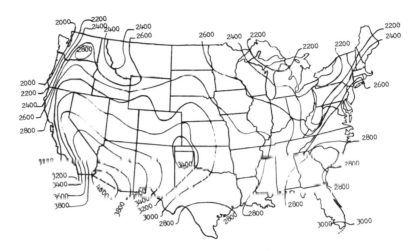

Figure 21-5. Average annual amount of sunshine in hours.

Table 21-4 shows some estimated values for k. They have not been verified empirically.

Table 21-4 Trial Values for Heating Estimate Constant

Annual Hours of Sunlight	k	Annual Hours of Sunlight	k
2,200	17.75	3,000	13.00
2,400	16.25	3,200	12.25
2,600	15.00	3,400	11.50
2,800	14.00		

In calculating degree-days for homes, a 65 degree F base temperature is used. For greenhouses that operate at lower temperatures, a lower base temperature must be used to determine the heating degree-days. Local weather bureaus may have degree-days based on 55 degrees F and 60 degrees F as well as the standard 65 degrees F. If not, a *reasonable* estimate may be made by direct proportion; that is, $55°/65° = 85$ percent and the DD for a 55°F base may be taken as 85 percent of the DD for a 65° base.

An example using the same greenhouse for which a heating system load was calculated is as follows:

$$q_f = q_t/\text{TD}$$
$$(\text{Total of } 217{,}843 \text{ Btu/hr})/60°\text{TD} = 3{,}630 \text{ Btu}/(\text{hr °F}).$$

Assume that the house is to be used for bedding plants for a period of 2,000 degree-days (based on 60 degrees F) in a 2,600-hour sunlight area and that oil with a net output of 98,000 Btu per gallon will be used.

$$F = q_f \, \text{DD} \, k/(\text{Btu/f})$$

$$3{,}630 \times 2{,}000 \times 15/98{,}000 = 1{,}111 \text{ gal of fuel oil required for that period}$$

VENTILATION

The exchange of air inside a greenhouse with air from outside is needed to lower the temperature, to reduce humidity, and to bring in fresh air to maintain the level of carbon dioxide. Ventilation is accomplished with either vents and doors or with fans.

Ridge and side vents are commonly used in glass houses. They depend on natural convection currents to move the air through the house.

Exhaust fans and inlet louvres are commonly used for plastic-covered houses because it is difficult to combine vents with the large sheets of plastic that are used. This is particularly true with the air-inflated, double-covered houses.

Vents or fans may be controlled either manually or with thermostats. As conditions can change rapidly, particularly during periods of partly cloudy weather, automatic controls are strongly recommended. Ventilation is most critical on bright, sunny days in mild weather when great quantities of solar heat must be removed. As shown in Figure 21-6, one air change per minute results in an inside temperature of about 10 degrees F (5 degrees C) above outside temperature. As this temperature difference is generally satisfactory, it is the ventilation rate that is commonly recommended. If lower temperatures are necessary, either shading or cooling or both may be used.

Fans should be rated at one-eighth of an inch (3 mm) static pressure. Winter ventilation, when it is required, should be at a rate of 10 to 20 percent of the summer maximum. In early spring or late fall, an intermediate rate is desirable to avoid chilling the plants from a sudden influx of cold air. These variations in rate of air movement may be obtained with multispeed fans or by operating only one of several fans in cold weather.

In most greenhouses, air is brought in through inlet louvres at one end and exhausted by fans at the opposite end. The inlet louvre area should equal 1.5 square feet per 1,000 cubic feet per minute (0.14m²/472

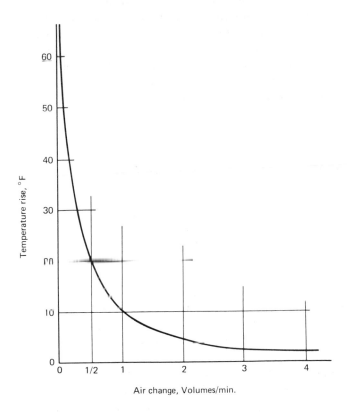

Figure 21-6. The influence of air exchange rate on temperature rise in greenhouses. (*Courtesy* Cooperative Extension Service, University of Kentucky)

L/s) and they should be motor controlled for positive action. The louvres at the exhaust fans need not be motorized.

Where natural ventilation systems are being used, the area of the vents at the ridge should be equal to one-sixth of the floor area and the side vents should total approximately the same. The ridge vents should open far enough to make a 60-degree angle with the roof.

COOLING GREENHOUSES

Under normal summer conditions the inside temperature will be higher than the outside even when shading material and a high level of ventilation are in use. If the resulting temperature is likely to reduce crop quality or result in serious plant damage, then cooling is desirable. Evaporative coolers are preferred over mechanical refrigeration because they are much less expensive. In addition they have the beneficial effect of raising the humidity which reduces plant wilting.

The most common evaporative cooling system consists of 2-inch (50-mm) thick pads of shredded wood fiber mounted in either a side or end wall. At least 1 square foot (0.093 m²) of pad area is required for each 150 cubic foot per minute (71 L/s) of fan capacity. Water is spread evenly over the pads from a manifold supplied from a sump with a float-controlled water level.

HEAT CONSERVATION IN GREENHOUSES

Greenhouses are designed to produce a crop under controlled conditions often involving high energy consumption. Heating costs represent a substantial part of the total cost of production and even relatively small savings can be significant. But efforts to save energy, which will limit yield or interfere with a critical production schedule, may not be economical. So it is imperative to examine the ways in which fuel consumption can be reduced without undermining the profit potential.

The greatest loss of heat is through the roof and walls. Various insulating techniques have been developed to curb this loss and thereby save energy.

Inflated double-layer PE can save up to 40 percent as compared to a single layer of PE. Used over fiberglass or glass houses, savings up to 50 percent are reported. However, the level of lighting is reduced about 15 percent and this in turn may reduce crop yields.

Movable, horizontal curtains or thermal screens that can be drawn over the plant area at night have shown considerable promise. In the event of a winter storm, they can be opened to allow enough heat loss to prevent snow accumulation. Fixed curtains are not recommended because of reduced light and possibly dangerous snow accumulation.

Concrete and masonry foundations, as well as asbestos-cement board perimeters used between supporting posts, are very poor barriers to heat transfer. One inch of foam insulation installed on either the inside or outside of the wall can reduce heat loss through these materials by 75 to 80 percent.

A number of innovative ideas are being investigated. They include pumping double walls full of foam or pellets at night and sucking them out again in the morning, building greenhouses with heavily insulated north walls, and using solar collectors and storages to supply a part of the necessary nighttime heat demand.

In constructing a new house, the selection of a well sheltered area can appreciably reduce heat loss from wind. In addition, tree windbreaks, located to the north and northwest and far enough away to avoid casting shadows on the house, provide permanent protection.

Maintenance plays an important role in heat conservation. Equipment that is kept in good condition will operate efficiently and houses that are kept tight will reduce heat loss. But these and other aspects of energy conservation in the greenhouse are a matter of management and not within the scope of this book.

SUN-HEATED PIT GREENHOUSES

The development of solar heating for greenhouses is still in the experimental stage. However, some of the ideas hold promise. The sun-heated pit house is a form of a solar greenhouse that has been in existence for many years. It uses the heat stored in the soil to keep the temperature in the house above freezing. In the 19th and early 20th centuries, large pits of this type were common on large estates in the North where tender tropical plants were wintered over.

The pit greenhouse is oriented east and west and the lower half is dug into the ground. It is often attached to another building, or the half of the roof that faces north is boxed in and heavily insulated. The span facing south is covered with glass, fiberglass or PE and normally heated only by the sun. On cold nights or cloudy days it is covered with a plastic foam pad to preserve the heat within the house. Drainage may be a problem that can be solved with a sump pump or properly installed drain tile.

GREENHOUSE BENCHES

The decision to use benches or to grow plants at ground level, either in flats or pots or in the floor soil, is largely determined by the crops to be produced, the shape of the house, and the management program. For example, tomatoes would probably be grown in the floor soil. Nursery stock containers might be arranged so as to completely fill the floor area. Cut flower crops are usually grown on benches filled with soil, while potted plants might be grown on open benches.

The use of benches however, has several advantages. They provide a comfortable working height, allow better air circulation and environmental control around the plants, and permit better disease and growth control.

Benches may be constructed of several different materials. Among the most satisfactory are corrugated asbestos-cement board, wood that has been pressure treated with water-borne preservatives, galvanized welded-wire fabric, and lath fence. Each has unique features and the choice depends on the manner in which the bench will be used. Support rails may be made of treated wood or galvanized pipe. Concrete blocks which can be easily leveled, make substantial supports.

ELECTRICAL AND WATER SYSTEMS

Electrical Service

In planning the electrical service for any building one must determine what equipment, operating simultaneously, will cause the peak demand for electrical power. In a greenhouse, the period of maximum ventilation is almost certain to cause the peak electrical demand. A close estimate of the load during this period is made by combining the running currents of all motors, including doubling the current for the largest motor. If other electrical equipment is likely to be operating at the same time, that should also be included.

Special care must be taken to insure that distribution lines between houses are of sufficient size to prevent more than a two to three percent voltage drop.

Alarms

An alarm to warn of a malfunction in the environmental control system is essential for any greenhouse with a valuable crop that may be easily damaged by a major change in temperature.

The failure of the electrical supply or the ventilating or heating equipment can ruin a greenhouse crop in a very short time. When one air change per minute is necessary for summer cooling, a devastating temperature rise can occur in a matter of minutes in the event of a ventilation failure. The reverse can occur with a heating failure on a windy zero night in winter.

A combination power- and temperature-sensitive alarm will insure the most rapid response. The alarm may be wired directly to a location where someone is always present, or in the case of greater distances, telephone lines can be leased for the purpose.

Watering

Hand watering, common in many operations, is facilitated by short hoses and several faucets rather than one long hose. Automatic bench-watering systems, in which nozzles are installed in lines along the edges of the benches, can be operated with a time clock. Potted plants may be watered more uniformly with a spaghetti tube system in which water is fed to each pot with a small sized tube extended from a larger distribution line.

PROBLEMS

21.1   Determine the heat loss from a gable roof greenhouse that is 18 feet (5.5 m) wide, 60 feet (18.3 m) long, 5 feet (1.5 m) to the eaves and has a rise of 6.3 feet (1.9 m). All surfaces are covered with a double layer of polyethylene. The greenhouse is located in an area with a design temperature of 10°F (−12°C) and must be maintained at a minimum of 60°F (15.6°C).

21.2   A 2-foot (0.6-m) diameter P.E. duct is used to distribute the air from the heater. If a velocity of 1,000 feet per minute (5.1 m/s) is maintained, what temperature rise is required to deliver the heat necessary to equal the loss determined in problem 21.1?

21.3   What fan capacity would be required for ventilation on a warm, sunny day?

21.4   An evaporative cooler is installed to match the ventilation rate found in problem 21.3. How much pad surface area will be required?

21.5   The air approaching the cooling pads is 95°F (35°C) and 60 percent relative humidity. If the moisture evaporates to produce 90 percent relative humidity as the air passes through the wet pad, what is the resulting air temperature?

REFERENCES

Aldrich, R.A. et al. *Energy Conservation in Greenhouses.* Ithaca, N.Y.: Northeast Regional Agricultural Engineering Service, 1977.

Aldrich, R.A. et al. *Hobby Greenhouses and Other Gardening Structures.* Ithaca, N.Y.: Northeast Regional Agricultural Engineering Service, 1976.

Duncan, G.A., and Walker, J.N. *Greenhouse Coverings.* University of Kentucky Cooperative Extension Service Bulletin AEN-10. Lexington, Ky. 1973.

Duncan, G.A., and Walker J.N. *Poly-tube Heating-Ventilation Systems and Equipment.* University of Kentucky Cooperative Extension Service Bulletin AEN-7. Lexington, Ky., 1973.

Walker, J.N., and Duncan, G.A. *Cooling Greenhouses.* University of Kentucky Cooperative Extension Service Bulletin AEN-28. Lexington, Ky., 1974.

Walker, J.N., and Duncan, G.A. *Greenhouse Structures.* University of Kentucky Cooperative Extension Service Bulletin AEN-12. Lexington, Ky., 1973.

Chapter Twenty-Two

Fruit, Vegetable, and Nursery Storage

APPLE STORAGE

Well designed and expertly managed storages allow high quality apples to be marketed during much of the year. Apples held in storage from a depressed market at the time of harvest to a strong market the following spring offer an opportunity for considerable economic benefit. To take advantage of this situation however, requires that only top quality fruit be stored and that careful attention be paid to the design, construction, and operation of the storage. Apple storages, particularly of the controlled-atmosphere (CA) type, represent a large investment and it is only when a high quality product is marketed that the storage becomes profitable.

Pears as well as apples respond well to long-term storage and much of the material covered for apples relates equally to pears. Other fruits such as grapes, cherries, plums, apricots, peaches, and strawberries are held for short periods in refrigerated storages during the marketing period.

Storage Requirements

Apples, like all fruits, are alive at the time of harvest and continue to live and ripen after picking. During the ripening process, complex changes take place in which the sugar in the apple is used up in the presence of oxygen. Water and CO_2 are produced and heat is generated. This process is spoken of as respiration and continues until the fruit is over-ripe and unpalatable. The rate of respiration varies according to temperature. Lowering the temperature retards respiration, while the rate increases two- or threefold for every 20°F (11°C) of temperature rise. Four days at 68°F (20°C) "ages" an apple the equivalent of three to four weeks at a storage temperature of 32°F (0°C). Therefore, for maximum storage life the importance of rapid cooling of apples to storage temperature can hardly be overemphasized.

Refrigeration capacity is designed so that the fruit moved into storage each day during the harvest season can theoretically be cooled to storage temperature. Actually the fruit does not reach the holding temperature in 24 hours, but if the system is not capable of removing that much heat it will fall behind the rate of harvest. As long as the storage refrigeration is adequate, hydrocooling of apples before storage offers no advantages.

A temperature of 30 to 32°F (−1 to 0°C) and a relative humidity of 85 to 88 percent is considered optimum for most apple varieties. A few varieties, such as McIntosh and Greenings, tend to deteriorate at temperatures below 35°F (1.7°C).

In addition to low temperature and high humidity, a reduction in the oxygen and an increase in the carbon dioxide in the atmosphere will slow down respiration and increase storage life. Controlled-atmosphere (CA) storages, in which both oxygen and carbon dioxide levels are maintained at approximately 3 percent, are of particular advantage for varieties that are injured by low storage temperatures. These storages have become very popular because of the long storage periods that are possible and the attractive marketing opportunities.

Air circulation is important to maintain uniform conditions throughout the storage room. Good controls and equipment are essential to reduce temperature and humidity fluctuations to a minimum as the system cycles on and off.

Storage Buildings

Site   A well drained site that is convenient to the orchard and not too far from the home is desirable, and if retail sales are anticipated, it should be near the highway. Provision for parking, receiving, and shipping, as well as a storage for empty containers will be needed. In addition, room should be allowed for expansion.

Layout and facilities   A service building will need to be constructed in connection with the storage. At a minimum it will serve as a location for refrigeration equipment and for receiving and loading out apples. Depending on the nature of the operation planned, it may be needed for much more. For example, storage for extra containers may be required, retail sales may be envisioned and if the total apple production is large enough, a complete grading and packing operation may need to be housed. This in turn will require more attention to insulation, heating, and special lighting. For example, deluxe cool-white fluorescent lamps are ideal for grading apples, while deluxe warm-white are better for a salesroom because of the additional red in the light.

Once the extent of the operation has been resolved, a flow diagram should be drawn to show the path of all traffic as apples are received, stored, handled, and shipped.

Although a square storage would be ideal from the standpoint of the ratio of surface area to volume, the practical width is limited by the framing system. A clear span of 40 to 60 feet (12 to 19 m) is a practical maximum. The total storage volume should be about 2½ cubic feet per bushel to be stored (2.86 m³/tonne). This allows for ceiling clearance and space between containers for ventilation.

Ceiling heights range from 18 to 22 feet (5.5 to 6.7 m) depending on container size and the number placed on a pallet. Although large sized storage rooms are more economical, when planning CA storages, some growers sacrifice some of the economy and choose to construct several smaller rooms which will allow greater flexibility in handling the needs of different varieties and in marketing over a longer period of time. Also, as soon as a room is empty, the refrigeration may be cut off.

Building construction There is a wide choice of materials suitable for use in the construction of cold storage buildings, each having individual advantages and limitations. Masonry blocks or precast concrete panel structures are inherently resistant to moisture and fire damage. Pole buildings are inexpensive. Wood-frame construction is medium in cost and easy to insulate. Clear spans of up to 50 feet (15 m) are practical with wood trusses. Steel frames with steel siding are usually the choice for wider buildings, although the installation of insulation may be more difficult.

Foundations should extend to below the frost level and be insulated to reduce heat transfer.

Level, concrete floors allow easy maneuvering of equipment and stacking of containers. The use of insulation in the floor is debatable. Eight to 10 inches of uniform gravel fill under the floor are desirable. If the water table is less than 10 feet (3 m) below the floor, the installation of rigid insulation under the concrete will improve refrigeration efficiency and prevent any possibility of freezing under the floor.

Insulation, Vapor Barriers and Gas Seals

A number of insulating materials have been used in the construction of apple storages. Their performance has been largely related to the success with which moisture has been excluded. Ordinary refrigerated apple storages present a difficult problem in that at harvest time it is warmer on the outside of the building, requiring a vapor barrier on the outside. However, during January and February, the outside temperature is likely to average lower than the inside and moisture tends to move outward into the insulation. Controlled-atmosphere storages further complicate the problem in that a gas-tight seal must be installed to allow the required levels of carbon dioxide and oxygen to be maintained. If a gas seal is installed on the inside of the wall, the vapor barrier on the outside must be exceptionally nonpermeable.

Approaches to solving the moisture problem have included the use of:

1.   Insulation sealed with a vapor barrier on both sides. This is satisfactory only if the seal is never damaged, a situation that is unlikely to prevail.

2.   A very permeable insulation, installed free-standing inside an outer shell that serves as structure, vapor seal, and gas seal. A plywood-covered building is sealed with five coats of sprayed-on PVC to a 0.030-inch (0.76 mm) thick layer. The glass fiber insulation installed inside is held in place with thin furring strips. During the early part of the storage period, the external seal prevents any moisture from reaching the insulation. During a short period in midwinter some moisture easily passes through the insulation, condenses on the cold plywood wall and drains back onto the storage floor.

3.   Closed-cell insulation which prevents entrance into or the passage of moisture through the insulating layer. It is still necessary to guard against moisture condensation at the boundary of the insulation and other materials.

At present, the most satisfactory method of excluding moisture from the insulation and producing an adequate gas seal at the same time is to use sprayed-on polyurethane insulation. Being closed-cell in nature, it not only excludes moisture but also serves as a gas seal when applied as a continuous layer. Three things must be kept in mind when installing sprayed-on polyurethane: (1) Precautions against fire must be taken during installation, (2) a thermal barrier surface must be installed so that no polyurethane is left exposed, thus reducing the fire hazard, and (3) for CA storages, the insulation should result in a continuous layer.

Figure 22-1 illustrates methods of insulating and sealing different types of storage walls and ceilings. In Figure 22-1A, the sprayed-on polyurethane provides continuous insulation and sealing over the entire wall and ceiling area. One-half inch (13 mm) of plaster offers physical protection and fire resistance. While cement plaster is harder, gypsum plaster offers slightly better thermal protection. The same insulation and sealing system may also be used on the inside of a plywood-surfaced frame wall.

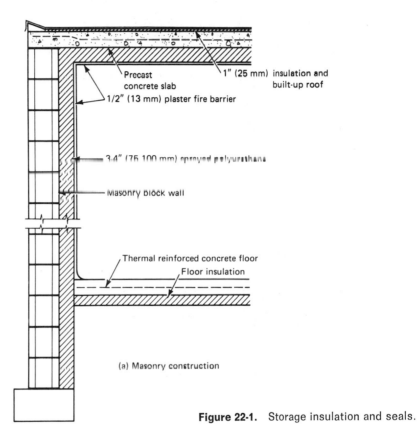

Precast
concrete slab

1" (25 mm) insulation and
built-up roof

1/2" (13 mm) plaster fire barrier

3-4" (75-100 mm) sprayed polyurethane

Masonry block wall

Thermal reinforced concrete floor
Floor insulation

(a) Masonry construction

Figure 22-1.   Storage insulation and seals.

Figure 22-1B shows the polyurethane sprayed on the outside of the plywood interior wall covering. This is done before the outside siding is installed. The plywood is installed on nailing strips on both the walls and ceiling. This leaves only small areas of contact that are not sealed with the polyurethane. This system could be used in either a pole building wall, as shown, or in standard stud construction. The nailing strips are required in either case. Plastic-coated or HDO plywood is used for the interior wall covering. All joints are filled with a nonhardening caulking material and sealed with a tape especially designed for CA storage applications.

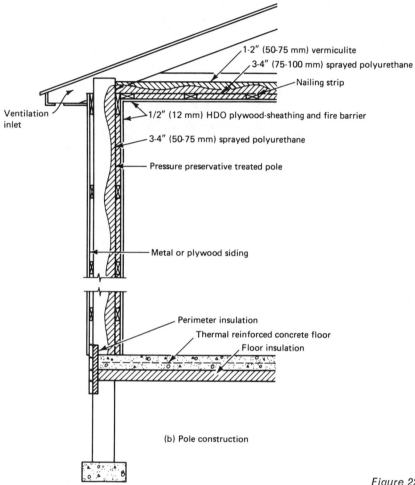

1-2" (50-75 mm) vermiculite

3-4" (75-100 mm) sprayed polyurethane

Nailing strip

Ventilation inlet

1/2" (12 mm) HDO plywood-sheathing and fire barrier

3-4" (50-75 mm) sprayed polyurethane

Pressure preservative treated pole

Metal or plywood siding

Perimeter insulation

Thermal reinforced concrete floor

Floor insulation

(b) Pole construction

Figure 22-1 continued

Three to 4 inches (75 to 100 mm) of polyurethane will produce a total R value of 20 to 26 (3.5 to 4.6) in any of these wall constructions. There are two reasons for choosing such a high R value. It reduces the refrigeration load and, more importantly, the temperature drop across the materials outside the insulation is small enough so that condensation is not likely to occur on the outside of the polyurethane even though outside vapor easily penetrates to that plane.

For example, assume an R_t of 20 (3.5) and an R for the concrete block of 1.45 (0.24). When the storage temperature is 32°F (0°C) and the outside temperature is 72°F (22.2°C), the humidity could rise to 90

percent before condensation would occur at the junction of the blocks
and the insulation.

$$(72° - 32°) \times 1.45/20 = 2.9°F \text{ drop across block}$$

$$72° - 2.9° = 69.1°F \text{ temperature at junction}$$

The relative humidity of 72°F (22.2°C) dry-bulb and 69.1°F
(20.6°C) dew point is 90 percent.

This condition is likely to occur only on a hot summer evening.

Only closed-cell, nonpermeable types of insulation are suitable for
installation on the outside of the gas seal.

The final test of a CA storage is the adequacy of the gas-tight seal.
This may be checked by blowing air into a storage to a pressure of at
least 1½ inches (38 mm) of water after which the pressure drop is
checked with a manometer. A small room should not drop to zero in less
than one hour and a larger room in less than half an hour.

Refrigeration

Refrigeration is needed to maintain storage temperature while at
the same time removing field heat at least as fast as apples are added
to the storage. The term *ton* is sometimes used in referring to the refrigeration load. It derives from the heat absorbed in melting one ton of ice
in 24 hours and equals 288,000 Btu per 24 hours, 12,000 Btu per hour or
200 Btu per minute. It is better to use Btu (kJ) when dealing with refrigeration loads.

Refrigeration load   The cooling load imposed on the system when
the storage is being filled comes from four sources:

1.   Heat transfer through the walls, ceiling, and floor.

2.   Field heat (that which is stored in the apples as they are
brought to the storage from the orchard).

3.   Heat of respiration given off by the apples.

4.   The service load resulting from lights, equipment, workers, and
air exchange through the open door.

Heat transfer through walls and ceilings is discussed in Chapter 14.

Field heat stored in the apples may be calculated using outside air
temperature, specific heat, and the average weight of apples added to the

storage each day. This represents the largest portion of the refrigeration load.

The heat of respiration varies with temperature. Table 22-1 provides estimated values for a number of fruits and vegetables including apples.

Table 22-1   Storage Conditions for Fruits and Vegetables

Product	Storage Temperature °F	°C	R.H. %	Heat of Respiration Btu/ton 24 hr	Watts/ tonne	Ventilation Rate
Apples	30–32	−1–0	90	700	9.4	High
Beets	32–40	0–4	95	1,800	24.2	Low
Cabbage	32	0	92	—	—	Low
Carrots	32–35	0–2	95	1,400	18.8	Low
Grapes	30–32	−1–0	85	900	12.1	Low
Onions	32	0	75	900	12.1	High
Peaches	31–32	−1–0	85	1,500	20.1	Low
Pears	29–32	−2–0	90	700	9.4	Low
Potatoes						
White	38–50	3–10	90	1,500	20.1	Medium
Sweet	50–60	10–15	85	1,000	13.4	Medium
Strawberries	31–32	−1–0	85	3,500	47.0	Low
Tomatoes						
Green	55–70	12–21	85	2,500	33.6	High
Ripe	45–50	7–10	85	—	—	High

The service load is usually taken as 10 percent of the sum of all other loads.

Experience has shown that the following refrigeration capacities are adequate for apples in most cases:

	Customary	SI
10-day filling period	12 Btu/hr per bushel	(0.16 W/kg)
15-day filling period	9 Btu/hr per bushel	(0.12 W/kg)
20-day filling period	8 Btu/hr per bushel	(0.10 W/kg)

Inasmuch as the field heat represents from one-half to two-thirds of the total load at the time of filling and is not repeated later, it is advisable to divide the refrigeration load between at least two compressors on a one-third to two-thirds basis. This will allow more efficient operation and provides a degree of safety factor in case of a breakdown.

Refrigeration principles   A mechanical refrigeration system works on the principle that if a vapor is compressed to a high pressure it will condense and give up its heat of vaporization to its surroundings and that when the pressure is reduced, the liquid again evaporates and absorbs heat from its surroundings. A refrigeration system consists of four main parts: (1) a pump or compressor, (2) a condenser (a heat exchanger that operates at high pressure and temperature and gives up its heat to the surrounding air or water), (3) an evaporator (a heat exchanger that operates at low pressure and temperature and absorbs heat from its surroundings), and (4) an expansion valve which is in fact a restriction in the line between the condenser and the evaporator. The evaporator is installed in the cold room and the condenser in a place where it can easily give up its heat, probably outdoors. With the system charged with a refrigerant, the compressor operates by drawing a low pressure on the evaporator where the refrigerant boils, evaporates, and picks up heat from the room air. At the same time, the cold gas is compressed to a high pressure and temperature in the condenser, where the refrigerant condenses and gives up its heat to the outside air. The expansion valve simply limits flow so that the pressure difference can be maintained on a continuous basis.

Either one of two refrigerants are used in the refrigeration system for apple storages: (1) Refrigerant 12, dichlorodifluoromethane, which is odorless, nontoxic, nonflammable, and is piped with copper tubing, and (2) Refrigerant 717, ammonia, which is toxic, has a strong pungent odor, burns at certain concentrations in air, and is piped with iron pipe. Of the two, ammonia is cheaper, more efficient, and because of a higher heat of vaporization, much less of the refrigerant is needed in the system so that all components are smaller. In general, ammonia may be preferable for large systems because of economy, and Refrigerant 12 for smaller systems because it is nontoxic and easier to handle.

Evaporators   The unit-cooler evaporator consisting of finned coils and a blower provides high capacity within minimal space. Ceiling-mounted unit coolers may be spaced in the storage to provide uniform cooling, or a larger cooler may supply the air for a duct system. Generally a tapered duct, sized to give a velocity of 800 to 1,000 feet per minute (4 to 6 m/s) would be installed along the center of the ceiling with openings on either side discharging toward the walls where the air settles along the wall, moves through the stacks toward the center aisle, and back to the blower. Air can be discharged for a maximum of about 33 feet (10 m). When distances are greater it is desirable to install additional ducts or more unit coolers.

Reversing ducts have been used in some installations to improve uniformity of temperature. The first apples in the airstream are cooled more than the last, so reversing the flow periodically reduces the effect.

Regardless of the type of evaporator and the air distribution system, it is important to have sufficient evaporator surface and to move enough air so that there is very little change in temperature through the cooler. This reduces to a minimum the moisture removed from the air. The change in air temperature through a cooler is called the "split" or "range." Experience has shown that 1,000 cubic feet per minute (472 L/s) will lose 200 Btu per minute (3516 W) with about a 10°F (5.6°C) split. The relationship is straight line for splits of 5 to 20°F (2.7 to 11°C).

If the evaporator and air flow are designed for a 10°F (5.6°C) split when maximum refrigeration is required during storage loading, the split will drop to about 2.5°F (1.4°C) after field heat has been removed. Table 22-2 compares temperature split and maximum relative humidity of the air passing through the cooler. Note that with a 10°F (5.6°C) split, the humidity is 62 percent. However, after the storage is loaded and the split can drop to about 2.5°F (1.4°C), the humidity is 90 percent and nearly ideal. The split can drop to 2.5°F (1.4°C) if the same amount of air is moving and the heat load has dropped by 75 percent.

Table 22-2   Relative Humidity vs Temperature Drop
Across an Evaporator
(32°F (0°C) entering air temperature)

| Temperature Drop | | Maximum |
°F	°C	Relative Humidity
1	0.56	96%
2	1.11	92%
3	1.67	88%
4	2.22	83%
6	3.33	76%
8	4.44	69%
10	5.55	62%

Evaporators maintaining a 32°F (0°C) room temperature will operate at about 15°F (8.3°C) below air temperature. Since this is well below freezing, moisture condenses out in the form of frost. Frost restricts both air flow and heat transfer and must be removed. Among the several automatic methods used are (1) warm water from the condenser which is fast and inexpensive but requires a drain, (2) electricity which is simple but costs more to operate, and (3) reverse refrigeration in which hot, compressed gas is fed back to the evaporator which is efficient but more costly to install.

With each of the methods of defrosting, it is important that the fan shut off and stay off until the coils are not only defrosted but are back down to operating temperature. This avoids circulating warm air which would cause unnecessary fluctuations in both temperature and pressure.

Condensers   Condensers may be either water or air cooled. Air cooling is used mainly for smaller condensers and is inefficient in hot weather. While water cooling is more efficient, either large amounts of water must be pumped and "wasted" or else an evaporative tower will be needed to cool the condenser water. It is advantageous to arrange to use the condenser heat to help provide the packing room heating needs.

Controlled Atmosphere Storages

A properly designed and managed CA storage allows the apple producer to maintain the quality of the apples until late spring or early summer when market prices are favorable.

Basically a CA storage is similar to any refrigerated storage except that it must be gas-tight (Figure 22-1). With the tight construction, it is possible to maintain a three to five percent oxygen level and a zero to five percent carbon dioxide level. In a gas-tight storage, this atmosphere will be produced by the respiration of the apples over a period of approximately two weeks. If unrestricted, the oxygen level would continue to drop and the carbon dioxide level rise. However, the carbon dioxide level is monitored and reduced as needed. Adequate oxygen may enter through leaks or with slight ventilation if the level drops too low. The storage is opened only when the fruit is marketed and at that time it is emptied within a few days.

CA generators are available that can produce the desired room conditions in a matter of days instead of weeks as required by natural respiration. The room can also be successfully opened, partially emptied, and resealed, although this practice increases storage costs.

Excess carbon dioxide is produced in a CA storage, making it necessary to check the level daily. The excess may be removed with a caustic soda scrubber, a water scrubber, fresh hydrated high-calcium spray lime, or a carbon dioxide adsorber. The caustic soda is highly corrosive and the system is difficult to handle. The water scrubber may lack capacity during the pull-down period. However, the use of the lime in combination with a water scrubber is economical and satisfactory. Bagged lime at the rate of three to five pounds per ton (1.5 to 2.5 kg/tonne) of fruit is placed in the storage room for this purpose. Although it is the most expensive method of removing excess carbon dioxide, carbon dioxide generators and adsorbers offer the most precise control over the atmosphere. The most recent of these systems makes use of catalytic oxygen burners and regenerating carbon dioxide adsorbers. These may be controlled manually or with automatic gas-sampling equipment. The automatic sampling equipment is expensive, but it may be used on several rooms and reduces to a considerable extent the manual monitoring of room atmosphere.

Early CA storages were equipped with a gas-expansion bag to limit pressure fluctuations. Today, with gas generators to maintain the correct atmosphere, a simple water trap allows pressure equalization.

Precautions   CA storages do not contain enough oxygen to support human life. Breathing equipment is necessary for anyone entering the storage for repairs. Help should always be nearby. When the room is opened for unloading, sufficient time must be allowed for the oxygen level to rise to 18 to 20 percent before workers enter the room for more than brief periods.

POTATO STORAGE

The need to maintain high quality potatoes over an extended period of time to supply both the fresh and processing markets has resulted in increased emphasis on the design, construction, and operation of potato storages.

Potatoes continue to release moisture, heat, and carbon dioxide throughout the storage period. Proper environmental conditions slow these life processes and reduce shrinkage, retard sprouting, and discourage the development of rot organisms. Inasmuch as the profit margin on stored potatoes is often small, ventilation, which is less expensive than refrigeration, is depended on for cooling to storage temperatures and to a large extent for maintaining a desirable temperature and humidity throughout the storage period.

Storage Buildings

Several types of buildings can serve adequately as potato storages, but they must incorporate certain important characteristics. The building should be easy to insulate and it should be resistant to the action of the very high humidity present throughout the storage period. In addition to the snow and wind loads typical of the region, there may be considerable force imposed on the walls by potatoes held in bulk storage. If the potatoes are held in bins, the bin walls must withstand the forces.

The combined requirements of considerable insulation and resistance to high, lateral loading make stud-frame construction the common choice. Neither pole frames nor masonry construction meet these requirements for above-grade storages. However, if a storage is to be built partly below grade, the use of concrete or masonry construction is advantageous. Soil and storage temperatures will be nearly equal, so insulation is not required below grade, and the lateral forces will be partially countered by the soil forces on the outside.

If the potatoes are piled directly against the building walls, the walls must be designed to include the additional forces. Table 22-3 provides the expected bending moments for a few bin and filling configurations. The values are based on lateral forces from potatoes, calculated with the expression:

$L = 17.8 + 8.52H - 0.18H^2$, where $L =$ the lateral force in lb/sq ft and $H =$ the depth of the potatoes in the bin (Schaper and Herrick, 1968).

Table 22-3   Bin-Wall Bending Moments for Potatoes

Customary Units Based on member spacing of 1 ft					SI Units 0.305 m				
Wall Height ft	Potato Depth ft	Sill Force lb	Plate Force lb	Bending Moment lb in.	Wall Height m	Potato Depth m	Sill Force N	Plate Force N	Bending Moment Nm
(Pile depth > bin width)									
10	8	261	123	6,150	3.1	2.4	1161	547	694
12	10	304	180	10,440	3.7	3.1	1610	801	1176
14	12	479	244	16,170	4.3	3.7	2131	1085	1823
16	14	603	316	23,560	4.9	4.3	2682	1406	2656
18	16	734	396	32,600	5.5	4.9	3264	1761	3685
(Bin width > 10 ft (3 m) and pile depth)									
14	12	525	267	17,706	4.3	3.7	2335	1188	2000
16	14	713	374	27,870	4.9	4.3	3171	1664	3146
18	16	929	501	41,240	5.5	4.9	4132	2228	4655

(From Schaper and Herrick, 1968.)

The use of the table in choosing a size and grade of a vertical member for a bin may be illustrated with an example. Assume a bin with 10-foot sides, 8 feet wide and filled to a depth of 8 feet. If studs are to be placed 16 inches on center, the required stud size is determined as follows:

From Table 22-3 the bending moment is found to be 6,150 pound inches based on a 1-foot spacing. For 16 inches, the BM $= 6,150 \times 1.33 = 8,200$ pound inches.

$$BM = F s \text{ (See chapter 11.)}$$

Assuming a 1,200 pound per square inch f (Table 11-1),

$$S = 8,200/1,200 = 6.8 \text{ in.}^3$$

Assuming 2-inch nominal material—(1½-inches actual),

$$S = 1/6 \, bd^2$$
$$d^2 = 6 \times 6.8/1.5$$
$$d = 5.22 \text{ in. (a 2 x 6 in. stud is adequate.)}$$

Bin or wall sills must be securely anchored in order to resist the lateral force transferred to them from the stud. In addition, the stud must be well anchored to the sill.

Storage foundations should extend below grade sufficiently to avoid any risk of frost damage. If the floor level in the storage is above the outside grade, it should be tied to the foundation wall with reinforcing to prevent outward collapse of the wall due to the high lateral force of the potatoes.

Storage floors should be of concrete, 6 inches (150 mm) thick, reinforced with 6- by 6-inch No. 6 gauge mesh and installed over well compacted gravel.

A clear-span roof design allows for maximum flexibility in arranging or moving bins. Lateral loads imposed by the potatoes must be considered in planning the roof framing.

The required storage capacity will depend on the manner in which the potatoes are handled, the ceiling clearance allowed, and whether or not bin fronts are used. An allowance of 2.5 cubic feet per bushel of potatoes to be stored should be adequate in most cases. (In SI units, that is the equivalent of about 400 kg/m³ or 2.5 m³/tonne.)

Since the angle of repose for potatoes is only about 37.5°, considerable storage capacity is lost if bin fronts are not used. In addition, bins that are filled level ventilate more evenly. The forces on bin fronts are similar to the wall sections. Planks dropped into channel guides on the corner posts of bins are usually satisfactory for short spans, but reinforced fronts are required for larger spans. A means of removing the bottom 1 foot (⅓ m) of the front is necessary to allow a conveyor, flume, or bulk scoop to start unloading the bin.

Environmental Control

The storing of potatoes can be divided into three periods, each having a particular function and requiring carefully managed conditions.

1. **Wound healing and curing (suberization) period**   A certain amount of injury and bruising inevitably occurs during harvesting. These fresh wounds are subject to infection from disease and rot organisms. To prevent infection of the damaged tubers, the potatoes are initially held at 55 to 60°F (13 to 16°C) and 90 to 95 percent relative humidity for a period of 7 to 14 days. During this period the skin toughens and a corky tissue forms over the wounds, reducing the chance for infection. If any disease is present, a lower temperature is required.

2. **Storage and holding period**   Potatoes have a natural dormancy

period lasting from 6 to 12 weeks after harvest. In storing potatoes under controlled conditions, the objective is to extend the dormant state as long as possible and to keep shrinkage at a minimum. As soon as the curing is finished, the temperature is reduced to that recommended for long-term storage. Minimum storage temperatures, however, are limited by the final use of the potatoes. For *seed stock*, 38 to 40°F (3.3 to 4.4°C) will delay sprouting for up to eight months. For *table stock*, 43 to 45°F (6 to 7°C) will allow several months of storage without serious sprouting. Lower temperatures would increase the storage period but at the risk of converting starch to sugar and thereby reducing table quality. For *processing stock*, a temperature of 45 to 50°F (7 to 10°C) is necessary to prevent discoloration and to keep the conversion of starch to sugar at a minimum. A chemical sprout inhibitor is required.

3. **Removal and grading period** Cold, brittle potatoes are easily damaged in handling. For this reason it is recommended that the potatoes be warmed to 50°F (10°C) for a few days before removal to prevent bruising and cracking. The heat of respiration given off by the potatoes will produce sufficient heat, providing the air vents are closed to prevent cool air from entering the storage.

A relative humidity of 85 to 90 percent throughout the storage period limits shrinkage to one-half to one percent per month. Humidities below 85 percent result in excessive shrinkage, less weight to market, and reduced quality. Humidities over 90 percent are apt to result in condensation on wall and ceiling surfaces in spite of considerable insulation in both areas.

Insulation Potatoes continue to produce heat throughout the storage period. A 24-hour production of 1,465 Btu per ton (1700 kJ/tonne) may be used for design purposes.

When the relative humidity is 91 percent in a storage at 45°F (7°C), the dew point temperature is only 1¼°F (0.7°C) below the dry-bulb or air temperature. If surface condensation is to be prevented, the R value achieved with insulation must limit the temperature difference between the air and the wall and ceiling surfaces to less than 1¼°F (0.7°C). Table 22-4 shows several levels of insulation R values and the outside temperature at which condensation is incipient.

The R values given in Table 22-4 will not only prevent condensation under most circumstances, but they will also limit heat loss to the point that the heat produced by the potatoes will maintain storage temperatures under design conditions and allow limited ventilation.

Vapor barrier Due to the very high humidity in the storage, the importance of a continuous vapor barrier between the insulation and the interior wall and ceiling surfaces cannot be overemphasized. Four or six

Table 22-4   Outside Temperatures at Which Condensation is
Incipient on Storage Surfaces
(Based on 45°F (7.2°C) and 91% RH)

| Outside Temperature | | R Value | |
Customary	SI	Customary	SI
20°F	−6.7°C	12.2	2.1
10°	−12.2°	17.1	3.0
0°	−17°	22.0	3.9
−10°	−23°	26.8	4.7
−20°	−41.8°	31.7	5.6
−30°	−57.7°	36.6	6.4

Ceiling R values should approximate table values.
Wall R values may be 0.75 of table values.

mil polyethylene, with all joints lapped and sealed and all holes repaired, will make a good barrier. In addition, the attic and the outside walls if possible should be ventilated.

Heat   If a storage, insulated as recommended, is at least one-half filled, little or no supplemental heat should be required. However, if storage doors are opened frequently, if potatoes must be warmed for handling, or if fresh air is needed for moisture control, then some additional heat may be needed. Usually 170 Btu per hour per ton (55 W/tonne) of supplemental heat is adequate.

Ventilation   The ventilation system in a storage performs three functions: (1) It brings in and distributes cool, fresh air to lower the temperature to storage levels, (2) it circulates air within the storage periodically to maintain uniform conditions, and (3) it introduces small quantities of fresh air periodically to correct the humidity or temperature.

During the initial cooling period, a fan capacity of 16 cubic feet per minute per ton (8.25 L/s per tonne) will insure rapid cool-down. Fans should deliver the necessary capacity at ½- to ¾-inch (13 to 19 mm) static pressure unless distribution ducts are undersized or potatoes are likely to be stored dirty. Either of these conditions will require a rating at 1 inch (25 mm) static pressure.

Air distribution control   As mentioned, the ventilation system must perform three functions. Each of these requires a somewhat different air distribution pattern. Of the numerous systems that have been used, probably the proportioning system that can be automatically controlled to circulate all fresh air, recirculate only storage air, or circulate any of several proportions of fresh and storage air, provides the best storage environment.

The operation of a proportioning system is complex, but Figure 22-2, showing the damper and fan locations, should help to illustrate

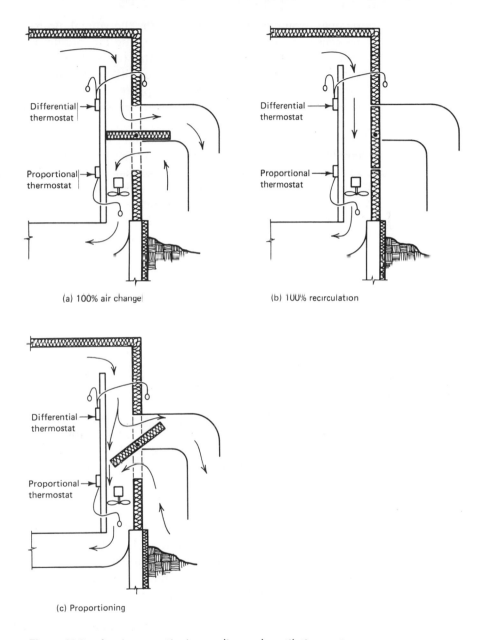

(a) 100% air change

(b) 100% recirculation

(c) Proportioning

Figure 22-2.   An air proportioning cooling and ventilation system.

how it functions. Soon after the potatoes are in the storage, rapid cool-down to storage temperature is desirable. Since the storage temperature would be quite warm and the outside air temperature still moderate, the damper would probably shift to the horizontal position allowing 100 percent fresh air to be brought in. During the middle of the day the outside temperature may rise above the temperature in the storage. The differential thermostat senses the condition and, overriding the proportioning thermostat, moves the damper to the vertical position until the outside temperature drops. A timer would continue to call for intermittent recirculation. When storage temperature is reached, the damper would shift to the vertical position and air would recirculate. Under these conditions a timer would operate the fan on an intermittent basis. Two to four hours per day is usually adequate. With mild outside temperatures, the potatoes will produce an excess of heat and the storage temperature will rise. Under these conditions the proportioning thermostat will tip the damper just enough so that cool air will temper the recirculating air and bring the storage temperature down.

When the storage temperature drops below normal, heat and recirculation are required. When humidity is too high, a small amount of fresh air can be admitted under control of a humidistat. This would probably drop the storage temperature enough to call for heat. Low humidities may be corrected antomatically with humidifiers installed in the duct and controlled by humidistats. However, as humidistats are rather undependable at high humidity levels, manual management may be substituted to adjust for humidity. A safety thermostat in the plenum can shut the system down and sound an alarm in the event that other controls fail to function correctly.

Air distribution   Air must be distributed through the potatoes with reasonable uniformity to maintain a quality product. Uneven air flow can cause pockets of high humidity that encourage rotting, or areas of either high or low temperature that cause premature sprouting or conversion of starch to sugar.

Distribution of the air has been achieved successfully with several different systems. One of the more common methods is through ducts cast in the concrete floor. Another is through rectangular or triangular shaped ducts installed on the floor surface. In addition, corrugated metal ducts or ducts built into bin partitions have been used. Whatever the choice, there are characteristics that should be embodied in the system if uniform distribution is to result.

1.   Delivery ducts under potatoes should be spaced 8 to 12 feet (2.5 to 3.7 m) apart.

2.   The maximum air velocity in either distribution or delivery ducts should be limited to no more than 1,000 feet per minute (5 m/s).

3.   *Distribution* ducts should be reduced in cross section after each branch opening in such a way that the velocity remains constant.

4. *Delivery* ducts may be tapered or stepped at 10-foot (3-m) intervals to maintain a uniform velocity, or the openings in the ducts may be restricted to provide enough static pressure for uniform distribution.

It has been demonstrated that if the total net area of the outlets in the delivery ducts is equal to the duct cross-section area, air will be distributed uniformly (Schaper, Cloud, and Lundstrum, 1974). However, if the potatoes rest on the openings as they would on the slotted cover of a cast-in-place floor duct, 75 percent of the opening area is covered. In this situation, a gross area of four times the duct cross-section area is required to provide the net area necessary to insure uniform air distribution without excessive static pressures.

Ducts cast in the floor that are a minimum of 20 inches (500 mm) wide will allow the use of a 16-inch (400-mm) conveyor in the duct for removing potatoes at the end of the season. To maintain a uniform air velocity, the cross-section area of the ducts may be reduced by decreasing the depth to a minimum of 14 inches (350 mm), also a limitation of the conveyor. Removable wood blocks may be used to further limit the cross-section area for air-flow control.

Curved metal corners installed in ducts at right-angle turns reduce turbulence and improve the uniformity of distribution.

Once the desired storage conditions have been achieved by moving air through the potatoes, some managers prefer to have the air move along the storage walls (Figure 22-3). This is called shell ventilation and maintains uniform room conditions while reducing air movement through the potatoes, resulting in somewhat less shrinkage.

Humidification In humid regions, nighttime relative humidities tend to be very high. Since it is primarily nighttime air that is used for cooling, satisfactory humidities are easily maintained during the initial stages of storage. In contrast, in some dry areas, nighttime humidities are so low that the fresh air tends to reduce storage humidity to an undesirably low level. Under these conditions, high capacity centrifugal humidifiers may be required. In marginal cases, duct bottoms may be kept covered with water or spray nozzles can be used to add moisture to the storage.

Monitoring equipment It is difficult to manage a storage without knowing what conditions actually exist within the bins of potatoes. Bin temperatures may be checked with the use of thermocouples buried in the potatoes during filling. The couples are inexpensive, but the portable potentiometer used with them costs several hundred dollars.

Thermisters are used with a much less expensive meter, and are very satisfactory for checking the temperature at 10 to 12 points.

Humidity may be checked with an inexpensive sling psychrometer although a motorized psychrometer is more convenient at a somewhat higher cost.

Figure 22-3. Potato storage air distribution ducts. Three center ducts are used for cool down. Two side ducts are available for shell ventilation during midwinter.

NURSERY STOCK STORAGE

Nursery plants have traditionally been lined out in fields or wooded areas where winter injury to evergreen foliage annually causes a considerable loss in salable plants. In the colder regions of the country, these plants are not available for the early spring market because of frozen ground.

These problems led to the growing of plants in containers which can be shipped as early as the market demands. But container growing introduced a new problem. Root damage to balled or containerized plants is much more common than to those left in the ground, especially among ornamentals including magnolias, dogwoods, and some hollys in which root damage occurs at 20°F (−7°C) or lower.

Both foliage and root damage can be avoided, however, by placing the container-grown plants in storage where a favorable environment is maintained. The growing demand for early spring sales of nursery stock has led to a considerable increase in the use of such winter storages.

Types of Storages

The two most common winter nursery storages are (1) temporary, plastic-covered structures erected over the area where the stock is growing, and (2) permanent buildings, often built partly below grade, insulated, and ventilated so that ideal environmental conditions may be maintained.

Plastic-covered storages   These are simple, inexpensive structures ranging from 3 feet (1 m) to 8 feet (2.5 m) high, consisting of hoop frames covered with polythylene (PE). The frames are covered in late fall and uncovered again in the spring. Since this type of storage is erected over the growing stock, it is unnecessary to handle the containers until the plants are ready to be marketed.

These PE-covered structures have worked well for storing hardy plants. They have also been reasonably successful for less hardy species by using supplementary management practices such as irrigation of the containers, covering the plants with one or two layers of PE film, and in some cases installing thermostatically controlled portable heaters. Clear, white, and black plastic covers have all been used on the hoop frames with similar results. Daytime temperatures are higher with the clear plastic, but nighttime temperatures are nearly equal for all three. In the absence of heat, the hoop frames may collapse under excessive snow loads. Temporary support at the midpoint of the arches ordinarily is adequate to prevent damage.

Permanent storages   Although investment in a permanent building is greater, and labor is required to move the plants into the storage, the opportunity to maintain ideal conditions and to assemble and ship plants easily and efficiently early in the spring has led to increased use of environmentally controlled storages.

While above-grade, insulated storages are generally satisfactory, the use of partially below-grade structures allows soil heat to assist in maintaining above freezing temperatures within the storage. Unlike potatoes, nursery stock produces negligible heat of respiration, so heavy insulation alone does not necessarily maintain the desired storage temperature. Uninsulated concrete floors and walls located well below grade should allow a minimum of 2 Btu per hour per square foot (6.3 W/m²) to pass into a 34°F (1°C) storage. On the average, this is enough so that with a well insulated ceiling and end wall, heat gain will exceed heat loss and occasional ventilation will be required to maintain storage temperature.

A winter nursery storage building includes the following recommended construction features:

1.   A well drained, sloping site to allow much of the building to be below grade.

2.   Twelve-foot (3.5-m) side walls of reinforced concrete, placed 10 feet (3 m) below grade. The walls must be anchored to large footings with reinforcing to resist lateral soil forces.

3.   A clear span of up to 50 feet (15 m) if wood trusses are desired.

4.   Insulation to an R of 20 (3.5) in the exposed end and ceiling. The maintenance of a high humidity means that vapor pressure will be higher inside the building than outside. Thus a vapor barrier should be installed between the ceiling and the insulation. To remove any moisture accumulation above the ceiling, large louvers should be installed in the gable ends of the building. An alternative means of avoiding moisture problems is to use a closed-cell insulation such as sprayed-on polyurethane or urea formaldehyde. Panels of polyurethane or polystyrene would also be suitable as long as a satisfactory covering is installed as a protection against fire. The upper part of the walls may be insulated with rigid insulation attached with an adhesive.

5.   An insulated door large enough to accommodate trucks and fork lifts.

6.   A ventilation system with an exhaust fan at one end of the storage with capacity to provide eight air changes per hour. Air is introduced through two or more motorized louvers at the opposite end of the storage and distributed through PE ducts suspended along the length of the ceiling. Ducts should be sized to carry air at 800 to 1,200 feet per minute (4 to 6 m/s) and each should have two rows of holes uniformly distributed along the length. The holes should be located to discharge down 30 degrees from the horizontal and be spaced 24 to 30 inches (600 to 750 mm) apart. A total area for all of the holes equal to one and one-half

to two times the cross-section area of the duct will provide sufficient velocity for good air distribution.

7. A ventilation system controlled by a pair of thermostats, one near the center of the storage that calls for ventilation whenever the storage temperature rises above 34°F (1°C) and one outside that prevents fan operation if the temperature is more than 34°F (1°C). An alternative and better control for the ventilation system is a single, differential thermostat that allows ventilation anytime it is required when the outside air is cooler than the inside.

8. Continuous air circulation provided with vertical stirring fans.

Handling the nursery stock within the storage will vary from place to place. However, pallets that can be stacked or placed on racks permit the use of a fork lift and allow for efficient use of the available storage space.

Although the plants do not need light during the storage season, adequate lighting is required for loading and unloading the storage.

An adjacent building, maintained at a higher temperature, makes a convenient and more comfortable location to ball bare-root stock and complete other winter and early spring operations.

PROBLEMS

22.1 An apple storage is to be built to hold 20,000 bushels (436 tonnes) equally divided into four rooms. Bulk boxes stacked 6 high will require 18 foot (5.5 m) ceilings. Recommend room dimensions for the storage. A bushel of apples weighs 48 pounds (21.8 kg).

22.2 The storage will be filled at the rate of 1,000 bushels (22 tonnes) per day. The average outside temperature is 65°F (18°C) and the storage temperature is 32°F (0°C). The walls and ceiling are insulated to an R of 25 (4.4) while the floor, also insulated, may be ignored since the heat loss through a floor is insignificant. The building, which includes an equipment room, is designed so that each storage room has one wall in common with another. Therefore, there is no heat exchange through that common wall. Determine the total refrigeration capacity required. Include room loss, field heat, heat of respiration and service loss.

22.3   Explain why it is desirable to have an evaporator with sufficient surface so that it can operate just a few degrees colder than room temperature.

22.4   An air-cooled potato storage is being designed to hold 10,000 bushels (273 tonnes). Recommend a ventilation rate and estimate the number of days that it will take to cool the potatoes to 40°F (4.4°C) if during 12 hours each day the outside temperature averages 38°F (3°C). Assume that the potatoes have a field temperature of 60°F (15.6°C) and that wall and ceiling heat transfer balances out to zero during the period. Field heat and heat of respiration should be included in the calculations. For purposes of calculation, it may be assumed that the potatoes average 45°F (7°C) during the cooling period and that the temperature of the air exhausted equals this temperature. Assume 70% relative humidity for both inlet and exhaust air.

22.5   A storage is being designed in which potatoes will be piled 12 feet (3.66 m) deep against the walls. The studs will be 14 feet (4.27 m) long and spaced 8 inches (200 mm) on center. There will be no bin partitions. Determine a satisfactory size of stud, assuming a safe fiber stress in bending of 1,000 pounds per square inch (6890 kPa).

REFERENCES

Havis, John R., and Fitzgerald, Robert D. *Winter Storage of Nursery Plants.* University of Massachusetts Cooperative Extension Service Publication 125. Amherst, Mass.: 1976.

Layer, J.W. *Refrigerated Farm Storage.* Cornell University Information Bulletin 16. Ithaca, N.Y.

Midwest Plan Service. *Structures and Environment Handbook.* MWPS-1. Ames, Iowa: Midwest Plan Service, 1977.

Patchen, Glenn O. *Storage of Apples and Pears.* U.S. Department of Agriculture, Agricultural Research Service Marketing Research Report 924. Washington, D.C., 1971.

Roberts, J.A. et al. *Bulk Potato Storage.* Canada Department of Agriculture Publication 1508. Ottawa, Ontario, Canada, 1974.

Sainsbury, G.F. *Cooling Apples and Pears in Storage Rooms*. U.S. Department of Agriculture, Agricultural Research Service Marketing Research Report 474. Washington, D.C., 1961.

Schaper, L.A., Cloud, Harold, and Lundstrum, Darnell. *An Engineering Evaluation of Potato Storage Ventilation Performance*. Paper 74-6509. St. Joseph, Mich.: American Society of Agricultural Engineers, 1974.

Schaper, L.A., and Herrick, J.F., Jr. *Lateral Pressures on Walls of Potato Storage Units*. U.S. Department of Agriculture, Agricultural Research Service Report 52-32. Washington, D.C., 1968.

Smock, R.M., and Blanpied, G.D. *Controlled Atmosphere Storage of Apples*. Cornell University Information Bulletin 41. Ithaca, N.Y.

Chapter Twenty-Three

Grain Storages, Silos, and Hay Storages

GRAIN

Grain may be grown on the farm and stored for use in livestock production, or it may be grown primarily for market and stored until it is sold. In either case, the construction of an adequate, efficient grain storage system requires a large investment and should not be undertaken without thorough planning.

One of the most important aspects of farm mechanization is materials handling. As the size of operation increases, the significance of materials handling also increases. The key to successful mechanization is the planning and organization of a materials "flow" pattern as it relates to machinery and equipment and to future expansion. Grain may be handled with a portable elevator and stored in one bin at the outset, but that one bin should be so located that additional bins can be constructed as needed where all of them can be served from a central elevating system.

Although there are several basic layout schemes for designing grain storage facilities and a number of types of handling equipment from which to choose, there are two principles of paramount importance that must be applied if the system is to operate efficiently and profitably:

1. It should always be possible to return the grain to the starting point for redistribution in a closed-loop system.

2. The system should be expandable without losing the closed-loop characteristic and with a minimum of additional equipment.

Centralization is a concept often recommended. A centralized layout meets the needs of both large and small operators and has the potential for expansion with a minimum of duplication of equipment. An arrangement enabling grain to be received, distributed, and returned to a central point keeps labor at a minimum. Equipment need not be moved and grain is easily transported to and from a single receiving and shipping point. However, a centralized layout requires a large initial investment. Although portable equipment may satisfactorily serve in several locations, as labor becomes increasingly costly, the centralized handling system becomes more economically feasible.

System Components

Grain is commonly moved through several component elements of a system linked together as a unit. It is essential that these elements be compatible, especially in capacity, or else surge bins must be added to take care of the uneven flow. In a continuous flow system, the lowest capacity unit controls the entire flow rate. It is best to locate this limiting unit at the beginning of the process. With evenly matched components, some surge allowance should be made for start-up or malfunction. A hopper located on the intake of each unit provides this insurance against plugging.

A typical flow pattern involves transportation from the harvester, off-loading, receiving, elevating, drying, storing, unloading, and either processing for feeding or transporting to a market. There are several alternative types of equipment from which to choose at almost every stage of the flow pattern. The problem is to select the most suitable system for a given operation and then choose the component parts that will fit and function together. A few of the alternatives will be discussed briefly.

Transporting Transporting with either a truck or wagon is satisfactory. However, the means of unloading should be compatible with the receiver. Gravity or hydraulic dumping is efficient and fast but the unloading rate must match the capabilities of the receiver.

Receiving Receiving the grain in a drive-over pit that can hold most of a load permits the use of a slow-speed elevator without holding up the transport vehicle. Lower cost tip-up or swinging hoppers have little surge capacity and can receive grain only as fast as the elevator takes it away.

Elevating   The use of a portable inclined auger or chain type elevator is undoubtedly the least expensive means of handling grain. A short and therefore not expensive high capacity conveyor used at the initial stage elevates the grain into a working bin. From there the grain may be sent to a dryer if necessary, or directly to the pit and from there on a slow-speed elevator to the storage bins.

A higher capacity, central-elevating system employs a vertical auger or bucket type elevator leg to lift the grain from the dump pit to a point where it can flow by gravity to a dryer or to one of up to four storage bins. The choice between an auger or a bucket elevator is based on capacity, cost, and efficiency. The auger will be least costly, but the bucket type will be more efficient and higher capacities are available if required.

Drying   This can be accomplished with several different systems at widely varying rates. This will be discussed separately.

Storing   Facilities for storing are selected primarily on the basis of the manner in which they will be used. Large, grade-level, flat-bottom bins, costing the least per bushel of capacity, are used for long-term storage of grain. A sweep auger in the bin bottom is required to unload the storage completely by mechanical means.

Where high moisture corn is harvested and not dried, it may be stored in a silo or treated chemically to prevent spoilage. In either case, it must be fed on the farm or sold locally for feeding purposes. High moisture corn may also be stored in a bunker silo if fed out by early spring. Considerable care should be taken in loading, packing, and sealing. Grinding the corn before storage is usually recommended. Conventional upright silos work well if at least 3 to 4 inches (75 to 100 mm) of corn are removed daily in warm weather. Sealed silos keep the losses of this rather high-value product to a minimum and can often be justified in spite of their high initial cost.

Small overhead hopper-bottom bins which unload by gravity flow are used as working bins to compensate for rapid unloading of grain, and to feed grinders or driers. They are used on a rotating basis whenever grain or feed is being handled.

Medium sized, grade-level or elevated hopper-bottom bins are used extensively for short-term feed storage. They may be refilled on a weekly or monthly cycle as required.

Unloading   The unloading of the bins is handled with horizontal conveyors that return the grain to the original receiving point. From there the vertical elevator moves it onto a truck, a working bin, or another storage bin. An alternative means of unloading storage bins is with auger or chain elevators that transfer grain directly from the bin to a truck for transport to market. Feed storage bins unload directly into a feeding conveyor or feed wagon.

Processing The processing of grain into feed on a livestock farm starts at the working bin. From there grain may be fed into a grinder, an automatic blender-grinder, or a transport grinder-mixer. The same center building that serves a cash-grain operation can, with careful initial planning, serve the processing operation needed for a livestock enterprise.

Feeding The flow in a grain-livestock operation is completed by feeding. A self-unloading wagon or one of the various types of conveyor feeders that distributes the ration uniformly along a feed bunk keeps labor at a minimum.

Planning the Layout

The site selected for a grain storage facility should be easily accessible with adequate room for expansion to at least double the initial size. A well drained site is essential since some of the conveying equipment will be installed below grade. In addition, heavy vehicles and equipment will require firm roadbeds in order to maneuver in the area. Grain storages produce considerable dust and noise, factors that influence the proximity to the home.

To illustrate the principle of a *centralized system* with room for expansion, a hypothetical grain handling center will be developed step by step from one bin to as many as six. An area 100 by 200 feet (30 by 60 m) is bisected at the 50- and 90-foot (15- and 27-m) points (Figure 23-1) to form four quadrants. The first bin is located in quadrant 1, 7 feet (2.2 m) from the X axis and 12 feet (3.6 m) from the Y axis. Initially a portable elevator is used with the single bin.

A second bin is constructed in quadrant 2, 2 feet (0.6 m) from the X axis and 12 feet (3.6 m) from the Y axis. As additional capacity is required, bins are built in quadrants 3 and 4 in the mirror-image positions shown.

Eventually the dump pit and elevator are constructed and housed within the center building. Space in the building adjacent to the elevator leg and beside the drive-thru is available for processing equipment to be used on a livestock farm.

The storages in quadrant 1 and 4 are spaced 14 feet (4.4 m) apart to allow room for a high speed dryer and work bin when they are required. Alternatively they may be placed next to the drive into the center building.

A noncentralized system is often a suitable option for the small grain operator or when initial investment must be kept to a minimum. Figure 23-2 shows three storage bins arranged to be filled from a single pit by swinging a slow-speed elevator. Grain may be off-loaded into a high-speed elevator and working bin combination. From the working bin, the grain may be directed to a dryer or directly to the low-speed elevator.

A number of grain handling system layouts and equipment components are shown in the Midwest Plan Service Handbook on Planning Grain and Feed Handling (Midwest Plan Service, 1968).

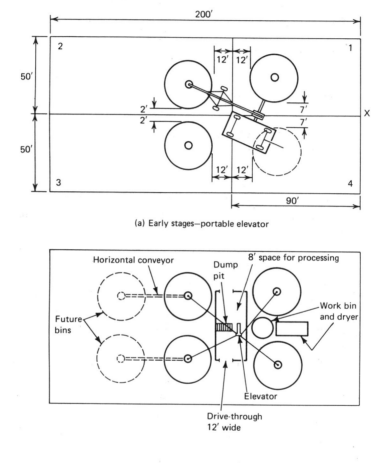

(a) Early stages—portable elevator

(b) Later stage

Figure 23-1.   Grain center layout.

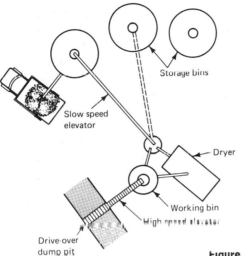

Figure 23-2.   Non-centralized grain storage system.

Drying Grain

Modern harvesting methods, late-maturing varieties and adverse weather conditions have encouraged the use of artificial drying systems. High initial investment and increasing energy costs make the selection of equipment and the management of drying and storage systems critical factors in the production of grain.

All drying operations require air flow and most depend on some added heat as well. The variation in systems is largely related to the amount of heat and the time required to remove the moisture. Grain may be dried in the bin by one of four basic methods:

1. Layer drying Damp corn is added to the storage in layers of 12 to 18 inches (300 to 450 mm) per day and dried by air warmed 5 to 20°F (3 to 11°C) above ambient temperature. This method is slow and requires careful attention to the rate of filling to avoid the growth of mold.

2. Batch drying Two to 3 feet (0.6 to 1 m) of corn are placed on a perforated floor in the bin and air at 100 to 120°F (38 to 49°C) is moved through the grain at 10 to 20 cubic feet per minute per bushel (130 to 260 L/s per m³). A drying rate of one-half to three-fourths percent per hour allows a 24-hour cycle. One and one-half to two hours of air circulation is required for cooling.

3. Dryeration   This is a term used to describe a process in which a batch of corn is dried to 16 to 18 percent moisture with high temperature air and then transferred to another bin where it stands for a few hours before it is cooled with a low-volume airstream. An additional three to four percent of moisture is removed in 8 to 10 hours of cooling. The capacity of the dryer is increased by transferring the cooling operation to another bin and this also reduces cracking damage to the corn.

4. Continuous-flow drying   This takes place in a bin or portable dryer with heated air blown through a column of slowly moving grain. Damp corn is added at the top while dry corn is removed at the bottom. Typical air temperatures are 180 to 220°F (82 to 105°C) and air-flow rates as high as 75 to 100 cubic feet per minute per bushel (1000 to 1350 L/s per m³). Cooling may be integral with drying or in a separate bin. A continuous flow system typically operates about 16 hours per day during the harvest season but may be operated continuously with a sufficiently large wet-grain bin.

The choice of a drying system depends on initial cost, energy cost, speed of harvesting, and the end use of the corn. As energy costs rise, the use of solar collectors (see Chapter 14) and low-temperature (layer) drying becomes more attractive. Corn for seed or market may not be heated to as high a temperature as corn for feed.

Summary

The number of alternative equipment systems to carry out each of the functions in a grain-flow process emphasizes the importance of long-range planning. Not only must the equipment be compatible in function but also in capacity. A slow conveyor in an otherwise fast system can slow down the whole system as well as cause mechanical breakdowns. Electric controls, wired in proper sequence, start equipment before any grain enters the system. Overload protection on all major motors in the system can be designed to shut down the whole system upon malfunction at any one point.

In materials handling equipment there are many parts moving at high speed. Shields are supplied by the manufacturer and should always be left in place. Hazards of any sort should be identified with easily seen warning signs. The adage, "Safety doesn't cost, it pays," is particularly true in the proximity of materials handling equipment.

SILAGE

To reap maximum profits, the beef and dairy farmer must provide a nutritionally balanced ration for his stock. The all-in-one ration, including a large percentage of silage, has led the way to achieving an efficient feeding program with a high degree of mechanization.

Ensiling forage crops such as corn, alfalfa, and grass, as well as some grains like high moisture corn, has become popular for a number of reasons:

1.   Harvesting high-moisture, immature crops in effect gives a longer growing season and the opportunity for increased yields.

2.   Weather damage is reduced because crops require less drying in the field.

3.   Forage crops stored as silage rather than as dry forage, can be handled more easily with mechanical and automated equipment.

4.   In many cases tests have shown that on a dry-matter basis, feed efficiency is higher with silage than with dry forage; that is for equal quantities of dry-matter fed either as silage or hay, that fed as silage produces greater animal gain.

These advantages seem to outweigh the disadvantages of the extra investment in storage structures that is often necessary and the labor involved to handle the extra weight of the high moisture crops. On many farms silage is either the only roughage fed, or it represents a high percentage of the total being used in the ration.

Silo Requirements

Top-quality silage results from a combination of high-quality forage, expertise in loading the silo, and a structure providing the necessary storage conditions. The following characteristics are essential for all silos, regardless of type.

1.   Sufficient wall strength to resist the lateral pressure of the silage.

2.   Tight, smooth, nonabsorbent walls that completely exclude air from the silage.

3.   A wall material that resists the effects of the acids in the silage.

4.   A means of sealing the exposed surface of the silage.

Types of Silos

There are several types of silos and a variety of materials used in their construction. Cost, adaptability to mechanization, and storage losses vary considerably.

Upright or tower silos   These silos have a long life and are well suited for mechanical unloading. They are filled with a blower and self-unloading truck or wagon. Packing is relatively easy and sealing the surface with a plastic cover is effective and not difficult.

Tower silos may be built of glass-coated steel, fiberglass-reinforced plastic, concrete or wood, with the cost decreasing in that order. The glass-coated steel and fiberglass silos are available as sealed structures with an expansion bag to allow for temperature-induced pressure variation. While the annual cost for these silos is considerably higher than for conventional silos, when properly managed, storage losses are minimal and with high value crops, the extra cost is justified.

Both monolithic concrete and concrete stave silos provide excellent storage conditions, and given proper care will last for years. Wood silos also provide good storage conditions, but they require more attention to maintain proper hoop tension.

Horizontal silos   These silos provide storage at considerably lower cost and are adaptable to self-feeding. However, they are not as easily automated and considerable care must be taken to properly pack and cover the silage to keep storage losses at an acceptable level. While it is not difficult to store corn silage with minimal losses, it takes great care to ensile grass successfully.

Horizontal silos are ordinarily built of concrete or pressure-preservative treated lumber. If built above grade, adequate bracing is essential (Figure 23-3 A & B). If concrete is used below grade, good drainage behind the walls is particularly important to prevent frost damage (Figure 23-4 A & B).

Stacks   Stacks may be used for short-term overflow storage, but losses are likely to be high.

Choosing a Silo

In considering what kind of silo to build and how to obtain the most efficient use, there are several factors to be kept in mind:

1. Type of silage to be stored Corn forage is relatively easy to ensile and can be stored successfully in any type of silo that is in good condition. Haylage, on the other hand, is lower in sugars and does not ferment as easily. Also it is more difficult to pack, and therefore is best stored in a tower silo. It is easiest to store haylage in a sealed silo, but careful packing and sealing the top surface with a weighted plastic cover will give good results in any tower silo.

2. Value of crop stored Crops grown for silage vary in nutritional and monetary value. Crops of high monetary value justify the greater investment in the more expensive types of storage which ordinarily have lower losses. Each percentage point saved is of greater dollar value with high-value crops. For example, a sealed, gas-tight storage should be considered for storing high-moisture shelled corn.

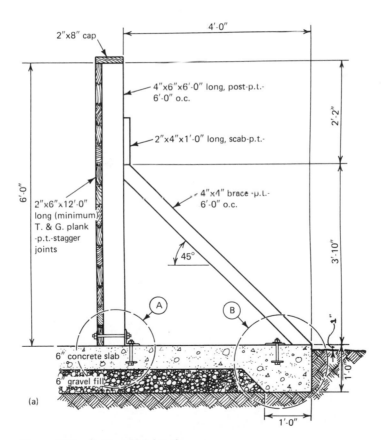

Figure 23-3. Bunker silo details.

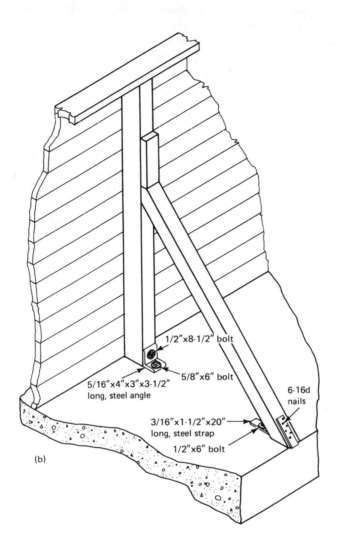

(b)

1/2"x8-1/2" bolt

5/8"x6" bolt

5/16"x4"x3"x3-1/2"
long, steel angle

6-16d
nails

3/16"x1-1/2"x20"
long, steel strap

1/2"x6" bolt

Figure 23-3 continued

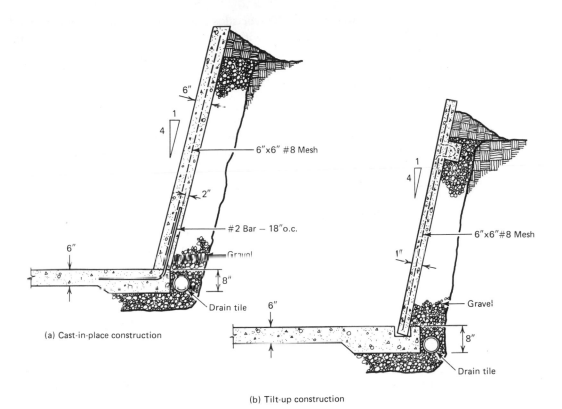

6"

1
4

6"x6" #8 Mesh

2"

#2 Bar – 18"o.c.

Gravel

6"

8"

Drain tile

(a) Cast-in-place construction

1
4

6"x6"#8 Mesh

1"

Gravel

6"

8"

Drain tile

(b) Tilt-up construction

Figure 23-4.   Concrete horizontal silo construction.

    3.   Possibility for multiple filling   Most operators use conventional, unsealed silos for corn silage and fill once a year in the fall. However, a gas-tight unit used to ensile haylage, being nearly empty in late May, can be filled for summer barn feeding and refilled again in late summer for winter feeding. The sealed silo may be refilled with other materials in almost any combination and in any season. However, to realize the benefits of multiple fillings and to justify the high investment in this type of silo, the unit should be no larger than is necessary to carry storage through from fall to spring filling. Filling the silo twice a year reduces to nearly half the storage cost per ton. On the other hand, if the silo has the capacity to carry a herd for the entire year, adding forage at two or three different times is meaningless from an economic standpoint. An exception to this would be the extra capacity installed in anticipation of herd expansion.

4. Feeding system   Tower silos equipped with unloaders are well suited for use in conjunction with a barn-feeding conveyor, concentrate meter and high-moisture corn crusher. Horizontal silos fit well with a tractor front-end loader and mixer wagon combination and offer considerable flexibility in the feeding program.

5. Available capital   The funds available or the cost of borrowed capital will influence the choice of storage facilities. Many operators with limited funds have used a temporary silo until sufficient funds were accumulated for a permanent silo or have built a less expensive, permanent, horizontal silo.

6. Storage losses   The moisture content, the quality of the silage stored, and management practices all influence storage losses. However, for the same quality of silage stored, the losses are also affected by the type of silo. The range of typical losses to be expected are:

Sealed upright silo	1—10%
Concrete upright silo	2—12%
Horizontal	10—25%
Stack	15—35%

The annual cost of a silo will run 13 to 15 percent of the original cost. The difference in annual cost, the expected storage loss, and the value of the product stored can be used to determine the type of storage that offers the lowest cost per ton of feed removed.

Site Selection and Layout

Good drainage is essential for all types of silos. In the case of tower silos, a large proportion of the silage load is transferred through the walls to the foundation. A firm, well drained soil is required to support the load. In the case of a below-grade, horizontal silo, good drainage behind the walls is necessary to prevent frost damage. Adequate drainage must be provided to remove excess juices and rainfall from the site and to divert surface water from draining into the silo. Firm ground will be required for heavy vehicular traffic handling the silage.

Silos must be located for convenient loading and unloading. During filling, wagons and trucks should be able to maneuver with a minimum of turning and backing. Unnecessary travel during the daily unloading can be eliminated by the careful placement of the silo in relation to the feeding area. This will depend on the type of animal housing and the method of feed distribution. Arranging tower silos and feed storages in a row so that one conveyor can "accumulate" a full ration is desirable.

Greater flexibility in location is possible with horizontal silos since they are usually used with a mixer wagon and a little extra distance is not critical. Care should be taken that the silos are not built in a place where the expansion of other facilities may be contemplated.

Tower Silos

The size and number of silos must be selected to match the requirements of the herd. The diameter of the silo is determined by the amount of silage fed daily, while the height and number of silos are determined by the amount fed annually. A suitable diameter will allow the removal of at least 2 to 3 inches (50 to 75 mm) of silage from the entire surface during the winter months and 3 to 4 inches (75 to 100 mm) in warm weather. Spoilage is likely to occur if less is removed. If a decision must be made between two silos that bracket the 2- to 4-inch (50 to 100 mm) removal rate, it is better to choose the one with the smaller diameter and prevent any loss. The height of a silo should not, however, be less than twice nor more than four times the diameter. The greater the depth of the silage, the greater the unit capacity and the higher the quality of the silage. Doubling the diameter increases total capacity four times, doubling the height triples the capacity, and doubling the height and the diameter increases the capacity 12-fold. The cost per ton drops rapidly as silos get taller and wider.

Silage weighs from 35 to 50 pounds per cubic foot (570 to 810 kg/m³) depending on type and depth. Table 23-1 provides estimated

Table 23-1 Capacity of Tower Silos

Depth of Silage		Mass in 10 ft (3 m) diameter silo		Silo Diameter		Multiplier*
feet	meters	ton	tonne	feet	meters	
20	6.1	27	24.5	12	3.7	1.44
24	7.3	35	31.8	14	4.3	1.96
28	8.5	44	40.0	16	4.9	2.56
32	9.8	53	48.2	18	5.5	3.24
36	11.0	63	57.3	20	6.1	4.00
40	12.2	74	67.3	22	6.7	4.84
44	13.4	85	77.3	24	7.3	5.76
48	14.6	95	86.4	26	7.9	6.76
52	15.9	108	98.2	28	8.5	7.84
56	17.1	120	109.1	30	9.2	9.00
60	18.3	132	120.0			

* Multiply mass for 10 ft (3 m) diameter by multiplier value to obtain mass for new diameter.

capacities of tower silos of various sizes. The height and number of silos needed may be determined with the help of the table. If more than one kind of feed is stored as silage, multiple silos allow all feeds to be used in the ration at the same time.

Tower silos require periodic maintenance to protect the inner surfaces from deterioration and to keep them airtight. Concrete and wood silos may be coated with raw linseed oil on a two-year schedule to protect and seal the surfaces. Epoxy coatings work well on concrete if applied before any damage has occurred. Seals around doors and openings should be checked for tightness. Maintenance of wood silos includes periodic tightening of hoops and guy wires.

During the filling of tower silos and for two weeks after filling, there is danger from silo gas. Silo gas is nitrogen dioxide, a yellowish-brown gas with an odor similar to some laundry bleaches. It is lethal to both animals and humans. Being heavier than air, the gas will settle to the stable level. As a safety precaution, it is wise to keep the silo shut off from the barn for 10 to 14 days after filling and to make certain that the barn is well ventilated. No one should enter a tower silo without first operating the blower for 15 to 20 minutes to purge any accumulation of silo gas. Two or more persons should be present for safety.

Horizontal Silos

Horizontal silos may be built 6 to 10 feet (2 to 3 m) or more in height and wide enough to allow a minimum amount of silage to be removed from the open face each day. Two to 3 inches (50 to 75 mm) is satisfactory in cold weather, but up to twice that much is desirable in the summer. Seven to 8 feet (2 to 2.5 m) is the maximum suitable height for self-feeding. The length is determined by the total silage needed for the year. Some farmers are reducing construction costs by building double silos with a common wall between them. Double silos also offer the flexibility of being able to feed out of one side while the other side is being filled. At the same time, there is less exposed area on the front surface, thus decreasing the possibility of spoilage. Horizontal silo capacity may be based on 35 pounds per cubic foot (570 kg/m^3).

Bunker silos should be built with tight, rigid walls and a solid floor. A simple design for a braced wall bunker silo constructed of pressure-preservative treated lumber is shown in Figure 23-3. Lining the silo with plastic each year insures a smooth, airtight surface against which to pack the silage.

Concrete horizontal silos installed below grade may be cast-in-place or "tilt-up." Although they are frequently built as essentially nonreinforced structures, it is common practice to use 6- by 6-inch (150 by 150 mm) No. 8 gauge mesh to reduce temperature stress cracks and to provide sufficient strength to lift the tilt-up panels into place. Carefully placed and well compacted gravel behind either the cast-in-place or tilt-up walls insures good drainage and adequate support to resist the lateral forces of the silage. Figure 23-4 shows a section of each type of construction. Figure 7-11 shows stages of tilt-up concrete construction.

Above-grade, horizontal, concrete silos must be designed as reinforced concrete structures. Sloping the sidewalls makes packing easier, but with smooth surfaces, vertical walls are satisfactory. The floor of the silo should be sloped for good drainage. A grade of 1:50 should be satisfactory for silos to be unloaded for feeding, but up to twice that much is desirable for self-feeding.

The most satisfactory material for covering horizontal silos is 4 or 6 mil polyethylene plastic, sealed with earth along the edges and with old tires placed as close as possible over the entire surface. In low to medium rainfall areas, molasses, hosed on the surface immediately after filling, has worked well. A 1½ to 2 gallons per square foot (60 to 80 l./m²) rate gives the best results but is economically feasible only when molasses costs not over 80 percent as much as corn.

Horizontal silos are often packed by driving a tractor back and forth over the fresh forage. The tractor wheel tread should be adjusted to its maximum width and extreme caution used in operating the tractor, particularly in a bunker type silo.

Silo Construction

Tower silo construction requires considerable know-how and equipment. It is a job for professionals. The design of concrete stave silos is detailed in Design Standards for Concrete Stave Silos (National Silo Association, 1974) which covers such design factors as foundations, loads, soil bearing, hoops, materials, stave design and testing, and construction tolerances. Sealed silos are usually installed by the manufacturer or a representative.

Horizontal silos are less complex than tower silos and may be constructed by general contractors or by farm labor.

HAY

Most hay is handled in conventional rectangular bales of 25 to 75 pounds (12 to 35 kg), large round bales of 1,000 to 2,000 pounds (450 to 900 kg), or stacks of one-half ton (tonne) or more. The use of elevators and conveyors allows the small bales to be stored in a variety of buildings, some of which may be many years old. When bales are stored in a random manner they can exert considerable lateral force against a barn wall, a fact that must be recognized when using an old barn or designing and building a new storage.

Although "big package" systems were designed for use in areas where light rainfall makes outside storage feasible, they have also become popular in high rainfall areas because of the improved labor efficiency. While some farmers tolerate the weather loss, which may exceed 10 percent, others find covered storages worthwhile.

Ground level drive-through structures not only allow handling equipment to place the packages directly into storage, but they offer protection at low cost. Pole structures with open sides permit the equipment to be driven through the building for unloading and later for loading out.

An open building of this type is subject to strong lifting forces from wind. Special attention must be paid to fastening trusses to poles and to anchoring the poles securely in the ground. On well drained sites, a slightly raised gravel floor may be satisfactory. If a concrete floor is necessary, it should slope to the sides to avoid any accumulation of water under the hay. A slope of 1:100 from the center should be adequate without affecting the stability of the hay piles.

Feeding out stacks or big bales should be under the controlled conditions of feed racks or fences. Without them, losses can be very high.

PROBLEMS

23.1   Determine the capacity of a circular grain bin 18 feet (5.5 m) in diameter and 16 feet (4.9 m) high.

23.2   Determine the approximate quantity of grain that can be dried daily in two bins, each 18 feet (5.5 m) in diameter, using the batch method and high temperature air.

23.3   A herd of 150 cows is fed a daily average of 67 pounds (30 kg) of corn silage per animal throughout the year. Make recommendations for the size and number of tower silos to provide adequate storage. Assume an average density of 44 pounds per cubic foot (714 kg/m³). Allow a minimum of 6 feet (2 m) extra height for settling of the silage after filling.

23.4   Make recommendations for the dimensions for a pole building to store 500 tons (455 tonnes) of baled hay.

REFERENCES

American Society of Agricultural Engineers. *Agricultural Engineers' Yearbook.* St. Joseph, Mich.: American Society of Agricultural Engineers, 1977.

Loewer, O.J. Jr., et al. *Layout of Grain Storage and Handling Facilities.* University of Kentucky Cooperative Extension Service AEN-1. Lexington, Ky., 1974.

Maddox, Robert L. "Questions Often Asked about Grain Drying," *Electricity on the Farm* Vol. 46, No. 4, 1973.

Midwest Plan Service. *Planning Grain-Feed Handling for Livestock and Cash-Grain Farms.* MWPS-13. Ames, Iowa: Midwest Plan Service, 1968.

National Silo Association, Inc. *Design Standards for Concrete Stave Silos.* Cedar Falls, Iowa: National Silo Association, Inc., 1974.

Pennsylvania State University Cooperative Extension Service. *Silage and Silos.* S.C. 80, The Pennsylvania State University Cooperative Extension Service, University Park, Pa. (no date).

Portland Cement Association. *Concrete Horizontal Silos.* Skokie, Ill.: Portland Cement Association, 1954.

Chapter Twenty-Four

Machinery Sheds, Farm Shops, and Fencing

MACHINERY SHEDS

The reliability of farm machines contributes to the timely completion of production operations. The complex machine that has been stored under cover and given a complete off-season checkup is much more likely to be ready to go when soil and weather conditions are optimum.

Machinery sheds do not come free. They represent an annual cost that must be justified. Economists and engineers alike have surveyed and analyzed the value of housing farm machinery with varying results. Often the machines checked were simple, heavy pieces such as plows and harrows that suffer only from a bit of rust when left outdoors. The results of such a survey would be quite different with complex machines such as balers, combines, and tractors. When precision machines are protected from the weather, several economic benefits accrue. Not only are repair costs and depreciation likely to be lower, but that intangible advantage of timeliness also has a monetary value. It is estimated, for example, that first-cutting hay decreases in value almost three percent per day after it reaches its peak quality. Late planting or harvesting reduces profits with most crops. It appears that when all factors are included, an investment in adequate machinery storage is justified.

The purpose of machinery storage is to offer protection from weather, theft, and vandalism, and to allow easy maintenance and adjustment of machines. To achieve these objectives, the design for a machinery storage should provide shelter from wind, rain and snow, sufficient space to maneuver and park individual pieces of equipment without undue shifting of other machines, and a firm, dry floor, preferably concrete, that facilitates moving machinery and prevents moisture damage. Doors should be large enough to permit safe and easy transfer of machines into and out of the storage and they should have adequate locks. A good lighting system is necessary for maintenance and repair operations.

Site Selection

Ordinarily the machinery storage and shop produce negligible pollution or nuisance and can be located relatively close to the farm home. As long as there is sufficient distance for fire safety, the proximity offers both convenience and additional protection from theft and vandalism. The site should offer good drainage and sufficient room for safe and easy maneuvering of large machines. Any service building should be located so that it adds to the attractive appearance of the farmstead. If possible, the machinery storage building should be oriented so that the front side faces away from the road and home to keep the equipment out of view. A blind of shrubbery will also improve the appearance.

Type and Shape of Building

There are three types of building layouts suitable for machinery storage. They vary in convenience, cost, and degree of protection (Figure 24-1).

1. Narrow, open-side shed Machines are backed in from one side. The side may be left open or protected with a series of rolling doors along part or all of the length of the building. Construction is simple and the least expensive. Inasmuch as machines are seldom moved after they are parked by the tractor, a gravel floor is probably more practical in this type of storage than in others. The building needs to be just high enough to accommodate the highest machine. It is important to face this building so as to minimize snow drifting.

2. Wide, open-side shed This design permits parking equipment in two rows. Machines are backed in as with the narrow shed to form one row and additional space for a second row is reached through a wide door located in the back half of the end wall. Floor, doors, height, and orientation would be similar to the narrow version.

3. Wide, enclosed shed This type might be classified as a drive-

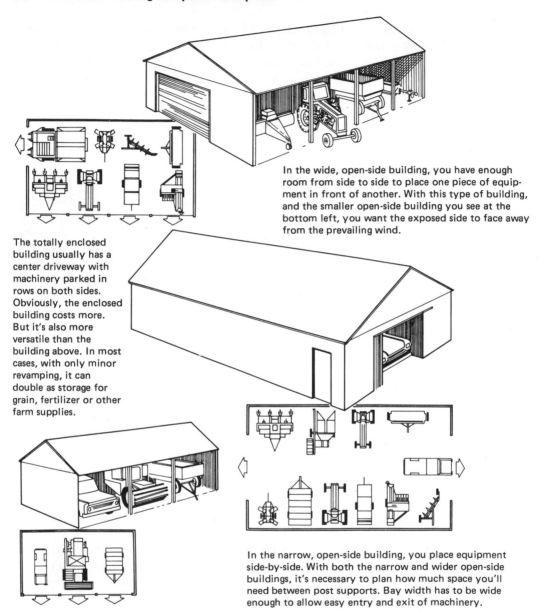

In the wide, open-side building, you have enough room from side to side to place one piece of equipment in front of another. With this type of building, and the smaller open-side building you see at the bottom left, you want the exposed side to face away from the prevailing wind.

The totally enclosed building usually has a center driveway with machinery parked in rows on both sides. Obviously, the enclosed building costs more. But it's also more versatile than the building above. In most cases, with only minor revamping, it can double as storage for grain, fertilizer or other farm supplies.

In the narrow, open-side building, you place equipment side-by-side. With both the narrow and wider open-side buildings, it's necessary to plan how much space you'll need between post supports. Bay width has to be wide enough to allow easy entry and exit of machinery.

Figure 24-1. Three main types of machinery storage. (*Courtesy* of International Harvester)

through shed. Although it is the most expensive, it offers the most protection. It should be 50 to 60 feet (15 to 20 m) wide to allow adequate room to maneuver a large machine. An extra door to allow entry without turning, simplifies storing and will usually save space. Doors and the central alley should be up to 20 feet (6 m) wide and 14 to 16 feet (4.4 to 5 m) high. Probably the greatest advantage of this type of building is the opportunity for easy access for temporary storage. Loaded trucks and wagons can be put under cover quickly and easily. The building is also available for short-term storage of seed, fertilizer, or newly harvested grain, even at the expense of pushing machines very close together or moving some outside temporarily.

Materials of Construction

Ordinarily temperature and air-moisture conditions are not a problem in a machinery storage. This broadens the choice of building materials. Attractive appearance, durability, and low maintenance are the main prerequisites. With the drive-through layout, clear-span construction is particularly important.

Lightweight construction such as pole and truss or rigid metal frame buildings are suitable. Almost any siding material may be used, but metal is attractive and offers some resistance to the spread of fire (Figure 24-2).

Figure 24-2.   Metal machinery shed. Doorways must be large enough for both the widest and highest machines. (*Courtesy* Butler Manufacturing Company)

Regardless of the type of building, there are some important construction details that are common to all. Since there is no thermal protection over the ground either inside or outside the shed, to avoid frost damage, foundations or piers need to be deeper than for most other buildings on the farm. While lightweight construction is suitable, care must be taken to provide adequate bracing and anchoring. A 5- to 6-inch (125- to 150-mm) concrete floor is highly desirable, but a well drained gravel floor is adequate and will save on investment.

Space Requirements

Every farm is unique in regard to space requirements, thus requiring individual planning. Table 24-1 lists typical dimensions for many farm machines. Using a scale of ¼ inch per foot (20 mm/m), rectangular, cardboard cutouts may be made for all the machines present on the farm or anticipated in the near future. Then, using ¼-inch (10-mm) graph paper as a background, the cutouts may be arranged to show how the machines might fit into a storage building.

Figure 24-3. Metal machinery shed interior. Adequate overhead clearance for large machinery is an important feature. (*Courtesy* Butler Manufacturing Company)

It is important to keep in mind that some implements or components cannot be moved easily. For example, the extra harvesting heads on a forage harvestor or combine are usually stored in the location where they are dropped off the machine. Plows, disks, and most mounted equip-

Table 24-1   Typical Machinery Dimensions

Machine	Feet		Meters	
	Length	Width	Length	Width
Tractors				
25–40 H.P.	12	6	3.7	1.8
40–70 H.P.	14	7	4.3	2.0
70–100 H.P.	15	8	4.6	2.4
4-wheel drive	16	10	4.9	3.0
Plows				
2 bottom	6	5	1.8	1.5
4 bottom	12	6	3.7	1.8
6 bottom	16	9	4.9	2.7
Tandem Disk				
7 ft	10	7	3.0	2.0
10 ft	11	10	3.4	3.0
14 ft	12	14	3.7	4.3
Grain Drill				
12 x 6	7	8	2.0	2.4
23 x 6	9	16	2.7	4.9
Corn Planter				
4 row	12	14	3.7	4.3
6 row	12	20	3.7	6.0
Sprayer	10	7	3.0	2.0
Mower	8	8	2.4	2.4
Rake	13	11	4.0	3.4
Self-propelled Windrower				
7 ft bar	10	10	3.0	3.0
12 ft bar	11	17	3.4	5.2
16 ft bar	12	20	3.7	6.0
Baler	17	13	5.2	4.0
Forage Harvester				
Extra Head	7	7	2.0	2.0
Blower	7	6	2.0	1.8
Combine				
Pulled, 8 ft	21	11	6.4	3.4
Self-propelled, 14 ft	24	16	7.3	4.9
Extra head, 4 row	7	12	2.0	3.7
Cotton Picker	20	11	6.0	3.4
Wagon	22	8	6.7	2.4
Manure Spreader	16	7	4.9	2.0
Manure Loader	14	6	4.3	1.8
Fertilizer Spreader	8	14	2.4	4.3
Pickup Truck	24	8	7.3	2.4

ment do not move easily and therefore space must be planned so that shifting is unnecessary. Finally, after all items are fitted into place, it is wise to add about 15 percent more space for equipment clearance and forgotten items. In addition, planning for future expansion is a good policy.

FARM WORKSHOPS

A well equipped farm shop is an essential service building for an efficiently operated agricultural enterprise. It increases the efficiency of the farm operation in several ways:

1. Fast and effective repairs are often possible in a short span of time, thereby avoiding expensive, prolonged breakdowns while waiting for a mechanic or parts.

2. Routine repairs and preventive maintenance of both equipment and buildings are possible during the off season or inclement weather. The year-round labor crew is kept busy, and expensive repairs by machinery dealers and contractors are reduced.

3. It is possible to build or modify some of the equipment to be used on the farm.

In summary, an adequate sized, well equipped farm shop can pay for itself over a period of time. However, a factor limiting the effectiveness of a shop should be not overlooked. If no one on the farm has the skill or the inclination to use the shop, it becomes a useless expense, or in some circumstances it may actually contribute to additional expense due to poorly finished work or to increased accidents due to careless procedures. The size of the shop and the equipment it houses should certainly be related to the skill and interest of the farm crew.

Site Selection

The farm shop is usually located in the hub of the farmstead traffic pattern. The site should be adequately drained to prevent water from accumulating in or around the shop. A distance of 150 feet (45 m) between the shop and other major structures provides room to maneuver and park large machinery nearby, reduces fire hazard, and allows for expansion.

Building Requirements

Lightweight, clear-span construction is satisfactory unless a hoist is to be supported from building frame members. In that case, the frame must be designed for the expected loads. Rigid frames, pole frames and trusses, or standard stud construction are all feasible. Metal siding is attractive, durable, and reasonable in cost. Wood, plywood, and punched hardboard interiors are convenient for developing wall storage areas. Some insulation is warranted to keep the building comfortable in winter and fire-resistant materials such as gypsum board or metal should be considered for the ceiling.

Space Requirements

The size of the shop will be determined by the amount of shop equipment, particularly floor power tools, and the size of the largest farm machine that will be serviced in the shop. A large, self-propelled combine, cotton picker or very wide machine such as a six-row corn planter may be excluded from this rule since they may be worked on outside or in the machinery shed. Although templates may be used to arrange and plan a shop layout, it may still be difficult to decide on the necessary work space around the shop equipment. The space may be effectively planned by first deciding on the size of an open service area in which to park a machine to be repaired, and then arranging the shop equipment, storage facilities, and heating system around that area. In most cases a minimum of 8 feet (2.5 m) should be allowed on one side and 5 feet (1.5 m) on the other. On farms with relatively small sized field equipment, a total of 24 feet (7.2 m) may be adequate, while on farms with large equipment, 28 to 30 feet (8.4 to 9 m) may be required. Thirty to 36 feet (9 to 10.8 m) of length will usually be minimal.

The layout will depend on personal preference and the type of work that is to be emphasized. However, there are a number of features that are recommended for all shops:

1. *A smooth concrete floor,* 4 inches (100 mm) thick in most areas, but 6 inches (150 mm) thick in the service area where large machines will stand. A portion of the open floor area should be installed with great care to have it flat and level. This can be useful in constructing or setting up projects. On the other hand, sloping the service area of the floor to a drain provides a place to wash down machinery and prevents the water from draining into the work or storage areas.

2. *A large concrete ramp* just outside the main entrance. This can be a very convenient place to work in mild weather. Natural lighting will be better than inside.

3. *An easily opened door* that is wide and high enough to accommodate large equipment. Fourteen feet (4.4 m) by 12 feet (3.7 m) high

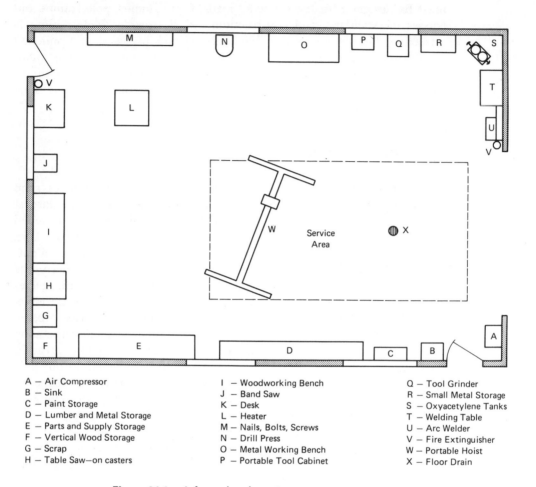

A — Air Compressor
B — Sink
C — Paint Storage
D — Lumber and Metal Storage
E — Parts and Supply Storage
F — Vertical Wood Storage
G — Scrap
H — Table Saw—on casters

I — Woodworking Bench
J — Band Saw
K — Desk
L — Heater
M — Nails, Bolts, Screws
N — Drill Press
O — Metal Working Bench
P — Portable Tool Cabinet

Q — Tool Grinder
R — Small Metal Storage
S — Oxyacetylene Tanks
T — Welding Table
U — Arc Welder
V — Fire Extinguisher
W — Portable Hoist
X — Floor Drain

Figure 24-4.   A farm shop layout.

is minimal. Overhead or rolling doors are preferable to hinged doors. The overhead type may be tighter and more convenient, but it tends to interfere with lights located in the area where it opens. A small door either in or adjacent to the large door is convenient. A second small door on the opposite side of the shop is an important safety factor in the event of a flash fire accident.

4. *Safety equipment,* such as that required by OSHA, should be provided even if not a legal requirement. Dry-powder fire extinguishers rated for B and C or A, B, and C fires should be located near the doorways and pails of dry sand placed strategically within the shop. All

machines should be equipped with guards, and safety goggles should be located at each machine where required. A first aid kit should be readily available.

5. *Adequate means for lifting machines.* Both hoists and jacks are convenient and may be used together on some jobs. Machine stands and wood blocking are an absolute necessity for use with any lifting equipment. A rolling A-frame hoist is convenient and much less expensive than constructing the roof framing strong enough to support heavy loads.

6. *A telephone or intercom system* for convenience and safety.

7. *A water supply and sink* for convenience and safety.

8. *A wall fan for general ventilation* and a flex tube to remove the exhaust fumes from an operating engine through a wall port.

9. *A large-capacity heating system* that is capable of raising the temperature to a comfortable level in a short time. The type of system is not important. However, ceiling-mounted heaters require no floor space and an automatic system that will keep the temperature above freezing is a protection for some supplies and the water system.

10. *Ample artificial lighting.* Although recommendations for window area range up to 20 percent of the floor area, artificial light is still required since shop work is often done on cloudy days or in the evening. Limiting the window area to five percent of the floor area while emphasizing a high level of artificial light is most practical. Up to 300 watt lamps spaced 10 to 12 feet (3 to 3.5 m) in each direction will provide good lighting. For the type of general lighting required in a shop, light colored wall and ceiling surfaces are more important than reflectors. Either fluorescent or incandescent lamps should be suspended above the front edge of the workbench and at each of the power tools. Portable lights than can be used in hard-to-reach areas are also a requirement.

11. *A minimum of a 100 ampere electrical service* and numerous electrical outlets for both 120 and 240 volts. The service entrance should have reserve capacity for future expansion.

12. *Location of the arc welder and compressed air supply near the main entrance.* This is convenient for use both outside on the ramp as well as inside the shop. Ventilation and fire safety are improved by using the welder near the open door.

13. *Careful placement of shop equipment* so that large or long pieces of material may be easily worked. Some power tools, a table saw for example, may be mounted on casters for storage next to the wall but for use in the middle of the room.

14. *Well organized storage space* for materials, supplies, parts, and manuals.

FENCING

Well built and maintained fences help to protect people from dangerous animals, crops from roaming animals, and animals from predators. Most states have laws relating to line fences dividing two properties as well as fences along highways and railroads. Good line fences help to make good neighbors by preventing disputes over crop damage. Fences may also be attractive additions to the farm home, but this discussion will be limited to fences related to the farm business.

Types of Fences

There may be no agricultural structure in the world with greater variety of design than the fence. Diversity of construction material as well as design seems limitless—from the prickly aloe hedge that surrounds the Zulu kraal in Africa and the beautifully woven sapling fences of eastern Europe, to the stone-walled pastures of Britain and the endless wire fences on New Zealand sheep stations; from the white board fences in Kentucky horse country to the electric fences on American dairy farms everywhere. A comprehensive study of fencing materials and design used throughout the world would be a fascinating study for the global traveler.

North America has had its own array of traditional fences, but developments in fencing have kept pace with other developments in modern agriculture. The picturesque rail fences and stone walls that surrounded the farms of colonial America have all but disappeared from the scene except for some use in landscaping home grounds. The development of a wide variety of fencing materials and construction methods now makes fencing available to meet the specific needs of all classes of livestock and the special requirements dictated by topography.

Woven-wire fencing   Figure 24-5 illustrates the five most common sizes of woven-wire fencing: 1155, 1047, 939, 832 and 726. The last two digits indicate the height in inches while the first one or two indicate the number of horizontal wires. For example, 1047 has 10 wires and is 47 inches (1,194 mm) high. The stay or vertical wires are 12 inches (305 mm) on center for the 1155 and 1047 and 6 inches (152 mm) on center for the others.

Woven-wire fences are used for sheep and hogs and are often recommended for cattle. If used for horses, a board is frequently used along the top to protect the fence and to give better visibility.

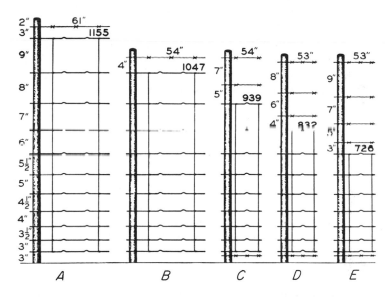

Figure 24-5. Standard types of woven wire fencing combined with barbed wire. (Farmer's Bulletin 2173, USDA)

Barbed-wire fencing Over the years barbed wire has been made in so many different styles that today it has become a collector's item. However, most barbed wire is now made from two strands of No. 12½ gauge wire twisted together with barbs made of No. 14 wire. Four-point barbs are spaced 5 inches (125 mm) on center and two-point barbs 4 inches (100 mm) on center.

Barbed wire is often used as bottom and top wires in combination with woven-wire fencing. The barbed wires discourage the animals from trying to push under the fence or from riding the fence down. Multiple strands of barbed wire may also be used alone as a fence. This is probably most satisfactory as a cattle fence.

Strand-cable fencing Zinc- or aluminum-coated, ⅜-inch (9.5-mm), 1 by 7 strand steel cable is used for constructing cattle yard fences. It allows maximum air movement across the yard.

Panel fencing Panel fencing is similar to woven-wire fencing, but the panels are made from heavier material, are rigid, and do not require stretching. The paneling comes in 16-foot (4.88-m) lengths and is suitable for lot fences for any type of livestock. Panels are installed on posts spaced 8 feet (2.44 m) or 5⅓ feet (1.63 m) on center with staples up to 2½ inches (64 mm) long depending on the post species.

Board fences Board fences are popular for horse paddocks and for working yards where animals are likely to be crowded into the fence. They usually prove to be too expensive for other areas.

Four-inch (100-mm) top posts, set 3 feet (1 m) deep in the ground, are spaced 6 feet (2 m) apart in crowded areas and 8 feet (2.4 m) apart in larger areas. Two- by 6-inch or 2- by 8-inch (38 by 140 or 38 by 184 mm) boards are nailed to the posts on the paddock side so that the stock will not loosen them. Two 16d spikes at each board-to-post contact is adequate.

Electric fencing Electric fences are usually used for controlling cattle. They may also be used for controlling pasture rotation for horses and other stock but with less dependability. Sheep in particular need to be trained to respect the fence. Electric fences are most useful for temporary applications such as managing pasture rotation, protecting hay stacks, and forming temporary lanes. They may also be used as the top wire on woven-wire fence to keep animals from riding the fence down, or as a single wire, mounted on standoffs, to keep animals from crowding a fence.

Fence Posts

Most posts are made of wood or steel, although fiberglass posts are now available and concrete posts are used on a limited basis. The choice of post depends on the type of fencing used, initial cost, durability, and ease of maintenance.

Steel posts Steel posts are easy to handle, easily driven into most soils, fireproof, and durable. They also protect stock by grounding the fence against lightning. Lightweight, steel posts are easily bent, especially under crowded conditions. Ordinarily they cost more than pressure-preservative treated (PPT) wood posts. However, most steel posts have at least a 25-year life expectancy.

Wood posts Wood posts are available in lengths of 5½ to 8 feet (1.7 to 2.8 m) and in diameters of 2½ inches (64 mm) and more. Minimum diameters are 2½ inches (64 mm) for line posts and 5 inches (125 mm) for corner or gate posts. The larger the top diameter, the stronger the post, and the more durable the fence.

Wood posts that are untreated have such a short life that they are satisfactory only for temporary fences. Only posts made from black locust or Osage orange are expected to last as long as 15 years. Other species should be treated to prevent decay and commercial pressure treatment is by far the most satisfactory.

However, if posts are produced on the farm, home treatment can increase the life of decay-prone species appreciably. Although there are a number of preservative materials and methods of introducing them to the posts, pentachlorophenol offers the best combination of effectiveness, reasonable cost, and ease of use. Complete directions for the process should be obtained before the trees are cut, and they must be followed carefully throughout. Briefly, the steps include cutting at the right season, removing bark completely, drying, calculating the amount of preservative required for one batch, soaking the posts until that amount (but no more) has been absorbed, draining, and drying before using.

Fiberglass posts Fiberglass reinforced plastic posts have been designed for use with electric or barbed-wire fencing. Fiberglass posts have the strength of steel but are light in weight. They bend under strain but return to their original position. They do not rust or rot, and they make insulators unnecessary when used with electric fencing.

Concrete posts Concrete posts are durable and, being large in diameter, make good gate or corner posts. They are also suitable for yard posts or they can be cast to be used with rails. They are usually cast 6 inches (150 mm) square and are reinforced with four No. 3 bars (⅜ inches or 10 mm) located in the corners.

Woven-Wire Fence Construction

1. Lay out the fence by first locating corners, ends, and gate openings.

2. Set corner and end posts and construct the necessary bracing as shown in Figure 24-6. A single anchor and brace assembly is satisfactory for fences up to 160 feet (50 m), but double bracing is recommended for lengths of 160 to 660 feet (50 to 200 m). Intermediate-braced line posts are needed for lengths over 660 feet (200 m).

3. For contour fencing, install braced line posts at 330-foot (100-m) intervals but only in straight sections. On rolling land it is recommended that braced line posts be installed at the crest and foot of each hill.

4. Wood anchor-posts may be driven or set in dug holes depending on equipment available and soil characteristics. In either case, they

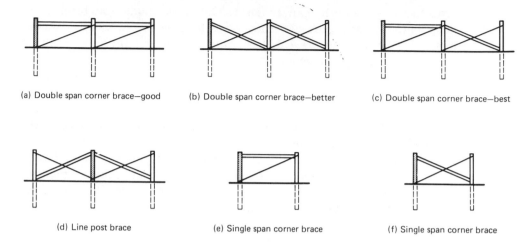

(a) Double span corner brace—good

(b) Double span corner brace—better

(c) Double span corner brace—best

(d) Line post brace

(e) Single span corner brace

(f) Single span corner brace

Figure 24-6.   Bracing methods for fencing.

should be set at least 3 feet (1 m) deep as they are subject to lifting as well as tipping forces. Steel anchor-posts and braces are set in concrete in order to get enough bearing surface. The concrete should extend below the frostline.

5.   Once the corner and end posts are in place, stretch a cord or a strand of barbed wire between them to establish a straight line as a guide for setting the line posts. A barbed wire is often used between the bottom of the woven-wire fence and the ground. When this is the case, use the barbed wire for the guide line. If the fence is built on the contour, the line will need to be staked out first.

6.   When the fenceline is established, locate and install the braced line-posts at 40-rod (200-m) intervals. Woven wire fencing is sold in 20-rod (100-m) rolls, so that on level land, two lengths will just reach to the braced posts. Each 40-rod (200-m) section is stretched and installed separately and each fence end wrapped around the center post. A continuous fence, simply spliced together and stapled to the post, is not as strong and will pull loose if damaged.

7.   Line posts have traditionally been spaced one rod (5 m) apart. However, there is no reason why cattle fences on flat land should not have a greater post spacing, while in heavy snow areas, a 13-foot (4-m) spacing will be more resistant to damage. Fences for hog lots will also require a closer post spacing to prevent the hogs from rooting under the

fence. Post spacing for fences built on the contour may be determined by limiting the offset of any post located between two alternate posts to 8 inches (200 mm).

8. Woven-wire fencing has tension crimping incorporated between the stay wires. This allows the fence to "give and take" with seasonal temperature changes. In tensioning a fence, use a hand puller—not a tractor—and pull until the crimp height is reduced by one-fourth to one-half.

9. Figure 24-7 illustrates the proper procedure for driving staples. Use 1 inch (25 mm) staples for very hard woods, 1½ to 1¾ inches (38 to 44 mm) for most others.

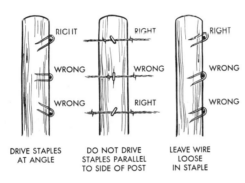

DRIVE STAPLES
AT ANGLE

DO NOT DRIVE
STAPLES PARALLEL
TO SIDE OF POST

LEAVE WIRE
LOOSE
IN STAPLE

Figure 24-7. Use of fence staples. (*Courtesy* Agricultural Extension Service, University of Minnesota)

10. The use of a metal post every 100 to 150 feet (30 to 45 m) will reduce the danger of lightning to stock and people.

Barbed-Wire Fence Construction

1. Corner, end, and line posts are located and spaced as with a woven-wire fence.

2. Use a reel support so that the wire may be unrolled. Never pull the wire off a stationary reel. Barbed wire should be stretched with hand pullers and stapled (Figure 24-5).

3. For cow-calf fences, four strands of barbed wire spaced 10 inches (250 mm) apart and 16 inches (400 mm) from the ground are adequate. For feeder cattle, the use of five strands started 12 inches (300 mm) from the ground is better. Barbed wire alone is not recommended for other stock.

Electric Fence Installation

1. Space lightweight posts as required to maintain wire clearance from the ground. Weeds, grass, and shrubbery must be cut to prevent grounding of the fence wire. Setting the posts far apart permits easier mowing under the fence.

2. Insulators prevent grounding the fence and rendering it ineffective. Choose insulators to match the type of post used (unnecessary with fiberglass posts). Gate wires should be charged through the hook so that the gate is not charged when it is open.

3. Only an Underwriters' Laboratories (UL) approved controller should be used. Whenever it is available, 120-volt power should be used since it will be dependable and less expensive than a battery. The ground rod will need to be driven 6 to 8 feet (2 to 2.5 m) deep in dry soil conditions.

4. For cattle, two wires spaced 20 inches (500 mm) apart and 16 inches (400 mm) above the ground are recommended. For swine, one wire at 6 to 8 inches (150 to 200 mm) is effective. For sheep, two barbed wires spaced 10 inches (250 mm) apart and 8 inches (200 mm) above the ground are usually satisfactory, but sheep should be trained to respect the fence immediately after shearing.

Specifications

The American Society of Agricultural Engineers has established a recommendation, ASAE R250.2, for farm fence construction (American Society of Agricultural Engineers, 1977). The quality of materials is largely based on ASTM tests while construction details are specified by ASAE. These recommendations are useful in writing specifications for fences to be installed on contract.

PROBLEMS

24.1   Make recommendations for a general type (closed or open) and size of machinery storage building for the following farm machines:

35 HP tractor	mower
100 HP tractor	forage harvester
6 bottom plow	blower
14 ft disk	two wagons

6 row corn planter   manure spreader
            sprayer   manure loader

24.2   Discuss your reasons for the type of building recommended in 24.1. Also make recommendations for a type of frame and for materials to be used for the roof and sidewall.

REFERENCES

American Assocation for Vocational Instructional Materials. *Building Farm Fences*. Athens, Ga.: American Association for Vocational Instructional Materials, 1962.

American Association for Vocational Instructional Materials. *Planning Farm Fences*. Athens, Ga.: American Association for Vocational Instructional Materials.

American Association for Vocational Instructional Materials. *Planning Machinery Protection*. Athens, Ga.: American Association for Vocational Instructional Materials, 1968.

American Society of Agricultural Engineers. *Agricultural Engineers Yearbook*. St. Joseph, Mich.: American Society of Agricultural Engineers, 1977.

Colvin, Thomas S. *Shop Planning*. Athens, Ga.: American Association for Vocational Instructional Materials, 1975.

Levi, Michael P. *Fence Posts for Farm and Home*. The North Carolina Agricultural Extension Service. Raleigh, N.C., 1974.

Moen, P.O. *Farm Workshops*. Canada Department of Agriculture Publication 1588. Ottawa, Ontario, Canada, 1976.

Neetzel, John R. *Building Better Farm Fences*. University of Minnesota Agricultural Extension Service Bulletin 272. St. Paul, Minn., 1955.

U.S. Department of Agriculture, *Farm Fences*. U.S. Department of Agriculture Farmers Bulletin 2173, 1961.

U.S. Department of Agriculture, *Preservative Treatment of Fence Posts and Farm Timbers*. U.S. Department of Agriculture Farmers Bulletin 2049, 1964.

Appendix

The National Bureau of Standards Technical Note 938, April, 1977 sets forth recommendations for the use of "le Système International d'Unités" (SI Units) in building design and construction. The following tables, which include the units most commonly used in building design and environmental control, are extracted to a large extent from this source.

Recommended units and symbols are used in all cases except for moisture transmission where no decision has yet been made. Inasmuch as the same letter may be used for more than one symbol, it is important to use the recommended form, that is, upper case, lower case or letter sequence. The following areas of possible confusion should be particularly noted:

c (centi); C (coulomb); °C (degree Celsius)
g (gram); G (giga)
k (kilo); K (kelvin)
m (milli); m (meter); M (mega)
n (nano); N (newton)
s (second); S (siemens)
t (metric tonne); T (tera); T (tesla)

Table A-1   Preferred Multiples, Submultiples, and Prefixes

Multiplication factor	Name	Symbol	Pronunciation
10^{12}	tera	T	*terra*ce
10^{9}	giga	G	jiga
10^{6}	mega	M	*mega*phone
10^{3}	kilo	k	*kilo*watt
10^{-3}	milli	m	*milli*tary
10^{-6}	micro	μ	*micro*phone
10^{-9}	nano	n	nan'oh
10^{-12}	pico	p	peek'oh

It is recommended that wherever feasible, prefixes be used so that values range between 1 and 1000.

Table A-2   SI Derived Units with Special Names

Quantity	Unit Name	Symbol	Formula
Frequency	hertz	Hz	Cycles/s
Force	newton	N	$kg \cdot m/s^2$
Gravitational force	newton	N	$kg \cdot 9.8\ m/s^2$
Pressure	pascal	Pa	N/m^2
Energy, Heat	joule	J	$N \cdot m$
Power	watt	W	J/s
Torque	newton meter (Do not use joule)	N·m	$N \cdot m$

Table A-3   Conversion from Customary to SI Units

Quantity	Preferred SI Units	Name	Customary to SI	
Length	m	meter	ft	$= 0.305$ m
	mm	millimeter	in.	$= 25.4$ mm
Area	m^2	square meter	sq ft	$= 0.093\ m^2$
	mm^2	square millimeter	sq in.	$= 645.16\ mm^2$
	ha	hectare	acre	$= 0.405$ ha
Volume	m^3	cubic meter	cu ft	$= 0.028\ m^3$
	mm^3	cubic millimeter	cu in.	$= 16\ 387\ mm^3$
Fluid Volume	mL	milliliter	fl oz. (U.S.)	$= 29.574$ mL
	L	liter	gal (U.S.)	$= 3.785$ L
			gal (U.K.)	$= 4.542$ L
			cu ft	$= 28.317$ L

Quantity	Preferred SI Units	Name	Customary to SI	
Velocity	m/s	meter per second	ft/min	= 0.005 m/s
	km/h	kilometer per hour	mph	= 1.609 km/h
Acceleration	m/s²	meter per second squared	ft/s²	= 0.305 m/s²
		acceleration due to gravity in U.S.	32.15 ft/s²	= 9.8 m/s²
*Mass**	kg	kilogram	lb	= 0.454 kg
	g	gram	oz	= 28.35 g
			grain	= 0.065 g
	t	tonne	ton (short)	= 0.907 t
Mass per Unit of Area				
	kg/m²	kilogram per square meter	lb/sq ft	= 4.882 kg/m²
Force	N	newton	lb	= 4.448 N
	kN	kilonewton	kip (1000 lb)	= 4.448 kN
Pressure	Pa	pascal	lb/sq ft	= 47.88 Pa
	kPa	kilopascal	lb/sq in.	= 6.895 kPa
	MPa	megapascal	kip/sq in.	= 6.895 MPa
Heat, Energy	kJ	kilojoule	Btu	= 1,055 kJ
	MJ	megajoule	kwh	= 3.6 MJ
Heat flow, Power				
	W	watt	Btu/hr	= 0.293 W
	kW	kilowatt	hp	= 0.746 kW
Temperature	°C	Celsius (ambient temp.)	°F	= 0.556 °C**
	K	kelvin (absolute and temp. diff.)	°F	= 0.556 K
Thermal Capacity				
	kJ/(kg·K)		Btu/(lb · °F)	= 4.187 kJ/(kg · K)
			kilocalorie	= 4.187 kJ
Illuminance	lx	lux	ft candle	= 10.764 lx

It is recommended that:

* The term *weight* be avoided. Scales are to be calibrated to read *mass* for the elevation of their location. Mass is constant while weight varies with elevation.

** Temperature may be converted from scale to scale as follows:

$$°C = (°F - 32) \cdot 5/9$$
$$°F = (°C \cdot 9/5) + 32$$
$$K = °C + 273.15$$

Table A-4   Conversion Factors for Multiple Units

Quantity	Customary to SI
Thermal Conductivity (k)	(Btu·in.)/(hr·ft²·°F) = 0.144 (W·m)/(m²·K)
Thermal Conductance (C,U)	Btu/(hr·ft²·°F) = 5.678 W/(m²·K)
Thermal Resistance (R)	(hr·ft²·°F)/Btu = 0.176 (m²·K)/W
Heat Flow (q)	Btu/(hr·ft²) = 3.155 W/m²
Permeability	(grains·in.)/(hr·ft²·in.Hg) = 0.017 (g·m)/(24h·m²·mmHg)
Permeance	grains/(hr·ft²·in.Hg) = 0.66 g/(24h·m²·mmHg)
Vapor Flow	grains/(hr·ft²) = 16.73 g/(24 h·m²)
Fluid Flow	ft³/min = 0.472 L/s

Index